RENEWALS 458-4574

WITHDRAWN
UTSA LIBRARIES

Visual Memory

OXFORD SERIES IN VISUAL COGNITION

Series Editors
Gillian Rhodes
Mary A. Peterson

Visual Memory

Edited by

STEVEN J. LUCK AND
ANDREW HOLLINGWORTH

OXFORD
UNIVERSITY PRESS
2008

OXFORD
UNIVERSITY PRESS

Oxford University Press, Inc., publishes works that further
Oxford University's objective of excellence
in research, scholarship, and education.

Oxford   New York
Auckland   Cape Town   Dar es Salaam   Hong Kong   Karachi
Kuala Lumpur   Madrid   Melbourne   Mexico City   Nairobi
New Delhi   Shanghai   Taipei   Toronto

With offices in
Argentina   Austria   Brazil   Chile   Czech Republic   France   Greece
Guatemala   Hungary   Italy   Japan   Poland   Portugal   Singapore
South Korea   Switzerland   Thailand   Turkey   Ukraine   Vietnam

Copyright © 2008 by Steven J. Luck and Andrew Hollingworth

Published by Oxford University Press, Inc.
198 Madison Avenue, New York, New York 10016
www.oup.com

Oxford is a registered trademark of Oxford University Press

All rights reserved. No part of this publication may be reproduced,
stored in a retrieval system, or transmitted, in any form or by any means,
electronic, mechanical, photocopying, recording, or otherwise,
without the prior permission of Oxford University Press.

Library of Congress Cataloging-in-Publication Data
Visual memory / edited by Steven J. Luck and Andrew Hollingworth.
p. cm. — (Oxford series in visual cognition; bk. 5)
Includes bibliographical references and index.
ISBN: 978-0-19-530548-7
1. Memory. 2. Visual perception. 3. Vision.
I. Luck, Steven J. (Steven John), 1963- II. Hollingworth, Andrew Richard.
BF371.V57 2008
153.1'32—dc22

2007048016

9 8 7 6 5 4 3 2 1

Printed in the United States of America
on acid-free paper

**Library
University of Texas
at San Antonio**

Contents

Contributors

Marvin M. Chun
Department of Psychology
Yale University

Gustavo Deco
Department of Technology
Universitat Pompeu Fabra

John M. Henderson
Psychology Department
University of Edinburgh

Andrew Hollingworth
Department of Psychology
University of Iowa

Glyn W. Humphreys
Behavioural Brain Sciences
School of Psychology
University of Birmingham

David E. Irwin
Department of Psychology
University of Illinois, Urbana-Champaign

Steven J. Luck
Center for Mind & Brain and Department of Psychology
University of California, Davis

Thomas J. Palmeri
Department of Psychology
Vanderbilt University

M. Jane Riddoch
Behavioural Brain Sciences
School of Psychology
University of Birmingham

Edmund T. Rolls
Department of Experimental Psychology
University of Oxford

Michael J. Tarr
Department of Cognitive and Linguistic Sciences
Brown University

Laura E. Thomas
Department of Psychology
University of Illinois, Urbana-Champaign

Nicholas B. Turk-Browne
Department of Psychology
Yale University

Visual Memory

Chapter 1

Visual Memory Systems

Andrew Hollingworth
University of Iowa

Steven J. Luck
University of California, Davis

This volume is devoted to the study of visual memory. In this introductory chapter, we summarize the various visual memory systems that are discussed in this volume, focusing on the nature of the representations used by these systems, their temporal dynamics, their neutral substrates, and their functional role in visually guided behavior. First, however, we consider what it is that makes a memory a *visual* memory and why it is worth devoting a volume to the topic of visual memory.

1.1 DEFINING VISUAL MEMORY

1.1.1 What Makes a Memory a Visual Memory?

As a first pass, one could posit that a visual memory is any memory for which the stored information was acquired initially by the visual system. However, such a definition would be too broad. For example, in reading, although initial acquisition occurs through the visual system, memory for the semantic or syntactic content of the materials cannot qualify as a visual memory, because such representations are likely to be abstracted away from the specific visual properties of the printed text. To qualify as a visual memory, then, the memory must retain properties of the original perceptual states generated when the memory was encoded.

A second possibility is that visual memories are imagistic: a representation of a previously viewed stimulus that retains the topographic and metric properties of the original perceptual states. Such a view of visual memory has been popular in the literature on mental imagery, in which memory for previous perceptual states is proposed to give rise to quasi-visual experience in a manner that retains the metric properties of early vision. Although mental images certainly count as visual memories (and are the focus of Chapter 9), this definition is too narrow. First, visual memories that retain the precise metric properties of early vision are extraordinarily fleeting and could not form the substrate of longer-term visual memory. Second, higher-level perceptual systems discard precise metric information in favor of more abstract representations (see Chapter 6). Third, higher-level visual systems, such as visual short-term memory, clearly retain visual information but in a format that is not inherently imagistic (see Chapter 3).

Thus, visual memory encompasses memory representations that maintain information about the perceptual properties of viewed stimuli, but the format in which that information is encoded can vary from low-level imagistic representations generated in early visual areas to higher-level visual representations stored further along the ventral stream and abstracted away from the precise spatial structure of early vision.

In practice, researchers have isolated visual memory by careful choice of stimuli and by attempting to eliminate the coding of information in a nonvisual format. To this end, researchers have frequently used novel, complex stimuli that do not map onto existing object categories and would be difficult to code in a nonvisual format. For example, the classic study of Phillips (1974) used a set of checkerboard stimuli constructed by randomly filling half of the cells of an 8×8 matrix, which could not plausibly have been encoded verbally. In studies using common, familiar objects and easily nameable stimuli, such as color patches, a concurrent verbal memory load or articulatory suppression are typically used to minimize the possibility of encoding the visual stimuli verbally. Interestingly, a verbal memory load has little or no effect on visual memory performance, indicating that verbal and visual memory do not draw upon a common limited-capacity resource (Scarborough, 1972; Vogel, Woodman, & Luck, 2001).

1.1.2 The Independence of Visual Memories

We do not, however, mean to suggest that visual memories are entirely independent from more abstract, conceptual memories. In the context of long-term memory, researchers such as Barsalou (e.g., Barsalou, 1999) and Martin (e.g., Martin & Chao, 2001) have argued that abstract, conceptual representations are linked to sensorimotor representations, such that activating the concept of *lemon* may activate visual representations of the color of lemons, olfactory representations of the scent of lemons, and motor representations of the act of puckering in response to the sour taste of lemons. However, these links between abstract concepts and sensorimotor representations are fully consistent with the proposal that the modality-specific sensorimotor representations have properties specific to the individual modalities. Thus, visual memories can be studied as a related class of representations without denying that they are linked to a larger conceptual network.

1.1.3 Why Focus on Visual Memory?

It is possible to slice the memory pie in many different ways, so why does this volume pull out a slice defined by the visual modality? There are two main reasons for this. First, highly refined methods have been developed to assess visual functioning in general, leading to an enormous wealth of information about the visual system. The field of vision science therefore provides extremely firm footing for researchers who attempt to study visual memory, footing that is absent for most other varieties of memory. The methods and concepts of vision science also provide a large degree of unity to the different issues addressed in this volume.

A second reason to focus on visual memory is that excellent animal models are available to provide a link between human visual memory and the underlying neural substrates. In particular, visual memory has been studied fairly extensively in macaque monkeys using paradigms that are related to the memory paradigms used in humans, providing much more detailed information than can be obtained from human neuroimaging data. Research on monkey neurophysiology thus plays an important role in many chapters in this volume.

1.2 VISUAL MEMORY SYSTEMS

Researchers have subdivided visual memory into three main subsystems: visual sensory memory, visual short-term memory (VSTM),[1] and long-term memory (LTM). We will provide an overview of each subsystem and then consider how they are related.

1.2.1 Visual Sensory Memory

Visual sensory memory can easily be experienced by going into a dark room with a flash camera and taking a picture. Although the camera's flashbulb will provide only a few milliseconds of illumination, the perception of the illuminated room will fade over a period of about half a second. Scientists had noted this phenomenon for many decades, but it was initially just a curiosity based on introspection. In perhaps the single most influential study in the history of visual memory, Sperling (1960) applied partial report methods to the study of sensory memory, beginning a long series of studies that have documented the existence and properties of this variety of memory (see Chapter 2 for a detailed exploration).

Visual sensory memory—later named *iconic memory* by Neisser (1967)—was originally thought to be a simple, precategorical, spatially mapped, picture-like image, and this view still dominates many textbook descriptions. However, decades of research have subdivided visual sensory memory into two main categories of persisting visual information, called *visible persistence* and *informational persistence*. Visible persistence gives rise to the phenomenological experience of a fading visual image, and it reflects the persisting activity of photoreceptors and neurons in the early stages of the visual system (probably through area V1). This aspect of visual sensory memory corresponds to the

---

1   The terms *visual short-term memory* and *visual working memory* typically are used
     to refer to the same memory system.

typical view of iconic memory, in which a detailed, picture-like, but relatively unprocessed representation of the world fades over time.

Ironically, however, visible persistence does not play a central role in Sperling's partial-report method, which instead depends primarily on informational persistence. Informational persistence is, as the name implies, the persistence of information following the offset of the stimulus but, although this information can be used to perform various tasks, it does not give rise to any phenomenological experience of a fading visual image. It can be divided into two subcomponents. One component is a spatially organized and precategorical representation that likely reflects gradually decaying activity in intermediate stages of visual cortex (e.g., area V4). A second component is a more abstract, categorized, and amodal representation.

Visual sensory memory probably plays little or no role in complex higher-level aspects of human cognition. Because this type of memory is fleeting, it is unlikely to support the accumulation of visual information over timescales relevant to postperceptual processing. In addition, because visible persistence is masked by new perceptual processing, it cannot support the comparison or integration of perceptual information across longer perceptual episodes. However, a short-lived memory is important for early and intermediate stages of visual perception. In general, sensory memory can be described as a temporal smoothing of the input signal that can allow information to be extracted over more extended periods of time. For example, photoreceptors gain much greater sensitivity by integrating photons over a period of time rather than producing brief but tiny responses to each photon. Higher-level memory systems, such as VSTM, draw upon sensory memory when consolidating perceptual information into more stable forms of memory.

1.2.2 Visual Short-Term Memory

Visual short-term memory maintains visual information from a small number objects in a relatively abstract, object-based format. The capacity of VSTM is limited to three or four objects for simple stimuli and one or two objects for more complex stimuli. These object representations are significantly abstracted away from the precise metric structure of early vision. Whereas iconic memory is strongly disrupted by changes in the retinal position of stimuli, VSTM is highly robust over changes in absolute position (Phillips, 1974) and fairly robust over changes in relative position (Jiang, Olson, & Chun, 2000). Object representations in VSTM can be bound to spatial locations, but VSTM itself does not appear to be inherently spatial in the sense of an array-format image. This likely reflects the fact that VSTM draws upon visual representations in regions of the ventral stream with relatively large receptive fields that provide only a coarse coding of location.

More specifically, VSTM representations appear to be implemented by means of sustained neural firing in the inferotemporal cortex (in monkeys) and the lateral occipital complex (in humans), along with sustained firing in prefrontal cortex (see Chapter 8). These areas will produce a sensory response to a stimulus and then maintain this response for several seconds after stimulus offset if required by the task. Earlier sensory areas, in contrast, appear to be unable to maintain high levels of activity following the termination of the stimulus.

The key functional feature of VSTM is its robustness across delay and across subsequent perceptual processing. Visual short-term memory representations can be maintained for many seconds and are largely impervious to visual masking. This allows VSTM to maintain information that spans perceptual episodes, bridging disruptions such as saccadic eye movements, blinks, and brief occlusion. This short-term bridging supports the comparison of perceptual information from objects separated in time and space, allowing people to compare visual objects to a remembered search target in the course of visual search, detect that an object has changed across a perceptual disruption, or note visual differences between two spatially separated objects. In addition, because consolidation of information into VSTM is strongly dependent on attention, the content of VSTM will reflect the moment-to-moment allocation of attention to goal-relevant objects during the performance of real-world tasks.

1.2.3 Visual Long-Term Memory

Visual short-term memory representations are robust over short periods of time, but the capacity limitations of VSTM preclude any significant accumulation of visual information over longer periods. In contrast, VLTM has a remarkably large storage capacity and highly robust retention. Single-trial learning of thousands of visual stimuli is possible, and such memory retains information about the specific visual form of objects and scenes. Visual long-term memory plays a central role in memory for the visual features of objects in the service of object and scene categorization (see Chapters 5 and 6). Visual long-term memory also is sensitive to statistical structure in visual input, which allows the visual system to utilize predictive contextual information in perception (see Chapter 7). For example, the learning of scene structure and object location facilitates visual search for an object, biasing search toward likely locations of the target. Finally, long-term environmental learning allows for the integration of visual and spatial information into large-scale, episodic representations of environments and events (see Chapter 5).

Whereas VSTM representations are maintained by means of sustained neural firing, VLTM representations are maintained by means of changes in the pattern and strength of the connections between neurons (see Chapter 8). These changes are thought to be implemented by means of structural changes in synaptic connections, which are responsible for the durability of VLTM representations. It has been notoriously difficult to find the actual storage locations of long-term memories in the brain, but most researchers believe that the memories are stored within the same systems that underlie perception (making it difficult to find cases of the loss of existing memories in the absence of perceptual deficits). Indeed, Chapter 6 argues that memory and perception are intrinsically interrelated.

1.2.4 Relations Among Visual Memory Subsystems

To what extent can these visual memory systems be considered independent? Each of the main visual memory systems—visual sensory memory, VSTM, and VLTM—has unique properties, especially in terms of capacity, duration, and abstractness. However, this does not mean that they are entirely independent. Sensory memory—especially insofar as it reflects an intrinsic aspect of perceptual representations—clearly provides information from which VSTM and VLTM representations are formed. Indeed, Chapter 3 argues that VSTM representations are best considered as high-level perceptual representations that have become stabilized by means of a limited-capacity attentional process. It is not yet known, however, whether these VSTM representations then become the starting point for VLTM representations. The influential working memory model of Baddeley and Hitch (1974) proposes that information need not pass through short-term memory to reach long-term memory, but this has not received much study in the visual domain. A few studies have asked whether VLTM representations influence VSTM storage, with most finding little or no interaction in this direction (see Chapter 3). However, we know of no direct tests of the hypothesis that VSTM representations provide the starting point for building VLTM representations. The alternative hypothesis is that VLTM representations are created directly from perceptual representations, whether or not they have been stabilized into VSTM representations. This will be an important question for future research.

REFERENCES

Baddeley, A. D., and Hitch, G. J. (1974). Working Memory. In *The Psychology of Learning and Motivation, Vol. VIII,* ed. G. H. Bower, 47–90. New York: Academic Press.

Barsalou, L. W. (1999). Perceptual symbol systems. *Behavioral and Brain Sciences* 22:577–660.

Jiang, Y., Olson, I. R., and Chun, M. M. (2000). Organization of visual short-term memory. *Journal of Experimental Psychology: Learning, Memory & Cognition* 2:683–702.

Martin, A., and Chao, L. L. (2001). Semantic memory and the brain: Structure and process. *Current Opinion in Neurobiology* 11:194–201.

Neisser, U. (1967). *Cognitive Psychology.* New York: Appleton-Century Crofts.

Phillips, W. A. (1974). On the distinction between sensory storage and short-term visual memory. *Perception & Psychophysics* 16:283–290.

Scarborough, D. L. (1972). Memory for brief visual displays of symbols. *Cognitive Psychology* 3:408–429.

Sperling, G. (1960). The information available in brief visual presentations. *Psychological Monographs* 74:(No. 498).

Vogel, E. K., Woodman, G. F., and Luck, S. J. (2001). Storage of features, conjunctions, and objects in visual working memory. *Journal of Experimental Psychology: Human Perception and Performance* 27:92–114.

Chapter 2

Visual Sensory Memory

David E. Irwin and Laura E. Thomas
University of Illinois

2.1 PHENOMENOLOGY OF VISUAL PERSISTENCE

Visual stimuli remain visible for some time after their physical offset. This can be demonstrated in a dark room by whirling a flashlight at arm's length in a circle in front of one's body; if the arm moves quickly enough, a continuous circle of light will be visible. The lingering phenomenal trace of a visual stimulus after its offset is usually called *visible persistence* (e.g., Coltheart, 1980) or *phenomenal persistence* (e.g., Turvey, 1978) and its existence has been known for centuries; according to Allen (1926), Aristotle made note of it over 2000 years ago. Inventors and engineers have taken advantage of the existence of visible persistence in devices such as television sets, computer monitors, and motion picture projectors; because of visible persistence, viewers "see" a continuous visual image when using these devices even though the actual physical stimulus is temporally discontinuous. Visible persistence differs from a retinal afterimage (like that produced by a photographer's flashbulb) in several ways; for example, visible persistence does not require an intense blast of light in order to be generated, it is briefer in duration, it is more easily masked by other visual stimuli, and it has the same contrast polarity as the originating stimulus (i.e., it is a positive, rather than a negative, image).

Visual stimuli not only remain visible for some time after their physical offset, but information about their characteristics also persists; that is, not only does something that looks like the physical stimulus continue to persist for a brief time after stimulus offset, but information can also be extracted from the stimulus for a brief time after its offset in much the same way as when the stimulus was physically present. This latter type of persistence is usually called *informational persistence* (e.g., Coltheart, 1980; Turvey, 1978). Once upon a time, visible persistence and informational persistence were thought to rely on the same underlying visual representation; in the last 25 years or so, it has become apparent that visible persistence and informational persistence reflect related but different aspects of visual sensory memory, however. The rest of this

9

chapter reviews the evidence behind this assertion and describes the current conception of these phenomena.

2.2 EARLY EXPERIMENTS ON VISUAL SENSORY MEMORY

Contemporary interest in the topic of visual sensory memory is due to the groundbreaking research of George Sperling (e.g., Sperling, 1960). The starting point for Sperling's research was the observation that when people are presented with a brief visual display, they believe that they see more than they can remember a short time later. For example, observers can usually report accurately four or five items after display offset, but they have the impression that more information than that is available to them but that it fades away before it can be reported. This intuition had been reported in the nineteenth century (e.g., Cattell, 1883; Erdmann & Dodge, 1898), but it was Sperling who devised a method for assessing it experimentally. In Sperling's experiments, subjects were usually presented with visual arrays of letters (for example, two or three rows of either three or four letters each) for a brief time (usually 50 ms). Under *whole-report* conditions, subjects were asked to report as many array items as they could in their proper spatial positions; consistent with previous investigators, Sperling found that subjects could report accurately approximately 4.5 letters under these conditions. To tap into the introspective feeling that more letters than that were available, however, Sperling developed a *partial-report* procedure in which a subset of the information in the array was cued for report (Fig. 2–1). For example, suppose the array contained three rows of four letters each; in the partial-report procedure the subject would be presented with a tone immediately after array offset that specified which one of the three rows in the array should be reported (e.g., a high-pitched tone would signal that the top row only should be reported, a medium-pitched tone the middle row only, and a low-pitched tone the bottom row only). Because the subject did not know which row would be probed for report on any given trial, Sperling reasoned that percent correct for an individual row could be used to estimate how much of the entire array was stored in memory before it faded away. For example, he found

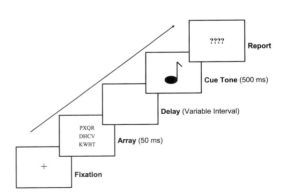

Figure 2–1. Sperling's (1960) partial-report procedure.

that, on average, subjects could report correctly a little more than three of the four letters in any individual row under partial-report conditions, corresponding to an accuracy rate of 76%. Based on this, he argued that, immediately after array offset, subjects must have had 76% of the entire array available to them, or 9.1 items in this case, considerably higher than the 4.5 items reported under whole-report conditions. Thus, Sperling's data confirmed the intuition that immediately following stimulus offset more information is available about a visual stimulus than can ordinarily be reported, and he proposed that this information is held in a quickly decaying visual information store (what later investigators termed *visual sensory memory*).

Averbach and Coriell (1961) reported similar results using a modified version of Sperling's partial report procedure (Fig. 2–2). In their experiments, subjects were presented with visual displays containing two rows of eight letters each. These arrays were presented for 50 ms, and then a visual bar marker was presented above or below one of the array positions and the subject named the letter designated by the marker. When the bar marker was presented simultaneously with array offset, average accuracy at reporting the cued letter was approximately 65%. Thus, based on Sperling's sampling logic, 65% of the 16 letters, or 10.4 letters, must have been available immediately after array offset.

In subsequent experiments, Sperling, Averbach and Coriell, and many other investigators discovered several important characteristics of this quickly decaying visual memory store. Several of these are described next.

2.2.1 Capacity

As described earlier, Sperling (1960) found that, on average, subjects had access to 9.1 out of 12 letters immediately after stimulus offset, and Averbach and Coriell (1961) found that 10.4 out of 16 letters were available. It takes time to interpret the partial-report cue and apply it to information in memory, however, so these values most likely underestimate the capacity of visual sensory memory because some information would decay during the cue-interpretation process. Sperling (1960) found that when the partial-report tone preceded the onset of the letter array by 50 ms, accuracy increased to 8.2 out of 9 and 9.8 out

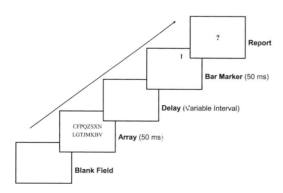

Figure 2–2. Averbach and Coriell's (1961) partial-report procedure.

of 12 letters. Averbach and Sperling (1961) found that approximately 17 out of 18 letters could be remembered under similar conditions. Using their bar-probe version of the partial-report task, Averbach and Coriell (1961) found that when the probe preceded the letter array by 100 ms accuracy increased to approximately 11.5 out of 16 letters. In a separate experiment, Averbach and Coriell (1961) estimated that detecting the bar marker and reading the cued letter took approximately 200–300 ms; presumably, accuracy would have been even higher in their experiment if the bar marker had preceded the letter array by more than 100 ms. Visual acuity limitations may also lower estimates of the capacity of sensory memory because letters in the periphery of a display are harder to resolve and thus harder to identify. Lateral inhibition in the visual pathway also makes it harder to identify letters that are flanked by other letters in the array; for example, Averbach and Coriell (1961) found that accuracy was highest for letters at the center and ends of each row in their arrays and lowest for letters in between. In sum, given the high levels of accuracy found when the partial-report probe cues memory shortly before or shortly after stimulus offset, plus the existence of visual factors that may artificially lower performance, it is generally assumed that the capacity of visual sensory memory is virtually unlimited (e.g., Dick, 1974).

2.2.2 Time Course

To estimate the time course of sensory memory, Sperling (1960), Averbach and Coriell (1961), and Averbach and Sperling (1961) delayed the presentation of the partial-report cue to determine how this affected partial-report performance. For example, in one experiment, Sperling presented the partial-report tone either immediately after array offset, or 150, 500, or 1000 ms after array offset. He found that accuracy decreased as probe delay increased; partial-report performance was superior to whole-report performance at delays of 0, 150, and 500 ms, but with a 1000-ms delay there was no difference in accuracy between partial-report and whole-report conditions. Averbach and Coriell (1961) also varied probe delay in their bar-probe version of the partial-report procedure and found that accuracy declined as probe delay increased from 0 to 200 ms after array offset, then asymptoted at approximately 30% for longer delays (Fig. 2–3), corresponding to an estimate of 4.8 letters available in memory (i.e., similar to what Sperling found in his whole-report condition). Thus, these pioneering studies converged in showing that visual sensory memory decays quickly, in less than a second. Averbach and Sperling (1961) found that the time course of sensory memory depends critically on the exposure parameters (e.g., luminance of the letter array and of the pre- and postexposure fields) that are used, however. For example, when a light field precedes and follows the letter array, then partial-report performance drops to the level of whole-report after .5 s; when a dark field precedes and follows the letter array, partial-report performance is superior for as long as 5 s. The fact that partial-report performance is sensitive to visual factors such as these implies that it measures a low-level sensory memory.

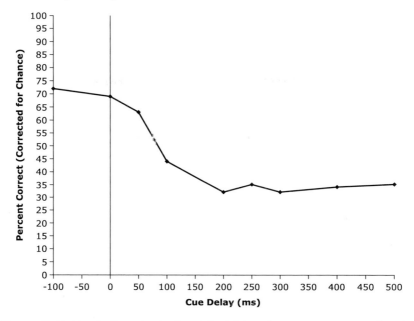

Figure 2–3. Results from Averbach and Coriell (1961). Percent correct as a function of cue delay (averaged across subjects) in a bar-probe partial report experiment.

2.2.3 Masking

As noted earlier, the luminance of the visual fields preceding and following a stimulus display affects the duration of the visual persistence following that display. The content contained in the pre- and postexposure fields also affects visual sensory memory. For example, in some of their experiments, Averbach and Coriell (1961) presented a circle around one of the previously occupied letter positions instead of a bar-marker to cue report. They found that the circle and the bar-marker were equally effective in cuing letter report if they were presented before array onset or simultaneously with array onset or array offset, but that the circle actually interfered with letter report if it was presented 100 ms after array offset; at longer delays, accuracy slowly improved to bar-marker levels. Phenomenologically, subjects reported seeing a circled letter at the short delays (i.e., an integrated representation of the two stimuli), but at longer delays the circle seemed to eliminate the letter. Averbach and Coriell referred to this latter phenomenon as *erasure*, but more generally it would seem to be an example of metacontrast masking (e.g., Kahneman, 1968). In another experiment, Averbach and Coriell presented a circle filled with grid lines at one of the letter locations; in this case, accuracy of letter report was lowest at the shortest cue delay and increased in a monotonic fashion as cue delay increased, because subjects had more time to identify the letter before it was masked. Similarly, Sperling (1963) showed that visual sensory memory was completely eliminated if a noise field (e.g., a jumble of random lines) was presented immediately after letter array offset. The existence of masking effects such as these implies that sensory memory is a low-level visual phenomenon; it is also generally viewed as a desirable property, in that it prohibits overlapping sensory images from interfering with each other over time.

By varying stimulus exposure duration and also the delay between stimulus offset and mask onset it is possible to compare information extraction from sensory memory with information extraction during stimulus presentation. For example, Loftus, Johnson, and Shimamura (1985) probed memory for stimuli whose exposure duration varied under conditions in which a mask was presented immediately after stimulus offset or after a 300-ms delay. They found that performance for a given exposure duration under delayed-mask conditions was virtually identical to performance in an immediate-mask condition in which the stimulus had been presented for 100 ms longer. They concluded that sensory memory is worth 100 ms of stimulus exposure time.

2.2.4 Attention

For a partial-report cue to be effective, it must quickly draw visual selective attention to the region of the display that is cued for report. Thus, visual bar-markers (e.g., Averbach & Coriell, 1961) or auditory tones that map onto specific regions of space (e.g., Sperling, 1960) are effective partial-report cues because they can be interpreted quickly and used to direct selective attention to the relevant region of sensory memory before it fades away. However, the fact that partial-report performance does not fall to zero when the partial-report cue is delayed for a long period of time implies that some period of nonselective readout (Averbach & Coriell, 1961) takes place in the absence of a cue. That is, before the cue is presented, subjects begin to read out from visual sensory memory any items that they can, but they then quickly shift their visual selective attention to the cued information when the cue is presented. In this way, they are able to perform reasonably well (i.e., at the level of whole-report performance, which also depends on nonselective readout) even when the partial-report cue is delayed past the time that visual sensory memory has decayed away (see Gegenfurtner & Sperling, 1993, for a comprehensive treatment of this phenomenon).

2.2.5 Representational Format

Several findings suggested that the format of sensory memory was indeed visual in nature. One source of evidence was subjects' introspective reports that they were "reading" a slowly fading stimulus trace. More compelling is the fact that the visual characteristics of the exposure fields presented before and after the stimulus array had a sizable effect on the duration of sensory memory, as discussed earlier. Several early studies also manipulated the physical and semantic characteristics of the items in the stimulus array as well as the nature of the partial-report cue and found that, in general, partial-report cues that selected items on the basis of some visuo-spatial characteristic yielded a partial-report advantage, whereas those that required some classification or categorization of stimulus items did not. For example, location (Averbach & Coriell, 1961; Sperling, 1960), color (Clark, 1969), brightness (von Wright, 1968), and shape (Turvey & Kravetz, 1970) were all found to be effective partial-report cues. However, if the partial-report cue signaled one to report only the letters from an array of letters and digits (e.g., Sperling, 1960; von Wright, 1968) or to report only the letters that ended in "ee" (Coltheart, Lea, & Thompson, 1974), then no partial-report superiority was found. These results were interpreted as showing that the information persisting from a stimulus array, and which the partial-report technique is capable of measuring, has only visual, and not semantic or phonological characteristics. In essence, sensory memory was thought to be a briefly persisting, literal image of the extinguished stimulus.

2.2.6 Summary

Based on the characteristics just described, the modal view (e.g., Coltheart et al., 1974; Dick, 1974; von Wright, 1972) of visual sensory memory was that visual information persists after stimulus offset in a precategorical, high-capacity, quickly decaying memory store that Neisser (1967) called *iconic memory* (Fig. 2–4). Not everyone agreed with this conception of visual sensory memory, however (see Long, 1980, for a comprehensive review). One criticism concerned the validity of comparing partial-report with whole-report performance. For example, Holding (1970, 1975a, 1975b) argued that output interference and cue anticipation, rather than the existence of a poststimulus memory store, might cause partial-report performance to be superior to whole-report performance in Sperling's (1960) paradigm, because fewer items need to

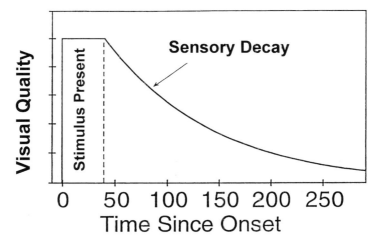

Figure 2–4. The traditional view of "iconic" memory, a raw sensory representation that begins at stimulus offset and decays quickly. Adapted with permission from Massaro, D. & Loftus, G. R. (1996). Sensory storage: Icons and echoes. In *Handbook of Perception and Cognition, Vol. 10*, eds. E. L. Bjork and R. A. Bjork, 68–101. New York: Academic Press. With permission from Elsevier.

be reported under partial-report conditions and subjects may be able to guess ahead of time which portion of the display to attend to. These criticisms were effectively refuted by several reviewers (e.g., Coltheart, 1975), however, because they fail to explain the decline in partial-report superiority with increasing cue delay. Furthermore, studies using the bar-probe technique (e.g., Averbach & Coriell, 1961) yield conclusions consistent with those of Sperling (1960), even though they don't involve comparisons between partial-report and whole-report conditions.

Other criticisms of the partial-report technique (and by extension, of the conclusions based on this technique regarding the properties of visual sensory memory) concern the type of stimuli that are usually employed and the time required to interpret and apply the partial report cue. With few exceptions, stimuli used in partial-report experiments are highly overlearned characters such as letters and numbers; this led some (e.g., Haber & Hershenson, 1973) to wonder whether the effects obtained in partial-report studies are specific to only linguistic information. In another vein, because subjects must decode the partial-report cue and direct selective attention appropriately before they can give their response, information in sensory memory may decay before subjects can attend to the appropriate stimulus characteristics (Crowder, 1976; Dick, 1974). This feature of the partial-report procedure may thus lead to an under-estimation of the amount and type of information in sensory memory. Consider the finding (described earlier) that only partial-report cues that select items on the basis of some visuo-spatial characteristic yield a partial-report advantage, whereas those that require some classification or categorization of stimulus items do not; this was interpreted to mean that the information stored in iconic memory was precategorical in nature—a raw, unprocessed visual image. Merikle (1980) argued that the difference in the effectiveness of these cues may instead result from differences in how easily attention can be directed to the relevant information in memory, however. For example, the items specified by a spatial cue are easily localized and tend to be close to each other (e.g., in the same row), whereas the items specified by a category cue are usually located at randomly selected positions in a display, thus requiring multiple shifts of atten-tion. Merikle (1980) found a partial-report superiority effect for a categorical cue (i.e., report letters versus report numbers) when partial-report and whole-report trials were intermixed (so that subjects did not know prior to cue presentation whether they would have to report all the items, only the letters, or only the numbers from the display); furthermore, this superiority declined with increasing cue delay and decreased at the same rate as when a spatial cue was used to cue report. Thus, he argued that visual sensory memory must not be only precategorical in nature.

More generally, it is worth noting that the partial-report technique does not measure directly the *visible* aspect of visual sensory memory, but rather what *information* persists after stimulus offset. Inferences based on this information are somewhat indirect and possibly open to multiple interpretations, as sum-marized earlier. So, partly in response to criticisms of this type, other proce-dures for studying visual persistence following stimulus offset were developed.

These techniques attempted to directly measure the visible properties of sensory memory instead of measuring the properties of information that persists after display offset.

2.3 VISIBLE PERSISTENCE

Several different techniques for measuring visible persistence (i.e., the phenomenal lingering trace of an extinguished stimulus) have been developed over the years, and the results from these studies agree with each other in many ways (for comprehensive reviews see Coltheart, 1980; Long, 1980). The major tasks and some representative findings are described next.

2.3.1 Judgment of Synchrony or Duration of Stimulus Technique

The judgment of synchrony (Coltheart, 1980) or duration of stimulus (Long, 1980) technique involves a two-part procedure in which the occurrence of a probe stimulus (e.g., an auditory click) is adjusted, so that its onset appears to be, first, simultaneous with the onset of a visual display, and then, simultaneous with the offset of the visual display. The difference between these two settings provides an estimate of the phenomenal duration of the visual display. This technique was introduced by Sperling (1967), but was used most extensively by Efron (1970a, 1970b, 1970c); Bowen, Pola, and Matin (1974); and Haber and Standing (1970). Using this procedure, the effect of various stimulus characteristics on the duration of stimulus persistence can be readily obtained. In general, the results from studies using this technique have shown that briefly presented visual stimuli persist for about 100–200 ms after their offset, but that persistence duration is affected by factors such as stimulus intensity, stimulus duration, and by the characteristics of the pre- and postexposure fields.

2.3.2 Phenomenal Continuity or Persistence of Form Technique

Another technique that relies on the phenomenal appearance of the stimulus is the phenomenal continuity (Coltheart, 1980) or persistence of form (Long, 1980) procedure. This method involves presenting a stimulus discontinuously in time and varying the interval between presentations; the stimulus appears continuous as long as its persistence outlasts the blank period between presentations. The temporal interval at which the stimulus no longer appears continuous is an estimate of the duration of its visible persistence. Haber and Standing (1969) used this technique by alternating presentations of a black circle and a blank field. They found that the circle appeared to be continuously present as long as the duration of the blank period was less than 250–300 ms. Meyer, Lawson, and Cohen (1975) used a slight variation of this technique in which the subject directly adjusted the duration of the blank field until the stimulus (a sinusoidal grating) appeared just continuous; this average duration was 177 ms. Another variation of this technique was used by Purcell and Stewart (1971). They presented subjects with a pair of brief light flashes separated by a variable period of time and asked them whether they saw one flash or two. They found that subjects perceived the two pulses as a single flash if the interval between them was no more than 60 ms.

A similar procedure was used in several *perception of simultaneity* studies performed during the 1960s. These studies presented parts of figures at varying intervals to determine the maximum interval at which the figure appeared to be continuously seen. Lichtenstein (1961), for example, found that four successively presented dots appeared to form a continuous diamond shape if the interval between the first and last dot was less than about 125 ms. Similar results were reported by Fraisse (1966) for letters within words, and by McFarland (1965) for sides of geometric figures. Loftus and Hanna (1989) used a variant of this technique in which subjects simply rated the subjective completeness of the stimulus parts on a scale from 1 to 4; these researchers found that completeness ratings decreased as the temporal separation between stimulus parts increased.

2.3.3 Moving Slit Technique

The moving-slit technique (Coltheart, 1980) is another method for studying visible persistence that is similar to the persistence of form technique. If a narrow slit is oscillated at the right speed in front of a figure, the entire figure will appear to be present even though only a narrow section of it is actually visible at any one time. This phenomenon is presumably due to the figure being "painted" across the retina, with retinotopic visible persistence (not necessarily located in the retina per se) from each section of the "painting" contributing to the appearance of a continuous figure. Haber and Standing (1969) used this method to obtain an estimate of persistence duration by finding the slowest slit-oscillation speed at which the figure was continuously visible. This value was approximately 300 ms, similar to what they observed using the phenomenal continuity technique described earlier.

2.3.4 Onset-offset Reaction Time Technique

Using the onset-offset reaction time technique, subjects are instructed to make a response (e.g., a key press) to the onset of a stimulus on some trials and to the offset of the stimulus on other trials (e.g., Briggs & Kinsbourne, 1972). The difference in reaction time between these judgments presumably depends on stimulus duration and also on visible persistence of the stimulus. As Coltheart (1980) noted, however, responses to "onsets" and to "offsets" are likely to differ because onsets are denoted by a steep rise time whereas the "offset" of a visibly persisting stimulus is extended in time. Thus, Coltheart concluded that it is not safe to use this technique to obtain estimates of the absolute duration of visible persistence, but that it might be useful for measures of relative duration.

2.3.5 Type I Versus Type II Measures of Persistence

All of the techniques just described can be criticized on the grounds that they rely on the subjective report of the observer, rather than on any objective response measure (Dick, 1974; Long, 1980). The problems associated with this form of measurement were discussed most clearly by Hawkins and Shulman (1979), who distinguished between what they called type I and type II persistence measures. Hawkins and Shulman observed that the concept of "stimulus offset" is actually somewhat ambiguous, and they suggested that subjects may use different criteria for "offset" in different experimental situations. For example, subjects might interpret "offset" to refer to the earliest indication that the stimulus has terminated, relying on a just-noticeable decrement in the visibility of the decaying stimulus trace (a type I measure of persistence). Hawkins and Shulman noted that some residual trace of the decaying stimulus might still be visible past the time that the initial decrement is observed, however; thus, if subjects interpret "stimulus offset" to refer to the last lingering trace of the extinguished stimulus (a type II measure of persistence), rather than to the earliest just-noticeable decrement in stimulus quality, then considerably longer estimates of persistence duration would be obtained. This might help explain the wide variation in estimates of persistence duration (60–300 ms) apparent in the studies described earlier.

2.3.6 Temporal Integration or Successive Field Technique

The temporal integration (Coltheart, 1980) or successive field (Long, 1980) technique for studying visible persistence does not rely on an observer's subjective experience, but rather on an objective response measure. This technique was first introduced by Eriksen and Collins (1967, 1968). Their procedure involved the presentation of two seemingly random dot patterns separated by a variable interval of time. The two dot patterns were constructed in such a way that, if they were physically superimposed, their dots formed a consonant-vowel-consonant nonsense syllable, even though neither dot pattern in itself contained any usable letter information. Thus, visible information from the first dot pattern had to persist throughout the interstimulus interval to be integrated with the second dot pattern in order for the nonsense syllable to be accurately identified. The temporal interval at which this integration became impossible provides an estimate of the duration of persistence of the first dot pattern. Eriksen and Collins found that accuracy at identifying the nonsense syllable decreased as the interval between the presentation of the two stimulus halves increased, until at interstimulus intervals (ISIs) of between 100 and 300 ms performance asymptoted near chance.

Variations of this procedure were used in a series of studies by Di Lollo and his colleagues (e.g., Di Lollo, 1977, 1978, 1980; Di Lollo & Wilson, 1978; Hogben & Di Lollo, 1974). For example, a typical experiment involved the presentation of 24 out of 25 dots from a 5 × 5 square matrix of dots (Fig. 2–5). The dots were presented in two frames of time, 12 dots per frame. The duration of the two frames was held constant at 10 ms, while the interval separating the two frames varied in time. The subjects' task was to report the location of the missing dot. Di Lollo found that performance was almost perfect when the stimulus onset asynchrony between the two frames of dots was 80 ms or less, but that accuracy decreased monotonically for durations longer than this until it was only slightly

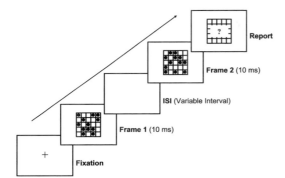

Figure 2–5. Hogben and Di Lollo's (1974) temporal integration procedure.

better than chance at 200 ms (Fig. 2–6). Furthermore, most of the errors that subjects made in this task were due to their reporting as missing a dot presented in frame 1, rather than in frame 2. It was as though information from the first frame persisted for 80 ms or so, then gradually decayed away.

The great advantage of the temporal integration technique over the other visible persistence measures described earlier is that it provides an objective estimate of persistence duration rather than a subjective one that might be influenced by shifts in subjects' criteria across experimental conditions. The temporal integration technique is not perfect, however, because under some

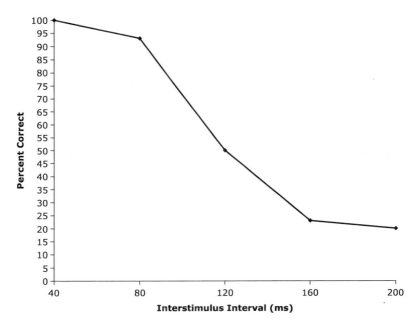

Figure 2–6. Results from Hogben and Di Lollo (1974). Percent correct as a function of interstimulus interval (averaged across subjects) in a temporal integration experiment.

conditions the presentation of the second frame of dots can interfere (rather than integrate) with persisting information from the first frame of dots. For example, Di Lollo and Hogben (1985, 1987) showed that accuracy in the temporal integration task was affected by the distance between individual dots; suppression of visible persistence occurred when the dots were close together, similar to what happens in metacontrast masking (e.g., Matin, 1975). Thus, under these conditions, the temporal integration technique most likely underestimates the duration of visible persistence. Furthermore, it has been shown that increasing the duration of the second frame of dots also lowers accuracy in the temporal integration task, suggesting that performance in this task does not rely only on visible persistence from the first frame of dots but also on the temporal correlation or degree of temporal overlap between the two frames of dots (Dixon & Di Lollo, 1994; Groner, Bischof, & Di Lollo, 1988; but see Francis, 1996, for an alternative view).

2.3.7 Summary

The partial-report technique assesses memory for the locations and identities of items in an array; information (i.e., informational persistence) about the visuo-spatial characteristics of these items seems to be available for approximately 500 ms after stimulus offset. In contrast, the visible persistence methods just described focus directly on the lingering visible trace of the display after its offset. Although no single technique is above reproach, the results obtained from these various methods have indicated clearly that a visible representation of the stimulus display persists for a short time (perhaps only 100 ms) after stimulus offset. Despite the differences in persistence duration estimated by partial-report and visible persistence tasks, prior to 1980, it was widely assumed that visible persistence tasks measured the same internal entity that was measured by partial report: a unitary, precategorical, high-capacity, quickly decaying visible memory (e.g., Coltheart, Lea, & Thompson, 1974; Dick, 1974; Neisser, 1967; von Wright, 1972). This view did not stand the test of time, however, for reasons we will describe next.

2.4 VISIBLE PERSISTENCE VERSUS INFORMATIONAL PERSISTENCE

The methods for studying sensory memory described in the preceding section differ on what aspects of persistence they measure. The partial-report technique is primarily a means of testing memory for item identity and item location, neither of which need be visual in character, whereas the visible persistence techniques require the presence of a visible trace of the stimulus. Thus, the difference in estimated persistence duration found in these two types of tasks might be due to the fact that they examine different attributes of the registered stimulus. In particular, the partial-report technique, which yields longer estimates of persistence, might access more than just raw visible persistence. Two pieces of evidence support this conjecture. One is that most errors in partial-report tasks are mislocation errors, rather than item intrusion errors (e.g., Dick, 1969; Irwin & Yeomans, 1986; Townsend, 1973); that is, when people make an error, they usually report an item that had appeared in the array, but not in the cued location. Furthermore, familiarity with the letter array has been found to reduce the number of intrusion, but not mislocation, errors (Mewhort, Campbell, Marchetti, & Campbell, 1981). These results indicate that the partial-report procedure accesses not just a raw sensory trace of the stimulus, but also a post-categorical store in which array items are identified and remembered quite well even though their locations are forgotten. Further evidence for a distinction between information measured by partial-report tasks and other visible persist-ence tasks is that performance in these tasks is affected differently by stimulus factors such as intensity, duration, and spatial frequency. In short, the stimulus persistence studied by the partial-report technique may be identifiably different from that indexed by the other persistence tasks described earlier, suggesting the presence of multiple levels of stimulus persistence following stimulus offset. This realization led several investigators (e.g., Coltheart, 1980; Di Lollo, 1980; Mewhort et al., 1981; Turvey, 1978) to challenge the widely held view that all information about a stimulus persists in a single, precategorical, high-capacity, quickly decaying "iconic" memory.

The simple, one-store view of visual sensory memory was criticized most thoroughly in a seminal paper by Coltheart (1980). Coltheart distinguished among three types of persistence that follow stimulus offset: *neural* persistence, due to residual activity in the visual pathway; *visible* persistence, or the phe-nomenal impression that the stimulus is still visibly present; and *informational* persistence, or knowledge about the visual properties of the stimulus that per-sist after its offset. Coltheart argued that visible persistence and informational persistence must be separate forms of visual memory. His argument was based on the fact that tasks requiring visible stimulus persistence (e.g., temporal integration tasks) show an inverse relationship between stimulus energy and duration of persistence, whereas tasks that don't require the presence of visible stimulus persistence, but only informational persistence (e.g., partial report tasks), do not. Specifically, the duration of visible persistence has been found to decrease with increasing stimulus duration in judgment of synchrony (Bowen, Pola, & Matin, 1974; Efron, 1970a, 1970b, 1970c; Haber & Standing, 1970), phe-nomenal continuity (Bowling & Lovegrove, 1980; Meyer & Maguire, 1981), and temporal integration tasks (Cohene, 1975; Di Lollo, 1977, 1980; Di Lollo & Wilson, 1978; Hogben & Di Lollo, 1974), but stimulus duration has little or no effect on persistence duration in most partial-report experiments (Di Lollo, 1978; Irwin & Yeomans, 1986; Loftus & Irwin, 1998; Yeomans & Irwin, 1985). Similarly, an inverse relationship between stimulus intensity and visible persist-ence has been found in judgment of synchrony tasks (Bowen et al., 1974; Efron, 1970c) and in phenomenal continuity tasks (Haber & Standing, 1969), but not in partial-report experiments (Adelson & Jonides, 1980; Eriksen & Rohrbaugh, 1970; Scharf & Lefton, 1970). Because visible persistence and informational persistence (as assessed by the partial-report technique) are affected differently by these various stimulus factors, Coltheart concluded that the two forms of persistence must reflect different underlying processes. He proposed that visible persistence is the result of neural persistence in the visual pathway, whereas informational persistence relies on a memory system that exists subsequent to stimulus identification.

Loftus and Irwin (1998) noted that Coltheart's conclusion that visible persistence and informational persistence are affected differently by stimulus duration and stimulus intensity was based on a comparison among experiments that differed on many dimensions (e.g., different subjects, different stimuli, different duration and intensity ranges, and so on). Given these many differences, Loftus and Irwin suggested that it was not completely clear that Coltheart's conclusion was correct. Loftus and Irwin thus examined subjects' performance in three tasks (temporal integration, subjective completeness ratings, and partial report) that measured some aspect of visible and/or informational persistence under experimental conditions that were as similar as possible. Stimulus duration and ISI were varied to determine whether these manipulations affected the three tasks in the same way. Loftus and Irwin found that subjective completeness ratings (i.e., ratings of whether the two stimulus halves in a temporal integration experiment or the letter array and the bar probe in a partial-report experiment appeared to entail one or two distinct temporal events) and accuracy in temporal integration were very highly correlated across experimental conditions, whereas subjective completeness ratings and partial-report accuracy were not. Using a form of dissociation logic called *state-trace analysis* (Bamber, 1979), Loftus and Irwin concluded that subjective completeness and temporal integration measure much the same thing (i.e., visible persistence), whereas subjective completeness and partial-report measure different things (visible persistence and informational persistence, respectively). These findings support Coltheart's conclusion that visible and informational persistence are separate forms of visual sensory memory.

Although not everyone agrees (see Long, 1980), Coltheart's view of visual sensory memory is now the dominant view in the field. Following Coltheart, the emphasis shifted to defining further the nature of the multiple components underlying visual sensory memory and their interactions with each other. This is considered next.

2.5 REPRESENTATIONAL FORMAT OF SENSORY MEMORY

2.5.1 Multistage Models of Sensory Memory

Di Lollo (1978, 1980) was one of the first to propose a two-state model of visual sensory memory. According to Di Lollo, the first state is activated by stimulus onset, sensitive to stimulus energy, retinotopically organized, and sensitive to masking. During this state, features are extracted and held in a precategorical format. The second state in Di Lollo's model begins approximately 100–150 ms after stimulus onset and, during this phase, display items are identified and stored in a postcategorical form that is nonvisible and immune to masking, with only poor coding of spatial position. The first state in Di Lollo's model corresponds well to Coltheart's conception of visible persistence, and the second state to informational persistence.

Campbell and Mewhort (1980; see also Mewhort, Campbell, Marchetti, & Campbell, 1981; Mewhort, Marchetti, Gurnsey, & Campbell, 1984) proposed a very similar *dual-buffer* model around the same time. According to this model, information from a display is first stored in a raw, precategorical format in a *feature buffer*. This raw information is transformed by an identification mechanism into an abstract, postcategorical representation that preserves the relative spatial positions of display items; this information is stored in a *character buffer*. Items are selected from the postcategorical character buffer when a partial-report cue is presented. Location information decays rapidly in the character buffer, causing mislocation retrieval errors in partial-report performance. According to the dual-buffer model, intrusion errors occur because of data corruption at the feature level. Masking is assumed to affect both buffers if mask presentation occurs within 150 ms of stimulus onset, producing both identification and localization failures. At longer delays, however, mask presentation is assumed to interfere with spatial information in the character buffer only, producing only mislocation errors.

The models of Di Lollo and of Mewhort and colleagues are alike in that they both assume that stimulus persistence is recoded into a postcategorical, nonvisual format shortly after stimulus onset, and that it is this nonvisual information that is measured by the partial-report technique. Yeomans and Irwin (1985) proposed instead that informational persistence might retain visual aspects of the stimulus long after stimulus onset. They suggested that information might persist in a visual memory (called the *visual analog representation*) that begins at stimulus offset and lasts for 150–300 ms, independently of exposure duration. This hypothetical visual analog representation differs from visible persistence in that it begins at stimulus *offset* rather than at stimulus onset, and its duration is independent of stimulus exposure duration; it differs from visual short-term memory (VSTM) in that it is maskable and has a short duration.

Irwin and Yeomans (1986) attempted to discriminate between the visual (Yeomans & Irwin, 1985) and nonvisual (e.g., Di Lollo, 1978, 1980; Mewhort et al., 1981) models of informational persistence. They did this by investigating what effect increasing stimulus exposure duration would have on masking. They reasoned that significant masking effects should be observed in partial-report even at long stimulus exposure durations if informational persistence relies on a visual memory that begins at stimulus offset. In contrast, if informational persistence reflects the translation of sensory features into abstract, nonvisual identity codes within 150 ms of stimulus onset, then masking should not be observed in partial-report at long stimulus exposure durations because all display information would be recoded into a nonmaskable form before stimulus offset. To test these predictions, 3 × 3 letter arrays were presented for exposure durations that ranged from 50 to 500 ms. Some time after array offset, a single-character mask was presented at one of the previously occupied letter positions. This mask cued the subject to report the entire row of the array containing the mask. Of interest was the effect of exposure duration and cue delay on report of the masked letter in the cued row relative to report of the nonmasked letters in that row. Irwin and Yeomans found that report of the masked letter was significantly worse than report of the nonmasked letters for cue delays of

0–150 ms, regardless of exposure duration. At cue delays longer than 150 ms, no difference was found in report of the masked and unmasked letters. These results supported the visual conception of informational persistence. Increasing exposure duration was also found to increase accuracy and to reduce intrusion errors, however, especially for the masked letters, suggesting that some recoding of stimulus information into nonvisual identity codes was also occurring. Based on these findings, Irwin and Yeomans concluded that informational persistence consists of at least two memory components: a relatively brief (i.e., no more than 150 ms) representation that begins at stimulus offset and that is visual (i.e., maskable) in nature (i.e., a visual analog representation), and a long-lasting, nonmaskable, postcategorical component. They proposed a new model of informational persistence that included elements of both the visual and non-visual models described earlier. This new model assumed that sensory information from a display is ultimately translated into nonvisual identity codes that have associated with them some abstract representation of spatial position. The longer a display is presented, the more time the translation process has to complete this recoding. However, the translation process can also operate on the contents of a visual analog representation of the display if the display is terminated before the translation process is complete; this representation begins at stimulus offset, has a duration of approximately 150 ms and, unless masked, it maintains form and location information about the display after stimulus offset in order to allow the translation process to extract further information about the stimulus.

Whereas the model of Irwin and Yeomans (1986) was concerned exclusively with describing the characteristics of informational persistence, Di Lollo and Dixon (1988) pointed out that a complete account of sensory memory must also examine the relationship between visible persistence and informational persistence and the role each play in visual memory tasks. They proposed that performance in tasks that require the maintenance of visuo-spatial information in memory is determined jointly by visible persistence and by the visual analog representation (as well as more durable memories that underlie asymptotic performance, such as short-term memory). In their conception, visible persistence is a primitive, visible copy that maintains a very precise spatial representation of the display, has a limited duration that begins at stimulus onset, and has a decay function that is described by a cumulative normal distribution. The visual analog representation, in contrast, is nonvisible and thus has less spatial precision, but it begins at stimulus offset and decays in an exponential fashion. Di Lollo and Dixon formulated a mathematical model based on these assumptions (as well as the assumption that visible persistence and the visual analog representation decay independently of each other) and found that it fit the data from two partial-report experiments very well. Further support for this *independent-decay* model was provided by Dixon and Di Lollo (1991) and by Di Lollo and Dixon (1992).

2.5.2 Visible Persistence Reconsidered

Just as the conception of informational persistence has evolved over time, so too has that of visible persistence. It has been known for decades that the visual system does not respond instantaneously to stimulus onset; rather, its response is delayed in time and can even extend significantly beyond stimulus offset (e.g., Kelly, 1961; Roufs, 1972). This is true at many levels of the visual pathway, from retina to striate cortex (e.g., Duysens, Orban, Cremieux, & Maes, 1985). The visual system thus acts as a linear temporal filter that smears a discrete stimulus into an extended sensory response (see Watson, 1986, for a review). Note that from this perspective the concept of stimulus persistence and "iconic decay" becomes somewhat uninteresting, because it is merely that part of the sensory response function generated by a stimulus that exists after stimulus offset (Fig. 2–7); what is more relevant is how particular experimental manipulations affect the entire sensory response function. Loftus and colleagues (Busey & Loftus, 1994; Loftus, Busey, & Senders, 1993; Loftus, Duncan, & Gehrig, 1992; Loftus & Hanna, 1989; Loftus & Hogden, 1988; Loftus & Irwin, 1998) adopted this notion in proposing a general theory to account for a variety of perceptual phenomena in vision. According to the theory, information is extracted at some instantaneous rate from the sensory response generated by a stimulus. The magnitude of the information extraction rate at any moment in time is determined by the product of the magnitude of the sensory response at that moment and the amount of unextracted information remaining in the stimulus. Phenomenological appearance is assumed to be determined by the rate of information extraction; the stimulus (or its "persistence") will be visible as long as the rate is sufficiently high. The theory accounts successfully for inverse duration and inverse intensity effects in visible persistence tasks because the

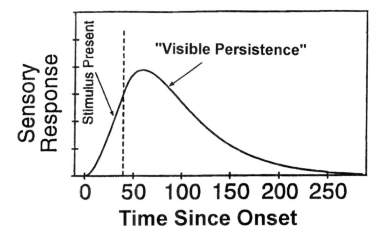

Figure 2–7. The response of the visual system to stimulus presentation can be characterized by a sensory response function that begins at stimulus onset but is smeared across time. According to this conception, "visible persistence" is merely that part of the sensory response function that exists after stimulus offset. Adapted with permission from Massaro, D. & Loftus, G. R. (1996). Sensory storage: Icons and echoes. In *Handbook of Perception and Cognition, Vol. 10*, eds. E. L. Bjork and R. A. Bjork, 68–101. New York: Academic Press/Elsevier.

amount of unextracted information remaining in the stimulus (and hence the rate of information extraction) will be less after stimulus offset for longer and for more intense stimuli.

Loftus and Irwin (1998) applied this model to three different measures of stimulus persistence: temporal integration, completeness rating, and partial-report. They assumed that the probability that two stimuli would appear to be contemporaneous (as judged by completeness rating) would be determined by the temporal correlation of their respective information acquisition rate functions (cf., Dixon & Di Lollo, 1994). They assumed further that temporal integration would be successful to the extent that two visual stimuli were perceived as contemporaneous. In contrast, partial report performance was assumed to be determined by the total amount of acquired information. Loftus and Irwin found that this theory fit their temporal integration and completeness rating data very well, but it was less successful at fitting the partial-report data. Thus, temporal integration and completeness rating, two prototypical "visible persistence" tasks, were accounted for well by a theory that views visible persistence as merely that part of a sensory response function that happens to follow stimulus offset. Partial-report requires an additional mechanism, however, namely the kind of visual analog and nonvisual identity code representations hypothesized to comprise informational persistence.

2.5.3 Summary

In summary, the simple one-store view of visual sensory memory that was widely accepted in the 1960s and 1970s has been replaced in light of substantial evidence that visible persistence and informational persistence have very different properties. It is now widely accepted that the visual system acts as a low-pass temporal filter that generates a sensory response, extended in time in response to the presentation of a discrete visual stimulus (e.g., Groner, Bischof, & Di Lollo, 1988; Dixon & Di Lollo, 1994; Loftus & Irwin, 1998; Loftus & Ruthruff, 1994; Sperling, 1964; Watson, 1986; Wolford, 1992); from this perspective, visible persistence is simply that portion of the sensory response function that exists after stimulus offset. But nonvisible information about the stimulus persists as well, in the form of a visual analog representation that is maskable and that maintains relatively precise shape and location information about the contents of a display for 150–300 ms (Irwin & Yeomans, 1986), and in the form of non-visual identity codes that are not maskable and that contain abstract postcate-gorical information about the elements in a display (Di Lollo, 1978; Mewhort, Campbell, Marchetti, & Campbell, 1981; Mewhort, Marchetti, Gurnsey, & Campbell, 1984).

2.6 RELATIONSHIP BETWEEN SENSORY MEMORY AND VISUAL SHORT-TERM MEMORY

Visual sensory memory has been distinguished from other, more durable forms of memory on the basis of its short duration, sensitivity to masking, and high capacity. The earliest investigators of visual sensory memory acknowledged at the outset that other forms of memory might contribute to performance in prototypical sensory memory tasks such as partial-report and temporal integration however, because performance in these tasks does not fall to chance levels even when long cue delays or ISIs are used (e.g., Averbach & Coriell, 1961; Sperling, 1960; Di Lollo, 1980). In partial-report tasks the long-lasting, durable memory is most likely auditory short-term memory (e.g., Sperling, 1963). In tasks such as temporal integration, in which random dot patterns are used as stimuli, however, it seems more likely that visual short-term memory (VSTM) is used. Phillips (1974) explicitly examined the relationship between visual sensory memory and VSTM by using a visual-matching or change-detection technique. In his experiments, subjects were presented with a visual block pattern created by lighting randomly selected cells in a square matrix (Fig. 2–8). This pattern was presented for 1000 ms, and after an ISI ranging from 20 to 9000 ms, a second block pattern was presented. This second pattern was either identical to the first or different by the addition or deletion of one block. Phillips found that accuracy was essentially perfect when only 20 ms separated the two patterns, and then declined as ISI increased (Fig. 2–9). Furthermore, accuracy at the 20-ms ISI was not affected by pattern complexity (i.e., the number of blocks in each pattern), whereas pattern complexity had a large effect on accuracy at the longer ISIs. In other experiments, he found that shifting one pattern with respect to the other (i.e., presenting the second pattern shifted horizontally by the width of one block) lowered accuracy considerably for ISIs less than 300 ms, but had no effect at longer ISIs. Presenting a visual mask (a checkerboard pattern) during the ISI also disrupted performance at short but not always at long ISIs. Phillips' results are consistent with the conclusion that at least two kinds of visual memory contribute to performance in this task. One is a high-capacity memory with a storage time of 100–300 ms, tied to spatial position and highly sensitive to masking; given that the first pattern in Phillips' experiments was presented for 1000 ms, well outside the time course of visible persistence, this first memory corresponds to informational persistence. The second kind of memory underlying performance in Phillips' experiments is a

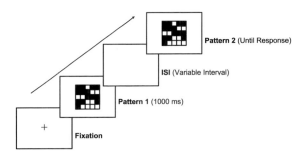

Figure 2–8. Phillips' (1974) change-detection procedure.

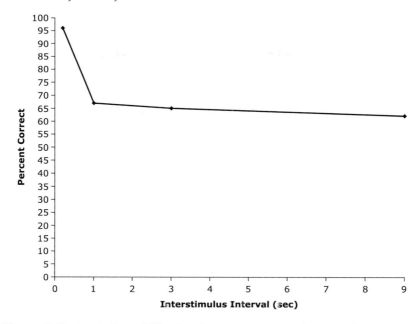

Figure 2–9. Results from Phillips (1974). Percent correct as a function of interstimulus interval (averaged across subjects) in a change-detection experiment.

limited-capacity memory that is not tied to spatial position and is relatively insensitive to visual masking, which corresponds to VSTM.

Irwin (1992c) extended Phillips' (1974) research by varying the duration of the first display as well as the duration of the interstimulus interval. In Irwin's experiments, a random dot pattern (usually 12 dots randomly chosen from a 5 × 5 dot matrix) was presented for some duration; then, some time later, a second pattern of 12 dots was presented that was either identical to the first pattern or different by the displacement of one dot. Subjects indicated whether the two patterns were identical or different, and their accuracy was measured. In one experiment, the first pattern was presented for either 20, 100, or 500 ms, and the second pattern was presented for 20 ms after an ISI that ranged from 10 to 5000 ms. When the first pattern had a short exposure duration (i.e., 20 ms), accuracy was low at the shortest ISI and increased as ISI increased from 10 to 300 ms. Accuracy was constant and quite high for ISIs of 300 to 500 ms, then accuracy declined but remained above chance as ISI increased from 500 to 5000 ms. In contrast, when the first pattern was presented for a longer duration (100 or 500 ms), accuracy was very high at the shortest ISI and decreased monotonically as ISI increased. Irwin attributed the poor performance at short ISIs for short duration patterns to visible persistence; when pattern duration was short and the ISI was short, the two patterns became temporally integrated into a single pattern and it was very difficult to discriminate same and different patterns. When the first pattern was presented for a longer duration, however, its visible persistence was less likely to result in temporal integration and, in fact, apparent motion of the displaced dot was very evident when the patterns were different. In a second experiment, Irwin found that shifting the second pattern, so that it occupied different retinal and spatial positions from the first pattern, lowered accuracy for both short- and long-duration patterns for ISIs as long as 300 ms, but had no effect on accuracy at longer separations. Presenting a masking stimulus during the ISI separating the two patterns interfered with both short- and long-exposure displays for ISIs as long as 250 ms. Another experiment showed that pattern complexity had no effect at ISIs below 1 s, but that accuracy was higher for simple displays than for complex displays at longer intervals.

Irwin (1992c) argued that this collection of results provided evidence for the existence of three distinct forms of visual memory: visible persistence, which is operative at short exposure durations and at short ISIs and sensitive to spatial displacements and masking but not to pattern complexity; informational persistence, which is operative at ISIs between 0 and 500 ms and sensitive to spatial displacement and masking but insensitive to exposure duration and pattern complexity (note that these properties are very similar to those of the visual analog representation observed in partial report experiments); and VSTM, which has a long duration and is insensitive to exposure duration, spatial displacement, and masking, but which has a limited capacity and hence is sensitive to pattern complexity. Visual short-term memory is discussed in more detail in Chapter 3.

2.7 ROLE OF SENSORY MEMORY IN REAL-WORLD VISION

As the cognitive revolution flourished in the 1960s, it became common for sensory memory to be viewed as the front end of the human information processing system; its purpose was to hold the contents of a visual display for some period of time after its offset to allow more time for other information processing mechanisms to operate on the contents of the stimulus (e.g., Neisser, 1967; Sperling, 1963). This view had its detractors, however; some objected to the notion that perception consists of a series of static "snapshots" (e.g. Turvey, 1977), others criticized the sometimes artificial nature of research in this area, such as the use of very brief (e.g., 50 ms) stimulus exposures (e.g., Neisser, 1976), and some argued that sensory memory was of little apparent value to normal perception (e.g., Haber, 1983). These criticisms may have had some validity when applied to the traditional notion of "iconic" memory, but they are less troublesome for the contemporary view of visual sensory memory, which distinguishes among different kinds of persistence following a stimulus event. From the perspective of linear-filter theories of vision, for example, nothing is mysterious or unnatural about visible persistence; it is merely that part of the sensory response function that outlasts the physical stimulus. Engineers and designers have certainly taken advantage of the existence of visible persistence in creating devices such as fluorescent light bulbs, television and computer displays, and motion picture projectors. Of course, no one would suggest that evolution provided the visual system with persistence in order that humans might watch television comfortably, but a number of other possible uses of sensory memory have been proposed, including the maintenance of perceptual continuity over time (e.g. Adelson, 1983; Dixon & Di Lollo, 1994; Wolford, 1992), the rapid detection of changes in the visual environment (e.g., Becker, Pashler, & Anstis, 2000; Dixon & Di Lollo, 1994; Phillips, 1983), and the perception of motion (e.g., Boynton, 1983).

It has also been suggested that some form of sensory memory might be useful in integrating information across successive eye fixations (e.g., Breitmeyer, Kropfl, & Julesz, 1982; Jonides, Irwin, & Yantis, 1982; McConkie & Rayner, 1976; Mewhort, Campbell, Marchetti, & Campbell, 1981). The eyes make rapid *saccadic* movements about three times each second to bring high-resolution foveal vision to bear on objects of interest in the environment; saccade durations are typically short, approximately 30 ms or so, whereas the fixations that separate successive eye movements are approximately 300 ms in duration (Rayner, 1978, 1998). Saccades create problems for perception because visual information sweeps across the retina during the eyes' movement, and the retinal contents of successive eye fixations are not identical. Despite these problems, the visual world appears to be unified, stable, and continuous; how this quality of perception is achieved is one of the classic problems in perception. At one time, it was thought that integration across saccades might rely on a form of visible persistence that was coded in spatial, rather than retinal, coordinates (e.g., Banks, 1983; Breitmeyer et al., 1982; Jonides et al., 1982; McConkie & Rayner, 1976; Trehub, 1977). For example, McConkie and Rayner (1976) proposed that the visible contents of each eye fixation were stored according to their positions in the environment (as opposed to their positions on the retina) in an *integrative visual buffer*. When the eyes moved, the contents of the new eye fixation were assumed to combine with the contents of previous fixations to produce an integrated representation of the visual environment. Subsequent research has failed to demonstrate the existence of spatiotopic visible persistence, however (see Irwin, 1992b, 1996 for reviews). Transsaccadic integration based on retinotopic visible persistence has been demonstrated (Irwin, Brown, & Sun, 1988; Irwin, Zacks, & Brown, 1990), but only when a brief display is presented immediately before the eyes move, and not when longer (and hence more naturalistic) exposure durations are employed And, of course, retinotopic transsaccadic integration is actually detrimental under normal viewing conditions because it leads to information at different spatial positions being combined in memory.

In sum, visible persistence appears to play no role in information integration across saccades under normal viewing conditions. What about informational persistence? The answer to this question is less clear, but some evidence suggests that something like the visual analog representation (i.e., a nonvisible, maskable representation that holds precise form and location information for a brief time) of Irwin and Yeomans (1986) might persist across saccades. For example, Palmer and Ames (1992) found that people can make very precise discriminations of line length across saccades, and Hayhoe, Lachter, and Feldman (1991) found that subjects could judge whether the spatial positions of single dots viewed in successive fixations formed a right triangle. In addition, McRae, Butler, and Popiel (1987) and Irwin (1992a) found small spatiotopic masking effects across saccades. Other results suggest that little informational persistence survives a saccade, however. For example, immediate memory across successive eye fixations appears to be limited to only four items (Irwin, 1992a; Irwin & Andrews, 1996), and it has a long duration (at least 5 s), is sensitive to stimulus complexity, and is stored in a location-independent format (Carlson-Radvansky & Irwin, 1995; Irwin, 1991). These results suggest that transsaccadic memory relies largely on VSTM (as well as visual long-term memory, as discussed in Chapters 4 and 5), rather than on any form of sensory memory. When saccades are made, sensory memory appears to be erased and replaced with the contents of the new eye fixation. Recent research indicates that the same is true for eyeblinks, as well (O'Regan, Deubel, Clark, & Rensink, 2000; Thomas & Irwin, 2006). The role of visual memory in integration across eye movements is discussed in more detail in Chapters 4 and 5.

2.8 NEURAL BASIS OF SENSORY MEMORY

Sensory memory appears to rely on neural persistence at many levels of the visual system. Electrophysiological recordings of rods and cones in the macaque have found that the photoreceptors continue to respond for some time after stimulus offset (Whitten & Brown, 1973a, 1973b, 1973c). In the early days (i.e., pre-Coltheart, 1980), some attempt was made to explain sensory memory purely in terms of persistence in the photoreceptors, especially the rods (e.g., Sakitt, 1975, 1976; Sakitt & Long, 1978, 1979a, 1979b), but subsequent research has disconfirmed this hypothesis. For example, color information persists throughout the delay period in partial-report experiments (Adelson, 1978; Banks & Barber, 1977), even when stimuli are matched for brightness, indicating that rods are not a necessary component of sensory memory. Partial-report superiorities have also been found when small letters (which the rod system would be unable to resolve) are used as stimuli, and under high-luminance conditions in which the rods are saturated and thus nonfunctioning (Adelson & Jonides, 1980). Thus, there is more to sensory memory than just the rod system. Adelson and Jonides (1980) argued that the cone system is also an unlikely candidate for being the sole locus of sensory memory, because both electrophysiological evidence (e.g., Baron, Boynton, & Hammond, 1979) and psychophysical analyses (e.g., Kelly, 1971; Sperling & Sondhi, 1968) suggest that cone persistence is no longer than 50–80 ms, considerably less than the estimates typically found in most sensory memory tasks.

Retinal ganglion cells also persist. For example, Levick and Zacks (1970) found that retinal ganglion cells in cats responded for at least 50–70 ms to stimuli that had durations as short as 8 ms. Subsequent research identified two distinct types of retinal ganglion cells that differ in their responsiveness to various aspects of a visual stimulus. One type of cell responds with a quick burst of activity at stimulus onset and at stimulus offset, but is relatively inactive while the stimulus is present. The second type of cell begins responding sometime after stimulus onset and continues to respond while the stimulus is present, gradually ceasing to respond after stimulus offset. These two types of cells were called *transient* and *sustained* cells, respectively (in contemporary terms, they correspond to M and P ganglion cells, respectively). Electrophysiological and psychophysical studies showed that these cells differed in a number of ways. For example, transient cells have faster conduction velocities and larger receptive fields than the sustained cells (Cleland, Levick, & Sanderson, 1973), and transient cells are more responsive to low spatial frequencies than to high—the reverse being true for sustained cells (Breitmeyer & Ganz, 1976). Evidence also suggests that transient activity can inhibit sustained activity, and vice versa (Breitmeyer, 1980; Singer & Bedworth, 1973). Breitmeyer (1980) proposed that interactions between transient and sustained channels could account for several aspects of performance in sensory memory tasks. For example, because transient activity precedes sustained activity by about 100 ms (Breitmeyer & Ganz, 1976), the presentation of two visual events within 100 ms of one another should lead to temporal integration, whereas longer intervals should lead to masking, just as Di Lollo (1980) has found in his temporal integration experiments.

Neural persistence has also been found in visual cortex (Duysens, Orban, Cremieux, & Maes, 1985). Duysens et al. found that cells in area 17 of the cat (corresponding to area V1 in humans) continue to respond after stimulus offset, and the duration of this persisting response is inversely related to stimulus duration. In this respect, these cortical neurons exhibit an inverse duration effect that parallels behavioral data that also show that visible persistence duration is inversely related to stimulus duration. Psychophysical evidence for the existence of cortical persistence comes from Engel's (1970) demonstration of stereoscopic persistence. Engel presented pairs of Julesz random-brightness stereograms to separate eyes and found that stereopsis was experienced if the second member of the pair was presented within about 80 ms of the offset of the first member of the pair. Once established, the stereoscopic sensation persisted for some 300 ms before the two stimuli had to be presented again to regenerate the phenomenon. These results suggest the existence of an 80-ms monocular persistence and a 300-ms binocular persistence of cortical origin.

Although visible persistence appears to rely on neural persistence throughout the early visual pathway, the neural correlates of informational persistence appear to involve higher-level visual areas. Few studies have explicitly investigated the neural basis of informational persistence, but a recent report by Keysers, Xiao, Földiák, and Perrett (2005) has shown that areas beyond V1 are involved. Humans in this study performed a task in which they viewed a target image and were then asked whether this target was present or absent in a rapid serial visual presentation (RSVP) stream of images under three different conditions. In the *short no-gap* condition, stimuli in the RSVP stream were shown for either 18 or 4 ms, with no breaks between successive stimuli. In the *long no-gap* condition, stimuli were shown for either 102 or 46 ms, once again with no breaks between stimuli. Finally, in the *gap* condition, stimuli were presented for the same durations as in the short no-gap condition (18 or 4 ms), but were separated by presentations of a blank screen for either 93 or 51 ms, such that the stimulus-onset asynchrony (SOA) was the same as for the long no-gap condition. The physical stimulus always remained on-screen until the next was presented in both of the no-gap conditions, leaving no opportunities for informational persistence; under gap conditions, however, it was conceivable that informational persistence might fill the gap and lead to performance similar to that observed under no-gap conditions. Participants' performance in this task indicated that this is exactly what happened; accuracy at detecting the presence/ absence of a target was the same for the gap and long no-gap conditions, indicating that informational persistence filled the gap as effectively as the physical target. Although the actual stimulus durations were equivalent for the short no-gap and gap conditions, performance in the short no-gap condition was poorer than either of the other two conditions, presumably because the rapid replacement of one stimulus with another in the short no-gap condition eliminated the possibility of using informational persistence to perform the task.

To investigate the neural correlates of informational persistence, Keysers et al. (2005) presented macaque monkeys with continuous RSVP streams of the same stimuli that the human participants had observed with the same three timing conditions (short no-gap, long no-gap, gap). They found that neurons in anterior superior temporal sulcus (STSa) of the macaque monkeys responded in ways that mirrored the accuracy patterns of the human participants. For example, neuronal responses were equal in the gap and long no-gap conditions, and responses in both of these conditions were stronger than those in the short no-gap condition. They proposed that informational persistence is due to persistence in STSa neurons and pointed out that the properties of these neurons can also account for other known psychophysical properties of informational persistence. For example, recall that informational persistence has a duration of several hundred milliseconds, and that this duration is independent of stimulus exposure duration; this is true of STSa neurons as well (Kovács, Vogels, & Orban, 1995; Rolls & Tovee, 1994). Informational persistence is maskable, and the persistence of STSa neurons is also known to be terminated by the presentation of a new stimulus (Keysers, Xiao, Földiák, and Perrett, 2001; Kovács et al., 1995; Rolls & Tovee, 1994). Finally, informational persistence represents identity information better than position information (as shown by the preponderance of mislocation errors over intrusion errors in partial-report, for example); STSa neurons are part of the ventral stream and thus are specialized for representing identity information as opposed to spatial position (e.g., they have relatively large receptive fields).

In sum, sensory memory appears to rely on neural persistence throughout the visual pathway. Precategorical, visible persistence is available early in the visual processing stream, whereas postcategorical information persists for longer durations in parts of the ventral stream. The neural mechanisms of visual memory are discussed in more detail in Chapter 8.

2.9 CONCLUSION

Although textbooks still typically portray visual sensory memory as a unitary, precategorical, high-capacity, quickly decaying visible memory, decades of research have shown that this simple view is incorrect. Rather, multiple forms of visual sensory memory exist, including visible persistence, a visual analog representation, and nonvisual identity codes (the latter two comprising informational persistence). The neural substrates of these phenomena are beginning to be understood, and research continues to investigate their role in many aspects of visual cognition.

ACKNOWLEDGMENTS

Preparation of this chapter was supported by NSF grant BCS 01–32292 to D. E. Irwin and by an NSF Graduate Research Fellowship to L. E. Thomas.

REFERENCES

Adelson, E. (1978). Iconic storage: The role of rods. *Science* 201:544–546.

Adelson, E. (1983). What is iconic storage good for? *Behavioral and Brain Sciences* 6:11–12.

Adelson, E., and Jonides, J. (1980). The psychophysics of iconic storage. *Journal of Experimental Psychology: Human Perception and Performance* 6:486–493.

Allen, F. (1926). The persistence of vision. *American Journal of Physiological Optics* 7:439–457.

Averbach, E., and Coriell, A. (1961). Short-term memory in vision. *Bell Systems Technical Journal* 40:309–328.

Averbach, E., and Sperling, G. (1961). Short-term storage of information in vision. In *Information Theory*, ed. C. Cherry, 196–211. London: Butterworth.

Bamber, D. (1979). State trace analysis: A method of testing simple theories of causation. *Journal of Mathematical Psychology* 19:137–181.

Banks, W. (1983). On the decay of the icon. *Behavioral and Brain Sciences* 6:14.

Banks, W., and Barber, G. (1977). Color information in iconic memory. *Psychological Review* 84:536–546.

Baron, W., Boynton, R., and Hammon, R. (1979). Component analysis of the foveal local electroretinogram elicited with sinusoidal flicker. *Vision Research* 19:479–490.

Becker, M., Pashler, H., and Anstis. S. (2000). The role of iconic memory in change-detection tasks. *Perception*, 29, 273–286.

Bowen., R., Pola, J., and Matin, L. (1974). Visual persistence: Effects of flash luminance, duration, and energy. *Vision Research* 14:295–303.

Bowling, A., and Lovegrove, W. (1980). The effect of stimulus duration on the persistence of gratings. *Perception and Psychophysics* 27:574–578.

Boynton, R. (1983). On "raw perception" of "the stimulus itself". *Behavioral and Brain Sciences* 6:15.

Breitmeyer, B. (1980). Unmasking visual masking: A look at the "why" behind the veil of "how." *Psychological Review* 87:52–69.

Breitmeyer, B., and Ganz, L. (1976). Implications of sustained and transient channels for theories of visual pattern masking, saccadic suppression, and information processing. *Psychological Review* 83:1–36.

Breitmeyer, B., Kropfl, W., and Julesz, B. (1982). The existence and role of retinotopic and spatiotopic forms of visual persistence. *Acta Psychologica* 52:175–196.

Briggs, G., and Kinsbourne, M. (1972). Visual persistence as measured by reaction time. *Quarterly Journal of Experimental Psychology* 24:318–325.

Busey, T., and Loftus, G. (1994). Sensory and cognitive components of visual information acquisition. *Psychological Review* 101:446–469.

Campbell, A., and Mewhort, D. (1980). On familiarity effects in visual information processing. *Canadian Journal of Psychology* 34:134–154.

Carlson-Radvansky, L. A., and Irwin, D. E. (1995). Memory for structural information across eye movements. *Journal of Experimental Psychology: Learning, Memory, and Cognition* 21:1441–1458.

Cattell, J. (1883). Über die Trägheit der Netzhaut und des Sehcentrums. *Philosophische Studien* 3:94–127.

Clark. S. (1969). Retrieval of color information from preperception memory. *Journal of Experimental Psychology* 82:263–266.

Cleland, B., Levick, W., and Sanderson, K. (1973). Properties of sustained and transient ganglion cells in the cat retina. *Journal of Physiology* 228:649–680.

Cohene, L. (1975). Iconic memory of dot patterns: Preliminary report. *Perceptual and Motor Skills* 41:167–170.

Coltheart, M. (1975). Iconic memory: A reply to Professor Holding. *Memory and Cognition* 3:42–48.

Coltheart, M. (1980). Iconic memory and visible persistence. *Perception and Psychophysics* 27:183–228.

Coltheart, M., Lea, C., and Thompson, K. (1974). In defense of iconic memory. *Quarterly Journal of Experimental Psychology* 26:633–641.

Crowder, R. (1976). *Principles of learning and memory*. Hillsdale, NJ: Erlbaum.

Dick, A. (1969). Relations between the sensory register and short-term storage in tachistoscopic recognition. *Journal of Experimental Psychology* 82:279–284.

Dick, A. (1974). Iconic memory and its relation to perceptual processes and other mechanisms. *Perception and Psychophysics* 16:575–596.

Di Lollo, V. (1977). Temporal characteristics of iconic memory. *Nature* 267:241–243.

Di Lollo, V. (1978). On the spatio-temporal interactions of brief visual displays. In *Studies in Perception*, eds., R. Day and G. Stanley, 39–55. Perth: University of Western Australia Press.

Di Lollo, V. (1980). Temporal integration in visual memory. *Journal of Experimental Psychology: General* 109:75–97.

Di Lollo, V., and Dixon, P. (1988). Two forms of persistence in visual information processing. *Journal of Experimental Psychology: Human Perception and Performance* 14:671–681.

Di Lollo, V., and Dixon, P. (1992). Inverse duration effects in partial report. *Journal of Experimental Psychology: Human Perception and Performance* 18:1089–1100.

Di Lollo, V., and Hogben, J. (1985). Suppression of visible persistence. *Journal of Experimental Psychology: Human Perception and Performance* 11:304–316.

Di Lollo, V., and Hogben, J. (1987). Suppression of visible persistence as a function of spatial separation between inducing stimuli. *Perception and Psychophysics* 41:345–354.

Di Lollo, V., and Wilson, A. (1978). Iconic persistence and perceptual moment as determinants of temporal integration in vision. *Vision Research* 18:1607–1610.

Dixon, P., and Di Lollo, V. (1991). Effects of display luminance, stimulus type, and probe duration on visible and schematic persistence. *Canadian Journal of Psychology* 45:54–74.

Dixon, P., and Di Lollo, V. (1994). Beyond visible persistence: An alternative account of temporal integration and segregation in visual processing. *Cognitive Psychology* 26:33–63.

Duysens, J., Orban, G., Cremieux, J., and Maes, H. (1985). Visual cortical correlates of visible persistence. *Vision Research* 25:171–178.

Efron, R. (1970a). Effects of stimulus duration on perceptual onset and offset latencies. *Perception and Psychophysics* 8:231–234.

Efron, R. (1970b). The minimum duration of a perception. *Neuropsychologia* 8:57–63.

Efron, R. (1970c). The relationship between the duration of a stimulus and the duration of a perception. *Neuropsychologia* 8:37–55.

Engel, G. (1970). An investigation of visual responses to brief stereoscopic stimuli. *Quarterly Journal of Experimental Psychology* 22:148–160.

Erdmann, B., and Dodge, R. (1898). *Psychologische Untersuchengen über das Lesen auf experimenteller Grundlage*. Halle: Niemeyer.

Eriksen, C., and Collins, J. (1967). Some temporal characteristics of visual pattern recognition. *Journal of Experimental Psychology* 74:476–484.

Eriksen, C., and Collins, J. (1968). Sensory traces versus the psychological moment in the temporal organization of form. *Journal of Experimental Psychology* 77:376–382.

Eriksen, C., and Rohrbaugh, J. (1970). Visual masking in multi-element displays. *Journal of Experimental Psychology* 83:147–154.

Fraisse, P. (1966). Visual perceptive simultaneity and masking of letters successively presented. *Perception and Psychophysics* 1:285–287.

Francis, G. (1996). Cortical dynamics of visual persistence and temporal integration. *Perception and Psychophysics* 58:1203–1212.

Gegenfurtner, K., and Sperling, G. (1993). Information transfer in iconic memory experiments. *Journal of Experimental Psychology: Human Perception and Performance* 19:845–866.

Groner, M., Bischof, W., and Di Lollo, V. (1988). A model of visible persistence and temporal integration. *Spatial Vision* 3:293–304.

Haber, R. (1983). The impending demise of the icon: A critique of the concept of iconic storage in visual information processing. *Behavioral and Brain Sciences* 6:1–10.

Haber, R., and Hershenson, M. (1973). *The psychology of visual perception*. New York: Holt, Rinehart, and Winston.

Haber, R., and Standing, L. (1969). Direct measures of short-term visual storage. *Quarterly Journal of Experimental Psychology* 21:43–54.

Haber, R., and Standing, L. (1970). Direct estimates of the apparent duration of a flash. *Canadian Journal of Psychology* 24:216–229.

Hawkins, H., and Shulman, G. (1979). Two definitions of persistence in visual perception. *Perception and Psychophysics* 25:348–350.

Hayhoe, M., Lachter, J., and Feldman, J. (1991). Integration of form across saccadic eye movements. *Perception* 20:393–402.

Hogben, J., and Di Lollo, V. (1974). Perceptual integration and perceptual segregation of brief visual stimuli. *Vision Research* 14:1059–1069.

Holding, D. (1970). Guessing behavior and the Sperling store. *Quarterly Journal of Experimental Psychology* 22:248–256.

Holding, D. (1975a). Doubts about iconic memory: A reply to Coltheart, Lea and Thompson. *Quarterly Journal of Experimental Psychology* 27:507–509.

Holding, D. (1975b). Sensory storage revisited. *Memory and Cognition* 3:31–41.

Irwin, D. E. (1991). Information integration across saccadic eye movements. *Cognitive Psychology* 23:420–456.

Irwin, D. E. (1992a). Memory for position and identity across eye movements. *Journal of Experimental Psychology: Learning, Memory, and Cognition* 18:307–317.

Irwin, D. E. (1992b). Perceiving an integrated visual world. In *Attention and Performance XIV: Synergies in Experimental Psychology, Artificial Intelligence, and Cognitive Neuroscience*, eds. D. E. Meyer and S. Kornblum, 121–142. Cambridge, MA: MIT Press.

Irwin, D. E. (1992c). Visual memory within and across fixations. In *Eye Movements and Visual Cognition: Scene Perception and Reading*, ed. K. Rayner, 146–165. New York: Springer-Verlag.

Irwin, D. E. (1996). Integrating information across saccadic eye movements. *Current Directions in Psychological Science* 5:94–100.

Irwin, D. E., and Andrews, R. (1996). Integration and accumulation of information across saccadic eye movements. In *Attention and Performance XVI: Information Integration in Perception and Communication*, eds. T. Inui and J. L. McClelland, 125–155. Cambridge, MA: MIT Press.

Irwin, D. E., Brown, J. S., and Sun, J.-S. (1988). Visual masking and visual integration across saccadic eye movements. *Journal of Experimental Psychology: General* 117:274–285.

Irwin, D. E., and Yeomans, J. M. (1986). Sensory registration and informational persistence. *Journal of Experimental Psychology: Human Perception and Performance* 12:343–360.

Irwin, D. E., Zacks, J. L., and Brown, J. S. (1990). Visual memory and the perception of a stable visual environment. *Perception and Psychophysics* 47:35–46.

Jonides, J., Irwin, D., and Yantis, S. (1982). Integrating visual information from successive fixations. *Science* 215:192–194.

Kahneman, D. (1968). Method, findings, and theory in studies of visual masking. *Psychological Bulletin* 70:404–425.

Kelly, D. (1961). Visual responses to time-dependent stimuli. II. Single-channel model of the photopic visual system. *Journal of the Optical Society of America* 51:747–754.

Kelly, D. (1971). Theory of flicker and transient responses, I. Uniform fields. *Journal of the Optical Society of America* 61:537–546.

Keysers, C., Xiao, D., Földiák, P., and Perrett, D. (2001). The speed of sight. *Journal of Cognitive Neuroscience* 13:90–101.

Keysers, C., Xiao, D., Földiák, P., and Perrett, D. (2005). Out of sight but not out of mind: The neurophysiology of iconic memory in the superior temporal sulcus. *Cognitive Neuropsychology* 22:316–332.

Kovács, G., Vogels, R., and Orban, G. (1995). Cortical correlate of pattern backward masking. *Proceedings of the National Academy of Sciences USA* 92:5587–5591.

Levick, W., and Zacks, J. (1970). Responses of cat retinal ganglion cells to brief flashes of light. *Journal of Physiology (London)* 206:677–700.

Lichtenstein, M. (1961). Phenomenal simultaneity with irregular timing of components of the visual stimulus. *Perceptual and Motor Skills* 12:47–60.

Loftus, G., Busey, T., and Senders, J. (1993). Providing a sensory basis for models of visual information acquisition. *Perception and Psychophysics* 54:535–554.

Loftus, G., Duncan, J., and Gehrig, P. (1992). On the time course of perceptual information that results from a brief visual presentation. *Journal of Experimental Psychology: Human Perception and Performance* 18:530–549.

Loftus, G., and Hanna, A. (1989). The phenomenology of spatial integration: Data and models. *Cognitive Psychology* 21:363–397.

Loftus, G., and Hogden, J. (1988). Picture perception: Information extraction and phenomenological persistence. In *The Psychology of Learning and Motivation Vol. 22*, ed., G. Bower. New York: Academic Press.

Loftus, G., and Irwin, D. (1998). On the relations among different measures of visible and informational persistence. *Cognitive Psychology* 35:135–199.

Loftus, G., Johnson, C., and Shimamura, A. (1985). How much is an icon worth? *Journal of Experimental Psychology: Human Perception and Performance* 11:1–13.

Loftus, G., and Ruthruff, E. (1994). A linear-filter theory of visual information acquisition with special application to intensity-duration tradeoffs. *Journal of Experimental Psychology: Human Perception and Performance* 20:33–55.

Long, G. (1980). Iconic memory: A review and critique of the study of short-term visual storage. *Psychological Bulletin* 88:785–820.

Matin, E. (1975). The two-transient (masking) paradigm. *Psychological Review* 82:451–461.

McConkie, G., and Rayner, K. (1976). Identifying the span of the effective stimulus in reading: Literature review and theories of reading. In *Theoretical Models and Processes of Reading*, eds. H. Singer and R. Ruddell, 137–162. Newark, DE: International Reading Association.

McFarland, J. (1965). Sequential part presentation: A method of studying visual form presentation. *British Journal of Psychology* 56:439–446.

McRae, K., Butler, B., and Popiel, S. (1987). Spatiotopic and retinotopic components of iconic memory. *Psychological Research* 49:221–227.

Merikle, P. (1980). Selection from visual persistence by perceptual groups and category membership. *Journal of Experimental Psychology: General* 109:279–295.

Mewhort, D., Campbell, A., Marchetti, F., and Campbell, J. (1981). Identification, localization, and "iconic memory": An evaluation of the bar-probe task. *Memory and Cognition* 9:50–67.

Mewhort, D., Marchetti, F., Gurnsey, R., and Campbell, A. (1984). Information persistence: A dual-buffer model for initial visual processing. In *Attention and Performance X*, eds. H. Bouma and D. Bouwhuis, 287–298. London: Erlbaum.

Meyer, G., Lawson, R., and Cohen, W. (1975). The effects of orientation-specific adaptation on the duration of short-term visual storage. *Vision Research* 15:569–572.

Meyer, G., and Maguire, W. (1981). Effects of spatial frequency specific adaptation and target duration on visible persistence. *Journal of Experimental Psychology: Human Perception and Performance* 7:151–156.

Neisser, U. (1967). *Cognitive psychology*. New York: Appleton-Century-Crofts.

O'Regan, J., Deubel, H., Clark, J., and Rensink, R. (2000). Picture changes during blinks: Looking without seeing and seeing without looking. *Visual Cognition* 7:191–211.

Palmer, J., and Ames, C. (1992). Measuring the effect of multiple eye fixations on memory for visual attributes. *Perception and Psychophysics* 52:295–306.

Phillips, W. (1974). On the distinction between sensory storage and short-term visual memory. *Perception and Psychophysics* 16:283–290.

Phillips, W. (1983). Change perception needs sensory storage. *Behavioral and Brain Sciences* 6:35–36.

Purcell, D., and Stewart, A. (1971). The two-flash threshold: An evaluation of critical duration and visual persistence hypotheses. *Perception and Psychophysics* 9:61–64.

Rayner, K. (1978). Eye movements in reading and information processing. *Psychological Bulletin* 85:618–660.

Rayner, K. (1998). Eye movements in reading and information processing: Twenty years of research. *Psychological Bulletin* 124:372–422.

Rolls, E., and Tovee, M. (1994). Processing speed in the cerebral cortex and the neurophysiology of visual masking. *Proceedings of the Royal Society of London B: Biological Sciences* 257:9–15.

Roufs, J. (1972). Dynamic properties of vision. II. Theoretical relationships between flicker and flash thresholds. *Vision Research* 12:279–292.

Sakitt, B. (1975). Locus of short-term visual storage. *Science* 190:1318–1319.

Sakitt, B. (1976). Iconic memory. *Psychological Review* 83:257–276.

Sakitt, B., and Long, G. (1978). Relative rod and cone contributions to iconic storage. *Perception and Psychophysics* 23:527–536.

Sakitt, B., and Long, G. (1979a). Cones determine subjective offset of a stimulus but rods determine total persistence. *Vision Research* 19:1439–1441.

Sakitt, B., and Long, G. (1979b). Spare the rod and spoil the icon. *Journal of Experimental Psychology: Human Perception and Performance* 5:19–30.

Scharf, B., and Lefton, L. (1970). Backward and forward masking as a function of stimulus and task parameters. *Journal of Experimental Psychology* 84:331–338.

Singer, W., and Bedworth, N. (1973). Inhibitory interaction between X and Y units in cat lateral geniculate nucleus. *Brain Research* 49:291–307.

Sperling, G. (1960). The information available in brief visual presentations. *Psychological Monographs* 74:1–29.

Sperling, G. (1963). A model for visual memory tasks. *Human Factors* 5:19–31.

Sperling, G. (1964). Linear theory and the psychophysics of flicker. *Documenta Ophthalmologica* 18:3–15.

Sperling, G. (1967). Successive approximations to a model for short-term memory. *Acta Psychologica* 27:285–292.

Sperling, G., and Sondhi, M. (1968). Model for visual luminance discrimination and flicker detection. *Journal of the Optical Society of America* 58:1133–1145.

Thomas, L., and Irwin, D. (2006). Voluntary eyeblinks disrupt iconic memory. *Perception and Psychophysics* 68:475–488.

Townsend, V. (1973). Loss of spatial and identity information following a tachistoscopic exposure. *Journal of Experimental Psychology* 98:113–118.

Trehub, A. (1977). Neuronal models for cognitive processes: Networks for learning, perception, and imagination. *Journal of Theoretical Biology* 65:141–169.

Turvey, M. (1977). Contrasting orientations to a theory of visual information processing. *Psychological Review* 84:67–88.

Turvey, M. (1978). Visual processing and short-term memory. In *Handbook of Learning and Cognitive Processes, Vol. 5*, ed. W. K. Estes, 91–142. Hillsdale, NJ: Erlbaum.

Turvey, M. and Kravetz, S. (1970). Retrieval from iconic memory with shape as the selection criterion. *Perception and Psychophysics* 8:71–172.

Von Wright, J. (1968). Selection in immediate visual memory. *Quarterly Journal of Experimental Psychology* 20:62–68.

Von Wright, J. (1972). On the problem of selection in iconic memory. *Scandinavian Journal of Psychology* 13:159–171.

Watson, A. B. (1986). Temporal sensitivity. In *Handbook of Perception and Human Performance Vol. 1*, eds. K. Boff, L. Kaufman, and J. Thomas. New York: Wiley.

Whitten, D., and Brown, K. (1973a). The time courses of late receptor potentials from monkey cones and rods. *Vision Research* 13:107–135.

Whitten, D., and Brown, K. (1973b). Photopic suppression of monkey's rod receptor potential, apparently by a cone-initiated lateral inhibition. *Vision Research* 13:1629–1658.

Whitten, D., and Brown, K. (1973c). Slowed decay of the monkey's cone receptor potential by intense stimuli, and protection from this effect by light adaptation. *Vision Research* 13:1659–1667.

Wolford, G. (1992). A model of visible persistence based on linear systems. *Canadian Psychology* 34:162–165.

Yeomans, J. M., and Irwin, D. E. (1985). Stimulus duration and partial report performance. *Perception and Psychophysics* 37:163–169.

Chapter 3

Visual Short-term Memory

Steven J. Luck
University of California, Davis

3.1 MEMORY SYSTEMS

3.1.1 Short-term Memory, Long-term Memory, and Working Memory

Memory researchers have made a distinction between short-term memory (STM) and long-term memory (LTM) systems for over 100 years (e.g., Calkins, 1898; Jacobs, 1887; James, 1890), and this distinction continues to play an important role in contemporary research on visual memory. The visual short-term memory (VSTM) system is generally thought to have four key properties that distinguish it from the visual long-term memory (VLTM) system. First, VSTM representations are created rapidly, with arrays of objects being encoded in VSTM at rates of 20–50 ms/item (Gegenfurtner & Sperling, 1993; Shibuya & Bundesen, 1988; Vogel, Woodman, & Luck, 2006). In contrast, VLTM representations are created more slowly, becoming richer and more robust as observers examine objects and scenes over periods of seconds (see Chapter 5). Second, VSTM representations are maintained by means of an active mechanism, implemented at the neural level by sustained neural firing while the memory is being maintained (see Chapter 8). In contrast, VLTM representations are maintained passively by means of structural modifications that lead to changes in synaptic strength. A consequence of this difference is that VSTM representations terminate when the active maintenance ends, whereas VLTM representations may persist indefinitely. Third, VSTM appears to have a highly limited storage capacity of just a few simple objects (Cowan, 2001; Phillips, 1974), whereas it is possible to store thousands of complex, real-world scenes concurrently VLTM (Nickerson, 1965; Standing, 1973). Fourth, each representation in VSTM contains a limited amount of information (Simons & Rensink, 2005), perhaps corresponding to one part or segment of an object (Sakai & Inui, 2002; Xu, 2002b), whereas VLTM representations can be very rich (see Chapter 5).

Much research on VSTM has taken place within the context of Baddeley's model of *working memory* (A. Baddeley & Logie, 1999; A. D. Baddeley, 1986; Baddeley & Hitch, 1974). In this model, modality-dependent short-term storage systems interact with a central executive, and the central executive links these short-term storage systems with perceptual, motor, and LTM systems.

The working memory model is sometimes viewed as being a competitor or successor to the concept of STM. However, the initial goal of the working memory model was not to replace the concept of STM but instead to shift the emphasis of research on STM away from the nature of the memory systems themselves and onto the role of these systems as buffers that are used in the service of cognitive tasks (see Baddeley, 1986). Thus, no conflict exists between research on VSTM and research on working memory, and it is reasonable to view VSTM as being the visual storage component of the working memory model. Because the idea of viewing VSTM as a buffer used by visual processes is attractive, this chapter will assume that the VSTM research being described refers to the visual storage component of a broader working memory system. However, because most recent VSTM research has not focused on the role of VSTM in performing cognitive "work," the term *visual short-term memory* will be used instead of *visual working memory* throughout the chapter. The role of VSTM as a temporary storage buffer for complex cognitive tasks will be considered at the end of the chapter.

3.1.2 Subdividing Visual Short-term Memory

A large amount of evidence indicates that verbal STM and visual STM are distinct memory stores. For example, brain damage can lead to a disruption of verbal STM without a disruption of visual STM and vice versa (De Renzi & Nichelli, 1975), and it is possible to occupy verbal STM with one task without impacting visual STM for another task and vice versa (Scarborough, 1972; Vogel, Woodman, & Luck, 2001).

A more controversial proposal, however, is that VSTM can be subdivided into two separate storage subsystems, one for spatial information and another for object identity information. One source of evidence for this proposal comes from interference studies, which assess the degree of interference between a memory task and a concurrent nonmemory task. These studies have shown that some concurrent tasks interfere with spatial memory performance but not with object memory, whereas other concurrent tasks interfere with object memory but not with spatial memory (Hyun & Luck, 2007; Logie & Marchetti, 1991; Tresch, Sinnamon, & Seamon, 1993; Woodman & Luck, 2004; Woodman, Vogel, & Luck, 2001). In addition, neuropsychological studies have shown that it is possible to disrupt object memory without disrupting spatial memory, or vice versa (De Renzi & Nichelli, 1975; Farah, Hammond, Levine, & Calvanio, 1988; Hanley, Young, & Person, 1991).

Another source of evidence comes from measurements of neural activity during the delay periods of spatial and object memory tasks (see Chapter 8 for a more extensive discussion). Studies of single-unit activity in monkeys have found delay activity in posterior parietal cortex in spatial memory tasks (e.g., Gnadt & Andersen, 1988), whereas the delay activity is observed in inferotemporal cortex in object memory tasks (e.g., Fuster & Jervey, 1981; Miller, Li, & Desimone, 1993). Similar results have been observed in human neuroimaging studies (e.g., Cohen, Perlstein, Braver, Nystrom, Noll, Jonides, & Smith, 1997; Courtney, Ungerleider, Keil, & Haxby, 1996; Courtney, Ungerleider, Keil, & Haxby, 1997; Smith & Jonides, 1997).

However, other evidence conflicts with the idea of separate spatial and object memory systems. In particular, areas of prefrontal cortex appear to show delay activity during both spatial and object memory tasks (Postle & D'Esposito, 1999; Rainer, Asaad, & Miller, 1998), although some evidence exists for segregation of spatial and object information in prefrontal cortex (Wilson, O' Scalaidhe, & Goldman-Rakic, 1993). In addition, task-irrelevant changes in object location can reduce memory accuracy for the identities of objects under some conditions (Jiang, Olson, & Chun, 2000), although no impairment is observed if the relative locations of objects are preserved (Irwin & Andrews, 1996; Phillips, 1974).

A reasonable way to reconcile these conflicting findings would be to propose that spatial and object representations are stored separately in posterior brain systems but are integrated in prefrontal cortex. Alternatively, prefrontal cortex may be involved in amodal executive functions that control the operation of posterior storage subsystems (Ranganath & Blumenfeld, 2005). It is also reasonable to suppose that the identity and location of a given object representation can be linked together when necessary, and this may be achieved by convergence of the information within prefrontal cortex or by means of functional links between the posterior storage subsystems. Thus, spatial and object representations in VSTM may be both segregated and interlinked, leading to different degrees of functional interaction depending on how they are tested.

3.2 MEASURING VISUAL SHORT-TERM MEMORY

Much recent VSTM research has sought to elucidate the properties of VSTM representations. However, these representations cannot be directly measured. Determining the properties of VSTM has proven to be somewhat like being given a wrapped present and trying to guess what it is without unwrapping it. To guess the contents of a wrapped box, you could shake the box, measure its size and weight, and even take an X-ray image of it. If those things do not work, you could try more drastic measures (e.g., palpating the box to feel the shape of its contents), but you might alter or destroy the present (e.g., changing a box of fruit into a box of fruit salad). You must also be careful not to confuse the packing materials with the present (e.g., a hard vase might be packed in soft tissue). By analogy, VSTM researchers must be careful not to use techniques that alter or destroy the memories as they are being measured and must distinguish between the memory representations and the processes used to create and use them.

These considerations have led many VSTM researchers to use *change-detection* tasks to study VSTM (see reviews by Rensink, 2002; Simons & Rensink, 2005). There are two main varieties of these tasks (Fig. 3–1). In *one-shot* change-detection tasks, observers view a brief *sample array*, which consists of one or more objects that the observers try to remember. After a brief *retention interval*, a *test array* is presented, and the observers compare the test array with the sample array (for a classic example, see Phillips, 1974). In most experiments, the test array

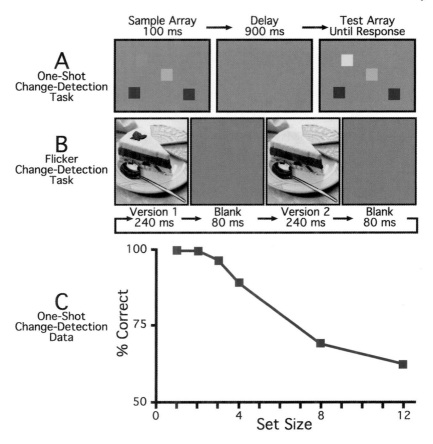

Figure 3–1. (**A**) Example of a change trial in a one-shot task. The green item in the sample array becomes a yellow item in the test array. (**B**) Example of a flicker task. A piece of chocolate is present on top of the cake in one version of the photograph but not in the other version. (**C**) Data from the study of Luck and Vogel (1997), using a one-shot color change-detection task similar to that shown in (A).

and sample array are identical on 50% of trials and differ in some subtle way on the remaining trials, and the observers simply make an unspeeded same–different response to indicate whether they noticed a difference. An example is shown in Figure 3–1A (based on the experiments of Luck & Vogel, 1997; Vogel, Woodman, & Luck, 2001). In this experiment, each sample array contains between one and 12 colored squares, and the test array is either identical to the sample array or differs in the color of one of the squares. Change-detection accuracy is typically near perfect for arrays with a small number of items and then decreases systematically as the number of items increases.

In *flicker* change-detection tasks, two slightly different versions of a given image alternate, separated by small blank periods, and observers respond as soon as they have detected the difference between the two versions. An example is shown in Figure 3–1B. In this example, a photograph of a slice of cake is presented for 240 ms, followed by an 80-ms blank period. A slightly altered version of the photograph is then presented for 240 ms, followed again by an 80-ms blank interval. This sequence repeats until the observer presses a button, indicating that the difference between the two photographs has been detected. The observer is then required to make some sort of response to demonstrate that the difference was actually detected (e.g., pointing to the difference). Even fairly substantial differences often require many alternations before being detected (see Chapter 5 of this volume for a discussion of the factors that combine to make change detection difficult in this task).

The main virtue of the change-detection paradigm is that the nonmemory processes involved in the task are relatively simple, making task performance sensitive primarily to the nature of the VSTM system. The role of perceptual processes can be minimized by the use of very simple and highly discriminable stimuli. The role of verbal memory systems can be minimized by using difficult-to-label stimuli or by using concurrent verbal tasks (like repeating "1-2-3-1-2-3 ...") that interfere with visual-to-verbal recoding (Besner, Davies, & Daniels, 1981; Murray, 1968). The role of response systems is minimized by using a simple, unspeeded 'change'/"no-change' response. Perhaps most importantly, the task does not require the observers to transform or manipulate the memories, as is necessary in tasks that require the observers to directly identify the items being held in memory. In verbal digit-span tasks, for example, the observers must hold a set of digits in memory briefly and then repeat them back to the experimenter; the process of reporting a given digit could disrupt the representations of the remaining digits, leading to a mischaracterization of the memory system. The change-detection task merely requires the observers to compare the memory representations with a new set of stimuli, most or all of which are the same as the items being held in memory. Although not completely trivial (see Hyun, 2006; Wilken & Ma, 2004), this task is relatively simple and can be performed quite rapidly.

A second virtue of the change-detection task is that it may closely resemble the way in which VSTM is used in the natural environment. As discussed in detail in Chapter 4 of this volume, the visual input is frequently interrupted by periods of suppressed visual processing caused by blinks and eye movements, and VSTM presumably plays an important role in comparing a memory representation of the visual input formed before the interruption with the new input that is visible after the interruption. Thus, the many change-detection findings described in the remainder of this chapter may be closely tied to a naturally occurring process of comparing VSTM representations with visual inputs, a process that presumably occurs many thousands of times each day (Hollingworth, Richard, & Luck, 2008).

3.3 THE STORAGE CAPACITY OF VISUAL SHORT-TERM MEMORY

Perhaps the most distinctive feature of VSTM is its small storage capacity. The first systematic exploration of VSTM capacity for simple features was performed by Luck and Vogel (1997) using the experimental paradigm shown in Figure 3–1A (see also the more detailed report by Vogel, Woodman, & Luck, 2001). Observers performed a change-detection task with arrays of one, two, three, four, eight, or 12 colored squares. A change was present on 50% of trials, and the observers simply reported whether or not they detected a change on each trial. The logic of the study was that, if observers had a memory capacity of K items, then they would perform perfectly when the set size (N) was $\leq K$. When $N > K$, the probability that the changed item happens to be one of the K items stored in VSTM is simply K/N, and the observers should always detect the change on those trials. However, on the remaining $(1 - K)/N$ trials, the observers will not know if an item has changed, and they will simply guess. Thus, performance should decline systematically as N exceeds K.

This general logic was formalized by Pashler (1988), who developed an equation for estimating K from the hit rate (H) and false alarm rate (F) in change-detection tasks. Pashler's equation was then improved by Cowan et al. (2005), and the resulting equation is simply: $K = N (H - F)$. It should be noted that this equation is similar to the equation for d' in the simple yes/no signal-detection procedure: $d' = Z(H) - Z(F)$. Both equations subtract the false alarm rate from the hit rate, but the d' equation first performs an inverse Z transformation, and the K equation multiplies this difference by the set size. If change and no-change trials are equally probable, and the observers do not have extreme response biases, d' and K are nearly perfectly correlated for a given set size.

In the experiment shown in Figure 3–1A, all observers were nearly 100% correct when the arrays contained one or two items, and most observers were also nearly 100% for arrays of three items (see Figure 3–1C). Almost all observers made errors at a set size of four, and mean accuracy declined systematically as the set size increased from three to 12 items. These results suggest that people are able to store only three to four simple, highly discriminable objects in VSTM. Similar results were obtained when the stimuli were oriented bars and the observers were asked to detect orientation changes rather than color changes. When the Pashler–Cowan K equation was applied to these data, the estimated average capacity was approximately three items.

Before accepting the conclusion that VSTM capacity for simple features is only three to four items, it was necessary to rule out some alternative hypotheses. First, it was necessary to demonstrate that performance was based on visual memory, with little or no contamination from verbal memory. That is, it is possible that the observers stored color names rather than (or in addition to) the actual colors and rehearsed these color names verbally. This possibility was examined by asking the observers to store two digits in verbal memory at the beginning of each trial, prior to the sample array, and then report these two digits at the end of the trial, after the test array. This concurrent verbal memory load had no significant impact on change-detection performance, but a subsequent experiment showed that it interfered a great deal with a verbal memory task. Thus, the original data were not contaminated by the use of verbal memory.

A second possibility is that, given that the sample array was presented for only 100 ms, the observers may have lacked sufficient time to encode the items in memory. That is, the limitation may have been on encoding speed rather than storage capacity. To test this, the duration of the sample array was increased to 500 ms. This fivefold increase in sample duration had no significant effect on performance, suggesting that performance was not limited by the time available for encoding.

A third possibility is that performance was limited by the comparison and decision processes rather than by storage capacity. To test this, a box was placed around one item in the test array, and the observers were told to report whether or not this item had changed. If there was a change, it was always the item in the box that changed, and this made it possible to restrict comparison and decision processes to a single item at any set size. This did not lead to any change in accuracy, indicating that performance and decision processes did not limit performance. However, if a box was placed around one item in the sample array, indicating that that was the only item that might change, performance improved considerably at large set sizes. In this case, the box limited the number of items that needed to be stored in memory, and the improved performance is therefore consistent with the proposal that performance in this task is limited primarily by storage capacity.

3.3.1 Conceptualizing Visual Short-term Memory Storage Capacity

Up to this point, the data shown in Figure 3–1C have been interpreted as evidence that VSTM can hold a small number of items, with the impaired performance at larger set sizes being a result of a failure to store all of the items in VSTM. This conceptualization of change-detection performance is embodied in the Pashler–Cowan K formula, and it is an example of a *high-threshold* approach to understanding psychophysical performance. That is, observers are assumed to have either a perfect representation of a given item or no representation at all, and when an item is represented, they are assumed to be perfectly accurate at determining whether or not that item changed.

High-threshold approaches do not usually do a good job of accounting for psychophysical performance, and approaches based on signal-detection theory are usually superior (Macmillan & Creelman, 1991). In signal-detection conceptualizations, noise in the stimulus (or in the representation) leads to uncertainty, and decisions are based on comparing the available evidence with a decision threshold. This approach has been applied to change detection by Wilken and Ma (2004). They proposed that observers form a noisy representation of each item in the sample array and compare each of these representations with the corresponding item in the test array. Because the representations are noisy, every representation will differ somewhat from the corresponding item in the test array, and it is therefore necessary to have an algorithm for deciding when the differences are big enough to report that a change was present. Two alternative algorithms were explored. One algorithm reports a change if the largest difference exceeds a threshold value; the other sums the differences and reports a change if this sum exceeds a threshold. The data could not distinguish between these alternatives. To account for the effects of set size on change-detection accuracy, Wilken and Ma (2004) proposed that the representations become noisier as the number of representations increases.

This model differs in two main ways from the high-threshold conceptualization of change-detection performance that is embodied in the Pashler–Cowan *K* equation. First, the Wilken and Ma conceptualization treats the representations as noisy, leading to the possibility of errors even when a given item is represented in VSTM. Second, the Wilken and Ma conceptualization assumes that all items are represented but that the representations become noisier (less accurate) at higher set sizes, whereas the Pashler–Cowan conceptualization assumes that a limited number of items are represented, with no reduction in the accuracy of the represented items as the number of items increases. The first of these differences is conceptually minor because the signal-detection and high-threshold approaches converge on the same predictions if the change magnitudes are sufficiently large. That is, if the degree of change between the sample and test arrays is very large relative to the noise level of the representations, then the Pashler–Cowan *K* equation will lead to the same quantitative predictions as a signal-detection model.

The second difference between the Wilken and Ma conceptualization and the Pashler–Cowan conceptualization is more fundamental, and these two conceptualizations are cases of two more general theoretical possibilities. One theoretical possibility, which I will call the *fixed-resolution hypothesis*, is that VSTM stores a relatively small number of representations and that the resolution of the representations does not vary as the number of representations increases. The other theoretical possibility, which I will call the *variable-resolution hypothesis*, is that VSTM can potentially store a very large number of representations, but the resolution of the representations decreases as the number of concurrently stored representations increases.

3.3.2 Fixed-resolution Representations and Slots

The fixed-resolution hypothesis is related to the old-fashioned notion of "slots" in memory that are analogous to slots in a physical filing system. Each slot has a particular size (corresponding to its resolution), and the number of slots is small and constant. It seems implausible that a massively parallel, distributed neural system such as the human brain contains a small set of structurally defined slots, but it is plausible that a small and discrete set of representations arises from the dynamics of neural interactions. Specifically, representations in VSTM may need to inhibit each other to avoid fusing together, and this inhibition may limit the number of concurrent representations in VSTM.

Indeed, this exactly what happens in a neural network model of VSTM developed by Raffone and Wolters (2001). This model is a case of the fixed-resolution hypothesis, but the limited number of representations that can be held in VSTM is a consequence of the dynamics of the system rather than a slot-like structural limitation. It should also be noted that the maximum number of representations that can be held in VSTM in such a system may vary from trial to trial. That is, because of noise in the system, the system might be able to maintain five representations on some trials but only two on others. Thus, the fixed-resolution hypothesis does not specify that K is invariant from trial to trial. This is important, because change-detection accuracy sometimes begins to fall from ceiling for set sizes below a given observer's average K. For example, an observer with a capacity of three items according to the Pashler–Cowan K equation might be slightly less accurate at a set size of three than at a set size of two, and this could be explained by positing that the observer sometimes held only two items in VSTM and sometimes held four items.

3.3.3 Variable-resolution Representations and Resources

The variable-resolution hypothesis is related to resource-sharing views of cognition (e.g., Navon, 1984; Navon & Gopher, 1979; Norman & Bobrow, 1976). According to this view, VSTM representations compete for a limited pool of some unspecified cognitive resource, and the resolution of a given representation will depend on the amount of this resource that is devoted to that representation. As more representations are concurrently stored in VSTM, the amount of the resource available for a given representation will decline, leading to a decrease in resolution (which is typically equivalent to an increase in noise).

The general class of resource-sharing models is highly flexible, and resource-sharing models have been difficult to rule out in a variety of domains (for examples in other domains, see Navon & Miller, 2002; Woodman & Luck, 2003). The main difficulty is that resource-sharing models are so flexible that they can often mimic other models. In the case of VSTM, for example, it is possible to devote all of the resource to a small subset of the objects in the sample array, yielding a high-resolution representation of three to four objects and essentially no representation of the other objects. This would be much like the fixed-resolution model, except that the resolution of the representations in the resource-sharing account would decline as the set size increased from one to three objects. But even this difference can be eliminated by adding the assumption that the resolution of a given representation is nonlinearly related to the amount of the resource devoted to that representation, with no appreciable decline in resolution until the amount of the resource becomes quite small. That is, changing the resource allocation for a given representation from 100% to 50% (corresponding to set sizes of one and two) may not change the resolution of the representation very much, whereas changing the resource allocation from 25% to 12.5% (corresponding to set sizes of four and eight) might change the resolution quite a bit. Thus, it may be impossible to falsify the entire class of variable-resolution models on the basis of psychophysical results even if the fixed-resolution model is correct.

3.3.4 Evidence for Fixed- Versus Variable-resolution Representations

Unfortunately, no definitive empirical tests of the fixed-resolution and variable-resolution hypotheses have been reported. Wilken and Ma (2004) found that a signal-detection approach provided a much better fit to change-detection results than a high-threshold approach; as discussed earlier, however, the fixed-resolution hypothesis does not necessarily imply a high-threshold conceptualization. This study did not attempt to test a sophisticated version of the fixed-resolution hypothesis in which a signal-detection conceptualization is applied to a small number of fixed-resolution representations. In particular, the results reported by Wilken and Ma can be quantitatively fit by a signal-detection model in which VSTM stores a small number of fixed-resolution representations (Zhang, 2007).

Support for variable-resolution representations was provided by Alvarez and Cavanagh (2004), who found that storage capacity was substantially lower for complex stimuli (e.g., three-dimensional cubes) than for simple stimuli (e.g., colored squares; Fig. 3–2). In this study, complexity was assessed objectively by examining visual-search performance for a given stimulus type and using the slope of the search function as a measure of complexity. This assumes that, all else being equal, visual-search slopes are greater for more complex objects than for less complex objects. As illustrated in Figure 3–2, Alvarez and Cavanagh observed that the search slope for a given set of objects was almost perfectly correlated with the storage capacity for that set of objects. Interestingly, the x-intercept of this function was 4.7 items, suggesting a maximum capacity of four to five items for the simplest possible object. From these results, Alvarez and Cavanagh concluded that it is possible to store more items in VSTM if they are simple than if they are complex, but that there also exists an absolute limit of four to five items. This conclusion is something of a hybrid between the fixed- and variable-resolution hypotheses: resolution may vary, but the number of concurrent representations is limited.

However, it would not be justified to conclude from these results that resolution is truly variable. As pointed out by Vogel et al. (2001), each "slot" in VSTM may store one part of an object rather than a whole object, and multipart objects such as those used by Alvarez and Cavanagh may require multiple "slots." In this scenario, observers would be able to store fewer multipart objects

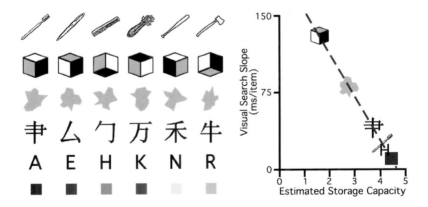

Figure 3–2. Stimuli and results from the study of Alvarez and Cavanagh (2004). Adapted by permission.

than single-part objects in VSTM even if the resolution of each "slot" was constant. In addition, Eng, Chen, and Jiang (2005) have provided evidence that much of the difference in estimated capacity between simple and complex objects in the Alvarez and Cavanagh study was due to errors in perceiving the complex objects; when encoding time was increased, the differences in capacity were reduced (but not eliminated). Similarly, Awh, Barton, and Vogel (2007) have provided evidence that the results of Alvarez and Cavanagh can be explained by variations in the similarity of the sample and test arrays rather than differences in the complexity of the items in the sample array.

Luck and Vogel (1997) described an experiment that provides some support for the fixed-resolution hypothesis. As described earlier, they found no significant effect of placing a box around one item in the test array, indicating that this item was the only item that might have changed. If an array of 12 items is stored in VSTM as a set of 12 very noisy representations, then a cue in the test array should have allowed the observers to reduce the number of decisions, thus reducing the probability of false alarms arising when a nonchanging item exceeds the threshold for reporting a change (see Palmer, 1990; Palmer, Ames, & Lindsey, 1993). However, if only three of the 12 items are stored in VSTM, and these representations are not very noisy, then this *decision noise* problem should be minimal, and adding a box around the one item that might have changed should not impact performance much. Because the box led to no change in accuracy, these results support the fixed-resolution hypothesis. However, this result is also compatible with the hypothesis of Alvarez and Cavanagh (2004) that resolution is variable as the number of objects increases from one to four, but a maximum of four to five objects can be stored in VSTM.

Zhang and Luck (in press) examined the resolution of VSTM representations more directly by asking observers to report the remembered color of an item by clicking on a color wheel, as in Wilken & Ma (2004), and by testing quantitative versions of the slot and resource theories. Zhang and Luck found that resolution remained constant as the set size increased between three and six objects and that observers simply had no information about the colors of many of the objects at set size six. Thus, it does not seem possible to store more than K items in VSTM. However, small improvements in performance were observed when the number of objects was reduced from three to one. Although this finding might seem to support the hypothesis of Alvarez and Cavanagh (2004), additional experiments and analyses demonstrated that these changes in performance could be explained quantitatively by a fixed-resolution slot model that made optimal use of the slots. Thus, the evidence is in favor of slot-like representations for simple features such as color.

3.3.5 Independent Versus Linked Representations

Another fundamental theoretical issue is whether each item is stored in an independent VSTM representation or whether VSTM stores a single hierarchical representation of the entire scene. These are not, however, mutually exclusive possibilities: Observers may store both a representation of the overall scene and

a set of independent representations of the individual items. Given the existence of parallel processing streams within the visual system, it would not be
surprising to find multiple VSTM representations of the same information, but
in different formats.

The most straightforward evidence regarding this issue was reported by
Jiang, Olson, & Chun (2000). As illustrated in Figure 3–3, they conducted a
color change-detection experiment. In one condition, the memory and test
arrays were identical except that a white box surrounded one item in the test
array and, on 50% of trials, one of the items changed color between the sample
and test arrays. In another condition, the configuration of the test array was
massively disrupted by removing all but one item, which was surrounded by a
white box and changed in color from the corresponding item in the sample
array on 50% of trials. Thus, observers in both conditions were signaled to
make a change-detection decision about the item surrounded by a white box,
but in one condition the rest of the items were eliminated. Accuracy was found
to be significantly higher when the configuration was not disrupted (74.4%
correct) than when it was disrupted by removing all but one of the items (64.5%
correct). Thus, the elimination of the configural information disrupted change-
detection performance. In a follow-up experiment, Jiang et al. spread the items
farther apart in the test array than in the sample array, but left the overall
configuration unchanged. Changing the relative locations of the items did not
disrupt performance compared to a condition in which the absolute locations
were unchanged. Similarly, Phillips (1974) and Carlson-Radvansky and Irwin
(1995) found that shifting the entire array between the sample and test arrays,
but maintaining the relative locations of the items, does not impair change-
detection performance. Similar results were observed by Hollingworth (2006)

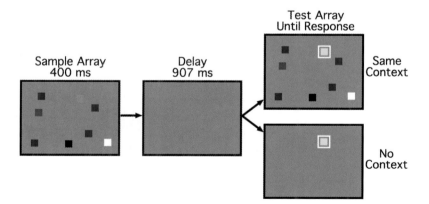

Figure 3–3. Stimuli from the study of Jiang et al. (2000). Observers performed a
color change-detection task. On *same-context* trials, all items from the sample array were
present, and the one item that might have changed was indicated by a white box. On
no-context trials, only the one item that might have changed was present in the test
array.

for complex objects presented within complex scenes. These results suggest that observers store the overall configuration of the sample array in VSTM, but that the configuration is encoded in relative rather than absolute coordinates.

How can this finding be reconciled with the evidence, described previously, for separable object and spatial VSTM storage subsystems? As discussed earlier, object and spatial information may be separately coded within parietal and inferotemporal areas, respectively, but may be coded together within prefrontal and/or medial temporal areas. Changes in spatial context would reduce the ability to use the combined representations, forcing observers to rely on the separated representations alone. Moreover, the combined representations may signal the presence of a change when the spatial context changes, even when object identity does not change, and this may lead to confusion. Indeed, Zimmer and Lehnert (2006) have provided evidence that a global spatial representation of the sample array is stored independently of the object identities, and a change in the spatial configuration interferes with change-detection performance because it produces a difficult-to-ignore change signal. For example, they found that changing the spatial context led to impaired change-detection performance for shapes even when the names of the shapes rather than the actual shapes were presented in the test array, suggesting that the interference arises at a non-visual stage. Nonetheless, because most natural tasks require object identity information to be combined with location information, it seems likely that these two sources of information are somehow combined in VSTM.

3.3.6 Why Is Visual Short-term Memory Capacity Limited?

Any serious theory of VSTM should go beyond describing the capacity limits of VSTM and explain *why* these limits exist. The most common explanation is that VSTM capacity is limited by the capacity of attention (e.g., Cowan, 2001). However, this just hands the problem to attention researchers rather than providing an explanation, and it is inconsistent with studies showing that attention can be diverted without reducing VSTM capacity (e.g., Fougnie & Marois, 2006; Woodman, Vogel, & Luck, 2001). This section will sketch an alternative explanation for capacity limits.

During visual perception, it is well known that each individual neuron in visual cortex will give its greatest response to a particular value of a particular dimension, with a more-or-less gradual fall-off in response as the stimulus moves away from that value. As an example, Figure 3–4 shows the orientation tuning curves of three neurons—labeled A, B, and C—with peak responses at 30 degrees, 40 degrees, and 50 degrees, respectively. Together, these three neurons can very accurately code interposed orientations by means of the relative firing rates of the neurons. For example, an orientation of 37 degrees might lead to firing rates of 30, 46, and 8 spikes/s in neurons A, B, and C, respectively. However, this *coarse coding* of orientation breaks down when multiple orientations must be represented simultaneously. For example, it is difficult to differentiate between a single oriented bar at 40 degrees and a 37-degree bar presented simultaneously with a 43-degree bar. A well-studied solution to this problem is

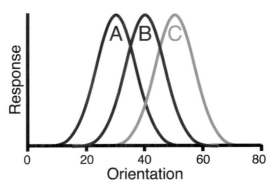

Figure 3–4. Example of orientation tuning in three neurons. The response for a given neuron is maximal at a particular orientation and then falls as the orientation moves away from this value. Many different orientations can be precisely represented by the relative activation levels of these three broadly tuned neurons.

to use a separate group of neurons—a *cell assembly* in the terminology of Hebb (1949)—to represent each bar. Each cell assembly would contain a complete set of neurons tuned to the different possible orientations, and the pattern of activity across the neurons within a cell assembly could precisely code the orientation of the bar being represented by that assembly. This is a well-known solution in the context of perception (see Luck & Beach, 1998, for an extended discussion), and it applies equally well to the representation of features in VSTM.

If feature values are represented in VSTM by units with overlapping tuning curves, with a separate cell assembly for each object being represented, then the capacity of VSTM would be limited by the number of cell assemblies that can be kept active simultaneously. If a fixed number of cell assemblies existed, permanently segregated from each other (in a functional sense), then this would be analogous to the idea of fixed slots.

Although no direct evidence rules out this possibility, the brain does not seem to be organized in such a static manner (even cortical topographic mapping is constantly shaped by experience rather than being static; Braun, Heinz, Schweizer, Wiech, Birbaumer, & Topka, 2001; Jenkins, Merzenich, Ochs, Allard, & Guc-Robles, 1990). However, it is possible that the brain forms cell assemblies dynamically, creating temporarily stable *attractor states* (for a dynamic systems account of VSTM, see Schutte, Spencer, & Schöner, 2003; Spencer, Simmering, Schutte, & Schöner, in press). It is easy to imagine that some mechanism is necessary to segregate the cell assemblies, so that they do not collapse into a single assembly that reflects an average of the values rather than the individual values. It may become more and more difficult to keep the cell assemblies segregated as the number of simultaneously active cell assemblies increases, and this could produce an effective limit on the number of assemblies that can be simultaneously active and hence the number of items that can be represented simultaneously in VSTM. Neurophysiological studies have indicated that posterior parietal cortex—and the intraparietal sulcus in particular—may be involved in this segregation process, because neural activity levels increase as the number of objects being retained increases, up to the individual observer's VSTM capacity level (Todd & Marois, 2004; Vogel & Machizawa, 2004; Xu & Chun, 2006).

This general hypothesis about the reason for capacity limits in VSTM is compatible with both the fixed-resolution, slot-like conceptualization of VSTM and the variable-resolution, resource-based conceptualization. The slot-like conceptualization would propose that the cell assemblies terminate or merge when too many objects are being represented, making it impossible to represent more than a handful of items at one time. The resource-like conceptualization would propose that interference increases as the number of cell assemblies increases, leading to less accurate representations but not to a limit on the number of simultaneously active assemblies. It is also possible to combine these ideas, postulating that accuracy declines as the number of cell assemblies increases, accompanied by the termination or merger of assemblies when the number gets too large, which would correspond to the hybrid hypothesis proposed by Alvarez and Cavanagh (2004).

3.4 THE NATURE OF VISUAL SHORT-TERM MEMORY REPRESENTATIONS

3.4.1 Features and Objects in Visual Short-term Memory

Treisman's influential *feature integration theory* of visual attention (Treisman, 1988; Treisman & Gelade, 1980) proposes that simple features are detected preattentively and that spatially focused attention is necessary to combine features into integrated object representations. Recent research has examined whether single features also have a different status from combinations of features in VSTM. Luck and Vogel (1997) used multifeature objects to test whether the capacity of VSTM is limited by the number of features that must be stored or by the number of objects. As shown in Figure 3–5, the observers in a change-detection task viewed a set of colored and oriented bars, and they were asked to remember the colors of the bars (because only the color could change), the orientations of the bars (because only the orientation change), or both the colors and the orientations of the bars (because either color or orientation could change). If capacity is limited by the number of features, then remembering both features of each of N objects should be as difficult as remembering a single feature of each of 2N objects. If, however, capacity is limited by the number of objects, then change-detection accuracy for N objects should be the same whether one feature or two features are remembered for each object. This is what was found: For a given number of objects, accuracy for remembering both color and orientation was the same as accuracy for remembering only color or only orientation. A follow-up experiment obtained the same pattern of results when the observers were asked to remember one versus four features

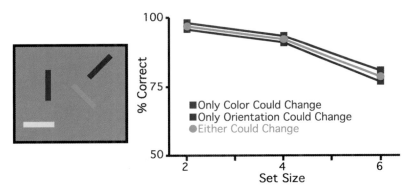

Figure 3–5. Stimuli and data from the study of Luck and Vogel (1997). In one condition, the observers were instructed to remember the colors of the items because only color could change between the sample and test arrays. In another condition they were instructed to remember the orientations because only orientation could change. In a third condition, they were instructed to remember both the colors and the orientations because either could change.

of object. This pattern mirrors the classic object-based attention findings of Duncan (1984), who found that attending to two features of an object was as easy as attending to a single feature. Indeed, Awh, Dhaliwal, Christensen, & Matsukura (2001) provided evidence that Duncan's effects occurred within VSTM representations rather than during the perception of the objects, so the findings of Luck and Vogel (1997) and Duncan (1984) probably reflect the same underlying mechanism.

On the basis of this pattern of results, Luck and Vogel (1997) proposed the *integrated-object hypothesis*, which states that the features of an object are stored together in a unitary VSTM representation rather than being stored independently. This should not be taken to imply that the features are stored in the same visual areas; instead, it implies that the neurons representing the features of an object are functionally linked and that VSTM capacity is limited by the number of these bound representations.

An alternative explanation for these results, however, is that each feature dimension is stored completely independently in VSTM (as proposed by Magnussen, Greenlee, & Thomas, 1996). If the memories for color and orientation do not draw from the same resource pool, then this can explain why performance was not impaired when the observers were required to remember both features. To rule out this possibility, Luck and Vogel (1997) tested a color–color condition, in which each object consisted of an inner square of one color and an outer square of another color. The observers were asked to remember the inner-square color in one condition, the outer-square color in a second condition, and both colors in a third condition. Change-detection accuracy was found to be equal across conditions. Because it is implausible to suppose that separate memory systems exist for the inner and outer colors, these results support the integrated-object hypothesis.

Unfortunately, this result has been difficult to replicate. Although it was replicated once in the same laboratory (see footnote 9 of Vogel, Woodman, & Luck, 2001), other laboratories found that performance was substantially worse when observers were required to remember both the inner and outer colors compared to when they were required to remember only the inner colors or only the outer colors (Olson & Jiang, 2002; Wheeler & Treisman, 2002). One possible explanation for the discrepancy is that perceptual processing may have been difficult in the two-color conditions of these subsequent experiments, whereas the color set used by Luck and Vogel (1997) and Vogel et al. (2001) was optimized for ease of perception. Indeed, Xu (2004) has shown that an object benefit for color–color combinations can be obtained when the two colors of an object are drawn from clearly different sets. Nonetheless, it is clear that the pattern observed by Luck and Vogel (1997)—equivalent performance for remembering one or two colors of a single object—can be obtained only under a limited set of conditions.

However, other sources of evidence have been reported that also support the integrated-object hypothesis. For example, Xu (2002a, 2002b) has conducted several studies of the sort shown in Figure 3–6, in which each object contained two parts, and performance was assessed in a connected condition (with abutting parts that form a clear object) and a disconnected condition (in which the parts were spatially separated to break up the appearance of a coherent object). When the observers were asked to remember the same feature dimension for both parts (as in the top row of Fig. 3–6), performance was approximately the same for the connected and disconnected conditions. In contrast, when the observers were asked to remember different feature dimensions for the two parts

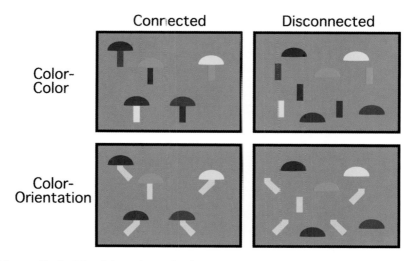

Figure 3–6. Stimuli from the study of Xu (2002b). In the conditions shown in the top row, the observers were asked to remember the colors of the mushroom tops and the stems. In the conditions shown in the bottom row, the observers were asked to remember the colors of the mushroom tops and the orientations of the stems.

(as in the bottom row of Fig. 3–6), performance was more accurate when the parts were joined into coherent objects. From these results, Xu (2002a, 2002b) concluded that multiple features can be stored in an integrated-object representation, but features from the same dimension compete with each other and cannot be stored together (see also Delvenne & Bruyer, 2004; Walker & Miles, 1999).

Evidence for integrated object representations was also obtained by Wheeler and Treisman (2002) with stimuli that are illustrated in Figure 3–7. In the *single-feature* conditions, the observers were asked to remember only the colors or only the shapes of the objects because only that dimension could change. In the *either* condition, the observers were asked to remember both the colors and the orientations, because either might change. These conditions were analogous to the conditions used by Luck and Vogel (1997) and shown in Figure 3–5. However, Wheeler and Treisman added a *binding* condition, in which a change consisted of a new combination of the feature values that were present in the sample array. For example, if the sample array contained a red square and a blue triangle, the test array might contain a blue square. Independent memories of color and shape would not be sufficient to detect a change in the binding condition, because the same features were present, but in different combinations. Accurate performance in this task therefore requires the formation of bound representations of color and shape. In contrast, changes in the other conditions were created by presenting a new feature value that had not been present in the sample array (e.g., a sample array containing red and blue, and a test array containing green).

Under the conditions shown in Figure 3–7, Wheeler and Treisman (2002) found that change-detection accuracy was nearly equivalent for the single-feature condition, the either condition, and the binding condition. Thus, there was no cost in performance when the observers were required to bind together the features of an object, consistent with the integrated-object hypothesis. However, impaired performance was observed in the binding condition in a different set of experiments in which the test array contained all the items from

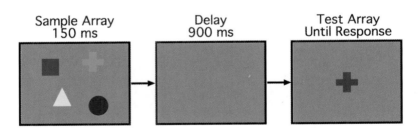

Figure 3–7. Example of a change trial in the binding condition of the study of Wheeler and Treisman (2002). In this condition, a change consisted of a recombination of the color and shape of two items (as shown here, the blue square and green cross became a green square and a blue cross). In the other conditions, a change consisted of a new feature value that was not present in the sample array.

the sample array rather than a single test item. From this pattern, Wheeler and Treisman concluded that bound-object representations can be formed as easily as single-feature representations, but the maintenance of bindings is more attention-demanding and is disrupted by the presence of multiple objects in the test array.

This hypothesis was tested directly by Johnson, Hollingworth, and Luck (2008), who interposed an attention-demanding visual-search task during the delay interval of a change-detection task. Although this interposed task did produce an impairment in change-detection performance, the impairment was no greater for the binding task than for the either task. Similar results were observed by Allen, Baddeley, and Hitch (2006), who used executive tasks rather than a search task to distract attention. Moreover, the Johnson et al. (2008) study failed to replicate Wheeler and Treisman's finding of a specific impairment in performance for the binding task when the test array contained multiple objects. Thus, no direct evidence suggests that the formation or maintenance of bound representations in VSTM is any more attention-demanding than the formation or maintenance of independent feature representations. Instead, the existing evidence indicates that VSTM representations always include all the features of an object.

However, this conclusion appears to apply only to single-part objects. As proposed by Xu (2002a, 2002b), when a given dimension must be stored for each part of a multipart object, the values along that dimension for the individual parts may compete with each other, leading to interference and poor memory. The representations of the individual parts may therefore be segregated from each other, and this segregation may cause each part to "fill a slot" (or to consume VSTM capacity). A single object of any substantial complexity (as measured by the number of competing parts) may therefore fill VSTM to its capacity.

The integrated-object hypothesis fits well with the idea that VSTM capacity is limited by the number of cell assemblies that can be simultaneously active. If the main limitation in VSTM is the need to avoid interference between cell assemblies, rather than the need to link together multiple neurons into each individual cell assembly, then VSTM capacity should be limited by the number of objects rather than the number of features (see Luck & Vogel, 1998). Indeed, the neural network model of Raffone and Wolters (2001) relies on cell assemblies to maintain information over time, and this model exhibits a storage capacity of three to four objects, irrespective of the number of features that defined each object.

3.4.2 Are Visual Short-term Memory Representations Simply Activated Visual Long-term Memory Representations?

Most general theories of working memory propose that working memory representations are activated LTM representations (see Miyake & Shah, 1999). Baddeley and Logie (1999), in contrast, have argued that working memory representations are more than activated LTM representations because we are able to dynamically construct working memory representations of things that have no corresponding LTM representation.

No one has yet developed detailed theories of the relationship between VSTM and VLTM representations of objects, but two general classes of hypotheses can be considered. One class of hypotheses would propose that VSTM representations are simply activated LTM representations. A specific version of this hypothesis, inspired by view-based theories of object perception (see Chapter 6), would propose that the brain computes the similarity between the to-be-remembered information and every visual representation in LTM (like the radial basis functions proposed for object recognition by Poggio & Edelman, 1990). Visual short-term memory would then consist of the maintenance of a vector of these similarity values. I call this the *LTM similarity vector hypothesis*, and an example is shown in Figure 3–8. In this example, a sample array of three oriented bars is represented in terms of its similarity to a variety of complex objects stored in LTM (the numbers represent the degree of similarity). This may seem like a computationally expensive storage mechanism, but the storage requirements could be minimized by retaining just those similarity values that are most diagnostic (in a manner analogous to using principal-components analysis to represent a multidimensional data set using only the components with the highest eigenvalues). The vector of values corresponding to a given object could be stored in the sort of cell assembly described earlier in this chapter.

A second class of hypotheses about VSTM storage, inspired by structural-description theories of object recognition (Biederman, 1987; Marr, 1982; see Chapter 6), would propose that VSTM representations are not linked to rich LTM representations. Instead, VSTM representations consist of structured sets of primitive components (e.g., orientations, colors, simple three-dimensional volumes, etc.). Thus, the sample array shown in Figure 3–5 would be represented as three bars in a specific spatial configuration, with each bar linked to an orientation value and a color value. I call this the *structured- primitives hypothesis*.

To my knowledge, no one has previously provided an explicit and detailed description of these two alternative classes of VSTM representational formats, and previous research does not provide conclusive evidence regarding them. The most relevant studies have examined whether familiarity influences the accuracy of change detection. If VSTM representations are stored as LTM

Sample Array   0.54   0.05   0.30   0.71   0.03   0.09

Figure 3–8. Example of the representation of a sample array in visual short-term memory (VSTM) as a vector of similarities to items stored in visual long-term memory (VLTM). The sample array is shown at left, and the other items are a subset of the available VLTM representations. The degree of similarity between the sample array and each VLTM item is shown under each VLTM item. For example, the jet in VLTM has a fairly high level of similarity because it contains parts that are similar in orientation to all three of the items in the sample array.

similarity vectors, then VSTM should be more accurate when the items being held in VSTM map directly onto strong and distinct LTM representations. The evidence to date has been mixed.

Pashler (1988) found that change-detection performance was no more accurate when the stimuli consisted of upright letters than when the letters were inverted. However, it is possible that even the inverted letters were so familiar that they could be well-represented in the form of links between VSTM and LTM (i.e., a ceiling effect on familiarity may have been present).

Olson and Jiang (2004) established familiarity on the basis of training and also found a lack of benefits of familiarity on change detection (see also Williams & Simons, 2000). The observers performed a location change-detection task in which the sample array consisted of a set of dots and the test array was identical or differed in the position of one dot. A set of six spatial configurations of dots was repeated 24 times each over the course of the experiment, intermixed with novel spatial configurations. As the observers experienced more and more trials with the repeating arrays, they could potentially form LTM representations of these arrays and thus detect changes by comparing the test array with the appropriate, activated LTM representation. However, the observers were found to be no more accurate for the repeating arrays than for the novel arrays. Thus, this study found no evidence that VSTM representations consist of activated LTM representations. However, to gain a benefit from LTM in this experiment, the observers would need to form accurate LTM representations of six highly similar dot arrays, each of which was repeated only 24 times; consequently, the LTM representations may not have been sufficiently strong to provide a benefit. Indeed, recognition performance for the repeated items at the end of the experiment was unimpressive (78% hits, 34% false alarms). Thus, this study cannot rule out the possibility that links from VSTM representations to strong LTM representations can produce enhanced change-detection performance.

Chen, Eng, and Jiang (2005) also found that training with a set of novel polygons did not produce enhanced change-detection performance for the trained items. The degree of training was much greater than in the Olson and Jiang (2004) study, and the observers were 88% correct at distinguishing between trained and untrained items at the end of the session. However, this is still not very impressive evidence of strong VLTM representations. Consider, for example, a typical person's VLTM representation of a toothbrush, which is developed over thousands of extended exposures. The kind of test used by Chen et al. (2006) to test memory would be equivalent to showing someone a toothbrush and asking if they had ever seen an object like that before. Obviously, performance would be at 100% correct for this sort of test, and a person's representation of a toothbrush would support accurate performance on much more difficult tests. Thus, although the results reported by Olson and Jiang (2004) and by Chen et al. (2006) clearly indicate that modest levels of familiarity do not improve change-detection performance, they do not provide strong evidence against the LTM similarity vector hypothesis.

Indeed, Buttle and Raymond (2003) were able to demonstrate improved change-detection performance by using highly familiar visual inputs. They tested observers with highly familiar faces (e.g., Prince Charles), with weakly familiar faces that were trained during a previous phase of the experiment, and with unfamiliar faces. Change detection was found to be more accurate for the highly familiar faces than for the weakly familiar and unfamiliar faces, but no difference was observed between weakly familiar and unfamiliar faces. Thus, high levels of familiarity do influence the accuracy of change detection. Although this result may indicate that VSTM representations consist of activated VLTM representations, there is an alternative explanation. Specifically, the benefit for highly familiar faces may have reflected the use of abstract, semantic, nonvisual memory representations rather than VSTM representations. That is, the observers could have remembered that they saw Prince Charles in some abstract manner rather than remembering anything about this particular picture of Prince Charles. Thus, the relationship between VSTM representations and VLTM representations remains an unresolved issue.

Neurophysiological studies of VSTM are broadly consistent with the similarity vector hypothesis. Specifically, VSTM representations appear to be implemented as elevated neural firing rates over the delay interval of the VSTM task (see Chapter 8 for more details), and this sort of delay activity is observed only in relatively high-level areas that are closely linked with LTM representations. For example, strong delay activity is observed in inferotemporal cortex but not in intermediate areas such as V4 (e.g., Chelazzi, Duncan, Miller, & Desimone, 1998; Chelazzi, Miller, Duncan, & Desimone, 2001; S. M. Courtney, Ungerleider, Keil, & Haxby, 1997; Todd & Marois, 2004). To accommodate such findings, the structured primitives hypothesis would have to postulate that the primitives are relatively abstract.

3.5 VISUAL SHORT-TERM MEMORY PROCESSES

Until this point, this chapter has focused on the nature of VSTM representations, largely neglecting the processes that create, maintain, and access these representations. This is a reflection of the research that has been done, which has focused much more on issues of representation than on issues of process. This section will describe what is known about the processes involved in creating and using VSTM representations.

3.5.1 The Creation of Visual Short-term Memory Representations

In old-fashioned box-and-arrow models of cognition (e.g., Atkinson & Shiffrin, 1968), STM representations are typically in a different box from perceptual representations, implying that perceptual representations are fed into one end of a memory-creation machine and STM representations come out the other end. An alternative and more contemporary view is that sensory inputs lead to the creation of a variety of perceptual representations, and some mechanism then stabilizes some of these representations, so that they can survive in the absence of incoming stimulation and remain active despite the presentation of new sensory inputs (see Chapter 8 and Schutte, Spencer, & Schöner, 2003; Spencer & Hund, 2002; Spencer, Simmering, Schutte, & Schöner, in press).

Jolicoeur and Dell'Acqua (1998) refer to the process of transforming transient perceptual representations into durable VSTM representations as *short-term consolidation*, by analogy to the consolidation process thought to occur in LTM. Vogel, Woodman, and Luck (2006) suggested that *vulcanization*—a process that makes raw rubber durable, so that it does not become brittle and breakable over time—might be an even more appropriate term.

As described in Chapter 8 it is relatively simple to design a neural network to maintain a representation once the input has been taken away. However, it is rather more complicated to do this in a controlled manner, so that some inputs are stored and others are not (Frank, Loughry, & O'Reilly, 2001). It is even more complicated to maintain multiple segregated cell assemblies, so that multiple items can be maintained simultaneously in VSTM (Raffone & Wolters, 2001). Thus, the process of transforming perceptual representations into VSTM representations may be nontrivial.

Indeed, research on VSTM consolidation has demonstrated that consolidation is a resource-demanding process. In the study of Jolicoeur and Dell'Acqua (1998), the observers were asked to store a small set of characters in VSTM at the beginning of each trial. After a variable-duration delay, a tone was presented, and the observers were required to rapidly press one of two buttons to indicate whether the tone was high- or low-pitched. If creating VSTM representations requires access to the same cognitive resources as pressing a button in a tone-discrimination task, then reaction times (RTs) for the tone task should be slowed when the tone is presented while the observer is in the process of creating the VSTM representations. Consistent with this hypothesis, RTs for the tone task were longer when the delay between the to-be-remembered characters was short than when it was long. Moreover, this slowing was present at longer delays when the observers were given more characters to store in VSTM. These results suggest that some sort of modality-nonspecific process is involved in both creating VSTM representations and making button-press responses to auditory stimuli. A limitation of this study, however, is that the observers may have stored the letters in a nonvisual STM system, perhaps involving subvocal articulation of the letters, and the slowing of RTs may have reflected interference between the manual response system and the articulatory system.

A different approach was taken by Vogel et al. (2006), who examined the consolidation process using a color change-detection task combined with an articulatory suppression procedure that discourages the use of verbal STM. As illustrated in Figure 3–9, an array of masks was presented at a variable interval after the sample array. If substantial time is required to transform a perceptual representation into a durable VSTM representation, then it should be possible to disrupt this process by masking the perceptual representation before the VSTM representation has been fully formed. Thus, change-detection performance should be impaired if the masks are presented shortly after the offset of the sample array but not if substantial time has passed between the sample array and the onset of the masks. Of course, the masks could also impair performance if they disrupted the process of forming the initial perceptual

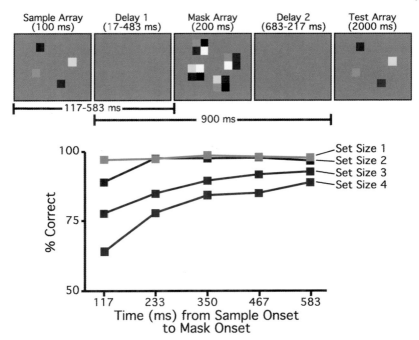

Figure 3–9. Stimuli and results from Experiment 1 of Vogel et al. (2006).

representation of the sample array, but the delays used in this study were long enough to prevent perceptual interference.

When the sample array contained a single item, Vogel et al. (2006) found that masks were ineffective at any of the sample-mask delays that were tested (ranging from 117 to 583 ms, measured from onset to onset). When the set size was increased to two items, masking was observed only at the shortest delay. As the set size was increased further, larger and longer lasting masking effects were observed (see Figure 3–9). Thus, the process of transforming perceptual representations into VSTM representations is limited in capacity, requiring more time as more items must be transformed. An additional experiment measured the Pashler–Cowan K value across a range of delays for a set size of four items, making it possible to assess the rate at which VSTM representations are created. For these simple colored squares, the consolidation rate was approximately 50 ms/item. That is, increasing the delay by 50 ms leads to the storage of an additional object's worth of information in VSTM. This same rate of consolidation is observed whether or not other items are being concurrently maintained in VSTM (Woodman & Vogel, 2005). However, it is not yet known whether this reflects the operation of a serial process that spends 50 ms consolidating each object in turn, or whether it reflects the operation of a parallel process that creates progressively more accurate and robust representations over time. It is also not yet known whether this process operates more slowly for more complex objects.

3.5.2 The Maintenance of Visual Short-term Memory Representations

Representations in VSTM can be maintained for several seconds without much cognitive effort. For example, it is possible to perform a difficult visual-search task during the retention interval of a color or form change-detection task with little or no disruption of either change-detection performance or search performance (Woodman, Vogel, & Luck, 2001). However, substantial interference is observed if the search task occurs during the retention interval of a spatial change-detection task (Woodman & Luck, 2004), which is consistent with the idea that spatial VSTM is used to avoid directing attention multiple times to the same spatial location (Castel, Pratt, & Craik, 2003). The converse pattern was observed when a mental rotation task was used rather than a visual-search task. The mental rotation of a letter—which presumably involves storing a representation of the letter in some sort of buffer and then rotating this representation— led to interference with a color change-detection task but not with a location change-detection task (Hyun & Luck, 2007). This suggests that object VSTM is used as a buffer to store shape representations while they are being rotated. More generally, the results of these experiments indicate that it is possible to perform a demanding cognitive task without disrupting representations in VSTM as long as the task does not require storing new representations in VSTM. Once formed, VSTM representations appear to persist without much cognitive effort.

However, VSTM representations may become degraded over time. Figure 3–10 shows five different types of degradation that are possible. First, the strength of the memory representation may decline gradually over time. Second, the precision of the memory representation may decrease over time. More specifically, there may be a progressive broadening of the range of values being represented, which in turn makes it difficult to know the exact value of the original item. For example, a 45-degree orientation may initially be represented by activation confined to units with a peak response at 45 degrees, but units with a slightly different tuning may also become activated over time. A decrease in precision and a reduction in amplitude may be functionally equivalent, because the ability to discriminate a feature value probably depends on the ratio of the amplitude of activation to the width of activation. Moreover, a decline in amplitude may eventually cause the representation to be lost, because a representation so broad that it has lost all information about the original value is functionally equivalent to a representation with zero amplitude.

Instead of becoming smaller or less precise, representations may drift over time. A drift may either be nonsystematic (labeled a *random walk* in Fig. 3–10; see Kinchla & Smyzer, 1967) or systematic (labeled *systematic drift*). Clear evidence of systematic drifts over time have been observed by Spencer and his colleagues, who showed that spatial VSTM representations may be attracted or repelled by spatial reference points (Simmering, Spencer, & Schöner, 2006; Spencer & Hund, 2002). Unless a drift is systematic, and the investigator knows the direction in which the drift might occur, the need to average over trials may make it impossible to distinguish between drifts and changes in amplitude

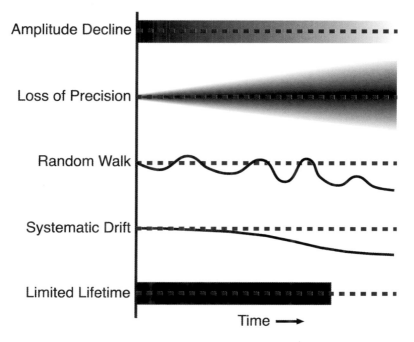

Figure 3–10. Examples of five different ways in which information may be lost from visual short-term memory over a period of seconds.

or precision. That is, the average representation may be strongest at the original value and progressively weaker at more distant values even if the single-trial representation maintains a constant amplitude and width but varies in value over time.

Gold, Murray, Sekuler, Bennett, and Sekuler (2005) developed a method for demonstrating that VSTM representations change systematically rather than randomly even if one does not know in advance the direction of the drift. They performed a change-detection task with texture patterns that were distorted by the addition of random noise. Different random noise was added to the sample and test arrays, but each trial was repeated in the second half of the session with the same noise that had been used in the first half. The observers were quite likely to make the same response on two identical trials, and the likelihood of this concordance did not decrease as the sample–test delay interval increased (even though overall accuracy decreased as the delay increased). This result demonstrates that the VSTM representations changed deterministically rather than randomly, consistent with the sort of systematic drift observed by Spencer and Hund (2002).

A final possibility is that representations may have a limited lifetime, suddenly terminating after a variable period. If this occurred, the average accuracy in a VSTM task would decline gradually over time even though the single-trial representations did not decline gradually. Moreover, VSTM representations might exhibit a combination of these different patterns. For example, a representation may drift systematically while becoming less precise, then suddenly terminate. To my knowledge, the possibility of limited lifetimes has never been addressed in the VSTM literature.

3.5.3 Comparing Visual Short-term Memory Representations with Perceptual Inputs

Visual short-term memory representations are maintained in an active form, eliminating the need for a distinct retrieval process (but see McElree, 2006). However, for VSTM representations to be useful for ongoing cognition, they must somehow be "read out" or accessed. In many cases, VSTM representations may be maintained for a period of time and then be used as the input to some other process (e.g., a LTM storage process, a response-selection process, etc.). The precise means by which a high-level internal representation becomes the input to a high-level internal process is difficult to study by means of behavioral techniques, and very little empirical research has been conducted on this topic.

However, change-detection tasks require that VSTM representations be accessed, and this task makes it possible to study at least one aspect of the general issue of VSTM access. In particular, the change-detection task requires the observer to compare a VSTM representation of the sample array with the incoming perceptual representation of the test array. The general issue of comparing two representations was studied extensively from the late 1960s to the early 1980s, although it was not typically framed as a VSTM issue. Much was learned and many interesting phenomena were discovered, but this line of research faded away and is not typically cited by contemporary VSTM researchers. Thus, this section will begin with a brief overview of this literature (see Farell, 1985 for a thorough review; see also Hyun, Woodman, Vogel, Hollingworth, & Luck, in press).

The original study of Egeth (1966) required observers to compare two objects, each defined by several features. However, to make close contact with the contemporary change-detection literature, this section will focus on experiments in which observers compare two arrays of items, each defined by a single feature. As illustrated in Figure 3–11A, for example, Taylor (1976) presented observers with two side-by-side arrays, each containing four letters. In the *any-difference* task, the observers pressed one button if *any* of the items in one array *differed* from the corresponding items in the other array, and they pressed a different button if all the items were identical. The number of differences ranged from zero to four, and the observers were required to make one response for zero differences and a different response for one to four differences. I refer to a difference between two corresponding items as a *critical feature* because a difference is the feature that distinguishes between the two response alternatives.

This task resembles the contemporary change-detection task except that (a) responses are speeded and RT is the primary dependent variable, (b) the number of differences is varied rather than the number of items, and (c) the arrays are presented simultaneously rather than sequentially. Although the simultaneous

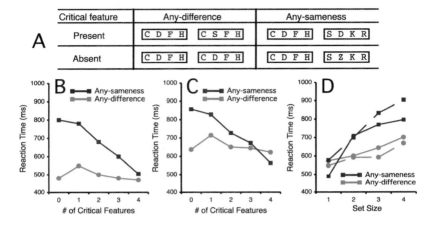

Figure 3–11. Stimuli (**A**) and results (**B**) from the study of Taylor (1976). (**C**) Results from a similar experiment by Hyun et al. (in press), using a sequential color change-detection task instead of a simultaneous letter change-detection task. (**D**) Results from an additional experiment by Hyun et al. (in press) in which the set size was varied, and the number of critical features was either zero (equivalent to a no-change trial in a standard change-detection experiment; shown in broken lines) or one (equivalent to a change trial in a standard change-detection experiment; shown in solid lines).

presentation might seem to obviate the use of VSTM, VSTM appears to be used for both sequential and simultaneous presentation (Scott-Brown, Baker, & Orbach, 2000). Indeed, it is likely that the observers foveated one array, stored it in memory, and then foveated the other array, comparing a VSTM representation of one array with the sensory input from the other array.

If observers perform this task by comparing each feature in serial, then RTs should be fastest when all four items differ and should become progressively slower as the number of critical features (differences) decreases. The slowest RTs should be obtained when the two arrays are identical, because the observer must verify that all four pairs of corresponding items are identical. As shown in Figure 11B, RTs did become slower as the number of critical features declined from four to one, but RTs were much faster on no-change trials than on one-change trials. This *fast-same* effect has been observed many times, with a variety of procedural variations (see Farell, 1985).

The Taylor (1976) study also included an *any-sameness* task (originated by Sekuler & Abrams, 1968), in which the observers made one response if the two arrays were completely different and another response if one or more items were identical between the two arrays (see Fig. 3–11). In this task, the critical feature is a *sameness* between two corresponding items. Although this task is just the obverse of the any-difference task, the pattern of results was quite different (see Fig. 3–11B). First, RTs become much longer when the number of critical features is small in the any-sameness task compared to the any-difference task.

Second, RTs do not become faster when the number of critical features is zero in the any-sameness task (which would be the analog of the fast-same effect in the any-difference task). As shown in Figure 3–11C, Hyun et al. (in press) have shown that the same pattern of results is obtained when the task is changed to be more like the contemporary change-detection task, using two sequential arrays of four colored squares rather than two simultaneous arrays of letters. Thus, the detection of sameness appears to be substantially more difficult than the detection of difference (unless sequential arrays are presented with a very short delay; Theeuwes, 2004).

To explain the greater difficulty of the any-sameness task, Hyun et al. (in press) proposed that the presence of a difference between a VSTM representation and a perceptual input in the change-detection paradigm is analogous to the presence of a distinctive feature in the visual-search paradigm. In visual search, a target defined by the presence of a feature can be detected rapidly, irrespective of set size, whereas a target defined by the absence of a feature is detected slowly, and RT increases steeply as the set size increases. For example, searching for a Q target among O distractors is very efficient because the observers can simply search for the presence of the line that distinguishes a Q from an O; however, search for an O target among Q distractors is very inefficient because the observers must find a circle that does not contain a line (Treisman & Souther, 1985). These results indicate that the presence of a simple feature can be detected by an unlimited-capacity parallel process, and additional research has shown that this detection leads to the rapid orienting of attention (Kim & Cave, 1995; Luck & Hillyard, 1994b). In contrast, the absence of a feature appears to require a slow, effortful, and possibly serial limited-capacity process (Treisman & Gormican, 1988; Woodman & Luck, 2003). Hyun et al. (in press) proposed that differences between VSTM representations and perceptual inputs can similarly be detected by a parallel, unlimited-capacity process, leading to the rapid allocation of attention, whereas the absence of a difference requires a limited-capacity process to be detected. More generally, the change-detection task can be considered a visual-search task in which the observer searches for a difference between the test array and a VSTM representation of the sample array.

Figure 3–11D shows RTs from an any-sameness task and an any-difference task in which the set size was varied and the number of critical features was either zero or one (as in most visual-search and change-detection tasks). The slope of the function relating RT to set size was much shallower in the any-difference task than in the any-sameness task. Moreover, the slope was substantially steeper on target-absent trials (i.e., zero critical features) than on target-present trials (i.e., one critical feature) in the any-sameness task, but not in the any-difference task. This parallels the pattern observed in visual-search tasks when the target is defined by the absence versus the presence of a feature. However, the slope of the function for the any-difference condition (50 ms/item) was still substantially steeper than that typically observed when observers look for a simple feature in a visual-search task (typically <15 ms/item).

Additional experiments by Hyun et al. (in press) explored whether the detection of a difference leads to a rapid shift of attention. In one experiment, shifts of attention were assessed by recording event-related potentials and measuring the *N2pc* component, a well-studied index of attention shifting that arises from extrastriate visual cortex (Hopf et al. 2006; Hopf et al., 2000; Luck, Girelli, McDermott, & Ford, 1997; Luck & Hillyard, 1994b; Woodman & Luck, 2003). A changed item in the test array was found to elicit an N2pc component beginning around 200 ms after the onset of the test array, indicating that the presence of a difference in a change-detection task triggers a shift of attention, just as simple features do in visual-search tasks (Luck & Hillyard, 1994a, 1994b). Moreover, the onset latency of the N2pc component remained constant as the set size increased from one to four items, just as N2pc onset latency remains constant as the set size increases in feature-search tasks (Luck & Hillyard, 1990). This is consistent with the proposal that an unlimited-capacity parallel process compares the VSTM representation of the sample array with the incoming test array, triggering a shift of attention when a difference is detected.

An additional experiment used eye movements as a measure of the time required to detect changes. In this experiment, a change was present on every trial, and the observers were required to make an eye movement to the changed item. The onset time of this saccade increased only slightly as the set size increased from two to four, with a slope of 12 ms/item. This provides further evidence that differences between VSTM representations and sensory inputs can be detected by an unlimited-capacity (or high-capacity) process.

Why, then, is the RT slope for change detection so much higher than the RT slope for feature-search tasks? It seems likely that a fast, unlimited-capacity process compares the VSTM representation with the sensory input, triggering a rapid shift of attention, but that a slower, limited-capacity process takes place before the observer makes a button-press response. This may be necessary because shifting attention to the changed item does not provide direct visual evidence that a change occurred. In visual search, the relevant features of the target become attended once attention shifts to it; in change detection, however, the relevant feature is the change, and this is not directly visible in the test array. Consequently, some kind of rechecking process may be necessary before high-level systems are willing to decide that a change had been present.

3.6 FUNCTIONS OF VISUAL SHORT-TERM MEMORY

As the preceding sections of this chapter indicate, VSTM is the subject of considerable research. Visual short-term memory also plays a key role in theories of visual attention, and several authors have argued that attention is necessary, in part, because of limitations in VSTM capacity (Duncan, 1980; Luck & Vecera, 2002; Vogel, Woodman, & Luck, 2005). With one exception, however, very little empirical or theoretical work has been done on the role of VSTM in cognition. The one exception is the proposed role of VSTM in integrating information across shifts in eye position (*transsaccadic integration*), which has been studied extensively. This role of VSTM is discussed fully in Chapter 4, so it will be discussed only briefly here, followed by a discussion of several other possible roles for VSTM in visual cognition.

3.6.1 The Role of Visual Short-term Memory in Transsaccadic Integration

Sudden shift of gaze (*saccades*) occur two to four times per second during reading and the viewing of natural scenes (see reviews by Rayner, 1984; Rayner & Pollatsek, 1987). Thus, the retinal input consists of stable snapshots lasting a few hundred milliseconds, interspersed with sudden shifts. Vision is suppressed during saccades, so we have no direct experience of the visual input sliding along the retinal input array (Matin, 1974). As discussed in Chapter 5, a stable internal representation of a complex scene is built up over time as the eyes move around the scene, which implies that some information about a given snapshot is retained and integrated with other snapshots. In addition, attention shifts to the intended saccade location prior to each eye movement (Deubel & Schneider, 1996; Hoffman & Subramaniam, 1995; Peterson, Kramer, & Irwin, 2004), and information from the attended location that was obtained prior to the saccade is integrated with information from the same environmental location after it has been fixated (Henderson, Pollatsek, & Rayner, 1987). Thus, an obvious need exists to retain information across saccades, and overwhelming evidence suggests that presaccade information is indeed retained and integrated with postsaccade information.

The remaining question, then, is whether the VSTM system described in the preceding portions of this chapter is the memory system in which the presaccade information is stored, so that it can be integrated with the postsaccade information. Irwin and his collaborators have argued in favor of this proposal (e.g., Irwin, 1991; Irwin, 1992; Irwin, 1993; Irwin & Andrews, 1996; Irwin & Gordon, 1998). To provide evidence for this proposal, they have conducted experiments in which observers perform VSTM tasks in which a memory must be formed prior to a saccade and then used after the saccade. For example, the observers may view a sample array, make a saccade, and then view a test array. In experiment after experiment, Irwin has shown that observers perform quite accurately in such tasks and, more importantly, that the pattern of performance is essentially identical to the pattern observed when no saccade is necessary.

These results indicate that VSTM could potentially be used for transsaccadic integration. That is, the memories stored in VSTM can survive a saccade, and observers can use VSTM to compare a sample and test array even if they are at different retinal locations because of a shift in eye position that occurs between sample and test. This is an important first step toward demonstrating that VSTM is used for transsaccadic integration. However, the fact that VSTM *could* be used for transsaccadic integration does not mean that it *is* used for transsaccadic integration. That is, no direct evidence shows that VSTM is used for transsaccadic integration outside of artificial laboratory tasks, and we do not yet know whether VSTM is responsible for the integration of presaccade information with postsaccade information.

3.6.2 The Role of Visual Short-term Memory in Establishing Correspondence Across Saccades

Rather than providing the presaccade information that is directly integrated with the postsaccade information, VSTM may play the even more fundamental role of making it possible to determine which objects in the presaccade input correspond to which objects in the postsaccade input. This *correspondence problem* must be solved if any integration is to occur, regardless of whether the information being integrated is stored in VSTM or some other memory system. Several investigators have proposed that the VSTM is used to establish correspondence between the presaccade and postsaccade inputs by matching the representation of the intended saccade target with the postsaccade sensory input (e.g., Currie, McConkie, Carlson-Radvansky, & Irwin, 2000; Henderson & Hollingworth, 1999). Once this correspondence has been established, the correspondence problem is easy to solve for the other objects by simply assuming that the relative locations of the objects remains relatively stable across the saccade (which is usually a reasonable assumption, given that saccades are quite brief). Until recently, however, this hypothesis has never received a direct test.

To examine this putative role of VSTM, Hollingworth, Richard, and Luck (2008) took advantage of the fact that saccades often fail to land on the intended object. Even in the simplest laboratory conditions, in which a single target appears on a blank screen and the observer must make a saccade to this object, the average error is approximately 10% of the saccade distance (Kapoula, 1985). Errors are presumably even larger during natural viewing, in which objects and the observer's head may be moving, sometimes unpredictably. When the eyes fail to land on the target, a fast and automatic correction occurs (Deubel, Wolf, & Hauske, 1982), which is presumably important under real-world conditions, so that important information is quickly foveated. When only a single object is visible, it is trivial to determine which object was the saccade target and to make an accurate correction. As illustrated in Figure 3–12, however, several objects may lie near the actual landing point under natural viewing conditions, making it more difficult to determine which object was the original saccade target and to make a correction to this location. Hollingworth et al. (2008) tested the hypothesis that a representation of the saccade target is stored in VSTM and then compared with the objects surrounding the postsaccade gaze location to determine which postsaccade object corresponds to the presaccade target. This is a special case of the more general hypothesis that VSTM is used to establish correspondence between the presaccade and postsaccade visual inputs.

To test this hypothesis, Hollingworth et al. (2008) modified an experimental paradigm that has been used previously to experimentally induce gaze errors (which makes it possible to study gaze corrections in a controlled manner). In a *baseline* condition, a single object in the periphery briefly expanded, signaling the observer to make a saccade to this object (Fig. 3–13). While the eyes were moving toward this target (and the visual input was suppressed), the position of the target shifted slightly, so that the eyes would not land on the target. Under these conditions, observers make a fast and automatic gaze correction, and

Figure 3–12. Example of the ambiguity that may occur following a saccade error in a complex natural scene. In this example, the observer is fixating the center of the child's face and then attempts to shift gaze leftward to the blue ball. However, gaze actually lands below this ball. Without some kind of memory of the saccade target (the blue ball), it would be impossible for the visual system to determine which item near the landing point was the original saccade target and then make an appropriate corrective saccade. Photo by Lisa Oakes.

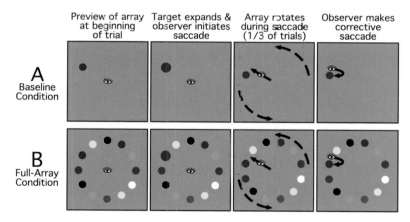

Figure 3–13. Stimuli from the baseline condition (**A**) and full-array condition (**B**) in the study of Hollingworth et al. (2008). The stimulus array is viewed at the beginning of the trial. After a delay, one item expands briefly, signaling that the observer should make a saccade to this item. On one-third of trials, the array rotates by a half position while the eyes are in flight, so that the eyes land halfway between the target and a distractor. The observer then makes a corrective saccade to the target item.

there is no ambiguity about the location to which gaze should shift. Thus, this condition provides a measure of the speed and accuracy of gaze correction when no memory of the saccade target is necessary. This condition was compared with a *full-array* condition, in which a circular array of colored disks was visible, one of which briefly expanded to indicate that the observer should make a saccade to this object. During the saccade, the entire array rotated by a half-position, so that gaze landed halfway between two disks (on average). In this condition, the postsaccade sensory input provides no information about which item was the original target, and the only way to solve this problem and make an accurate gaze correction is to compare a memory of the presaccade input with the postsaccade input.

Despite the lack of visible cues in the postsaccade input, the observers made a gaze correction to the correct item on 98% of trials in the full-array condition (they were 100% correct in the baseline condition). Moreover, the onset of the corrective saccade was only 39 ms slower in the full-array condition than in the baseline condition. Thus, the need to use memory resulted in only a small decrease in the speed and accuracy of the corrective saccades. Indeed, the modest slowing may have reflected the fact that a nearby competitor was present in the full-array condition rather than the time required to consult a memory representation of the target. Additional experiments demonstrated that these memory-guided corrective saccades are largely automatic and unconscious: When asked to avoid making a correction, the observers often made a correction even though they reported that they did not make a correction. An additional experiment tested the hypothesis that VSTM is the memory system used to guide these corrections. In this experiment, the gaze-correction task was interposed during the retention interval of a change-detection task. Significant interference was observed between gaze-correction performance and change-detection performance, indicating that the same memory system (VSTM) is used for both tasks. No interference was observed, however, when the gaze-correction task occurred during the retention interval of a verbal STM task. Together, these results support the proposal that VSTM is used to establish correspondence between presaccade and postsaccade visual inputs, a task performed by the visual system tens of thousands of times each day. Indeed, this important and extremely frequent use of VSTM may have been the main driving force behind the development of VSTM (both ontogenetically and phylogenetically).

3.6.3 Other Functional Roles of Visual Short-term Memory

Visual short-term memory is presumably also used in real-world tasks outside the domain of gaze control and transsaccadic integration. This section considers some of these other functional roles.

One likely role for spatial VSTM is to keep track of locations and regions that have already been attended in visual-search tasks. *Inhibition-of-return* experiments have shown that RTs are slowed when a target is presented at the location to which attention was previously drawn by a peripheral transient, and this effect has been interpreted as a reflection of a mechanism that biases attention away from previously attended locations, so that new locations can be searched (Posner & Cohen, 1984). In support of this interpretation, studies using visual-search tasks have confirmed that attention avoids revisiting previously searched locations (Klein, 1988, 2000). It appears that the visual system can exhibit inhibition at several previously attended locations over a period of a few seconds, at least under some conditions (e.g., Snyder & Kingstone, 2001; Tipper, Weaver, & Watson, 1996), which is consistent with the use of VSTM to maintain these locations. Moreover, the inhibition is reduced when spatial VSTM is occupied by a concurrent task (Castel, Pratt, & Craik, 2003). More generally, substantial interference is observed when a visual-search task is presented during the retention interval of spatial change-detection task (Woodman & Luck, 2004), but minimal interference is observed when a visual-search task is presented during the retention interval of a color or form change-detection task (Woodman, Vogel, & Luck, 2001). Thus, spatial VSTM (but not object VSTM) plays an important role in visual search, most likely being used to keep track of previously searched locations, so that they are not searched again.

Object VSTM, in contrast, may serve as a buffer in which object representations are held while they are being manipulated. As discussed earlier, the object VSTM system is used as a buffer for representations of objects during mental rotation. This VSTM system presumably plays a similar role in other tasks that require the manipulation of perceptual representations.

As discussed earlier in this chapter, the change-detection task requires a comparison of a VSTM representation with a perceptual input, and this points toward a real-world role of VSTM. Specifically, many high-level cognitive operations rely on the ability to make comparisons among representations (for a review, see Markman & Gentner, 2000), and the ability to compare visual objects may play an important role in the learning of object categories (Gentner & Namy, 1999). Consider, for example, an infant in a room with two dogs and a cat. As the infant fixates one animal after another, the process of determining the similarities between the two dogs and the differences between the dogs and the cat may require that the infant remember the visual features of the previously fixated animal and compare them with the features of the currently fixated animal. This sort of comparison process may be important for both children and adults as they try to perceive the similarities and differences among objects that are present in the same scene but do not both fall into the high-resolution fovea. Thus, VSTM may play a key role in the acquisition of long-term knowledge from the visual environment.

REFERENCES

Allen, R. J., Baddeley, A. D., and Hitch, G. J. (2006). Is the binding of visual features in working memory resource-demanding? *Journal of Experimental Psychology: General* 135:298–313.

Alvarez, G. A., and Cavanagh, P. (2004). The capacity of visual short-term memory is set both by information load and by number of objects. *Psychological Science* 15:106–111.

Atkinson, R. C., and Shiffrin, R. M. (1968). Human memory: A proposed system and its control processes. In *The Psychology of Learning and Motivation: Advances in Research and Theory Volume 2*, ed. K. W. Spence, 89–195. New York: Academic Press.

Awh, E., Barton, B., and Vogel, E. K. (2007). Visual working memory represents a fixed number of items regardless of complexity. *Psychological Science* 18:622–å628.

Awh, E., Dhaliwal, H., Christensen, S., and Matsukura, M. (2001). Evidence for two components of object-based selection. *Psychological Science* 12:329–334.

Baddeley, A., and Logie, R. H. (1999). Working memory: The multiple-component model. In *Models of Working Memory* (Vol. 28–61), eds. A. Miyake and P. Shah. Cambridge, UK: Cambridge University Press.

Baddeley, A. D. (1986). *Working Memory*. Oxford: Clarendon.

Baddeley, A. D., and Hitch, G. J. (1974). Working Memory. In *The Psychology of Learning and Motivation, Vol. VIII*, ed. G. H. Bower, 47–90. New York: Academic Press.

Besner, D., Davies, J., and Daniels, S. (1981). Reading for meaning: The effects of concurrent articulation. *Quarterly Journal of Experimental Psychology*, 33A:415–437.

Biederman, I. (1987). Recognition by components: A theory of human image understanding. *Psychological Review* 94:115–147.

Braun, C., Heinz, U., Schweizer, R., Wiech, K., Birbaumer, N., and Topka, H. (2001). Dynamic organization of the somatosensory cortex induced by motor activity. *Brain* 124:2259–2267.

Buttle, H., and Raymond, J. E. (2003). High familiarity enhances visual change detection for face stimuli. *Perception and Psychophysics* 65:1296–1306.

Calkins, M. W. (1898). A study of immediate and delayed recall of the concrete and of the verbal. *Psychological Review* 5:451–456.

Carlson-Radvansky, L. A., and Irwin, D. E. (1995). Memory for structural information across eye movements. *Journal of Experimental Psychology: Learning, Memory, and Cognition* 21:1441–1458.

Castel, A. D., Pratt, J., and Craik, F. I. (2003). The role of spatial working memory in inhibition of return: evidence from divided attention tasks. *Perception and Psychophysics* 65(6):970–981.

Chelazzi, L., Duncan, J., Miller, E. K., and Desimone, R. (1998). Responses of neurons in inferior temporal cortex during memory-guided visual search. *Journal of Neurophysiology* 80:2918–2940.

Chelazzi, L., Miller, E. K., Duncan, J., and Desimone, R. (2001). Responses of neurons in macaque area V4 during memory-guided visual search. *Cerebral Cortex* 11:761–772.

Chen, D., Eng, H. Y., and Jiang, Y. (2006). Visual working memory for trained and novel polygons. *Visual Cognition* 14:37–54.

Cohen, J. D., Perlstein, W. M., Braver, T. S., Nystrom, L. E., Noll, D. C., Jonides, J., et al. (1997). Temporal dynamics of brain activation during a working memory task. *Nature* 386(6625):604–608.

Courtney, S. M., Ungerleider, L. G., Keil, K., and Haxby, J. V. (1996). Object and spatial visual working memory activate separate neural systems in human cortex. *Cerebral Cortex* 6:39–49.

Courtney, S. M., Ungerleider, L. G., Keil, K., and Haxby, J. V. (1997). Transient and sustained activity in a distributed neural system for human working memory. *Nature* 386:608–611.

Cowan, N. (2001). The magical number 4 in short-term memory: A reconsideration of mental storage capacity. *Behavioral and Brain Sciences* 24:87–185.

Cowan, N., Elliott, E. M., Saults, J. S., Morey, C. C., Mattox, S., Ismajatulina, A., et al. (2005). On the capacity of attention: Its estimation and its role in working memory and cognitive aptitudes. *Cognitive Psychology* 51:42–100.

Currie, C., McConkie, G., Carlson-Radvansky, L. A., and Irwin, D. E. (2000). The role of the saccade target object in the perception of a visual stable world. *Perception and Psychophysics* 62:673–683.

De Renzi, E., and Nichelli, P. (1975). Verbal and nonverbal short-term memory impairment following hemispheric damage. *Cortex* 11:341–354.

Delvenne, J.-F., and Bruyer, R. (2004). Does visual short-term memory store bound features? *Visual Cognition* 11:1–27.

Deubel, H., and Schneider, W. X. (1996). Saccade target selection and object recognition: Evidence for a common attentional mechanism. *Vision Research* 36:1827–1837.

Deubel, H., Wolf, W., and Hauske, G. (1982). Corrective saccades: Effect of shifting the saccade goal. *Vision Research* 22:353–364.

Duncan, J. (1980). The locus of interference in the perception of simultaneous stimuli. *Psychological Review* 87:272–300.

Duncan, J. (1984). Selective attention and the organization of visual information. *Journal of Experimental Psychology: General* 113:501–517.

Egeth, H. (1966). Parallel versus serial processing in multidimensional stimulus discrimination. *Perception and Psychophysics* 1:245–252.

Eng, H. Y., Chen, D., and Jiang, Y. (2005). Visual working memory for simple and complex visual stimuli. *Psychonomic Bulletin and Review* 12:1127–1133.

Farah, M. J., Hammond, K. M., Levine, D. N., and Calvanio, R. (1988). Visual and spatial mental imagery: Dissociable systems of representation. *Cognitive Psychology* 20(4):439–462.

Farell, B. (1985). "Same"–"different" judgments: A review of current controversies in perceptual comparisons. *Psychological Bulletin* 98:419–456.

Fougnie, D., and Marois, R. (2006). Distinct capacity limits for attention and working memory. *Psychological Science* 17:526–534.

Frank, M. J., Loughry, B., and O'Reilly, R. C. (2001). Interactions between frontal cortex and basal ganglia in working memory: A computational model. *Cognitive, Affective, and Behavioral Neuroscience* 1:137–160.

Fuster, J. M., and Jervey, J. P. (1981). Inferotemporal neurons distinguish and retain behaviorally relevant features of visual stimuli. *Science* 212:952–954.

Gegenfurtner, K. R., and Sperling, G. (1993). Information transfer in iconic memory experiments. *Journal of Experimental Psychology: Human Perception and Performance* 19(4):845–866.

Gentner, D., and Namy, L. (1999). Comparison in the development of categories. *Cognitive Development* 13:487–513.

Gnadt, J. W., and Andersen, R. A. (1988). Memory related motor planning activity in posterior parietal cortex of macaque. *Experimental Brain Research* 70:216–220.

Gold, J. M., Murray, R. F., Sekuler, A. B., Bennett, P. J., and Sekuler, R. (2005). Visual memory decay is deterministic. *Psychological Science* 16:769–775.

Hanley, J. F., Young, A. W., and Person, N. A. (1991). Impairment of the visuo-spatial sketch pad. *Quarterly Journal of Experimental Psychology* 43A:101–125.

Hebb, D. O. (1949). *Organization of Behavior: A Neuropsychological Theory*. New York: Wiley, Inc.

Henderson, J. M., and Hollingworth, A. (1999). The role of fixation position in detecting scene changes across saccades. *Psychological Science* 10:438–443.

Henderson, J. M., Pollatsek, A., and Rayner, K. (1987). The effects of foveal priming and extrafoveal preview on object identification. *Journal of Experimental Psychology: Human Perception and Performance* 13:449–463.

Hoffman, J. E., and Subramaniam, B. (1995). The role of visual attention in saccadic eye movements. *Perception and Psychophysics* 57:787–795.

Hollingworth, A. (2006). Scene and position specificity in visual memory for objects. *Journal of Experimental Psychology: Learning, Memory, and Cognition* 32:58–69.

Hollingworth, A., Richard, A. M., and Luck, S. J. (2008). Understanding the function of visual short-term memory in human cognition: Transsaccadic memory, object correspondence, and gaze correction. *Journal of Experimental Psychology: General 137:163–181.*

Hopf, J.-M., Luck, S. J., Boelmans, K., Schoenfeld, M. A., Boehler, N., Rieger, J., et al. (2006). The neural site of attention matches the spatial scale of perception. *Journal of Neuroscience* 26:3532–3540.

Hopf, J.-M., Luck, S. J., Girelli, M., Hagner, T., Mangun, G. R., Scheich, H., et al. (2000). Neural sources of focused attention in visual search. *Cerebral Cortex* 10:1233–1241.

Hyun, J.-S. (2006). *How Are Visual Working Memory Representations Compared with Perceptual Inputs?* Iowa City: University of Iowa Press.

Hyun, J.-S., and Luck, S. J. (2007). Visual working memory as the substrate for mental rotation. *Psychonomic Bulletin and Review* 13:154–158.

Hyun, J.-S., Woodman, G. F., Vogel, E. K., Hollingworth, A., and Luck, S. J. (in press). The comparison of visual working memory representations with perceptual inputs. *Journal of Experimental Psychology: Human Perception and Performance.*

Irwin, D. E. (1991). Information integration across saccadic eye movements. *Cognitive Psychology* 23(3):420–456.

Irwin, D. E. (1992). Memory for position and identity across eye movements. *Journal of Experimental Psychology: Learning, Memory, and Cognition* 18:307–317.

Irwin, D. E. (1993). Perceiving an integrated visual world. In *Attention and Performance XIV: Synergies in Experimental Psychology, Artificial Intelligence, and Cognitive Neuroscience*, ed. D. E. K. S. Meyer, 121–142. Cambridge, MA: MIT Press.

Irwin, D. E., and Andrews, R. V. (1996). Integration and accumulation of information across saccadic eye movements. In *Attention and Performance XVI*, T. Inui and J. L. McClelland, eds., 125–155. Cambridge, MA: MIT Press.

Irwin, D. E., and Gordon, R. D. (1998). Eye movements, attention and trans-saccadic memory. *Visual Cognition* 5(1–2):127–155.

Jacobs, J. (1887). Experiments on "prehension". *Mind* 12:75–79.

James, W. (1890). *The Principles of Psychology*. New York: Holt.

Jenkins, W. M., Merzenich, M. M., Ochs, T., Allard, T., and Guc-Robles, E. (1990). Functional reorganization of primary somatosensory cortex in adult owl monkeys after behavioral controlled tactile stimulation. *Journal of Neurophysiology* 63:82–104.

Jiang, Y., Olson, I. R., and Chun, M. M. (2000). Organization of visual short-term memory. *Journal of Experimental Psychology: Learning, Memory and Cognition* 2:683–702.

Johnson, J. S., Hollingworth, A., and Luck, S. J. (2008). The role of attention in the maintenance of feature bindings in visual short-term memory. *Journal of Experimental Psychology: Human Perception and Performance* 34:41–55.

Jolicoeur, P., and Dell' Acqua, R. (1998). The demonstration of short-term consolidation. *Cognitive Psychology* 36(2):138–202.

Kapoula, Z. (1985). Evidence for a range effect in the saccadic system. *Vision Research* 25:1155–1157.

Kim, M.-S., and Cave, K. R. (1995). Spatial attention in visual search for features and feature conjunctions. *Psychological Science* 6:376–380.

Kinchla, R. A., and Smyzer, F. (1967). A diffusion model of perceptual memory. *Perception and Psychophysics* 2:219–229.

Klein, R. (1988). Inhibitory tagging system facilitates visual search. *Nature* 334:430–431.

Klein, R. (2000). Inhibition of return. *Trends in Cognitive Science* 4(4):138–147.

Logie, R. H., and Marchetti, C. (1991). Visuo-spatial working memory: Visual, spatial or central executive? *Advances in Psychology* 80:105–115.

Luck, S. J., and Beach, N. J. (1998). Visual attention and the binding problem: A neurophysiological perspective. In *Visual Attention*, R. D. Wright ed., 455–478). New York: Oxford University Press.

Luck, S. J., Girelli, M., McDermott, M. T., and Ford, M. A. (1997). Bridging the gap between monkey neurophysiology and human perception: An ambiguity resolution theory of visual selective attention. *Cognitive Psychology* 33:64–87.

Luck, S. J., and Hillyard, S. A. (1990). Electrophysiological evidence for parallel and serial processing during visual search. *Perception and Psychophysics* 48:603–617.

Luck, S. J., and Hillyard, S. A. (1994a). Electrophysiological correlates of feature analysis during visual search. *Psychophysiology* 31:291–308.

Luck, S. J., and Hillyard, S. A. (1994b). Spatial filtering during visual search: Evidence from human electrophysiology. *Journal of Experimental Psychology: Human Perception and Performance* 20:1000–1014.

Luck, S. J., and Vecera, S. P. (2002). Attention. In *Stevens' Handbook of Experimental Psychology: Vol. 1: Sensation and Perception*, 3rd ed., S. Yantis, ed. New York: Wiley.

Luck, S. J., and Vogel, E. K. (1997). The capacity of visual working memory for features and conjunctions. *Nature* 390:279–281.

Luck, S. J., and Vogel, E. K. (1998). Response from Luck and Vogel (Response to commentary by Nelson Cowan). *Trends in Cognitive Sciences* 2:78–80.

Macmillan, N. A., and Creelman, C. D. (1991). *Detection Theory: A User's Guide.* New York: Cambridge University Press.

Magnussen, S., Greenlee, M. W., and Thomas, J. P. (1996). Parallel processing in visual short-term memory. *Journal of Experimental Psychology: Human Perception and Performance* 22:202–212.

Markman, A. B., and Gentner, D. (2000). Structure mapping in the comparison process. *American Journal of Psychology* 113:501–538.

Marr, D. (1982). *Vision: A Computational Investigation into the Human Representation and Processing of Visual Information.* San Francisco: Freeman.

Matin, E. (1974). Saccadic suppression: A review and an analysis. *Psychological Bulletin* 81:899–917.

McElree, B. (2006). Accessing recent events. In *The Psychology of Learning and Motivation* (Vol. 46), B. H. Ross, ed., pp. 155–200. San Diego: Academic Press.

Miller, E. K., Li, L., and Desimone, R. (1993). Activity of neurons in anterior inferior temporal cortex during a short-term memory task. *Journal of Neuroscience* 13:1460–1478.

Miyake, A., and Shah, P. (Eds.). (1999). *Models of Working Memory.* Cambridge, UK: Cambridge University Press.

Murray, D. J. (1968). Articulation and acoustic confusability in short-term memory. *Journal of Experimental Psychology* 78:679–684.

Navon, D. (1984). Resources--a theoretical soup stone? *Psychological Review* 91:216–234.

Navon, D., and Gopher, D. (1979). On the economy of the human processing system. *Psychology Review* 86:214–255.

Navon, D., and Miller, J. (2002). Queuing or sharing? A critical evaluation of the single-bottleneck notion. *Cognitive Psychology* 44:193–251.

Nickerson, R. S. (1965). Short-term memory for complex meaningful visual configurations: A demonstration of capacity. *Canadian Journal of Psychology* 19:155–160.

Norman, D. A., and Bobrow, D. G. (1976). On the analysis of performance operating characteristics. *Psychological Review* 83(6):508–510.

Olson, I. R., and Jiang, Y. (2002). Is visual short-term memory object based? Rejection of the "strong-object" hypothesis. *Perception and Psychophysics* 64:1055–1067.

Olson, I. R., and Jiang, Y. (2004). Visual short-term memory is not improved by training. *Memory and Cognition* 32:1326–1332.

Palmer, J. (1990). Attentional limits on the perception and memory of visual information. *Journal of Experimental Psychology: Human Perception and Performance* 16:332–350.

Palmer, J., Ames, C. T., and Lindsey, D. T. (1993). Measuring the effect of attention on simple visual search. *Journal of Experimental Psychology: Human Perception and Performance* 19:108–130.

Pashler, H. (1988). Familiarity and visual change detection. *Perception and Psychophysics* 44:369–378.

Peterson, M. S., Kramer, A. F., and Irwin, D. E. (2004). Covert shifts of attention precede involuntary eye movements. *Perception and Psychophysics* 66:398–405.

Phillips, W. A. (1974). On the distinction between sensory storage and short-term visual memory. *Perception and Psychophysics* 16:283–290.

Poggio, T., and Edelman, S. (1990). A network that learns to recognize three-dimensional objects. *Nature* 343:263–266.

Posner, M. I., and Cohen, Y. (1984). Components of visual orienting. In *Attention and Performance X*, eds. H. Bouma and D. G. Bouwhuis, 531–556. Hillsdale, NJ: Erlbaum.

Postle, B. R., and D'Esposito, M. (1999). "What" then "where" in visual working memory: An event-related fMRI study. *Journal of Cognitive Neuroscience* 11:585–597.

Raffone, A., and Wolters, G. (2001). A cortical mechanism for binding in visual working memory. *Journal of Cognitive Neuroscience* 13:766–785.

Rainer, G., Asaad, W. F., and Miller, E. K. (1998). Selective representation of relevant information by neurons in the primate prefrontal cortex. *Nature* 393:577–579.

Ranganath, C., and Blumenfeld. (2005). Doubts about double dissociations between short- and long-term memory. *Trends in Cognitive Sciences* 9:374–380.

Rayner, K. (1984). Visual selection in reading, picture perception, and visual search: A tutorial review. In *Attention and Performance X: Control of Language Processes*, eds. H. Bouma and D. Bouwhuis, 67–96). Hillsdale, NJ: Erlbaum.

Rayner, K., and Pollatsek, A. (1987). Eye movements in reading: A tutorial review. *Attention and Performance* (Vol. XII), ed. In M. Coltheart. Hillsdale: Erlbaum.

Rensink, R. A. (2002). Change detection. *Annual Review of Psychology* 53:245–277.

Sakai, K., and Inui, T. (2002). A feature-segmentation model of short-term visual memory. *Perception* 31:579–590.

Scarborough, D. L. (1972). Memory for brief visual displays of symbols. *Cognitive Psychology* 3:408–429.

Schutte, A. R., Spencer, J. P., and Schöner, G. (2003). Testing the dynamic field theory: Working memory for locations becomes more spatially precise over development. *Child Development* 74:1393–1417.

Scott-Brown, K. C., Baker, M. R., and Orbach, H. S. (2000). Comparison blindness. *Visual Cognition* 7(1–3):253–267.

Sekuler, R. W., and Abrams, M. (1968). Visual sameness: A choice time analysis of pattern recognition processes. *Journal of Experimental Psychology* 77:232–238.

Shibuya, H., and Bundesen, C. (1988). Visual selection from multielement displays: Measure and modeling effects of exposure duration. *Journal of Experimental Psychology: Human Perception and Performance* 14:591–600.

Simmering, V. R., Spencer, J. P., and Schöner, G. (2006). Reference-related inhibition produces enhanced position discrimination and fast repulsion near axes of symmetry. *Perception and Psychophysics* 63:1027–1046

Simons, D. J., and Rensink, R. A. (2005). Change blindness: Past, present, and future. *Trends in Cognitive Sciences* 9:16–20.

Smith, E. E., and Jonides, J. (1997). Working memory: A view from neuroimaging. *Cognitive Psychology* 33:5–42.

Snyder, J. J., and Kingstone, A. (2001). Multiple location inhibition of return: When you see it and when you don't. *Quarterly Journal of Experimental Psychology* 54A:1221–1237.

Spencer, J. P., and Hund, A. M. (2002). Prototypes and particulars: Spatial categories are formed using geometric and experience-dependent information. *Journal of Experimental Psychology: General* 131:16–37.

Spencer, J. P., Simmering, V. R., Schutte, A. R., and Schöner, G. (in press). What does theoretical neuroscience have to offer the study of behavioral development? Insights from a dynamic field theory of spatial cognition. In *Emerging Landscapes of Mind: Mapping the Nature of Change in Spatial Cognitive Development*, eds. J. Plumert and J. P. Spencer. London: Oxford University Press.

Standing, L. (1973). Learning 10,000 pictures. *Quarterly Journal of Experimental Psychology* 25:207–222.

Taylor, D. A. (1976). Stage analysis of reaction time. *Psychological Bulletin* 83:161–191.

Theeuwes, J. (2004). No blindness for things that do not change. *Psychological Science* 15:65–70.

Tipper, S., Weaver, B., and Watson, F. (1996). Inhibition of return to successively cued spatial locations: A commentary on Pratt and Abrams (1995). *Journal of Experimental Psychology: Human Perception and Performance* 22:1289–1293.

Todd, J. J., and Marois, R. (2004). Capacity limit of visual short-term memory in human posterior parietal cortex. *Nature* 428:751–754.

Treisman, A. (1988). Features and objects: The fourteenth Bartlett memorial lecture. *Quarterly Journal of Experimental Psychology* 40:201–237.

Treisman, A., and Gormican, S. (1988). Feature analysis in early vision: Evidence from search asymmetries. *Psychological Review* 95:15–48.

Treisman, A., and Souther, J. (1985). Search asymmetry: A diagnostic for preattentive processing of separable features. *Journal of Experimental Psychology: General* 114:285–310.

Treisman, A. M., and Gelade, G. (1980). A feature-integration theory of attention. *Cognitive Psychology* 12:97–136.

Tresch, M. C., Sinnamon, H. M., and Seamon, J. G. (1993). Double dissociation of spatial and object visual memory: Evidence from selective interference in intact human subjects. *Neuropsychologia* 31(3):211–219.

Vogel, E. K., and Machizawa, M. G. (2004). Neural activity predicts individual differences in visual working memory capacity. *Nature* 428:748–751.

Vogel, E. K., Woodman, G. F., and Luck, S. J. (2001). Storage of features, conjunctions, and objects in visual working memory. *Journal of Experimental Psychology: Human Perception and Performance* 27:92–114.

Vogel, E. K., Woodman, G. F., and Luck, S. J. (2005). Pushing around the locus of selection: Evidence for the flexible-selection hypothesis. *Journal of Cognitive Neuroscience* 17:1907–1922.

Vogel, E. K., Woodman, G. F., and Luck, S. J. (2006). The time course of consolidation in visual working memory. *Journal of Experimental Psychology: Human Perception and Performance* 32:1436–1451.

Walker, P., and Miles, R. (1999). The object-based representation of partially occluded surfaces in short-term visual memory: evidence from image combination. *Memory and Cognition* 27:553–560.

Wheeler, M., and Treisman, A. M. (2002). Binding in short-term visual memory. *Journal of Experimental Psychology: General* 131:48–64.

Wilken, P., and Ma, W. J. (2004). A detection theory account of change detection. *Journal of Vision* 4:1120–1135.

Williams, P. E., and Simons, D. J. (2000). Detecting changes in novel, complex three-dimensional objects. *Visual Cognition* 7:297–322.

Wilson, F. A. W., O' Scalaidhe, S. P., and Goldman-Rakic, P. S. (1993). Dissociation of object and spatial processing domains in primate prefrontal cortex. *Science* 260:1955–1958.

Woodman, G. F., and Luck, S. J. (2003). Serial deployment of attention during visual search. *Journal of Experimental Psychology: Human Perception and Performance* 29:121–138.

Woodman, G. F., and Luck, S. J. (2004). Visual search is slowed when visuospatial working memory is occupied. *Psychonomic Bulletin and Review* 11:269–274.

Woodman, G. F., and Vogel, E. K. (2005). Fractionating working memory: Consolidation and maintenance are independent processes. *Psychological Science* 16:106–113.

Woodman, G. F., Vogel, E. K., and Luck, S. J. (2001). Visual search remains efficient when visual working memory is full. *Psychological Science* 12:219–224.

Xu, Y. (2002a). Encoding color and shape from different parts of an object in visual short-term memory. *Perception and Psychophysics* 64:1260–1280.

Xu, Y. (2002b). Limitations of object-based feature encoding in visual short-term memory. *Journal of Experimental Psychology: Human Perception and Performance* 28:458–468.

Xu, Y. (2004). *An Object Benefit for Encoding Two Within-Dimension Features in Visual Short Term Memory.* Paper presented at the 45th Annual Meeting of the Psychonomic Society, Minneapolis, MN.

Xu, Y., and Chun, M. M. (2006). Dissociable neural mechanisms supporting visual short-term memory for objects. *Nature* 440(7080):91–95.

Zhang, W. (2007). *Resolution and capacity limitations in visual working memory: A new approach.* Iowa City: University of Iowa Press.

Zhang, W., and Luck, S. J. (in press). Discrete fixed-resolution representations in visual working memory. *Nature.*

Zimmer, H. D., and Lehnert, G. (2006). The spatial mismatch effect is based on global configuration and not on perceptual records within the visual cache. *Psychological Research* 70:1–12.

Chapter 4

Eye Movements and Scene Memory

John M. Henderson
University of Edinburgh

4.1 INTRODUCTION

Many, if not most, of our daily activities are informed by vision. The visual world guides behavior and thought by interacting with what we have previously seen and learned and what we are thinking about and trying to accomplish. That is, visual perception interacts with learning, memory, and cognition. An important limitation on visual processing is that visual acuity is variable across the visual field, with the very highest resolution and color sensitivity limited to a very small region at the center of fixation. In a sense, at any given moment, the visual system is confronted with detailed input at the center of view and a progressively blurry and monochromatic view beyond. The visual system maximizes the visual sensitivity of central vision by directing fixation through the scene via very rapid saccadic eye movements.

Given the constraints imposed by limited acuity and frequent eye movements, a critical question in vision and visual cognition is how the visual–cognitive system combines the information collected in successive views into a more complete composite representation. The creation of such a representation requires the storage of some type of information across each saccade, with representations generated from consecutive fixations integrated in some way. Furthermore, such representations would have to be retained in some form of online memory over multiple fixation–saccade cycles to be integrated over the entire course of scene viewing. Finally, once constructed, such representations might be stored in longer-term memory, so that they would be available to support future viewing, perceptual learning, and other cognitive activities such as thinking, reasoning, and language use (Henderson & Ferreira, 2004a).

On the one hand, given the difficulties that arise in generating a composite representation, one might hypothesize that such a representation is never built. Indeed, this view has been popular among some theorists (O'Regan, 1992; O'Regan & Noë, 2001). Alternatively, this chapter reviews the evidence supporting the view that representations are retained and combined across eye movements and over extended time. I will specifically consider representations that are generated over three time periods: across fixations (transsaccadic memory), over multiple fixation–saccade cycles (active online scene memory), and over the longer term (long-term scene memory). This basic taxonomy is summarized in Table 4–1. I use these memory categories for expository purposes to help organize the literature around function; I make no claim that retention and integration over these different time scales necessarily require separate structural memory stores. In fact, one might argue that transsaccadic memory and online scene memory are both forms of short-term memory (STM) (Irwin & Andrews, 1996), or that online and long-term scene memory are both forms of long-term memory (LTM; Hollingworth, 2004). Also, rather than attempt an exhaustive review of the literature, I highlight some of the critical studies as I see them, with particular attention to recent experiments from my laboratory concerning saccadic eye movements and visual memory. My conclusion is that a composite scene representation that includes relatively detailed (although not sensory or iconic) visual information is generated and retained in memory across eye movements and over time as a natural consequence of active, dynamic scene perception.

4.2 EYE MOVEMENT BASICS

This chapter focuses on saccadic eye movements. Saccadic eye movements comprise two temporal phases: *fixations*, in which gaze position is held relatively still; and *saccades*, in which the eyes move rapidly from one fixation location to another (Fig. 4–1). Saccadic eye movements are very fast (700–900 deg/sec can be observed, e.g., Carpenter, 1988) and, due to a combination of visual masking and central suppression, visual uptake of pattern information is essentially shut down during the saccade, a phenomenon known as *saccadic suppression* (Thiele, Henning, Buishik, & Hoffman, 2002; Matin, 1974; Volkman, 1986; Volkman, Schick, & Riggs, 1968). Evidence also suggests that some cognitive processes, particularly those associated with spatial cognition, are suppressed during

Table 4–1. Three Functional Epochs of Memory Related to Eye Movements

Functional Memory Type	Supports	Event	Time Scale
Transsaccadic memory	Transsaccadic information integration	One saccade	Tens of milliseconds
Active online scene memory	Short-term online episodic scene representation	Current perceptual episode	Seconds
Long-term scene memory	Long-term episodic and generalized (schematic) scene representations	Beyond current perceptual episode	Minutes, hours, days, years

saccades (Irwin, 2004). Saccadic suppression implies that useful pattern information is acquired from complex scenes only during fixations. The quality of the visual information available during a fixation falls off rapidly and continuously from the center of gaze due to the optical properties of the cornea and lens and the neuroanatomical structure of the retina and visual cortex.

The highest quality visual information is acquired from the foveal region of a viewed scene, a spatial area subtending roughly 2 degrees of visual angle at and immediately surrounding the fixation point. The fovea is centered at the optical axis of the eye and contains a dense array of cones with minimal spatial summation. Although the cones require a relatively high level of luminance to operate, they support the perception of color and fine detail. Furthermore, a disproportionately large amount of primary visual cortex is devoted to the fovea, providing the neural machinery needed for initial visual computation that can take advantage of the high-resolution input from the fovea.

The fovea must be oriented rapidly and accurately to ensure that important stimuli in the environment receive the highest quality visual analysis as information is required for ongoing vision, cognition, and action. On average, the eyes move to a new fixation position during scene viewing about three times each second, although there is a good deal of variability in the durations of fixations in a given image within individuals as well as across individuals (Castelhano & Henderson, in press; Henderson, 2003; Henderson & Hollingworth, 1998; Rayner, 1998), and some evidence suggests that these distributions may also differ depending on whether the viewer is examining a scene depiction or a real environment (Land & Hayhoe, 2001). Two important issues for understanding eye movements during scene perception are where a fixation tends to be directed and how long it typically remains there.

Eye movements during scene perception are intelligent in the sense that fixations are directed to scene regions that are task-relevant from moment to moment. Eye movement control therefore draws not only on the current visual input, but also on cognitive systems (Henderson, 2007). Henderson and Ferreira (2004b) provided a typology of the knowledge available to the human gaze control system (Table 4–2). This knowledge includes information about a specific scene that can be learned over the short term in the current perceptual encounter (short-term episodic scene knowledge) and over the longer term across multiple encounters (long-term episodic scene knowledge); scene schema knowledge or generic semantic and spatial knowledge about a particular type of scene (Mandler & Johnson, 1977); and task-related knowledge, including general gaze-control policies or strategies relevant to a given task (e.g., fixate the rear-view and side-view mirror before passing) and decisions based on ongoing task needs (e.g., fixate the teacup to put the spoon in it; Land & Hayhoe, 2001).

Exactly what factors determine which areas of a scene will be fixated? Research on eye movement control in scene perception has tended to focus on the influence of visual factors, with computational and psychophysical investigation highlighting image properties (e.g., first-order factors such as contrast and higher-order factors such as connected edges) that correlate with human

Table 4–2.   **Knowledge Sources in Memory Influencing Eye Movements During Scene Viewing**

Knowledge Source	Description	Example
Short-term (online) episodic scene knowledge	Specific knowledge about a particular scene in the current perceptual episode	My coffee cup is on my desk next to my telephone where I just put it.
Long-term episodic scene knowledge	Specific knowledge about a particular scene retained over time	When I return from a meeting, I remember that I left my coffee cup on my desk next to my telephone.
Scene schema knowledge	Generic knowledge about a particular category of scene	Coffee cups are found on flat surfaces like tables and desks.
Task knowledge	Generic knowledge about a particular category of task	When searching for my coffee cup, I don't need to look at the floor.

Adapted from Henderson and Ferreira, 2004b.

fixation locations (Itti & Koch, 2001; Parkhurst & Neibur, 2003). The goal of this research program has been to predict human fixation locations based on image properties alone. However, because of the intelligence of active scene perception, it is becoming clear that this approach is limited (Henderson, 2007). Of course, this is not to say that the visual stimulus plays no role in gaze control; some internal spatial map must exist, over which saccades are planned, and cognitive factors are generated in part from the scene that is currently present. Importantly, however, selecting fixation locations is primarily a function of *cognitive relevance*; that is, cognitive systems engaged in scene interpretation interacting with task considerations, rather than by inherent differences in the image properties themselves (Henderson, Brockmole, Castelhano, & Mack, 2007; Torralba, Oliva, Castelhano, & Henderson, 2006).

Another important aspect of gaze control is the length of time that a given fixation remains in a given location (*fixation duration*). The average duration of an individual fixation during scene viewing is about 330 ms, but there is a good deal of variability around this mean both within an individual and across individuals. An important issue in active scene perception is the degree to which this variability can be accounted for by visual and cognitive factors associated with the currently fixated scene region. The influence of visual and cognitive factors on fixation duration has been heavily investigated in the study of reading and language processing (Henderson & Ferreira, 2004a; Rayner, 1998), but has generally been overlooked in the literature on gaze control in scenes (Henderson, 2003). Conclusions about the distribution of attention over a scene can differ markedly when fixation position is weighted by fixation duration, because the distribution of processing time across a scene is a function of both the spatial distribution of fixations and their individual durations (Henderson, 2003). The degree to which individual fixation durations (rather than summed durations) in scene viewing are directly and immediately influenced by ongoing visual and cognitive factors has not been systematically investigated, but we have recently collected data in my lab suggesting that a large proportion of scene fixations are under direct and immediate stimulus control (Henderson & Pierce, in press).

In summary, humans use knowledge about the world to intelligently guide fixation through a scene. Cognitive systems interact with each other and with the scene image to determine where the eyes fixate. At the same time, as we will see, where the eyes land and how long they remain there have a profound effect on what is encoded and remembered from a scene.

4.3 EYE MOVEMENTS AND VISUAL MEMORY

4.3.1 Transsaccadic Memory

I noted in the section on Eye Movement Basics that the location of the fixation point changes in a scene once every 330 ms on average. What type of representation is retained in memory across a saccade from one fixation to the next? How is that retained information combined with information acquired during the subsequent fixation? For example, consider the saccade to the faucet in Figure 4–1. What type of representation is retained about the faucet during the saccade, and how is that representation combined with the new information taken in once the eyes land on it?

4.3.1.1 Spatiotopic sensory fusion

One hypothesis with a long history is that high-resolution sensory images are stored across saccades, with images from consecutive fixations integrated to form a composite sensory image (for reviews see Bridgeman, Van der Hejiden, & Velichkovsky, 1994; McConkie & Currie, 1996). Traditionally, this *spatiotopic fusion hypothesis* (Irwin, 1992b) has been instantiated by models in which a sensory (i.e., a precise, highly detailed, metrically organized, precategorical) image is generated during each fixation and stored in a temporary buffer, with sensory images from consecutive fixations spatially aligned and fused in a system that maps a retinal reference frame onto a spatiotopic frame (Breitmeyer, Kropfl, & Julesz, 1982; Davidson, Fox, & Dick, 1973; Duhamel, Colby, & Goldberg, 1992; Feldman, 1985; Jonides, Irwin, & Yantis, 1982; McConkie & Rayner, 1976; O'Regan & Lévy-Schoen, 1983; Pouget, Fisher, & Sejnowski, 1993; Trehub, 1977). In such models, the composite image formed during consecutive fixations is aligned by tracking the extent of the saccade (via afferent or efferent pathways) or by comparing the similarity of the individual images.

The notion of transsaccadic sensory fusion derives most directly from the intuition that visual stimuli linger beyond their physical presence. This can be experienced, for example, in the form of visual afterimages. The notion that a persisting visual representation or "icon" might support continuing visual

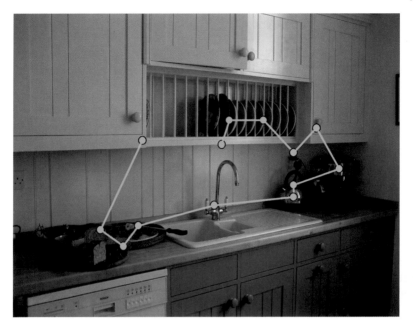

Figure 4–1. Example of an eye movement scan pattern over a photograph of a real-world scene. The lines represent saccades, and the points at which the lines change direction represent fixations.

processing was brought to the attention of modern cognitive psychology in a classic study by Sperling (1960). The well-known finding is that estimates of the visual information available from a brief visual display are much greater when individual items are probed (partial report) than when participants are asked to describe the entire display (full report). Furthermore, the partial-report advantage declines rapidly as the delay between display offset and probe onset increases. These results suggest that, immediately after the termination of a visual display, a large amount of information is available, but that this information is rapidly lost.

Subsequent studies revealed that "iconic memory" (Neisser, 1967) comprises a number of separable processes (Coltheart, 1980). Specifically, Coltheart suggested that *visible persistence* is the visual trace experienced as an image and is a consequence of lingering neural activity in early visual pathways, whereas *informational persistence* is based on a trace that is not experienced as an image but that nevertheless is available to influence performance. Visible persistence supports visual fusion, is influenced by factors such as the intensity and duration of the stimulus, and lasts for a maximum of about 100 ms (Di Lollo, 1980; Eriksen & Collins, 1967). Informational persistence is brief, nonvisible, precategorical, maskable, and independent of the duration of the stimulus (Irwin & Brown, 1987; Irwin & Yeomans, 1986). Finally, performance on traditional "iconic memory" tasks can also be influenced by a third memory system, visual short-term memory (VSTM), which is relatively long lasting, postcategorical, nonmaskable, and limited in capacity to about five items in these types of tasks (Irwin & Brown, 1987; Irwin & Yeomans, 1986). See Chapter 2 for a more detailed review and discussion of this literature.

Given the duration of a typical saccade (on the order of 20–80 milliseconds), both visible and informational persistence are potentially available to support transsaccadic sensory fusion, were these forms of persisting traces to reside in a spatiotopically organized memory buffer. However, despite this potential, evidence from a variety of paradigms has unambiguously provided evidence against the existence of spatiotopic sensory fusion across saccades. Perhaps the most convincing evidence arises from direct demonstrations that viewers are unable to fuse simple visual patterns from one fixation to the next. In these studies, viewers are required to integrate a presaccade and postsaccade pattern to successfully accomplish the task. If visual patterns can be fused in a spatiotopically based sensory memory system, then performance should be similar in a transsaccadic condition, in which the environmental spatial position of the patterns is maintained but retinal position is displaced due to a saccade, and a condition in which position in both retinal and environmental spatial reference frames is maintained within a fixation.

For example, when two dot patterns forming a matrix of dots are presented in rapid succession at the same retinal and spatial position within an eye fixation, a single fused pattern is perceived and performance (e.g., identification of a missing dot from the matrix) can be based on this percept (Di Lollo, 1977; Eriksen & Collins, 1967; Irwin, 1992a; Phillips, 1974). However, when the two patterns are viewed with similar timing parameters at the same environmental position but different retinal positions across a saccade, no such fused percept is experienced, even though the timing is appropriate for visible persistence (Coltheart, 1980; Irwin, 1992a) and performance is dramatically reduced (Bridgeman & Mayer, 1983; Irwin, 1991; Irwin, Brown, & Sun, 1988; Irwin, Yantis, & Jonides, 1983; Irwin, Zacks, & Brown, 1989; Jonides, Irwin, & Yantis, 1983; O'Regan & Lévy-Schoen, 1983; Rayner & Pollatsek, 1983).

Another interesting example of the failure of spatiotopic sensory fusion was provided by O'Regan and Lévy-Schoen (1983). In this study, participants were presented with a set of letter features in the parafovea during one fixation, and the complementary set of features in a subsequent fixation following a saccade. When fused, the features formed a word. Participants were unable to report the word across a saccade, although the task is trivial with the same display timing within a fixation. If a spatiotopically organized visual buffer were operating across saccades, based either on visible or informational persistence, one would expect that performance in the transsaccadic version of these fusion tasks would approach that of the within-fixation condition.

A different type of evidence against transsaccadic spatiotopic fusion comes from studies of visual masking. Within a fixation, a *visual mask* disrupts processing of visible and informational persistence. If these types of persistence can linger across a saccade within a spatiotopic buffer, then similar spatiotopic masking should be observed from fixation to fixation. Initial tests of this prediction suggested that such masking does in fact occur (Davidson, Fox, & Dick, 1973). Subsequent investigation, however, demonstrated that this masking effect is retinotopic rather than spatiotopic (Irwin, Brown, & Sun, 1988; Irwin et al., 1990; Van der Heijden, Bridgeman, & Mewhort, 1986), again providing evidence against transsaccadic spatiotopic fusion. For more extensive reviews of this research, see Irwin (1992b), Irwin and Andrews (1996), Pollatsek and Rayner (1992), and Rayner (1998).

If the visual information acquired from successive fixations is fused into a single composite sensory image, then displacements of the viewed world during a saccade should be highly noticeable and troublesome because fusion would then result in nonaligned input from the two fixations. Contrary to this prediction, Bridgeman, Hendry, and Stark (1975) demonstrated that a scene could be spatially displaced during a saccade with no conscious experience that the stimulus had shifted position, and with little or no disruption to the performance of a visual task. This insensitivity to spatial displacement across saccades has subsequently been replicated many times (e.g., Bridgeman & Stark, 1979; Currie, McConkie, Carlson-Radvansky, & Irwin, 2000; Henderson, 1997; Irwin, 1991; Mack, 1970; McConkie & Currie, 1996; Verfaillie, De Troy, & Van Rensbergen, 1994; Whipple & Wallach, 1978).

Changes to other visual properties are similarly difficult to detect across a saccade. For example, readers are insensitive to changes in the visual properties of text from fixation to fixation (McConkie & Zola, 1979). In these experiments, text was made up of characters of alternating case. During a given saccade, the case of all characters was exchanged. These case changes were typically not noticed by readers and had very little, if any, effect on reading rate or comprehension. Similar insensitivity to changes in visual features of an image across a saccade has been shown with pictures of objects and scenes. For example, Henderson (1997) found that it was very difficult for observers to detect a change to the specific contours of an object from fixation to fixation. In this study, participants were asked to fixate a point on a computer screen. A line drawing of an object was then presented to the right of fixation. About half of the contours of the object were presented; the other contours were occluded by black stripes. The participant executed a saccade to the object as soon as it appeared. During the saccade, the object remained exactly the same, changed to reveal the complementary set of contours, shifted one stripe width in position, or changed to a different object. The participant was asked to indicate whether any change had occurred. Participants failed to detect the majority of contour changes or position shifts. Other visual changes to objects, such as enlargements and reductions of size, also often go unnoticed when they take place during a saccade (Henderson, Pollatsek, & Rayner, 1987; Pollatsek, Rayner, & Collins, 1984).

Henderson and Hollingworth (2003a) reported results for full scenes similar to those of Henderson (1997). In this saccade-contingent global display change study, participants viewed pictures of real-world scenes while their eye movements were recorded. Scenes were presented as an alternating pattern of scene strips and occluding gray bars, as in the Henderson study (1997). Each time a viewer's eyes crossed an invisible software-defined boundary, the display changed, so that the occluding gray bars revealed the occluded parts of the scene, and the previously visible scene areas became occluded by gray bars. The display changes always took place during saccades, so that they were not accompanied by visual transients. With this manipulation, every pixel and every local visual feature in the scene was changed each time a change took place, although higher-level visual scene properties (e.g., surface color, viewpoint, direction of lighting and shadow, object shape, spatial relationships, and so on) remained the same across the changes. Viewers were told to view the scenes to prepare for a later memory test, but were also told about the nature of the changes and asked to press a button whenever they noticed one. If a point-by-point representation could be retained and evaluated across saccades, then these scene changes should have been highly salient and easy to detect. In contrast, in two experiments, the change detection rates were extremely low (15 of the 13 participants detected fewer than 8% of the changes), suggesting that point-by-point representations were not retained and integrated across saccades during scene perception. Insensitivity to global scene changes across saccades has also been replicated with image brightness and image contrast (Henderson, Brockmole, & Gajewski, 2008).

4.3.1.2 The blanking effect

Deubel and colleagues have reported an interesting exception to the just-noted studies (Deubel & Schneider, 1996; Deubel, Schneider, & Bridgeman, 1996, 2002; see also Gysen, Verfaillie, & De Graef, 2002). As just discussed, when a saccade target is displaced during a saccade, it is very difficult for a viewer to detect the displacement. However, Deubel et al. have shown that when the post-saccade display is blanked for a brief period of time (50–300 ms) prior to appearance of the displaced target, then detection of the displacement improves dramatically. These results suggest that the saccade target position is in fact retained across the saccade. Furthermore, these results hold when the stimulus is presented in an otherwise dark room, suggesting that the stored saccade target position can be updated based on an extraretinal signal. Deubel et al. have suggested that relatively precise information is typically carried across a saccade, but that this information is then overwritten when new information is acquired at the beginning of the next fixation. That is, when the availability of the information in the next fixation is delayed by introducing a brief blank period, evidence for the survival of the information acquired in the previous fixation can be obtained. Although provocative, it is not yet clear whether this retained information has any functional significance in transsaccadic scene processing. In typical viewing, the current scene is present immediately at the beginning of each new fixation, and so precise information about target position would be overwritten.

4.3.1.3 Retinal fidelity, cortical magnification, and saccadic spatial compression

In addition to the empirical data just reviewed, which argues against transsaccadic spatiotopic fusion, logical reasons also exist to suspect that fusion would not be implemented by the visual system as a solution to the perceptual stability and transsaccadic integration problems. Many of these issues were summarized by O'Regan (1992). For example, because acuity drops quickly from the fixation point, and because more cortical tissue is devoted to the central part of the retina than to parafoveal and peripheral regions, the mapping of a sensory image acquired outside the fovea to a sensory image acquired at the fovea would not be a trivial problem. Essentially, the system would be faced with fusing a low-resolution, blurry, and spatially distorted image with a highly detailed and more uniform image. Such a mapping would require a difficult transformation of one or the other of the images, a process that would seem to violate the spirit of the fusion hypothesis. Another recent phenomenon that is problematic for the sensory fusion hypothesis is the spatial mislocation and apparent compression of the visual image that occurs prior to and during a saccade (Kaiser & Lappe, 2004; Ross, Morrone, & Burr, 1997; see Ross, Morrone, Goldberg, & Burr, 2001, for review). These results again suggest that a precise representation of the spatial properties of an image is not carried from one fixation to the next.

4.3.1.4 Summary

Overall, empirical and logical considerations strongly suggest that sensory images are not retained and visually integrated or fused across saccades.

4.3.2 Transsaccadic Information Integration

The overall insensitivity of the visual system to pattern changes from one fixation to the next provides strong evidence against a spatiotopic sensory fusion account of transsaccadic perception. Given these findings, and other related results suggesting that the visual system is similarly insensitive to visual changes across brief visual disruptions, some theorists proposed the extreme opposite to sensory fusion. In the "grand illusion" hypothesis (Noë, Pessoa, & Thompson, 2000), no visual information at all is retained from one fixation to the next. For example, O'Regan (1992; O'Regan & Noë, 2001) proposed that, because the world can serve as its own memory, the visual system need not keep track of any visual information from fixation to fixation. Similar ideas were proposed by other theorists from a variety of perspectives (e.g., Ballard, 1996; Bridgeman, Van der Hejiden, & Velichkovsky, 1994; Churchland, Ramachandran, & Sejnowski, 1994; Dennet, 1991). Based on demonstrations that visual search for a given target in a given location does not become more efficient with high levels of experience with that item at that location when it is a nontarget search distractor, Wolfe (1999) argued that there are no perceptual consequences of having attended and perceived specific objects in the environment. On this view, once attention is withdrawn from an object, no lingering perceptual representation remains to be integrated in the next fixation (see also Rensink, 2000a, 200b). Although this view has some merit, in that it is clear that no strictly sensory image is retained from fixation to fixation (as reviewed earlier), it is also clear (as reviewed later; see also Chapter 5) that relatively precise but abstract visual representations can be retained and integrated transsaccadically over both short and longer time scales, including representations of search distractors (e.g., Beck, Peterson, Boot, Vomela, & Kramer, 2006; Castelhano & Henderson,

2005; Kristjansson, 2000; McCarley, Wang, Kramer, Irwin, & Peterson, 2003; Williams, Henderson, & Zacks, 2005).

To begin with, there is good evidence that visual information coded in an abstract format survives from fixation to fixation and is functional in subsequent visual processing. For example, Irwin and colleagues demonstrated in a transsaccadic partial-report task that the perceptual properties of up to four visual patterns can be retained across a saccade (Irwin & Andrews, 1996). Irwin has argued that the properties of this transsaccadic memory are consistent with VSTM. Furthermore, many studies have shown that the information acquired from a visual stimulus (e.g., a word or object) during one fixation can speed or otherwise facilitate subsequent processing of that stimulus during the next fixation. Early clear evidence for this transsaccadic information integration came from studies of word recognition and reading (McConkie & Rayner, 1975; Rayner, 1978; Rayner, McConkie, & Zola, 1980), followed by similar evidence from object recognition (Henderson, 1992b; Henderson, Pollatsek, & Rayner, 1987, 1989; Pollatsek, Rayner, & Collins, 1984; Pollatsek, Rayner, & Henderson, 1990). The retention and integration of nonsensory representations is typically referred to in the literature as transsaccadic *information* integration to distinguish it from transsaccadic *visual* integration.

An early example of transsaccadic information integration involves the study of word reading (Rayner, 1978; see also Rayner et al., 1978; Rayner et al., 1980). Participants began each trial looking at a fixation point. A word "preview" then appeared at varying distances from fixation, and the participant immediately moved his eyes to that preview. Using a saccade-contingent display change technique, the preview changed during the saccade to a target word that the participant named as quickly as possible. The distance of the preview from initial fixation and the similarity of the preview to the target word were manipulated. The important finding was that a preview benefit, or facilitation in naming latency, was observed when the target was shown prior to the saccade compared with when a control string (e.g., a string of x's) was presented. Furthermore, the preview benefit extended to partial previews, including previews that overlapped with the target only in the initial and final letters. Similar effects are observed in natural connected reading rather than word naming. The literature on transsaccadic information integration and preview benefits for words is now extensive, and it continues to be a heavily studied topic in the reading literature. Strong evidence suggests that transsaccadic information integration during reading involves representations at a variety of levels of abstraction, including abstract (nonsensory) letter codes and word-length information, as well as phonological representations (Pollatsek, Lesch, Morris, & Rayner, 1992; Henderson, Dixon, Peterson, Twilley, & Ferreira, 1995). For a comprehensive review of this literature, see Rayner (1998).

The preview paradigm used in reading has also been extended to the study of information integration across saccades during object recognition. In transsaccadic object identification studies, the situation shown in Figure 4–1, in which a saccade takes the eyes from one location in the scene to the faucet, is simplified by presenting just the faucet (or at most one or two other objects) prior to and following the saccade. The main result is that participants are faster to identify an object when a preview of that object is available extrafoveally prior to a saccade (i.e., the faucet is present prior to the saccade to that location) than when no preview is available at that location (i.e., an empty box or a meaningless shape is presented at that location instead) (e.g., Gajewski & Henderson, 2005a; Henderson, 1992b, 1994, 1997; Henderson, Pollatsek, & Rayner, 1987, 1989; Henderson & Siefert, 1999; Pollatsek, Rayner, & Collins, 1984; Pollatsek, Rayner, & Henderson, 1990). Furthermore, preview benefits for objects can be affected by visual changes such as replacement of one visual token with another token of the same conceptual type (such as changing from one coffee cup to another, Henderson & Siefert, 2001) and mirror reflections (Henderson & Siefert, 1999, 2001). These influences of visual change on preview benefit are more pronounced when the spatial location of the target object remains constant compared with when the location changes (Gajewski & Henderson, 2005a; Henderson, 1994; Henderson & Anes, 1994; Henderson & Siefert, 2001).

Together, these results suggest that the visual properties of objects are preserved in the representations retained across saccades, that these representations are at least partially tied to spatial position, and that the preserved representations are functional during the subsequent fixation. Returning to an earlier point, it is important to note that these visual representations are not sensory. That is, representation of detailed visual information does not imply the preservation of a point-by-point iconic image. As discussed earlier, sensory representation implies a complete, precise, precategorical, maskable, and metrically organized image of the visual scene (Irwin 1992b; Neisser, 1967; Sperling, 1960). In contrast, a postsensory visual representation is an imprecise, postcategorical, nonmaskable, and noniconic visual description encoded in the vocabulary of visual computation. This same distinction maps onto the distinction in the iconic memory literature between visual and informational persistence on the one hand, and VSTM on the other (Irwin, 1992b; see also Coltheart, 1980). Importantly, abstract visual representations are still visual in the sense that they represent visual properties such as object shape and viewpoint, albeit in a nonsensory format. An example of a nonsensory representation of shape is a structural description (e.g., Biederman, 1987; Marr, 1982; Palmer, 1977; see Chapter 6). Additional evidence suggests that shape may be encoded and retained across saccades in this representational format (Carlson-Radvansky, 1999; Carlson-Radvansky & Irwin, 1995;). Another example of an abstract visual representation is a hierarchical feature representation (e.g., Riesenhuber & Poggio, 1999). Importantly, abstract visual representations of this sort are neither sensory, nor are they equivalent to conceptual representations (which encode semantic properties) or linguistic descriptions.

In summary, empirical evidence strongly suggests that nonsensory information, including visual description, is retained and integrated across saccades.

4.3.3 Active Memory and Online Scene Representations

In this section, I consider scene representations that are kept active in memory over the course of the current perceptual episode lasting several seconds and multiple fixation–saccade cycles.

4.3.3.1 Change detection and "change blindness"

In general, when the local transient motion signals that usually accompany a visual change are unavailable because the change takes place during a saccade, sensitivity to what would otherwise be a highly visible change is reduced and, in the extreme case, eliminated. This fact has already been discussed here in the section on transsaccadic memory. In the early 1990s, this basic result was extended to picture viewing and, in a striking initial demonstration of the effect in photographs of scenes, George McConkie presented data at two workshops demonstrating that change detection can be remarkably poor for what otherwise would seem to be obvious changes such as additions and deletions of central objects in scenes (McConkie, 1990, 1991; see Grimes, 1996; McConkie & Currie, 1996). Subsequent experiments showed that the effect could also be observed when the change took place during a simulated saccade (i.e., when a blank field was inserted between two scene images, Rensink, O'Regan, & Clark, 1997), a phenomenon that came to be known as "change blindness" (Simons, 2000). These results led some to call into question the idea that a detailed visual representation is constructed online in memory during scene viewing (e.g., O'Regan, 1992; Rensink, 2000a, 2000b; Wolfe, 1999).

During the past several years, it has become clear that the original interpretation of poor change detection during scene viewing was incorrect and that relatively detailed online visual memory representations can be observed in change-detection experiments (for more extensive review, see Henderson and Hollingworth, 2003b, Chapter 5). Several key findings emerged from these studies. First, change detection can be very good when steps are taken to ensure that a changing item (e.g., an object in a scene) is fixated before and after the change, suggesting that memory encoding and retrieval play a central role in change detection (Henderson & Hollingworth, 1999b, 2003c; Hollingworth, 2003; Hollingworth & Henderson, 2002; Hollingworth, Williams, & Henderson, 2001). Second, viewers can fixate many intervening scene regions and objects between an initial fixation on a prechange object and the first refixation of the (now changed) object and still detect the change (Hollingworth & Henderson, 2002). These delayed change detections establish that online visual scene representations survive potential decay over time and potential interference from other fixated objects. Third, other factors known to affect memory, such as semantic consistency (Friedman, 1979), also influence change detection across fixations (Hollingworth, Williams, & Henderson, 2001), as predicted by the view that change detection is supported by memory. Fourth, explicit change detection often significantly underestimates the degree to which online visual representations are retained in memory, and the time a viewer spends looking at an object (gaze duration) is often elevated on a changed object even when the change is not reported (Hayhoe, Bensinger, & Ballard, 1998; Henderson & Hollingworth, 2003c; Hollingworth & Henderson, 2002; Hollingworth, Williams, & Henderson, 2001). Therefore, participants' failure to report a change cannot be taken as evidence that the information needed to detect that change was unavailable (see also Fernandez-Duque & Thornton, 2000; Williams & Simons, 2000).

Given the potential difficulty of interpreting change-detection failure, Hollingworth and Henderson (2002) developed a forced-choice memory test to directly investigate viewers' online memory for objects in scenes. Participants studied photographs of real-world scenes while their eye movements were monitored. Following the start of each trial, the computer waited until the target object had been fixated at least once, assuring that the object had been attended prior to the memory test. Then, during a saccade to a different object on the other side of the scene, the target object was obscured by a pattern mask. The onset of the mask coincided with the saccade, so the target object was not attended at the time the mask appeared. Following the appearance of the mask, a forced-choice memory test was given in which two object alternatives were displayed sequentially in random order within the scene: the original target and a distractor object. The distractor was either a different token from the same basic-level category (token discrimination) or a version of the target object rotated 90 degrees in depth around the vertical axis (orientation discrimination). Performance in this memory test was very good for both token discrimination and orientation discrimination. Again, on many trials, viewers fixated multiple objects between the last fixation on the target object and the onset of the mask (and consequent initiation of the forced-choice test), but performance did not differ statistically as a function of the number of intervening fixations. As in the change detection experiments, these results suggest that online representations are relatively stable in memory.

In summary, contrary to proposals based on change blindness, visual object representations are not lost upon the withdrawal of attention. At the same time, change detection is clearly mediated by attention, presumably because attention is needed to (a) encode prechange and postchange representations, (b) retrieve from memory the prechange representation following the change, and (c) enable comparison of the two. In the transsaccadic change-detection paradigm, the same change is much more easily detected when it occurs during a saccade toward the changing object (Currie et al., 2000; Hayhoe et al., 1998; Henderson & Hollingworth, 1999b, 2003c) than during a saccade away from that object (Henderson & Hollingworth, 1999b, 2003c; Hollingworth et al., 2001). Similarly, transsaccadic information integration is heavily weighted toward the saccade target (Gajewski & Henderson, 2005a; Henderson, 1994; Henderson & Anes, 1994; Irwin & Andrews, 1996), at least partly due to the fact that attention is allocated to the saccade target prior to a saccade (Deubel & Schneider, 1996; Henderson, 1993; Henderson, Pollatsek, & Rayner, 1989; Hoffman & Subramanian, 1995; Irwin & Gordon, 1998; Irwin & Zelinsky, 2002; Kowler et al., 1995; Rayner, McConkie, & Ehrlich, 1978; Shepherd et al., 1986). In the change-blindness literature, detection of change is better in the flicker paradigm for scene regions rated to be of higher interest (Rensink et al., 1997), for semantically unexpected objects (Hollingworth & Henderson, 2000), at locations to which attention has been explicitly directed (Scholl, 2000), and at locations near fixation (Hollingworth, Schrock, & Henderson, 2001). All of these results are consistent with the need for attention in change detection.

4.3.3.2 Eye movements and short-term memory

Although it is clear that online memory is able to store a large amount of information about the current scene, evidence also suggests that this memory system is susceptible to the same sorts of memory constraints typically associated with STM. For example, Irwin and Zelinsky (2002) showed that a recency effect is obtained for objects viewed in simplified scenes. In this experiment, each image contained seven toys in a baby's crib. Participants' eye movements were recorded during display viewing, and the display was terminated after a set number of fixations ranging from one to 15. After the display terminated, a location was cued and the participant reported the object that had appeared there. Two critical results were observed. First, capacity for position-identity pairs was relatively low at about five, even following 15 fixations on the image, consistent with estimates of the capacity of STM. Second, performance for the object about to be fixated was best, followed by the last two fixated objects, followed by objects fixated three or more fixations earlier. This pattern demonstrates a recency effect in memory performance tied to fixation behavior, with an advantage for recently fixated objects (see also Tatler, Gilchrist, & Land, 2005).

In a related experiment, Zelinsky & Loschky (2005) investigated in more detail the nature of the recency effect related to eye fixations. Participants again viewed nine objects in three simplified scenes (crib, workbench, and table), and memory for one of the objects was probed following display offset. This time, though, the cue was shown only after a predetermined target and a predetermined number of subsequent objects had been fixated. Following display offset and the location cue, four objects were displayed, and the participant had to indicate which one of them had appeared at the cued location. Memory was examined as a function of the number of intervening objects fixated and the number of intervening fixations between target fixation and display offset. Consistent with Irwin and Zelinsky (2002), memory dropped steeply as the number of intervening objects increased from one to three. Following three intervening objects, memory performance reached an asymptote, with memory performance still well above chance following four or more intervening objects (65% versus chance rate of 25%). This latter result is consistent with the good longer-duration memory results observed for objects in full real-world scenes later discussed in the section on long-term scene memory.

The Zelinsky and Loschky results seem to be at odds with the report in the scene literature discussed earlier, suggesting little evidence for a serial position effect for objects viewed in real-world scenes (Hollingworth & Henderson, 2002). To explain the difference, Zelinsky and Loschky (2005) noted that it may be important to examine memory performance as a function of intervening objects rather than as a function of intervening fixations. Another potentially important difference between the Zelinsky and Loschky (2005) and Hollingworth and Henderson (2002) studies, though, is the nature of the memory task itself. Zelinsky and Loschky probed memory for specific object-location pairings for a small repeated set of objects distinguished only by their locations from trial to trial, whereas Hollingworth and Henderson probed memory for the visual details of a unique object within a unique scene on each trial.

In an experiment designed to further investigate the characteristics of VSTM and the role of serial position in memory for objects in real-world scenes, Hollingworth (2004) used a "follow-the-dot" task to direct participants' attention through scenes. In each trial, a dot moved sequentially through the scene, and participants were told to follow the dot. As in Zelinsky and Loschky (2005), one object in each scene was predefined as the target. After the dot had landed on the target, it continued to move to another one to nine additional objects. Following the sequence of dots, the target object was visually masked and participants were asked to report which of two displayed versions of the target object, differing only in visual detail, had appeared in the scene. A recency effect was observed, with better memory for the visual details of the target when only one or two additional objects intervened between attention to (dot on) the target and the memory test. Memory performance for target objects followed by three to nine intervening objects was very good and remained stable over those serial positions. In a subsequent study, Hollingworth (2005) showed that there was additional loss of visual information about objects from 200 ms after a scene's appearance (presumably equivalent to the three to nine intervening object condition in Hollingworth, 2004) and 24 h following scene viewing, although performance remained well above chance even in the 24-hour condition. Together, these results suggest that a VSTM component to online scene memory results in a recency effect, but that scene memory for visual detail also remains relatively robust over extended time.

In another type of paradigm designed to investigate the functional use of STM in scene perception, Gajewski and Henderson (2005b) presented participants with a scene comparison task. This task is similar to the "spot the differences" children's game in which similar scenes are shown side-by-side. In our case, the images were computer-rendered real-world scenes, and each scene pair contained only one difference. Previous research suggested that in a visuo-motor task involving copying a pattern of blocks, participants used a "just-in-time" strategy of encoding only the information that was directly and immediately relevant for the next move in the copying task (Ballard, Hayhoe, & Pelz, 1995). In the spot-the-differences task, we asked whether participants would buffer three to four items in one scene before checking the corresponding objects in the other scene, as might be expected based on the capacity of STM, or whether instead they would use a one-by-one encode-and-compare strategy, as would be expected in a "just-in-time" strategy in which participants encode the minimal amount of information at each step (Ballard et al., 1995).

In the first two experiments, participants made same–different judgments in response to simultaneously presented pairs of scenes that were identical or differed by one object. In Experiment 1, the objects were either the same or different in type (e.g., coffee cup versus apple) or token (e.g., two different coffee cups), or an object was deleted. The nature of the difference was randomly ordered. In Experiment 2, only the type and token differences were used, and they were blocked, so that participants always knew the nature of the difference they were searching for. In both experiments, the number of fixations per scene glance and the number of fixations intervening between glances to corresponding objects across the two scenes suggested that the primary strategy adopted by participants was to encode and maintain one object at a time in STM. The same pattern of results was observed in a third experiment using word and object arrays rather than scenes. Overall, the results suggested a strong general "just-in-time" bias to use minimal memory capacity when critical task-relevant information could be sampled directly with eye movements.

4.3.3.3 An online memory inconsistency?

It may appear that we have something of an inconsistency in the conclusions we have reached for online scene memory. On the one hand, online scene memory has a large capacity for visual detail. On the other hand, in the scene comparison task, participants used the absolute minimum of available STM capacity to conduct the task (Gajewski & Henderson, 2005; see also Ballard et al., 1995). How can the apparent large capacity of online scene memory and the apparent limited functional capacity of STM during scene viewing be reconciled? I suggest that, although online memory capacity is large, viewers prefer to use external rather than internal memory whenever possible. Two factors lead to this preference. First, it is likely that directing the eyes to the external world is less capacity-demanding than memory search. Second, using the world as an external memory is also less error-prone than internal memory, even when internal memory is very good. That is, unless memory is 100% accurate, it is always going to provide less information than the world itself. Both of these points are similar to those that have been made by proponents of no-memory search and perception, but these proponents have taken the point to the extreme conclusion that no internal memory/representation exists at all. As argued earlier, this is simply not a tenable theoretical stance given the existing empirical evidence. The position taken here is that a visuo-cognitive system can have very good memory and still be biased to resample the world when that option is available, because eye movements are often computationally cheaper than memory search and are the only way to ensure error-free (within the bounds of perceptual capacity) information (see also Oliva, Wolfe, & Arsenio, 2004). This view accommodates both a strategy of sampling (and resampling) the world when it is available (Ballard et al., 1995; Gajewski & Henderson, 2005a; Gilchrist & Harvey, 2000; Horowitz & Wolfe, 1998; Oliva et al., 2004) and the existence of relatively robust, detailed, and long-lasting scene memory.

4.3.3.4 Memory effects on eye movements

Another method that can be used to study the presence and functional significance of scene memory is to examine its influence on eye movements themselves. The majority of the research reviewed earlier has focused on the online object representations that are retained in active memory. Castelhano and Henderson (2007) set out to determine whether the global scene representations generated in an initial scene glimpse can affect subsequent eye movements during search after a delay and, if so, whether the memory representations that support such an effect encode visual information.

It is well known that an initial scene glimpse is sufficient to provide information about general scene category and gist (Potter, 1976), spatial layout (Sanocki & Epstein, 1997), and central object identities (Thorpe, Fize, & Marlot., 1996). Furthermore, there is good evidence that eye movements during visual search through arrays of simple stimuli can draw on memory acquired from similar displays during previous search (Gibson, Li, Skow, Brown, & Cooke, 2000; Kristjánsson, 2000; Peterson, Kramer, Wang, Irwin, & McCarley, 2001; Shore & Klein, 2000). Testing whether the initial scene glimpse affects eye movements raises a difficulty, however, because if the complete scene remains visible during subsequent fixations, then it is not possible to determine whether eye movement control decisions are based on information acquired during the initial glimpse or based on information acquired in those subsequent fixations.

To allow for both manipulation of the first scene glimpse and extended scene viewing involving saccadic eye movements, while at the same time restricting scene information available following the initial glimpse, we developed a "Flash-Preview Moving-Window" paradigm (Castelhano and Henderson, 2007). This new paradigm combined the brief tachistoscopic viewing method typically used in scene gist experiments with the moving window technique typically used to investigate eye movements under restricted viewing conditions. Participants were asked to search for target objects in scenes while their eye movements were recorded. Prior to presentation of the search scene, a scene preview was presented for 250 ms, and the nature of that preview was manipulated. A mask was then shown for 50 ms, followed by the name of the search target for 2 s. The total delay between offset of the preview and onset of the limited-view search scene was therefore 2050 ms and included visual masking and cognitive work (reading the target word and committing it to STM). The search then took place with the search scene visible only through an eye-contingent moving window with a 2-degree diameter centered at fixation.

In this paradigm, evidence for scene memory would be revealed by increased search efficiency (as measured by eye movement behavior) following the brief preview of the search scene compared with a control preview. We called this increased efficiency *scene-preview benefit*. We found clear scene-preview benefit in four experiments, with shorter search times, fewer eye fixations, and a shorter overall saccade path to the search target following the search scene preview compared to the control preview. This benefit held up whether or not the search target was actually present in the preview, suggesting that the benefit was not simply due to locating the target from the preview. Instead, general scene information useful for finding the target during the subsequent search was acquired and retained from the initial preview. Interestingly, no scene-preview benefit was observed when the preview was a different exemplar of the search scene category (e.g., if the search scene was a kitchen, a different kitchen), suggesting that the benefit was due to visual information more specific than generic scene identity or gist. Finally, we found that the benefit was not related to precise metrical information. Equivalent scene-preview benefit was observed from a search scene preview that was 25% the size of the search scene itself. These results suggest that a nonmetrical scene representation that preserves visual detail is generated during an initial scene glimpse, that this representation lingers in a relatively stable form in memory over the current perceptual episode, and that such memory representations can be functional in guiding behavior.

4.3.4 Eye Movements and Long-term Scene Memory

In this section, I consider the relationship between eye movements, scene representations, and long-term scene memory. I take long-term scene memory to involve the representations that linger once the current perceptual episode is over. For example, if the current perceptual episode involves turning on the faucet in the kitchen depicted in Figure 4–1, what continues to reside in memory about the faucet, and more generally about the other objects on the countertop and in the room once you have left it? There is little controversy that LTM retains general schematic and semantic information about viewed scenes (e.g., I was in a dining room, and it contained a dining room table). A more controversial question, though, has been the extent to which long-term scene memory also retains representations of visual detail.

Classic scene memory research demonstrated surprisingly good LTM for scene detail (Nickerson, 1965; Shepard, 1967; Standing, Conezio, & Haber, 1970). In an early study of eye movements and long-term memory, Nelson and Loftus (1980) showed that memory for object detail was highly related to fixation position. Participants studied line drawings of scenes while their eye movements were recorded. A later memory test was given in which participants were required to discriminate objects that had originally appeared in the scenes from visually similar foil objects. Memory performance was highly related to the proximity of the closest fixation during initial viewing to the critical object, with very good visual memory performance when the nearest fixation fell on the critical object but near-chance performance when the closest fixation was 1.8 degrees or more away.

In the study described earlier in this chapter related to online memory, Hollingworth and Henderson (2002) also tested LTM for individual objects after those objects had been fixated during initial scene viewing. A difficult forced-choice discrimination memory test was given for specific target objects between 5 and 30 min after the scenes were removed from view. Similar to the online memory test described in the online scene memory section, for each studied scene, participants viewed two versions in the test session: one that was identical to the studied scene and a distractor scene that differed only in the target object. The distractor object was a different conceptual type, a different token of the same conceptual type, or the same object rotated in depth. This longer retention interval did not cause much of a decrement in discrimination performance compared to online discrimination, both of which were very good. The similarity between discrimination performance in the online and

LTM tests suggests that visual object representations are stable after fixation and attention are removed from an object, at least over the retention intervals we tested. In Hollingworth's (2004) "follow-the-dot" study, after all the scenes had been viewed, a test was given requiring participants to detect token differences in particular objects that had appeared in the scenes. Participants were able to perform well above chance. In a subsequent study, Hollingworth (2005) showed that these results held up over 24 h for both token changes and orientation changes, suggesting that visual long-term scene memory is relatively stable over time.

4.3.4.1 Eye movements and incidental visual learning

A lingering concern with the studies described earlier is the possibility that the observed results arise from the use of viewing instructions that stress scene memorization. That is, it is possible that detailed visual scene representations can be generated and retained in memory when viewers engage in intentional memory encoding (either to prepare for a later memory test or to prepare for change detection), but that these representations are not typically generated incidentally during natural scene perception. If this hypothesis were correct, then the evidence for good visual memory performance obtained in prior studies might be dismissed as irrelevant to normal scene viewing.

If detailed visual memory is only generated under intentional memorization instructions, then evidence for the preservation of the visual details of previously viewed objects should only be observed in intentional memorization tasks. Conversely, viewing tasks for which intentional memory encoding is unnecessary should produce no visual representation in memory. On the other hand, if detailed visual representations are typically generated and stored in memory as a natural consequence of scene perception, then evidence for the long-term preservation of visual detail should be found in both intentional and incidental memorization conditions. To test these two hypotheses, we have conducted two sets of experiments to examine the nature of the visual representations of objects generated incidentally over the course of viewing (Castelhano & Henderson, 2005; Williams, Henderson, & Zacks, 2005).

In Williams et al. (2005), participants searched through arrays of real-world objects while their eye movements were recorded. Each array contained 12 unique full-color photographs of objects from a wide variety of conceptual categories. In each trial, participants were asked to count the exemplars of a specific category, such as yellow birds. Arrays contained three types of distractors: category distractors (birds that were not yellow), color distractors (yellow objects that were not birds), and unrelated distractors (objects that were neither yellow nor birds). After all of the arrays had been searched, participants were given a surprise forced-choice visual memory test in which they had to discriminate objects that had appeared in the arrays from memory foils that were different tokens of the same object class. For example, if the test object from an array were a yellow bird, the foil would be a different yellow bird. This test therefore required that relatively detailed visual information be preserved in memory. The memory task was designed to eliminate the contribution of context and semantic information to performance by presenting targets and foils that fit the same semantic description. Because of the surprise nature of the visual memory test, any learning that occurred during the search portion of the experiment was incidental.

Three critical findings resulted. First, preserved visual memory was observed for all three types of objects (search targets, color distractors, and unrelated distractors). This finding is remarkable because participants did not anticipate a memory test during the search task (so learning was completely incidental) and because the memory test was very stringent: test objects were presented without the context within which they were initially viewed—in the center of the display rather than where they originally appeared—and the foils were very similar to the targets. All of these factors would serve to depress memory performance (Chapter 5). Second, memory was graded, with best visual memory for the search targets, intermediate memory for the related distractors, and poorest memory for the unrelated distractors. Third, this pattern was mirrored in the eye movement data; search targets received the greatest number of fixations and the most fixation time, followed by related (color or category) distractors, followed by unrelated distractors. These latter results suggest that fixation during encoding is related to the strength of the resulting memory representation. This finding is reminiscent of Friedman's (1979) observation that expected objects in scenes receive less fixation time than unexpected objects (see also De Graef et al., 1990; Henderson, Weeks, & Hollingworth, 1999; Hollingworth, Williams, & Henderson, 2001) and show poorer memory when tested later. However, the results in our study were a bit more interesting: When eye movement behavior was directly compared to memory performance via linear regression, it became clear that search targets were remembered better than would be expected from the number of looks or total fixation time they received. Specifically, although a relationship existed between fixation time and memory performance for all types of objects, memory for search targets was better than memory for distractors when fixation behavior was statistically controlled. Thus, although eye fixations and the consequent opportunity for memory encoding was highly related to later memory performance, it was not the only factor at work. In short, this study clearly demonstrated that representations of the visual details of objects are generated and retained incidentally over the long term during visual search.

In a related study, we also examined memory performance for visual information obtained either intentionally or incidentally from objects in real-world scenes (Castelhano & Henderson, 2005). In three experiments, participants viewed scenes while engaged in an incidental-learning visual search task or an intentional-learning memorization task. After both viewing tasks had been completed, a memory test for a critical object in each scene was administered, although no memory test was anticipated by the participants during the visual search task. In the memorization task, participants were instructed to view the scenes in preparation for a difficult memory test that would require knowledge of the details of specific objects. In the visual search task, participants were instructed to find a specific target object in each scene, and they were not told that they would receive a memory test.

The memory test always focused on the visual properties of a critical object drawn from each scene. Unlike the Williams et al. (2005) study, the critical test objects for the search scenes were never the search targets. In the first experiment, the memory test involved discriminating between a previously seen critical object and a matched foil object of the same basic-level category type. In the second experiment, participants had to discriminate between the previously viewed orientation of the critical object and a mirror-reversed distractor version of that same object. In both of these experiments, all participants took part in both the memorization and visual search conditions. In a third experiment, the first experiment was replicated but each participant was given only one of the two initial viewing tasks (memorization or search) to ensure that there was no contamination from the memorization condition to the visual search condition. The main question in the three experiments was whether LTM for visual information would be observed for objects that were incidentally encoded during scene search.

In all three experiments, memory performance was above chance. Furthermore, no evidence suggested that memory was better in the intentional than in the incidental learning condition. Again, as in Williams et al. (2005), the study involved a relatively stringent test of visual memory. Memory performance was based on a total of only 10 s of viewing time per scene and an average of less than 1 s of total fixation time on each critical object. During the memory test, the tested objects (and their matched foils) were presented alone on a blank screen without any indication of which scene they had come from or where in each scene they had appeared. The retention interval varied between approximately 4 and 20 min between initial scene viewing and object test, depending on where in the randomized sequence each scene and memory test appeared. Furthermore, the total number of objects likely to have been encoded across all of the scenes was large. Using conservative estimates of object encoding, Castelhano and Henderson (2005) estimated that between 373 and 440 objects were fixated and processed on average by each participant in each of the three experiments. All of these factors would work against finding evidence for memory of visual detail (Chapter 5), yet such evidence was clearly obtained. Again, these results strongly suggest that visual representations are generated and stored in LTM as a natural consequence of scene viewing.

4.3.4.2 Eye movements and savings effects in scene viewing

Another way to assess the nature of scene memory is to study savings in scene learning as a consequence of prior views. For example, in studies of contextual cueing (Chun & Jiang, 1998; see Chapter 7), participants search for a target (e.g., backward L) within arrays of similar items (e.g., forward Ls). Repeated exposure to a consistent arrangement of target and distractors leads to progressively faster search for the target. Strikingly, these learning effects occur despite observers' inability to explicitly discriminate between repeated and novel displays at the conclusion of the experiment.

In a recent series of experiments, we have investigated the nature of contextual cueing when the context comprises a real-world scene. In an initial set of experiments, we demonstrated that the basic contextual cueing effect can be observed with real-world scenes, although unlike classic contextual cueing, the repetition of scenes tends to be noticed by the participant (Brockmole & Henderson, 2006a). In these experiments, participants searched for and identified a target letter embedded in scene photographs. Search time within novel scenes remained relatively consistent across trials, whereas search time within repeated scenes decreased across repetitions. We also found that repetition of inverted scenes, which made the scene more difficult to identify, greatly reduced the rate of learning, suggesting that semantic information concerning object and scene identity was learned and then used to guide attention.

In a second set of experiments, we investigated the role of global and local contexts for contextual cueing in naturalistic scenes (Brockmole, Castelhano, & Henderson, 2006). Participants were presented with a sequence of trials in which they searched for and identified an arbitrarily located target letter within computer-rendered illustrations of realistic scenes. Rendered scenes were used instead of photographs because they enabled us to independently manipulate local and global contexts. Local context was defined as a group of objects in close spatial proximity to the target (e.g., a coffee table containing a few objects), and the remainder of the scene constituted the global context. In a first experiment, we found that the learned locations of letters embedded within scenes transferred when local information was altered, but not when global information was changed. In a second experiment, we showed that the target locations were learned more slowly when local but not global information was repeated across trials than when global but not local information was repeated. Thus, with real-world scenes, participants are biased to associate target locations with global contexts, contrary to the local precedence typically observed in classic contextual cueing (Jiang & Wanger, 2004; Olson & Chun, 2002).

Finally, in a third set of experiments, we used eye movements to assess the degree to which scene-level contextual cueing was based on general schematic knowledge versus more precise knowledge of spatial layout (Brockmole & Henderson, 2006b). Participants were again shown photographs of scenes that contained consistently but arbitrarily located letter targets, allowing target positions to be associated with scene content. Learned scenes were then unexpectedly mirror-reversed, spatially translating visual features as well as the target across the display while preserving the scene's identity and gist. Mirror-reversals produced a cost in search as the eyes initially moved toward the position in the display in which the target had previously appeared. The cost was not complete, however; when initial search failed, the eyes were quickly directed to the target's new position. These results suggest that, in real-world scenes, shifts of attention are initially based on learned associations with scene identity and subsequent attention shifts are guided by more detailed information regarding scene and object layout, supporting the conclusion that these latter types of information accumulate and are retained in memory.

Melcher (2001; Melcher & Kowler, 2001) used a different type of paradigm to investigate long-term scene memory via savings over scene repetitions. In these experiments, participants were presented with minimal scenes made up of computer-rendered rooms with furniture, each of which supported 12 critical objects. These displays were presented for brief durations (1, 2, or 4 s) and immediately tested for object content. Some displays were repeated on a later trial, and savings in learning was measured by subsequent memory performance. Memory performance improved with display repetition, suggesting a LTM system that survived across time and interference from intervening items. Unfortunately, however, memory was assessed with free recall verbal report, leaving open the possibility that performance was based on verbal coding of visual properties (Hollingworth, 2003). Continual testing after each item may have further encouraged such a strategy. An additional difficulty with interpreting these studies is that the same items were tested across display repetitions, raising the possibility that repetition savings were due to the test repetition itself, for example, because of differential attentional focus during scene viewing based on prior test.

More recently Melcher (2006) modified the procedure to overcome the issue of test repetition. Again, the study investigated longer-term memory for visual details (object color, object location, background) of pictures of scenes. In the first experiment, participants viewed a scene photograph, and the accumulation of visual information in memory was tested. Following initial presentation of each scene, participants were either given an immediate memory test or continued to the next trial. Accumulation of scene information across viewings was then investigated following the second scene presentation for those scenes that were not initially tested. As in the earlier studies, repetition followed several intervening trials and so was unlikely to be supported by online memory. Memory for probed information was found to increase with total scene viewing time whether that time was continuous or was due to scene repetition. This method took care of the problem of testing each scene more than once. Again, however, memory probes were in the form of verbal questions and multiple-choice answers, leaving the verbal recoding problem. In Experiment 2, scenes were initially shown for either 1 or 10 s. In the repetition condition, a 10- to 60-second delay (filled by a reading task or a VSTM task) was followed by a 1-second repetition of the scene. Again, memory was tested by the three questions used in the first experiment, but an additional forced-choice object discrimination task was added in which participants had to distinguish which of three conceptually identical objects had been shown. The main result was again that memory was facilitated by repetition. This effect held across delay duration and fill task, and for the visual discrimination test. These results provide converging evidence with contextual cueing that visual information from a scene is retained in LTM and is available to provide savings during later views.

4.4 SCENE REPRESENTATION, VISUAL MEMORY, AND PERCEPTUAL EXPERIENCE

Given the clear evidence, both historically and recently, for the creation and storage of visual object and scene representations, we might ask what leads theorists to posit the lack of such representations (e.g., O'Regan & Nöe, 2001). I believe this difference of perspective on scene representation has its roots in two traditions in the study of visual perception. The first tradition is concerned to a large extent with trying to explain perceptual phenomenology. Why do we experience red in the way we do? How is it that we experience a stable visual world despite the presence of saccadic eye movements? And, most relevantly here, why and how do we experience a complete, detailed, full-color visual world despite the fact that (a) the retinas cannot deliver this high-fidelity input within a given fixation, and (b) the visual system cannot fuse together discrete retinotopic images to generate a composite internal picture?

The second tradition, which is reflected most strongly in cognitive psychology as well as in much of computer vision, is concerned with the nature of the representations that are available for visual and cognitive computations (and implemented in the brain in the case of human cognition), without concern for whether they give rise to perceptual experience or are open to awareness. Rather than asking what gives rise to the experience of stability across saccades (for example), those studying vision within this tradition instead tend to ask about the nature of the internal representations generated across saccades regardless of whether those representations are directly experienced or play a causal role in generating experience. In the case of scene memory and representation, the issue from a cognitive perspective concerns the nature of the scene representations (if any) that are generated over the course of multiple fixations and stored in memory, again without regard for which of, or even whether, these representations give rise to perceptual experience.

The problem arises when data bearing on issues in the first tradition (visual experience) are used as evidence bearing on issues in the second tradition (internal representation and computation). In the case of scene perception, the specific problem concerns claims about the nature of visual representation that are made purely on the basis of reported experience. As stated most recently and forcefully by O'Regan and Noë (2001) based on change blindness (it is not difficult to find similar strong statements from other investigators in this field), "Indeed there is no "*re*"-presentation of the world inside the brain ... " (O'Regan & Nöe, 2001). But we know, and have known for a very long time in cognitive psychology, that what people experience (or can report) is not necessarily a very good indication of what the brain represents. A good example of this has already been discussed in this chapter: Participants are typically unaware that patterns are repeated or that they are learning regularities during contextual cueing experiments, but the behavioral data demonstrate unambiguously that they are. Cognitive science is rife with similar examples across a range of areas. In fact, it is commonplace that people do not experience, are not aware of, and cannot report the nature of their cognitive processes. (If they could, cognitive psychologists would be out of a job.) Those of us who study the processes and consequences of eye movements know that participants are very often completely shocked to find out that they are moving their eyes in fast hops rather than smoothly across a page of text or over a picture. In the memory literature, the dissociation between report and representation is sometimes captured by the theoretical distinction between explicit and implicit memory.

More directly relevant to the issue of eye movements and scene representation and memory, change blindness demonstrates that viewers can be unaware of (or unable to report) what would otherwise appear to be salient changes to a viewed scene. At the same time, as demonstrated in our research and summarized in this chapter, behavioral consequences of such changes can be observed even when they are not reported. The clearest example of this is increased fixation time on a changed object in the absence of explicit report (e.g., Hayhoe et al., 1998; Henderson & Hollingworth, 2003b; Hollingworth & Henderson, 2002; Hollingworth, Williams, & Henderson, 2001). The increased fixation times, which can be on the order of several hundred milliseconds, are themselves neither under conscious control nor consciously experienced (again, most participants in eyetracking experiments are unaware of the nature of their eye movements). These fixation time differences unambiguously demonstrate that there is more to internal representation than conscious experience would lead one to believe. It is therefore dangerous to draw any strong conclusions about internal visual representation or computation based solely on perceptual phenomenology.

4.5 CONCLUSION

In this chapter, I reviewed the literature concerned with the types of memory systems that are relevant for understanding the object and scene representations generated during scene viewing. I focused on three memory epochs important for understanding how scene representations are generated dynamically across multiple eye movements: transsaccadic memory, active online memory, and LTM. I argued that the evidence supports the conclusion that relatively detailed visual representations are retained over the short and long term. Furthermore, I presented evidence strongly suggesting that these representations are generated incidentally as a natural consequence of scene viewing. Taken as a whole, the evidence strongly supports the view that relatively detailed visual representations are generated and stored in memory during active real-world scene perception.

ACKNOWLEDGMENT

Preparation of this chapter was supported by funding from the Army Research Office (W911NF-04-1-0078; the opinions expressed in this article are those of the authors and do not necessarily represent the views of the Department of the Army or any other governmental organization). Thanks to Fernanda Ferreira and to past members of the Visual Cognition Lab (especially James Brockmole, Monica Castelhano, Daniel Gajewski, Andrew Hollingworth, Michael Mack, Aaron Pearson, and Carrick Williams) for their contributions to the experiments and ideas summarized here.

REFERENCES

Ballard, D. (1996). On the function of visual representation. In *Vancouver Studies in Cognitive Science 5: Perception*, ed. K. Akins, 111–131. New York: Oxford University Press.

Ballard, D. H., Hayhoe, M. M., and Pelz J. (1995). Memory representations in natural tasks. *Journal of Cognitive Neuroscience* 7:66–80.

Beck, M. R., Peterson, M. S., Boot, W. R., Vomela, M., and Kramer, A. F. (2006). Explicit memory for rejected distractors during visual search. *Visual Cognition* 14:150–174.

Biederman, I. (1987). Recognition-by-components: A theory of human image understanding. *Psychological Review* 94:115–147.

Biederman, I., Mezzanotte, R. J., and Rabinowitz, J. C. (1982). Scene Perception: detecting and judging objects undergoing relational violations. *Cognitive Psychology* 14:143–177.

Breitmeyer, B. G., Kropfl, W., and Julesz, B. (1982). The existence and role of retinotopic and spatiotopic forms of visual persistence. *Acta Psychologia* 52:175–196.

Bridgeman, B., Hendry, D., and Stark, L. (1975). Failure to detect displacements of the visual world during saccadic eye movements. *Vision Research* 15:719–722.

Bridgeman, B., and Mayer, M. (1983). Failure to integrate visual information from successive fixations. *Bulletin of the Psychonomic Society* 21:285–286.

Bridgeman, B., and Stark, L. (1979). Omnidirectional increase in threshold for image shifts during saccadic eye movements. *Perception and Psychophysics* 25:241–243.

Bridgeman, B., Van der Hejiden, and Velichkovsky (1994). A theory of visual stability across saccadic eye movements. *Behavioral and Brain Science* 17:247–292.

Brockmole, J. R., Castelhano, M. S., and Henderson, J. M. (2006). Contextual cueing in naturalistic scenes: Global and local contexts. *Journal of Experimental Psychology: Learning, Memory, and Cognition* 32:699–706.

Brockmole, J. R., and Henderson, J. M. (2005a). Prioritization of new objects in real-world scenes: Evidence from eye movements. *Journal of Experimental Psychology: Human Perception and Performance* 31:857–868.

Brockmole, J. R., and Henderson, J. M. (2005b). Object appearance, disappearance, and attention prioritization in real-world scenes. *Psychonomic Bulletin and Review* 12:1061–1067.

Brockmole, J. R., and Henderson, J. M. (2006a). Using real-world scenes as contextual cues for search. *Visual Cognition* 13:99–108.

Brockmole, J. R., and Henderson, J. M. (2006b). Recognition and attention guidance during contextual cueing in real-world scenes: Evidence from eye movements. *Quarterly Journal of Experimental Psychology* 59:1177–1187.

Carlson-Radvansky, L. A. (1999). Memory for relational information across eye movements. *Perception and Psychophysics* 61:919–934.

Carlson-Radvansky, L. A., and Irwin, D. E. (1995). Memory for structural information across eye movements. *Journal of Experimental Psychology: learning, memory, and Cognition* 6:1441–1458.

Carpenter, R. H. S. (1988). *Movements of the Eyes*. London: Pion.

Castelhano, M. S., and Henderson, J. M. (2005). Incidental visual memory for objects in scenes. *Visual Cognition: Special Issue on Scene Perception* 12:1017–1040.

Castelhano, M. S., and Henderson, J. M. (in press a). Stable individual differences across images in human saccadic eye movements. *Canadian Journal of Experimental Psychology*.

Castelhano, M. S., and Henderson, J. M. (2007). Initial scene representations facilitate eye movement guidance in search. *Journal of Experimental Psychology: Human Perception and Performance, 33*, 753-763.

Chun, M. M., and Jiang, Y. (1998). Contextual cueing: Implicit learning and memory of visual context guides spatial attention. *Cognitive Psychology* 36:28–71.

Churchland, P. S., Ramachandran, V. S., and Sejnowski, T. J. (1994). A critique of pure vision. In *Large-scale Neuronal Theories of the Brain*, eds. C. Koch and J L. David, 23–60. Cambridge, MA: MIT Press.

Coltheart, M. (1980). Iconic memory and visible persistence. *Perception and Psychophysics* 27:183–228.

Currie, C., McConkie, G., Carlson-Radvansky, L. A., and Irwin, D. E. (2000). The role of the saccade target object in the perception of a visually stable world. *Perception and Psychophysics* 62:673–683.

Davidson, M. L., Fox, M. J., and Dick, A. O. (1973). Effect of eye movements on backward masking and perceived location. *Perception and Psychophysics* 14:110–116.

De Graef P, Christiaens D, d'Ydewalle G. 1990. Perceptual effects of scene context on object identification. *Psychological Research* 52:317–329.

Dennett, D. C. (1991). *Consciousness Explained*. Boston: Little, Brown.

Deubel, H., and Schneider, W. X. (1996). Saccade target selection and object recognition: Evidence for a common attentional mechanism. *Vision Research* 36:1827–1837.

Deubel, H., Schneider, W. X., and Bridgeman, B. (1996). Postsaccadic target blanking prevents saccadic suppression of image displacement. *Vision Research* 36:985–996.

Deubel, H., Schneider, W. X., and Bridgeman, B. (2002). Transsaccadic memory of position and form. *Progress in Brain Research* 140:165–180.

Di Lollo, V. (1977). Temporal characteristics of iconic memory. *Nature* 267:241–243.

Di Lollo, V. (1980). Temporal integration in visual memory. *Journal of Experimental Psychology: General* 109:75–97.

Duhamel, J. R., Colby, C. L., and Goldberg, M. E. (1992). The updating of the representation of visual space in parietal cortex by intended eye movements. *Science* 255:90–92.

Eriksen, C. W., and Collins, J. F. (1967). Some temporal characteristics of visual pattern recognition. *Journal of Experimental Psychology* 74:476–484.

Feldman, J. A. (1985). Four frames suffice: a provisional model of vision and space. *Behavioral and Brain Sciences* 8:265–289.

Fernandez-Duque, D., and Thornton, I. M. (2000). Change detection without awareness: Do explicit reports underestimate the representation of change in the visual system? *Visual Cognition* 7:323–344.

Friedman, A. (1979). Framing pictures: The role of knowledge in automatized encoding and memory for gist. *Journal of Experimental Psychology: General* 108:316–355.

Gajewski, D. A., and Henderson, J. M. (2005a). The role of saccade targeting in the transsaccadic integration of object types and tokens. *Journal of Experimental Psychology: Human Perception and Performance* 31:820–830.

Gajewski, D. A., and Henderson, J. M. (2005b). Minimal use of working memory in a scene comparison task. *Visual Cognition* 12:979–1002.

Gibson, B. S., Li, L., Skow, E., Brown, K., and Cooke, L. (2000). Searching for one versus two identical targets: When visual search has a memory. *Psychological Science* 11:324–327.

Gilchrist, I. D., and Harvey, M. (2000). Refixation frequency and memory mechanisms in visual search. *Current Biology* 10:1209–1212.

Grimes, J. (1996). On the failure to detect changes in scenes across saccades. In *Perception: Vancouver Studies in Cognitive Science*, ed. K. Akins, 89–110). Oxford: Oxford University Press.

Gysen, V., Verfaillie, K., and De Graef, P. (2002). The effect of stimulus blanking on the detection of intrasaccadic displacements of translating objects. *Vision Research* 42:2021–2030.

Hayhoe, M. M., Bensinger, D. G., and Ballard, D. H. (1998). Task constraints in visual working memory. *Vision Research* 38:125–137.

Henderson, J. M. (1992a). Object identification in context: The visual processing of natural scenes. *Canadian Journal of Psychology: Special Issue on Object and Scene Processing* 46:319–342.

Henderson, J. M. (1992b). Identifying objects across eye fixations: Effects of extrafoveal preview and flanker object context. *Journal of Experimental Psychology: Learning, Memory, and Cognition* 18:521–530.

Henderson, J. M. (1992c). Visual attention and eye movement control during reading and picture viewing. In *Eye Movements and Visual Cognition: Scene Perception and Reading*, ed. K. Rayner, 260–283. New York: Springer-Verlag.

Henderson, J. M. (1993). Visual attention and saccadic eye movements. In *Perception and Cognition: Advances in Eye Movement Research*, eds. G. d'Ydewalle and J. Rensbergen, 37–50). Amsterdam: Netherlands Science Publishers.

Henderson, J. M. (1994). Two representational systems in dynamic visual identification. *Journal of Experimental Psychology: General* 123:410–426.

Henderson, J. M. (1996). Visual attention and the attention-action interface. In *Perception: Vancouver Studies in Cognitive Science*, ed. K. Aikens 290–316. Oxford: Oxford University Press.

Henderson, J. M. (1997). Transsaccadic memory and integration during real-world object perception. *Psychological Science* 8:51–55.

Henderson, J. M. (2003). Human gaze control in real-world scene perception. *Trends in Cognitive Sciences* 7:498–504.

Henderson, J. M. (2007). Regarding scenes. *Current Directions in Psychological Science* 16:219–222.

Henderson, J. M., and Anes, M. D. (1994). Effects of object-file review and type priming on visual identification within and across eye fixations. *Journal of Experimental Psychology: Human Perception and Performance* 20:826–839.

Henderson, J. M., Brockmole, J. R., Castelhano, M. S., and Mack, M. (2007). Visual saliency does not account for eye movements during visual search in real-world scenes. In *Eye Movements: A Window on Mind and Brain*, eds. R. van Gompel, M. Fischer, W. Murray, and R. Hill. Oxford: Elsevier.

Henderson, J. M., Brockmole, J. R., and Gajewski, D. A. (2008). Differential detection of global luminance and contrast changes across saccades and flickers during active scene perception. *Vision Research, 48*, 16–29.

Henderson, J. M., Dixon, P., Petersen, A., Twilley, L. C., and Ferreira, F. (1995). Evidence for the use of phonological representations during transsaccadic word recognition. *Journal of Experimental Psychology: Human Perception and Performance* 21:82–97.

Henderson, J. M., and Ferreira, F. (2004a) (eds.). *The Interface of Language, Vision, and Action: Eye Movements and the Visual World*. New York: Psychology Press.

Henderson, J. M., and Ferreira, F. (2004b). Scene perception for psycholinguists. In *The Interface of Language, Vision, and Action: Eye Movements and the Visual World*, eds. J. M. Henderson and F. Ferreira. New York: Psychology Press.

Henderson, J. M., and Hollingworth, A. (1998). Eye movements during scene viewing: An overview. In *Eye Guidance in Reading and Scene Perception*, ed. G. Underwood, 269–283). Oxford: Elsevier.

Henderson, J. M., and Hollingworth, A. (1999a). High-level scene perception. *Annual Review of Psychology* 50:243–271.

Henderson, J. M., and Hollingworth, A. (1999b). The role of fixation position in detecting scene changes across saccades. *Psychological Science* 10:438–443.

Henderson, J. M., and Hollingworth, A. (2003a). Global transsaccadic change blindness during scene perception. *Psychological Science* 14:493–497.

Henderson, J. M., and Hollingworth, A. (2003b). Eye movements, visual memory, and scene representation. In *Analytic and Holistic Processes in the Perception of Faces, Objects, and Scenes*, eds. M. A. Peterson and G. Rhodes, 356–383. New York: Oxford University Press.

Henderson, J. M., and Hollingworth, A. (2003c). Eye movements and visual memory: Detecting changes to saccade targets in scenes. *Perception and Psychophysics* 65:58–71.

Henderson, J. M., and Pierce, G. L. (in press). Eye movements during scene viewing: Evidence for mixed control of fixation durations. *Psychonomic Bulletin & Review*.

Henderson, J. M., Pollatsek, A., and Rayner, K. (1987). The effects of foveal priming and extrafoveal preview on object identification. *Journal of Experimental Psychology: Human Perception and Performance* 13:449–463.

Henderson, J. M., Pollatsek, A., and Rayner, K. (1989). Covert visual attention and extrafoveal information use during object identification. *Perception and Psychophysics* 45:196–208.

Henderson, J. M., and Siefert, A. B. (1999). The influence of enantiomorphic transformation on transsaccadic object integration. *Journal of Experimental Psychology: Human Perception and Performance* 25:243–255.

Henderson, J. M., and Siefert, A. B. C. (2001). Types and tokens in transsaccadic object identification: Effects of spatial position and left-right orientation. *Psychonomic Bulletin and Review* 8:753–760.

Henderson, J. M., Weeks, P. A. Jr., and Hollingworth, A. (1999). Effects of semantic consistency on eye movements during scene viewing. *Journal of Experimental Psychology: Human Perception and Performance* 25:210–228.

Hoffman, J. R., and Subramanian, B. (1995). The role of visual attention in saccadic eye movements. *Perception and Psychophysics* 57:787–795.

Hollingworth, A. (2003). Failures of retrieval and comparison constrain change detection in natural scenes. *Journal of Experimental Psychology: Human Perception and Performance* 29:388–403.

Hollingworth, A. (2004). Constructing visual representations of natural scenes: The roles of short- and long-term visual memory. *Journal of Experimental Psychology: Human Perception and Performance* 30:519–537.

Hollingworth, A. (2005). The relationship between online visual representation of a scene and long-term scene memory. *Journal of Experimental Psychology: learning, Memory, and Cognition* 3:396–411.

Hollingworth, A., and Henderson, J. M. (2000). Semantic informativeness mediates the detection of changes in natural scenes. *Visual Cognition (Special Issue on Change Blindness and Visual Memory)* 7:213–235.

Hollingworth, A., and Henderson, J. M. (2002). Accurate visual memory for previously attended objects in natural scenes. *Journal of Experimental Psychology: Human Perception and Performance* 28:113–136.

Hollingworth, A., Schrock, G., and Henderson, J. M. (2001). Change detection in the flicker paradigm: The role of fixation position within the scene. *Memory and Cognition* 29:296–304.

Hollingworth, A., Williams, C. C., and Henderson, J. M. (2001). To see and remember: Visually specific information is retained in memory from previously attended objects in natural scenes. *Psychonomic Bulletin and Review* 8:761–768.

Horowitz, T. S., and Wolfe, J. M. (1998). Visual search has no memory. *Nature* 357:575–577.

Irwin, D. E. (1991). Information integration across saccadic eye movements. *Cognitive Psychology* 23:420–456.

Irwin, D. E. (1992a). Memory for position and identity across eye movements. *Journal of Experimental Psychology: Learning, Memory, and Cognition* 18:307–317.

Irwin, D. E. (1992b). Visual memory within and across fixations. In *Eye Movements and Visual Cognition: Scene Perception and Reading*, ed. K. Rayner, 146–165. New York: Springer-Verlag.

Irwin, D. E. (2004). Fixation location and fixation duration as indices of cognitive processing. In *The Interface of Language, Vision, and Action: Eye Movements and the Visual World*, eds. J. M. Henderson and F. Ferreira. New York: Psychology Press.

Irwin, D. E., and Andrews, R. (1996). Integration and accumulation of information across saccadic eye movements. In *Attention and Performance XVI: Information Integration in Perception and Communication*, eds. T. Inui and J. L. McClelland, 125–155. Cambridge, MA: MIT Press.

Irwin, D. E., and Brown, J. S. (1987). Tests of a model of informational persistence. *Canadian journal of Psychology* 41:317–338.

Irwin, D. E., Brown, J. S., and Sun, J. (1988). Visual masking and visual integration across saccadic eye movements. *Journal of Experimental Psychology: General* 117:276–287.

Irwin, D. E., and Gordon, R. (1998). Eye movements, attention and trans-saccadic memory. *Visual Cognition* 5:127–155.

Irwin, D. E., and Yeomans, J. M. (1986). Sensory registration and informational persistence. *Journal of Experimental Psychology: Human Perception and Performance* 12:343–360.

Irwin, D. E., Yantis, S., and Jonides, J. (1983). Evidence against visual integration across saccadic eye movements. *Perception and Psychophysics* 34:49–57.

Irwin, D. E., Zacks, J. L., and Brown, J. S. (1990). Visual memory and the perception of a stable visual environment. *Perception and Psychophysics* 47:35–46.

Irwin, D. E., and Zelinsky, G. J. (2002). Eye movements and scene perception: Memory for things observed. *Perception and Psychophysics* 64:882–895.

Itti, L., and Koch, C. (2001). Computational modeling of visual attention. *Nature Reviews Neuroscience* 2:194–203.

Jiang, Y., and Wagner, L. C. (2004). What is learned in spatial contextual cueing: Configuration or individual locations? *Perception and Psychophysics* 66:454–463.

Jonides, J., Irwin, D. E., and Yantis, S. (1982). Integrating visual information from successive fixations. *Science* 215:192–194.

Jonides, J., Irwin, D. E., and Yantis, S. (1983). Failure to integrate information from successive fixations. *Science* 222:188.

Kaiser, M., and Lappe, M. (2004). Perisaccadic mislocalization orthogonal to saccade direction. *Neuron* 41:293–300.

Kowler, E., Anderson, E., Dosher, B., and Blaser, E. (1995). The role of attention in the programming of saccades. *Vision Research* 35:1897–1916.

Kristjánsson, A. (2000). In search of remembrance: Evidence for memory in visual search. *Psychological Science* 11:328–332.

Land, M. F., and Hayhoe, M. (2001). In what ways do eye movements contribute to everyday activities? *Vision Research* 41:3559–3565.

Mack, A. (1970). An investigation of the relationship between eye and retinal image movements in the perception of movement. *Perception and Psychophysics* 8:291–298.

Mandler, J. M., and Johnson, N. S. (1977). Some of the thousand words a picture is worth. *Journal of Experimental Psychology: Human Learning and Memory* 2:529–540.

Marr, D. (1982). *Vision*. San Francisco: Freeman.

Matin, E. (1974). Saccadic suppression: A review and an analysis. *Psychological Bulletin* 81:899–917.

McCarley, J. S., Wang, R. F., Kramer, A. F., Irwin, D. E., and Peterson, M. S. (2003). How much memory does oculomotor search have? *Psychological Science* 14:422–426.

McConkie, G. W. (1990). *Where vision and cognition meet*. Paper presented at the Human Frontier Science Program Workshop on Object and Scene Perception, Leuven, Belgium.

McConkie, G. W. (1991). Perceiving a stable visual world. In *Proceedings of the Sixth European Conference on Eye Movements*, eds. J. Van Resnbergen, M. Devijver, and G. d'Ydewalle, 5–7. Leuven, Belgium: Laboratory of Experimental Psychology.

McConkie, G. W., and Currie, C. B. (1996). Visual stability while viewing complex pictures. *Journal of Experimental Psychology: Human Perception and Performance* 22:563–581.

McConkie, G. W., and Rayner, K. (1975). The span of the effective stimulus during a fixation in reading. *Perception and Psychophysics* 17:578–586.

McConkie, G. W., and Rayner, K. (1976). Identifying the span of the effective stimulus in reading: Literature review and theories of reading. In *Theoretical Models and Processes in Reading*, eds. H. Singer and R. B. Ruddell, 137–162. Newark, DE: International Reading Institute.

McConkie, G. W., and Zola, D. (1979). Is visual information integrated across successive fixations in reading? *Perception and Psychophysics* 25:221–224.

Melcher, D. (2001). The persistence of memory for scenes. *Nature* 412:401.

Melcher, D. (2006). Accumulation and persistence of memory for natural scenes. *Journal of Vision* 6:8–17.

Melcher, D., and Kowler, E. (2001). Visual scene memory and the guidance of saccadic eye movements. *Vision Research* 41:3597–3611.

Neisser, U. (1967). *Cognitive Psychology*. East Norwalk, CT: Appleton-Century-Crofts.

Nelson, W. W., and Loftus, G. R. (1980). The functional visual field during picture viewing. *Journal of Experimental Psychology: Human Learning and Memory* 6:391–399.

Nickerson, R. S. (1965). Short-term memory for complex visual configurations: A demonstration of capacity. *Canadian Journal of Psychology, 19*, 155-160.

Noë, A., Pessoa, L., and Thompson, E. (2000). Beyond the grand illusion: What change blindness really teaches us about vision. *Visual Cognition* 7:93–106.

Oliva, A., Wolfe, J. M., Arsenio, H. C. (2004). Panoramic search: The interaction of memory and vision in search through a familiar scene. *Journal of Experimental Psychology: Human Perception and Performance* 30:1132–1146.

Olson, I. R., and Chun, M. M. (2002). Perceptual constraints on implicit learning of spatial context. *Visual Cognition* 9:273–302.

O'Regan, J. K. (1992). Solving the "real" mysteries of visual perception: The world as an outside memory. *Canadian Journal of Psychology Special Issue: Object perception and scene analysis* 46:461–488.

O'Regan, J. K., and Lévy-Schoen, A. (1983). Integrating visual information from successive fixations: Does trans-saccadic fusion exist? *Vision Research* 23:765–768.

O'Regan, J. K., and Noë, A. (2001). A sensorimotor account of vision and visual consciousness. *Behavioral and Brain Sciences* 24:939–1031.

Palmer, S. E. (1977). Hierarchical structure in perceptual representation. *Cognitive Psychology* 9:441–474.

Parkhurst, D. J., and Niebur, E. (2003). Scene content selected by active vision. *Spatial Vision* 16:125–154.

Peterson, M. S., Kramer, A. F., Wang, R. F., Irwin, D. E., and McCarley, J. S. (2001). Visual search has memory. *Psychological Science* 12:287–292.

Phillips, W. A. (1974). On the distinction between sensory storage and short-term visual memory. *Perception and Psychophysics* 16:283–290.

Pollatsek, A., Lesch, M., Morris, R. K., and Rayner, K. (1992). Phonological codes are used in integrating information across saccades in word identification and reading. *Journal of Experimental Psychology: Human Perception and Performance* 18:148–162.

Pollatsek, A., and Rayner, K. (1992). What is integrated across fixations? In *Eye Movements and Visual Cognition: Scene Perception and Reading*, ed. K. Rayner, 166–191. New York: Springer-Verlag.

Pollatsek, A., Rayner, K., and Collins, W. E. (1984). Integrating pictorial information across eye movements. *Journal of Experimental Psychology: General* 113:426–442.

Pollatsek, A., Rayner, K., and Henderson, J. M. (1990). Role of spatial location in integration of pictorial information across saccades. *Journal of Experimental Psychology: Human Perception and Performance* 16:199–210.

Potter, M. C. (1976). Short-term conceptual memory for pictures. *Journal of Experimental Psychology: Human Learning and Memory* 2:509–522.

Pouget, A., Fisher, S. A., and Sejnowski, T. J. (1993). Egocentric spatial representation in early vision. *Journal of Cognitive Neuroscience* 5:150–161.

Rayner, K. (1978). Eye movement latencies for parafoveally presented word. *Bulletin of the Psychonomic Society* 11:13–16.

Rayner, K. (1998). Eye movements in reading and information processing: 20 years of research. *Psychological Bulletin* 124:372–422.

Rayner, K., McConkie, G. W., and Ehrlich, S. (1978). Eye movements and integrating information across fixations. *Journal of Experimental Psychology: Human Perception and Performance* 4:529–544.

Rayner, K., McConkie, G. W., and Zola, D. (1980). Integrating information across eye movements. *Cognitive Psychology* 12:206–226.

Rayner, K., and Pollatsek, A. (1983). Is visual information integrated across saccades? *Perception and Psychophysics* 34:39–48.

Rensink, R. A. (2000a). Seeing, sensing, and scrutinizing. *Vision Research* 40:1469–1487.

Rensink, R. A. (2000b). The dynamic representation of scenes. *Visual Cognition Special Issue: Change blindness and visual memory* 7:17–42.

Rensink, R. A., O'Regan, J. K., and Clark, J. J. (1997). To see or not to see: The need for attention to perceive changes in scenes. *Psychological Science* 8:368–373.

Riesenhuber, M., and Poggio, T. (1999). Hierarchical models of object recognition in cortex. *Nature Neuroscience* 2:1019–1025.

Ross, J., Morrone, M. C., and Burr, D. C. (1997). Compression of visual space before saccades. *Nature* 386:598–601.

Ross, J., Morrone, M. C., Goldberg, M. E., and Burr, D. C. (2001). Changes in visual perception at the time of saccades. *Trends in Neuroscience* 24:131–121.

Sanocki, T., and Epstein, W. (1997). Priming spatial layout of scenes. *Psychological Science* 8:374–378.

Scholl, B. J. (2000). Attenuated change blindness for exogenously attended items in a flicker paradigm. *Visual Cognition Special Issue: Change blindness and visual memory* 7:377–396.

Shepard, R. N. (1967). Recognition memory for words, sentences, and pictures. *Journal of Verbal Learning and Verbal Behavior* 6:156–163.

Shepherd, M., Findlay, J. M., and Hockey, R. J. (1986). The relationship between eye movements and spatial attention. *Quarterly Journal of Experimental Psychology* 38A:475–491.

Shore, D. I., and Klein, R. M. (2000). On the manifestation of memory in visual search. *Spatial Vision* 14:59–76.

Simons, D. J. (2000) (ed.). *Change Blindness and Visual Memory, A Special Issue of Visual Cognition.* Hove: Psychology Press.

Sperling, G. (1960). The information available in brief visual presentation. *Psychological Monographs* 74:29.

Standing, L., Conezio, J., and Haber, R. N. (1970). Perception and memory for pictures: Single-trial learning of 2500 visual stimuli. *Psychonomic Science* 19:73–74.

Tatler, B. W., Gilchrist, I. D., and Land, M. F. (2005). Visual memory for objects in natural scenes: From fixations to object files. *The Quarterly Journal of Experimental Psychology* 58A:931–960.

Thiele, A., Henning, M., Buischik, K., Hoffman, P. (2002). Neural mechanisms of saccadic suppression. *Science* 295:2460–2462.

Thorpe, S. J, Fize, D., and Marlot, C. (1996). Speed of processing in the human visual system. *Nature* 381:520–522.

Torralba, A., Oliva, A., Castelhano, M. S., and Henderson, J. M. (2006). Contextual guidance of eye movements and attention in real-world scenes: The role of global features in object search. *Psychological Review* 113:766–786.

Trehub, A. (1977). Neuronal models for cognitive processes: Networks for learning, perception and imagination. *Journal of Theoretical Biology* 65:141–169.

Van der Heijden, A. H. C., Bridgeman, B., Mewhort, D. J. K. (1986). Is stimulus persistence affected by eye movements? A critique of Davidson, Fox, and Dick (1973). *Psychological Research* 40:179–181.

Verfaillie, K., De Troy, A., and Van Rensbergen, J. (1994). Transsaccadic integration of biological motion. *Journal of Experimental Psychology: Learning, Memory, and Cognition* 20:649–670.

Volkmann, F. C. (1986). Human visual suppression. *Vision Research* 26:1401–1416.

Volkman, F., Schick, A., and Riggs, L. (1968). Time course of visual inhibition during voluntary saccades. *Journal of the Optical Society of America* 58:1310–1414.

Whipple, W. R., and Wallach, H. (1978). Direction-specific motion thresholds for abnormal image shifts during saccadic eye movement. *Perception and Psychophysics* 24:349–355.

Williams, P., and Simons, D. J. (2000). Detecting changes in novel, complex three-dimensional objects. *Visual Cognition Special Issue: Change blindness and visual memory* 7:297–322.

Williams, C. C., Henderson, J. M., and Zacks, R. T. (2005). Incidental visual memory for targets and distractors in visual search. *Perception and Psychophysics.*

Wolfe, J. M. (1999). Inattentional amnesia. In *Fleeting Memories*, ed. V. Coltheart, 71–94. Cambridge, MA: MIT Press.

Zelinsky, G. J., and Loschky, L. C. (2005). Eye movements serialize memory for objects in scenes. *Perception and Psychophysics* 67:676–690.

Chapter 5

Visual Memory for Natural Scenes

Andrew Hollingworth
The University of Iowa

5.1 INTRODUCTION

How do people perceive and remember the complex environments they typically inhabit? In this chapter, I review research examining visual memory for complex, natural environments. Given that we spend most of our waking lives perceiving and behaving within complex scenes, our memory for visual scenes is certainly one of the core issues that a science of human cognition must address. Yet, scene memory is a relatively young field, with much of the research conducted over the last 10-15 years. Current research questions are broad and fundamental: Do we have a memory for the visual properties of scenes? If so, how precise is that memory, and what is its capacity? How is memory for scenes structured? How does the visual system detect changes to the environment? How does scene memory support real-world behaviors? What is the relationship between visual memory and conscious perception? Although these questions are by no means answered in full, it is now possible to provide a broad account of how visual information is acquired from a scene and stored in memory. The chapter is divided into two main sections. The first concerns the use of visual memory to construct online representations of natural scenes (i.e., the representation produced as one is actively viewing a scene). The second concerns longer-term scene memory stored after a scene is no longer in view.

The representation of natural scenes requires visual memory. Scene perception is spatially dynamic and temporally extended. There is far too much information in a complex scene to be perceived in a single glance, and thus our attention is sequentially directed to subregions of a scene as viewing unfolds. Under natural conditions, shifts of attention are typically accomplished by movements of the eyes (and head and body) so as to direct the high-resolution region of the retina—the fovea—to individual objects of interest. Eye movements allows us to obtain high-resolution visual information from objects (e.g., enabling us to read the label on a soup can) but also serve to specify objects in the world as the targets of actions such as grasping (Hayhoe, 2000; Land, Mennie,

& Rusted, 1999). During brief eye movements, vision is suppressed (Matin, 1974), and perceptual input is further disrupted by frequent blinks. Memory is required to span these disruptions, and memory is required to accumulate (and perhaps integrate) information acquired sequentially from local scene regions. Further, if our previous experience within scenes is to influence our subsequent behavior (e.g., remembering where the phone is located within one's office so as to reach for it without searching), information about the structure and content of a scene must be stored robustly across the sometimes extended delays between encounters with a particular scene. Thus, memory plays an important role not only within our moment-to-moment perceptual interactions with a scene but also over much longer time scales that allow perceptual learning to guide behavior.

Before discussing the role of visual memory in the representation of natural scenes, it is necessary to briefly review current knowledge regarding the basic properties of visual memory systems (much of which is reviewed in detail elsewhere within this volume). Visual memory appears to be composed of four different memory stores: visible persistence, informational persistence, visual short-term memory (VSTM), and visual long-term memory (VLTM). Visible and informational persistence are often grouped together as *iconic memory* or *sensory persistence* (Coltheart, 1980). Visible persistence and informational persistence preserve a precise, high-capacity, sensory trace that is generated across the visual field but is highly volatile (Chapter 2). Visible persistence is phenomenologically visible (one sees a stimulus as visibly present after it has been removed), but its duration is extraordinarily brief. Visible persistence decays within approximately 80–100 ms after the onset of a stimulus (Di Lollo, 1980). Informational persistence is a nonvisible sensory trace that is maintained for approximately 150–300 ms after stimulus offset (Irwin & Yeomans, 1986). Both visible persistence and informational persistence are highly susceptible to interference from new sensory processing (i.e., they are susceptible to backward masking). Visual short-term memory maintains a small number of higher-level visual representations that are abstracted away from precise sensory information. It has a limited capacity of three to four objects (Irwin, 1992; Luck & Vogel, 1997; Chapter 3) and lacks the metric precision of sensory persistence (Irwin, 1991; Phillips, 1974). However, VSTM is not subject to significant backward masking (Pashler, 1988; Phillips, 1974) and can be maintained over durations on the order of seconds (Phillips, 1974) and across saccades (Hollingworth, Richard, & Luck, 2008; Irwin & Andrews, 1996). Visual long-term memory maintains visual representations similar to those maintained in VSTM but is capable of accumulating visual information from scores of individual objects (Hollingworth, 2004, 2005c). Of the four visual memory stores, only visible persistence directly supports visual phenomenology. Other forms of visual memory maintain visual information, but they do not directly generate visual experience. With the exception of brief visible persistence, visual memory is not visible.

5.2 THE ONLINE REPRESENTATION OF NATURAL SCENES

Recent research on the online perceptual representation of scenes has focused on four main issues: the amount of detail stored in a scene representation, the role of attention in the encoding of scene information into memory and its maintenance in memory, the memory systems used to construct scene representations, and the relationship between scene representation and conscious experience. These issues have come to the fore in the literature surrounding the phenomenon of change blindness. Before discussing that literature and its implications for understanding the online representation of natural scenes, it is necessary to discuss the visual memory systems that could potentially contribute to online scene representation.

5.2.1 Visual Memory Systems Contributing to Online Scene Representation

Much of the work in the area of online scene perception has sought explain why we see the world as complete, detailed, and seamlessly present when the input to vision is incomplete, lacking in precision (except at the fovea), constantly shifting on the retina, and frequently disrupted by saccades and blinks (for a review, see O'Regan, 1992). Early theories sought to explain the perception of a complete and detailed visual world by positing that a representational analog of that experience must exist: an internal visual representation containing detailed visual sensory information across the visual field. In this view, visible, high-resolution sensory representations (visible persistence) are retained and integrated across eye movements (Davidson, Fox, & Dick, 1973; Jonides, Irwin, & Yantis, 1982; McConkie & Rayner, 1975) (see Chapters 2 and 4). Over the course of viewing, high-resolution sensory representations from multiple fixated regions could be integrated to form a precise, sensory image of the external world, which would then serve as the substrate for our experience of seeing a complete and detailed visual world.

This sensory-image hypothesis—and more generally the idea that conscious visual experience is based on the construction of complete sensory models (Palmer, 1999)—has been highly influential, but it has foundered both on theoretical and empirical grounds. The basic assumption that we see a complete and detailed visual world across the visual field is actually false, and therefore does not require an explanation. When we look at the world, we see detail at the center of gaze, but our experience of peripheral visual stimuli is fuzzy and indistinct. We see a complete and detailed visual world only in the very loose sense that we are typically unaware that peripheral vision is poor (Dennett, 1991). But, it only takes a slight effort (keeping one's eyes still and attending to the quality of peripheral vision) to realize that, at any given moment, peripheral objects are poorly resolved. This is true even for peripheral objects that were fixated earlier (from which high-resolution information could have been acquired and retained under a sensory-image hypothesis). Despite being fixated earlier, these peripheral objects appear just as fuzzy and indistinct as objects that have never been fixated. No visible, high-resolution sensory information was retained from the earlier fixation on the object, and no global sensory image was formed. At best, we can say that we see the world *as being* detailed and complete, which is true (Cohen, 2002); the world itself is indeed detailed and complete. But humans never see all of that detail at once, and therefore there is no need to posit a representational substrate for the perception of a complete and detailed visual world.

Empirical evidence has also failed to support sensory-image hypotheses. First, visible sensory representations persist for such a short period of time that they could not possibly survive long enough to support sensory integration over the course of scene viewing (Averbach & Coriell, 1961; Coltheart, 1980; Di Lollo, 1980; Sperling, 1960; Chapter 2 of this volume). Second, direct tests of sensory integration across eye movements have failed to find any capability for such integration (Henderson & Hollingworth, 2003b; Irwin, 1991; Irwin, Yantis, & Jonides, 1983; O'Regan & Lévy-Schoen, 1983; Rayner & Pollatsek, 1983; Chapter 4 of this volume), and tests of integration within a fixation have found no evidence of integration over the time scales necessary to construct a global sensory image of a scene (Di Lollo, 1980; Hollingworth, Hyun, & Zhang, 2005; Jiang, 2004).

Thus, if scene representations are constructed at all from the incomplete, shifting, and frequently disrupted input that characterizes natural vision, that construction must depend on robust, higher-level visual memory systems of VSTM and VLTM. Note that neither VSTM nor VLTM maintains visual representations that are directly visible, and thus the study of scene representation is necessarily removed to some extent from the study of conscious visual perception.

5.2.2 Change Blindness Effects and Theories of Online Scene Representation

The phenomenon of change blindness has shaped recent thinking on the role of visual memory in scene perception. The change blindness literature has provided converging evidence that scene representations are not precise, sensory images. And, given the absence of sensory-specific scene representation, change blindness has spurred investigation of what precisely *is* represented during the visual perception of complex environments.

In change blindness studies, participants often fail to detect otherwise salient changes when detection requires visual memory. This has been achieved either by introducing an interstimulus interval (ISI) between differing images (Rensink, O'Regan, & Clark, 1997), by introducing a change to an image during an eye movement (Grimes, 1996; Henderson & Hollingworth, 1999, 2003b), or by occluding a change with a physical object (Simons & Levin, 1998). In one of the best-known change blindness papers, Rensink et al. presented photographs of real-world scenes and introduced a change to a portion of the image on each trial, such as the deletion of the chimney on a building, illustrated in Figure 5–1. The original and changed images were separated by a brief ISI. The change was repeated by alternating the two images until the participant detected the change (i.e., the chimney would disappear, then reappear, then disappear, and so on). Rensink et al. found that, for many changes, participants required extended viewing (often more than 30 s) before they detected the change. In a real-world change paradigm, Simons and Levin (1998) found that many participants did not report noticing the replacement of one person for another when the

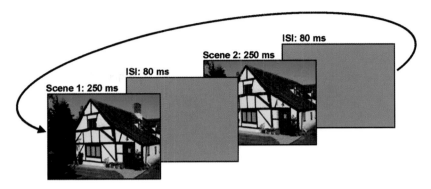

Figure 5–1. Illustration of the "flicker task" introduced by Rensink et al. (1997) and used extensively to study change blindness. The Scene 1 and 2 differ in the presence of the chimney. The change sequence was repeated until the participant detected the change.

replacement was introduced during a period of disruption. An experimenter asked an unwitting participant for directions on campus. During the conversation, confederates briefly occluded the view of the participant, and the experimenter was replaced by a different experimenter. Approximately 50% of participants failed to detect the change. In a transsaccadic change detection paradigm by Henderson and Hollingworth (2003b), participants were almost entirely insensitive to changes that altered the entire pictorial content of a scene image when the change was introduced during a saccade. A scene was partially occluded by a set of vertical bars (as if viewing the scene from behind a picket fence). The bars shifted during saccades, so that all visible portions of the scene became occluded and all occluded portions visible. Despite these global image changes, which were highly salient to observers when not synchronized with saccades, participants saw a perfectly stable and unchanging scene.

Clearly, such insensitivity to changes across perceptual disruptions provides further evidence that the visual system does not construct a complete, low-level sensory representation of a scene. But what is represented during visual scene perception? Proposals have spanned a wide range of theoretical possibilities.

5.2.2.1 The non-representationalist account

O'Regan (1992; O'Regan & Noë, 2001) has argued that essentially no role exists for visual memory in scene representation, because the world itself acts as an "outside memory." The basic idea is that, because the outside world is generally stable, the information it contains can be reliably and efficiently acquired whenever it is needed by simply shifting attention and the eyes to the appropriate location in the world. Given that the information resides in the world, the storage of that information in the brain would be redundant, and thus the use of memory is minimal, explaining why participants have such difficulty detecting changes in change blindness studies when detection requires memory.

Further, our experience of seeing a stable visual world across disruptions such as saccades is not generated by the integration of visual representations across saccades but rather by anticipating the perceptual consequences of a motor action (the saccade).[1] This view draws heavily from ecological approaches to vision (Gibson, 1979), particularly with respect to the claims of minimal perceptual representation and the importance of motor processes in perception.

It is certainly true that the world contains much more detail than could ever be remembered, and it is also certainly true that eye movements are used to acquire that information when it is needed (Hayhoe, 2000; Land et al., 1999). However, the claim that scene representation depends entirely on an outside memory fails to account for the clear benefits of having an internal memory. An outside memory is of limited use if one cannot remember where the relevant information is located. If I wish to acquire information about the current time of day, that acquisition is made much more efficient if I remember where the clock is located, so that I can direct gaze to the appropriate location rather than search for the clock. In addition, memory for the perceptual properties of objects allows us to compare perceptual information over time (that dog was sitting earlier but is now standing), allows us to classify objects and scenes into meaningful categories (Chapter 6), allows us recognize individual objects based on their perceptual features (my notebook is the one with the blue cover, not the one with the red cover), and so on. Moreover, empirical evidence, reviewed later, demonstrates that humans have a quite astonishing ability to remember visual properties of scenes. Thus, the rather extreme position taken by O'Regan finds little support.

5.2.2.2 The functionalist account

Ballard, Hayhoe, and colleagues (Ballard, Hayhoe, & Pelz, 1995; Ballard, Hayhoe, Pook, & Rao, 1997; Hayhoe, 2000) have argued that visual scene memory during common, real-world tasks is typically limited to the attended information necessary to support moment-to-moment actions. That is, the visual system minimizes memory demands by representing only the immediately task-relevant information, with eye movements used to acquire this information when it is needed. This approach depends on some of the same assumptions held by O'Regan (that the world serves as an outside memory that is probed when needed) and is consistent with theories claiming a central role for attention in scene representation (Rensink, 2000). This view is primarily supported by evidence that fixation position is tied closely to the immediate task at hand. For example, in a task requiring participants to copy a block pattern (Ballard et al., 1995), instead of memorizing the entire pattern to be copied, participants adopted a local strategy, whereby each individual block was fixated prior to copying, consistent with proposal that the internal representation of the block pattern was acquired locally and in sequence, so as to minimize memory demands.

---

1   There has yet to be a clear account of how anticipating the perceptual consequences of motor actions would lead to a seamless experience of the visual world.

5.2.2.3 Attention-based accounts: Coherence theory

Rensink (Rensink, 2000, 2002; Rensink et al., 1997) and others (Becker & Pashler, 2002; Wheeler & Treisman, 2002) have also argued that the visual representation of scenes is minimal, with visual representation limited to the currently attended object. This view, which is best exemplified by Rensink's *coherence theory* (Rensink, 2000), can be distilled into the following set of claims. First, low-level vision produces a description of the visual field in terms of *proto-objects*: volatile, transient collections of low-level sensory features. Proto-objects are proposed to decay very quickly after visual stimulation is removed and are highly susceptible to backward masking. In the context of change detection, proto-objects are not by themselves sufficient to detect a change, because they will typically have decayed prior to the appearance of the changed image, or, if they have not yet decayed, sensory processing of the new image will mask them. Given the sensory properties attributed to proto-objects, the concept appears equivalent to visible persistence (i.e., high-capacity, visible, fleeting, and susceptible to masking). Second, coherence theory holds that visual attention enables the consolidation of proto-objects into a coherent, robust representation that does not immediately decay and is not susceptible to backward masking (i.e., VSTM). Finally, coherence theory holds that attention is necessary to maintain coherent object representations in VSTM. Once attention is removed from an object, the coherent object representation comes unbound, and the object dissolves back into its constituent proto-object features. Although Rensink claims that coherent visual representation is limited to the currently attended object, he does allow that other forms of representation may be retained robustly from a complex scene. In particular, the gist (or basic identity of a scene, such as "kitchen" or "airport") is remembered robustly, as well as the abstract spatial organization of the scene, or layout. But neither of these representations preserves information about the visual details of individual objects in the scene.

Much of coherence theory is consistent with prior research and theory. The earliest research on visual sensory memory (Averbach & Coriell, 1961; Sperling, 1960) found that low-level sensory representations were generated across the visual field, but after stimulus removal, these low-level representations were fleeting and highly susceptible to masking. However, three or four items could be attended and consolidated into a more stable memory store (which we now term VSTM) that could support report at longer delays. The transience and volatility of sensory representations has been a background assumption in the visual memory literature for the last 45 years. Thus, the novelty of coherence theory lies not in the claim that sensory representations are fleeting (Averbach & Coriell, 1961; Coltheart, 1980; Di Lollo, 1980; Sperling, 1960), or in the claim that attention supports the binding of low-level features into a coherent object representation (Treisman & Gelade, 1980), or in the claim that attention enables consolidation of visual information into VSTM (Averbach & Coriell, 1961; Chun & Potter, 1995; Irwin, 1992; Schmidt, Vogel, Woodman, & Luck, 2002; Sperling, 1960), but rather in the claim that object representations come unbound when attention is withdrawn, leaving no trace of the coherent object representation that had been previously formed. As a result, visual representations do not accumulate as attention is oriented from object-to-object within a scene, and visual scene representations are impoverished, leading to change blindness.

5.2.2.4 Visual short-term memory–based accounts

Irwin (Irwin & Andrews, 1996; Irwin & Zelinsky, 2002) has proposed that higher-level visual representations (abstracted away from precise sensory features) of previously attended objects accumulate in VSTM as the eyes and attention are oriented from object to object within a scene. However, this accumulation is limited to the capacity of VSTM: five or six objects at the very most (Irwin & Zelinsky, 2002). As new objects are attended and fixated, and new object information is entered into VSTM, representations from objects attended earlier are replaced. The scene representation is therefore limited to objects that have been recently attended. This proposal is based on evidence that memory for the identity and position of letters in arrays does not appear to accumulate beyond VSTM capacity (Irwin & Andrews, 1996) and that memory for the positions of real-world objects, which improves as more object are fixated, does not improve any further when more than six objects are fixated (Irwin & Zelinsky, 2002).

5.2.2.5 Visual short-term memory/long-term memory accounts

Based on existing evidence of excellent long-term memory (LTM) for pictorial stimuli (Nickerson, 1965, 1968; Shepard, 1967; Standing, 1973; Standing, Conezio, & Haber, 1970), Hollingworth and Henderson (2002) proposed that both VSTM and VLTM are used to accumulate higher-level visual representations of objects during scene viewing, enabling the construction of scene representations that maintain visual information from many individual objects. In this view, attention is necessary to bind sensory features into coherent object representations (Treisman & Gelade, 1980), and attention is required to consolidate object representations into VSTM (Averbach & Coriell, 1961; Schmidt et al., 2002). The higher-level visual representation of an object, activated in VSTM, is associated with a position within a spatial representation of the scene, forming an object file (Hollingworth, 2006, 2007; Irwin & Zelinsky, 2002; Kahneman, Treisman, & Gibbs, 1992; Zelinsky & Loschky, 2005). Object representations are also consolidated into VLTM. As subsequent objects are attended and fixated, representations of objects attended earlier are replaced by new object representations in VSTM (Irwin & Zelinsky, 2002). However, the VLTM representation is retained robustly and accumulates with visual representations from other previously attended objects. Thus, over the course of scene viewing, VSTM and VLTM support the construction of a relatively elaborate representation of the scene, with higher-level visual representations of individual objects episodically linked to the larger scene representation through the binding of object representations to scene locations. In this account, change blindness is not necessarily symptomatic of impoverished scene representation.

5.2.2.6 Evaluation of theories

The theoretical accounts of change blindness and scene representation are highly divergent. However, most theoretical accounts emerging from the change blindness literature (and related work on visual memory) have two basic claims in common: (a) Low-level visual sensory representations are fleeting, and (b) attention is critical for the consolidation of visual object representations into a more stable store (VSTM, and perhaps VLTM) that is sufficient for change detection. The differences concern the fate of visual representation after attention is withdrawn from an object, with competing claims that coherent visual representations are immediately lost with the withdrawal of attention (Rensink, 2000; Wheeler & Treisman, 2002), that visual representations can be stored briefly within limited-capacity VSTM (Irwin & Zelinsky, 2002), and that visual representations can also be stored robustly in VLTM (Hollingworth, 2004; Hollingworth & Henderson, 2002). The commitments as to whether visual representations accumulate during scene viewing generate significant differences in the proposed richness of visual scene representations, with attention-based accounts proposing that scene representations are highly impoverished (limited to the attended object), VSTM-based accounts proposing that scene representations are limited to three or four higher-level objects representations, and VSTM/LTM accounts proposing that, given the extraordinarily large capacity of VLTM, scene representations have the potential to be highly elaborate (not "elaborate" in the sense of a complete, low-level sensory image, of course; rather, elaborate in the sense of accumulating many higher-level visual object representations).

The principal evidence cited in support of the idea that the removal of attention from an object leads to the disintegration of coherent object representations—and thus that attention to an object when it changes is necessary to detect the change—comes from the original *flicker paradigm* experiments by Rensink et al. (1997). In those studies, objects were classified as of "central interest" or "marginal interest" based on ratings provided by a separate group of participants. Changes to central-interest objects were detected more quickly than changes to marginal-interest objects. Rensink et al. reasoned that because participants would be more likely to attend to central-interest objects, facilitated change-detection performance for those objects indicated that attention was necessary for change detection. This logic is not particularly strong, however, because Rensink et al. had no means to measure or control where attention was allocated at any given time. Thus, although the results imply that there might be a relationship between attention and change detection, the nature of that relationship cannot be determined from the Rensink et al. method. As a stronger test of the role of attention in change detection, Scholl (2000) used an attention capture method to control where attention was allocated during a flicker paradigm. Detection of changes to objects that abruptly appeared or had a singleton color feature—and thus should have recruited attention—was facilitated. This result does indeed demonstrate that attention facilitates change detection, but that prediction is generated by all theoretical accounts under consideration, as it is well established that attention is necessary for the consolidation of perceptual information into VTSM. The Rensink et al. and Scholl studies do not address the critical question of whether sustained attention is necessary to maintain coherent object representations in memory.

Wheeler and Treisman (2002) sought to examine, directly, the role of attention in the maintenance of coherent visual object representations. They examined memory for objects composed of two features (e.g., shape and color) in a VSTM change-detection task. Participants saw a random array of objects, followed by a brief ISI and a test image. In the *feature memory* condition, participants were required to remember both features, as either color or shape might change. In the critical *binding memory* condition, participants were required to detect a change in the binding of features (e.g., two objects switched colors). Wheeler and Treisman found that memory for the binding of features was impaired relative to memory for individual features, but only when the entire array was presented at test. When a single item was presented at test, no binding deficit occurred. Wheeler and Treisman argued that the presentation of the entire array at test led to attentional distraction and the withdrawal of attention from the items in VSTM, in turn causing the bound object representations to disintegrate into their constituent features, generating a deficit in memory for binding. However, the experiments reported by Wheeler and Treisman do not represent a strong test of the hypothesis that attention is necessary to maintain feature binding, because attention was not directly manipulated. Although it is possible that presenting the full array at test led to attentional distraction, no compelling reason exists to think this was so, especially given that other studies have found higher change-detection performance when the full array is presented at test, compared with when a single test object is displayed (Hollingworth, 2007; Jiang, Olson, & Chun, 2000).

More recent work has indicated that attention is not necessary for the maintenance of coherent, bound object representations in memory. Gajewski and Brockmole (2006) found that explicit recall of objects in a VSTM task did not exhibit any significant loss of feature binding when attention was engaged by a peripheral cue. Johnson, Hollingworth, and Luck (2008) attempted to replicate the Wheeler and Treisman (2002) result, but found no decrement in binding memory when comparing full array test with single object test. More importantly, Johnson et al. directly manipulated attention in a VSTM change-detection task. During the delay between presentation of the study array and test array, participants completed a demanding visual search task that required serial shifts of attention to search array elements. The introduction of this search task lowered memory performance overall, but there was no specific decrement in memory for feature binding. Finally, Allen, Baddeley, and Hitch (2006) found no specific decrement in binding memory when participants performed an attentionally demanding executive task. Thus, although attention might be necessary to bind perceptual features initially into a coherent object representation (Treisman & Gelade, 1980), sustained attention is not necessary to maintain that binding in visual memory. As a result, it is possible that visual object representations accumulate in memory as attention is shifted from object-to-object within a scene.

Within the context of real-world scene perception and memory, Hollingworth and Henderson (2002) examined the accumulation of visual object representations after the withdrawal of attention. Eye movements were monitored while participants viewed computer-generated depictions of real-world scenes. The computer waited until the participant had fixated a target object in the scene (to ensure it had been attended). Later in viewing, the target object was changed during a saccade directed to a different object in the scene. Because visual attention is shifted to the goal of a saccade prior to the initiation of that eye movement (e.g., Hoffman & Subramaniam, 1995), the target object was no longer attended when the change occurred. The target object was changed either by rotating it 90 degrees in depth (rotation change) or by replacing it with another object from the same basic-level category (token change) Neither change altered the basic-level identity of the target. Coherence theory (Rensink, 2000; Wheeler & Treisman, 2002) predicts that these object changes should not have been detected, because attention had been withdrawn from the target prior to the change. Yet, participants successfully detected token and rotation changes on a significant proportion of trials, demonstrating that visual object representations accumulate in memory during scene viewing. Figure 5–2 shows the events in a sample trial of this experiment.

In a converging experiment (Hollingworth & Henderson, 2002), a previously fixated object was masked during a saccade to a different object in the scene. Two object alternatives were then displayed sequentially at the target location. One alternative was the original target object, and the other was either a different token or different orientation distractor. The target was no longer attended when it was masked, yet participants performed the discrimination tasks at rates above 80% correct. Further, accurate discrimination performance was observed even when multiple fixations on other objects intervened between the fixation of the target and the test. When more than nine fixations on other objects intervened between target fixation and test, token-discrimination performance was 85% correct, and orientation-discrimination performance was 92% correct. Memory for the visual details of previously attended objects was robust across shifts of attention and of the eyes.

The experiments in Hollingworth and Henderson (2002) depended on the relationship between eye position and attention (that attention covertly precedes the eyes to a saccade target). Hollingworth (2003) used an abrupt onset cue at a nontarget location, which captured attention (Yantis & Jonides, 1984), to ensure that attention was not allocated to the target when it was masked before the test. Again, visual memory performance was highly accurate for objects that had been, but were no longer, attended.

Visual memory for objects during scene viewing depends on higher-level visual memory systems: VSTM and VLTM. To examine the relative contributions of VSTM and VLTM, Hollingworth (2004) used a serial position manipulation to control the sequence of objects fixated and attended within a scene. On each trial of this *follow-the-dot* paradigm, participants followed a green dot as it visited a series of objects in a scene. Participants shifted gaze to fixate the object most recently visited by the dot. After the dot sequence, a target object

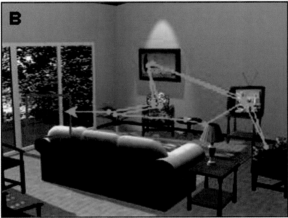

Figure 5–2. Sample trial in Hollingworth and Henderson (2002, Experiment 2). Participants viewed each scene for 20 s. They were instructed to prepare for a memory test and to press a button if one of the objects changed during viewing. The three panels show the eye movement scanpath divided into three sequential periods. Dots represent fixations and lines saccades. **Panel A.** The participant began the trial and fixated the target object (television) on the eleventh fixation. **Panel B.** After target fixation, an invisible change-triggering region was activated (*marked in red*). The participant continued to fixate objects, including refixations on the target. During the saccade that crossed into the change-triggering region, the target object was rotated 90 degrees in depth.

Figure 5–2. (*continued*) Panel C. After target rotatior, the change was not detected immediately. Significantly later in viewing, the participant happened to refixate the television, and the change was de-ected at that point.

was masked, and memory for the visual form of the target was tested in an orientation- or token-discrimination task. The dot appeared on the target object either relatively early in viewing or relatively late. There was a reliable recency effect, characteristic of retention in VSTM (Murdock, 1962; Phillips & Christie, 1977). This recency advantage was limited to the last two objects fixated in the scene (see also Zelinsky & Loschky, 2005). However, objects examined earlier than two objects before the test were remembered at rates well above chance, and no further forgetting occurred. Performance was equivalent for objects fixated between three objects before the test and 10 objects before the test. At 10 objects before the test, visual memory easily exceeded the three-to four-object capacity of VSTM. This robust pre-recency memory therefore suggests a VLTM component to online scene representation. In summary, VSTM appears to support memory for the visual form of the last two objects fixated and attended in a scene, with memory for objects attended earlier in viewing supported by VLTM.

What about claims that the visual representation of scenes is limited to immediately task-relevant objects (e.g., Ballard et al., 1997)? It is certainly true that attention and the eyes are directed in a moment-by-moment fashion to goal-relevant objects (Hayhoe, 2000; Land et al. 1999; Yarbus, 1967). And, given that attended objects are prioritized for consolidation into VSTM, the moment-by-moment content of VSTM is likely to be closely related to the current task (Ballard et al., 1995; Hayhoe, Bensinger, & Ballard, 1998) and to reflect the most recently attended objects (Hollingworth, 2004). Even for an attended object, changes to task-relevant properties (e.g., color in a color sorting task) are detected more reliably than changes to task-irrelevant properties (Droll, Hayhoe, Triesch, & Sullivan, 2005; Triesch, Ballard, Hayhoe, & Sullivan, 2003), suggesting task specificity in memory for object attributes.

Although it is clear that task has a large influence on scene memory, scene representation is not limited to task-relevant information, and, in fact, longer-term scene memory, retained long after it has ceased to be immediately task relevant, is critical for efficient future behavior. Before starting a real-world task, such as making a sandwich or tea, participants exhibit a "surveying" behavior, in which they scan the environment, presumably to encode the layout of the scene, the perceptual properties and identities of objects, and their locations (Aivar, Hayhoe, Chizk, & Mruczek, 2005; Hayhoe, Shrivastava, Mruczek, & Pelz, 2003; Land & Hayhoe, 2001). During the task itself, eye movement behavior shows evidence of memory derived from these familiarization behaviors. In addition, task-irrelevant properties of scenes are often robustly represented in memory. In the original block copying task of Ballard et al. (1995), participants were sensitive to changes in the color of blocks that were not currently being manipulated (Hayhoe et al., 1998). In addition, Castelhano and Henderson (2005; see also Williams, Henderson, & Zacks, 2005) found robust incidental memory for the visual form of individual objects in a search task. In this study, participants first completed a visual search task through images of real-world scenes. Then, they were given a surprise memory test for the visual form of individual objects. Memory for attended target objects (which had been but were no longer task-relevant) and attended distractor objects (task-irrelevant) was significantly above chance and did not differ. Finally, long-term perceptual learning has effects on perceptual processing, such as search efficiency, long after that information has ceased to be immediately task-relevant (Chun & Jiang, 2003). Thus, visual memory (presumably LTM) is used to construct representations of the spatial structure of a scene that can guide subsequent behavior and to accumulate visually specific information from attended objects.

It is now well established that coherent visual object representations are preserved in memory and accumulate after the withdrawal of attention. Recently, Rensink (Rensink, 2002; Simons & Rensink, 2005) has proposed that, whereas sustained attention might not be necessary to detect that a change has occurred, attention *is* necessary for the experience of seeing dynamic change. This distinction depends on phenomenology. According to Rensink, "... the detection of dynamic change refers to the perception of the transformation itself: The change is perceived as a dynamic visual event" (Rensink, 2002, p. 249). In contrast, detection of completed change (i.e., that a change has occurred) refers to one's ability to detect a difference but without the phenomenology of actually seeing the change happen. But, in change blindness studies, changes typically occur in a single step across some sort of disruption; that is, changes do not occur in real time. Even if one has the (illusory) experience of "seeing the change occur," that experience can be generated only by first detecting that a change has occurred across the disruption, in precisely the same way that one can only perceive apparent motion *after* having detected that the object has changed location. Thus, the most basic operation in change detection is to detect that a change has occurred. Whether one "sees the change as occurring" is secondary to the basic representational issue of how the difference was detected in the first place. Further, Rensink (2002) has proposed that the phenomenology of "seeing a change occur" might be driven by the retention of low-level informational persistence across the disruption, whereas detecting that a change has occurred would be based on higher-level visual representations abstracted away from sensory persistence. This distinction does not appear particularly plausible. Informational persistence, unlike visible persistence, is not directly visible, and thus would seem an inappropriate substrate for conscious experience of dynamic change (visible persistence itself is not a plausible option, given its extraordinarily rapid decay). In addition, informational persistence is highly susceptible to masking, yet the addition of a pattern mask in the ISI of the standard flicker paradigm does not have any significant influence on the experience of "seeing a change occur." Thus, no direct evidence exists to suggest that seeing a change occur and detecting that a change has occurred depend on different forms of visual memory or are differentially dependent on attention.[2]

---

2   Consider the following informal experiment. An initial and changed scene image (250 ms each) were presented in a flicker paradigm, with an ISI of either 200 ms, 1 s, or 5 s. In each case, the participant was attending the changing object throughout (because it was specified at the beginning of the trial). Participants reported having a strong impression of "seeing the change occur" at 200-millisecond ISI, a weaker impression at 1-second, and no impression of "seeing the change occur" at 5-second ISI (at least according to the 10 people who viewed this demonstration). What accounts for the difference in phenomenology? Attention does not account for the difference, because in all cases the change was to an attended object. Differential retention of visible persistence cannot account for the difference, because a 450-millisecond SOA (250 ms stimulus plus 200 ms ISI) is already well beyond the temporal range of visible persistence. Differential retention of informational persistence cannot account for the difference, because the addition of a pattern mask during the ISI does not change the phenomenology. Differential retention in VSTM does not account for the difference, because VSTM studies have shown robust retention over ISIs as long as 10 s (Vogel, Woodman, and Luck, 2001), and in this very informal experiment, participants only had one object to remember, and they correctly described the nature of the change on all trials.

   The difference in phenomenology appears to depend simply on the delay between the initial and changed images. At short ISIs, the visual system can attribute the difference to a point in time within a brief window, generating the strong sense that it just happened, now. The change really did just happen, as if in the blink of the eye. But at longer ISIs, no such precise temporal attribution is possible. If I look at and attend an object, have my view occluded for 5 s, and then it reappears, changed, I can detect that it is different (just as in the case of shorter ISI), but I cannot pinpoint with any precision when it changed within that 5 s interval, so there is no strong impression of the change occurring right in front of me, now. This would also apply to the case in which I attend to an object, attend elsewhere, and then re-attend the (now changed) object and notice a difference (Hollingworth and Henderson, 2002). It is the length of the delay that controls whether one "sees a change occur," not any fundamental difference in attention or visual memory.

5.2.2.7 Understanding change blindness

Evidence of robust visual memory for the visual details of scenes leads one to consider why change blindness would ever be observed in the first place. Change blindness is rarely absolute. For example, Grimes and McConkie (Grimes, 1996) found that some changes introduced during eye movements were detected by only 25% of participants, whereas others were detected by as many as 80% of participants. Similarly, Simons and Levin (1998) found that approximately 50% of participants failed to detect the replacement of one person for another. But even if participants do often detect changes, they also fail to detect changes that would seem to alter precisely the types of information found to be retained robustly in visual memory. For example, the appearance and disappearance of a chimney in a flicker paradigm should certainly be detectable by the retention of a higher-level visual representation in VSTM or VLTM. Why do participants often fail to notice this sort of change?[3]

5.2.2.7.1 Failures of encoding.   One of the principal causes of changes blindness is encoding failure. Change blindness may occur in many circumstances because the local information from the target object has yet to be encoded when a change occurs. Hollingworth and Henderson (Hollingworth & Henderson, 2002; Hollingworth, Schrock, & Henderson, 2001) examined change detection performance as a function of whether the target object had been fixated prior to the change. Changes to previously fixated objects were detected at rates well above chance. However, changes to objects that had not been fixated were detected at a rate no higher than the false-alarm rate, suggesting that without direct fixation, information sufficient to detect a change was rarely encoded. In a LTM paradigm, Nelson and Loftus (1980) also found that memory performance for unfixated objects was near chance. These findings are consistent with evidence that attention is necessary to consolidate perceptual information into memory (e.g., Schmidt et al., 2002). It may take participants many seconds to fixate each of the potentially changing objects in a scene. In a paradigm introducing a single change, if the object is changed before it has been fixated, it is hardly surprising that such a change was not detected; the visual system simply has not had an opportunity to form a robust visual memory representation of that object. In a repeating change paradigm, such as the flicker paradigm, relatively long delays before change detection could be caused, to a significant extent, by the fact that participants require a fairly long time to fixate the changing object.

Although attention to and fixation of the changing object before the change may be necessary to detect most changes, it is not necessarily sufficient to detect a change. In many cases, participants fail to detect changes to objects that were previously attended and fixated. For example, in the Hollingworth and Henderson (2002) experiments, detection of changes to previously fixated objects was well above chance, but it was nowhere near perfect. In the studies by Simons, Levin,

---

3   See Simons (2000) for further discussion of the causes of change blindness.

and colleagues (Levin & Simons, 1997; Levin, Simons, Angelone, & Chabris, 2002; Simons & Levin, 1998), in which one person is replaced by another during a disruption, it is almost certain that the original person (and the original person's face) was fixated before the change, yet these changes were often missed. Finally, O'Regan, Deubel, Clark, and Rensink (2000) introduced scene changes during blinks. Changes were missed even when the changing object was fairly close to the current fixation position. Thus, failures to attend to and fixate the changing object before the change cannot entirely account for change blindness.

5.2.2.7.2 Failures of retention. Clearly, forgetting occurs in visual memory, which contributes to change blindness. The most dramatic forgetting is the rapid loss of low level sensory information following a visual event (Averbach & Coriell, 1961; Coltheart, 1980; Di Lollo, 1980; Sperling, 1960). Although changes certainly would be detected more reliably if sensory information was retained robustly and integrated across the times scales and disruptions characteristic of natural vision, we have long known that such retention and integration do not occur (Di Lollo, 1980; Irwin et al., 1983).

Another possible cause of retention failure and change blindness, identified by Rensink (2000), is the *overwriting* of old visual memory representations with new perceptual representations (see Loftus, Miller, & Burns, 1978 for a similar proposal of overwriting in visual memory). In this view, when a change is introduced, perceptual processing of the changed object or region overwrites the original information (unless the object is attended), generating change blindness. The critical test of this proposal is whether participants can remember properties of the original object after an undetected change: Was the original information overwritten? Several studies now indicate that, contrary to the overwriting hypothesis, participants reliably remember perceptual properties of the original object after an undetected change (Angelone, Levin, & Simons, 2003; Mitroff, Simons, & Levin, 2004; Simons, Chabris, Schnur, & Levin, 2002; Varakin, Levin, & Collins, 2007). In a method inspired by McCloskey and Zaragoza (1985), Hollingworth (unpublished data) tested memory for the visual form of the original object after an undetected change. Eye movements were monitored as participants viewed scenes. After an object was fixated, it was replaced during a saccade by an object from a different category (e.g., a toaster replaced by a mixer). On trials in which the participant did not detect the change, two forms of memory test were administered. Memory for the original object (toaster) was tested in a two-alternative, forced-choice (2AFC) test, with the original object and a different token version of that object (a different toaster) as the alternatives. Similarly, memory for the new object (mixer) was tested in a 2AFC test, with the new object and a different token version of the new object (a different mixer) as the alternatives. Contrary to the prediction of the overwriting hypothesis, memory performance was significantly more accurate for the original object than for the new object. Although it is certainly possible that new perceptual information interferes with old, generating some degree of forgetting, new perceptual processing does not necessarily overwrite existing visual memory representations.

To further examine the issue of forgetting in scene memory, Hollingworth (2005c) compared memory for the visual form of individual objects during online scene viewing and after a delay of one trial, when the scene had been removed for approximately 90 s. In both cases, participants remembered visually specific details accurately. Critically, there was absolutely no loss of memory for object detail: Memory performance was actually numerically higher after a one-trial delay than during online scene viewing. With longer delays of 30 min and 24 h (Hollingworth, 2004, 2005c), significant forgetting of object detail begins to be observed. Thus, over the time scales typical of change blindness studies (on the order of a minute or two, at most), low-level sensory information is being forgotten constantly, but there appears to be minimal further forgetting in visual memory.

5.2.2.7.3 Failures of retrieval and comparison.   Even if one forms a visual memory representation sufficient to detect a change, that memory must be retrieved and compared with current perceptual information in order to detect the change. Early change blindness studies assumed that explicit report of change provided an exhaustive measure of visual memory. However, a number of converging sources of evidence show that explicit change detection underestimates visual memory and that retrieval and comparison failures are a significant cause of change blindness.

Changes may go undetected despite accurate memory when the changed object is not attended or fixated after the change. In Hollingworth and Henderson (2002), detection of object change was often delayed until the object happened to be refixated later in viewing, as illustrated in Figure 5–2. Such a delay, if observed in a flicker paradigm, could be taken as evidence of extended change blindness, yet the ultimate detection of the change demonstrated that participants had a memory representation of the relevant object. That representation was not retrieved and compared with current perceptual information until the eyes were directed back to the (now changed) object.

Hollingworth (2003) examined the role of retrieval and comparison failure in change blindness using a post-cue manipulation. After viewing a scene, a target object in the test scene was either the same, rotated, or replaced by a different token. The target object was either post-cued by a green arrow or not post-cued (the latter method is typical of change blindness experiments). In the no–post-cue condition, participants had to determine whether any object in the scene had changed, potentially requiring many individual comparisons. In the post-cue condition, participants needed only to compare the cued object with memory. If change blindness is caused by failed retrieval and comparison, then change detection should have been improved when retrieval and comparison demands were minimized by the post-cue. Indeed, significantly higher change-detection performance was observed in the post-cue condition.

Converging evidence of retrieval and comparison failure comes from three studies conducted by Simons, Levin, and colleagues. In Simons et al. (2002), an experimenter carrying a basketball engaged a participant in conversation. The basketball was covertly removed during a disruption, and the participant was then asked to report any odd events or changes. If such general questions did not yield report of the removed basketball, the participant was given a direct instruction to describe the basketball (the removal of which had not been noticed). Participants could then often report specific perceptual details of the basketball, demonstrating that they had sufficient memory to detect the change but had not retrieved that information and compared it to perceptual information during the interaction. Similarly, Angelone et al. (2003) found that when participants failed to detect the replacement of one person for another, they could discriminate the original person in a forced-choice test at levels above chance. Finally, Varakin et al. (2007) demonstrated that a fairly large proportion of participants remembered the original color and the changed color of a binder that the participant had used in a real-world event, but the participants did not compare these two pieces of information to detect the change.

5.2.2.7.4 Implicit detection and threshold mechanisms.   Finally, preserved memory in the face of change blindness is observed using measures more sensitive than explicit report of change (for a review, see Thornton & Fernandez-Duque, 2002). For example, when a change is not reported, fixation durations on a changed object are longer than on the same object when it has not changed (Hayhoe et al., 1998; Henderson & Hollingworth, 2003a; Hollingworth, Williams, & Henderson, 2001; Ryan, Althoff, Whitlow, & Cohen, 2000).

Effects of unreported change on indirect measures may be generated by threshold mechanisms for attributing visual discrepancy to a change in the world. Dynamic vision often introduces perceptual discrepancies that could have been generated either by internal error or by external change. For example, when making a saccade to an object, the eyes often fail to land on the target of the eye movement (Deubel, Wolf, & Hauske, 1982; Hollingworth et al., 2008; Kapoula, 1985). After the completion of such an eye movement, the saccade target object is not at the center of gaze. This discrepancy could be due to the inaccuracy of the eye movement (internal error), but it could also be due to the movement of the target object during the saccade (external change). By shifting saccade targets during saccades, researchers have discovered that the visual system sets a threshold for attributing positional discrepancy to external change. If the displacement of the saccade target is greater than approximately one-third of the distance of the saccade, participants perceive the target to have moved, attributing the discrepancy to change in the world (Bridgeman, Hendry, & Stark, 1975; McConkie & Currie, 1996). Below that threshold, a corrective saccade is executed to bring the saccade target onto the fovea, but participants are rarely aware of the displacement or of the corrective saccade. Thus, for small discrepancies that are likely to have been caused by error in occulomotor mechanisms, the visual system does not attribute the discrepancy to a change in the world, and participants do not perceive the target object to have moved. They are "blind" to the change despite the fact that the visual system was sensitive to the discrepancy. Further, if additional cues indicate that the external world has changed, participants are more likely to attribute positional discrepancy to a shift of the saccade target, and explicit awareness of the shift is dramatically improved (Deubel, Schneider, & Bridgeman, 1996). In the Deubel at al. study, the saccade target was shifted, and on a portion of trials, it was also deleted for a few hundred ms once the eyes landed. This target "blanking" meant that no object was visible when the eyes landed, clearly indicating that the visual world had changed. When the target object reappeared, participants were much more sensitive to spatial displacement than when the target object was fully visible throughout the trial.

Threshold mechanisms are also observed in the phenomenon of insensitivity to incremental change (Hollingworth & Henderson, 2004; Simons, Franconeri, & Reimer, 2000). In a flicker paradigm, Hollingworth and Henderson (2004) gradually rotated an entire scene, with each image changed by 1 degree of orientation in depth. Participants were remarkably insensitive to these gradual changes. They often came to treat significantly different views of a room as an unchanged continuation of the initial view.[4] Nevertheless, memory was sensitive to the difference between views. With rotation, memory came to reflect the recent, changed state of the scene rather than the initial state. This implicit updating of memory to reflect scene changes meant that comparison typically operated over similar representations. The current image was compared with memory for the most recent image(s). As a result, the discrepancy between perceptual information and memory tended to be very small, falling below threshold for explicit detection. Although memory was sensitive to the fact that the image had changed, individual comparisons rarely exceeded threshold for explicit awareness of change, thus yielding change blindness.

In summary, recent evidence suggests that participants fail to detect changes because they have not fixated and attended the changing object prior to the change and thus have not had an opportunity to encode information sufficient to detect a change, because they have not retrieved or compared a memory representation to current perceptual information, and because evidence of discrepancy falls below threshold for signaling a change in the world. Change blindness is also caused by forgetting, but after the initial loss of sensory persistence, visual memory is surprisingly resistant to decay and interference.

5.3 LONGER-TERM SCENE MEMORY

5.3.1 Capacity and Visual Specificity

Early work on LTM for scenes was primarily targeted at estimating the capacity of memory for pictures. Initial studies of picture memory demonstrated that humans possess a prodigious ability to remember pictures presented at study

---

4   Similar insensitivity to gradual change is observed for changes in the global brightness of a scene image (Hollingworth, 2005b). In this study, the scene image began as fairly dim (as if viewing a darkened room with a low-intensity light source). Gradually, the room brightened. Many participants failed to detect the change even when the room image was so bright that surface details were lost (as if the room were floodlit).

(Nickerson, 1965, 1968; Shepard, 1967; Standing, 1973; Standing et al., 1970). For example, Standing et al. (1973) tested LTM for 2560 photographs of various subject matter. Shortly after study, memory for a subset of 280 images was tested in a 2AFC test, with mean discrimination performance of approximately 90% correct. Nickerson (1968) presented 200 black-and-white photographs for 5 s each. Memory was essentially perfect after a 1-day delay and was still well above change after a delay of almost 1 year. In the most remarkable demonstration of capacity, Standing (1973) presented each participant with 10,000 photographs for 5 s each (which required 5 days of study!). At the end of the fifth day, a subset of images was tested in a 2AFC task. Recognition performance was 86% correct, which suggested the retention of approximately 6800 photographs in memory.

Although studies of memory capacity demonstrate that scene memory is specific enough to successfully discriminate between thousands of different items, they do not identify the nature of the stored information supporting this performance. Based in part on change blindness effects, recent discussions of the picture memory literature have tended to ascribe high-capacity picture memory to retention of scene gist rather than to retention of the visual details of the photographs (Chun, 2003; Potter, Staub, & O'Connor, 2004; Simons, 1996).

However, evidence that long-term picture memory preserves specific visual information comes from the Standing et al. (1970) study. Memory for the left–right orientation of studied pictures was tested by presenting studied scenes at test either in the same orientation as at study or in the reverse orientation. It is unlikely that the orientation of a picture could be encoded using a purely con-ceptual representation of scene gist, as the meaning of the scenes did not change when the orientation was reversed. However, participants were able to correctly identify the initially viewed picture orientation 86% of the time after a 30-minute retention interval. Thus, the Standing et al. study demonstrates that in addition to being accurate enough to discriminate between thousands of studied pictures, VLTM for scenes is not limited to the gist of the scene or to the identities of individual objects.

To examine the capacity of VLTM for the visual details of individual objects in natural scenes, Hollingworth (2004) used the follow-the-dot method but delayed the token change detection test until the end of the session, after all scenes had been viewed. In this condition, more than 400 objects, on average, were examined between target examination and test. Of course, participants did not know which of these objects would be tested until the test occurred. Token change did not alter the gist of the scene, or even the identity of the target object; detection required memory for the perceptual details of the object. Despite these considerable memory demands, participants performed the token-change detection task at a rate well above chance (68% correct), which was only moderately lower than change-detection performance when object memory was tested during scene viewing. Change-detection perform-ance (both for token changes and orientation changes) remains above chance even after a delay of 24 h (Hollingworth, 2005c). To put this in concrete terms, after having viewed 48 different scenes and hundreds of individual objects, and after a delay of 24 h, participants can still detect that a single object (e.g., a pen on a cluttered desk) has changed orientation. Clearly, VLTM in not limited to scene gist. See Chapter 6 for converging evidence that LTM maintains significant visual detail in the service of object recognition.

5.3.2 The Episodic Structure of Scene Representations

Our memory for natural environments is inherently episodic, forming the visual contextual structure within which to organize memory for objects and events. Thus, one of the central issues in scene memory research is the manner by which larger, episodic representations of scenes are formed from the local and sequential acquisition of visual information that comprises natural visual. For example, if I fixate a pen and encode visual information about its color, orientation, and so on, and if later I fixate a coffee cup in the same room and also encode information about its visual properties, how are the two visual memory representations bound into a more comprehensive representation of the larger office scene (if they are at all)? Research on the episodic structure of visual memory initially focused on understanding the types of schematic information (i.e., scene schemas) that could serve to structure visual memory. More recent research has examined spatial context as a central organizing structure in visual memory. We turn to each of these literatures next.

5.3.2.1 Context effects and schemas

Since the 1970s, a central theoretical construct in the field of picture and scene memory has been the scene schema (Biederman, Mezzanotte, & Rabinowitz, 1982; Brewer & Treyens, 1981; Friedman, 1979; Intraub, 1997; Mandler & Ritchey, 1977; Pedzek, Whetstone, Reynolds, Askari, & Dougherty, 1989). Schema representations have been proposed as supporting memory for categories of scenes (e.g., a kitchen schema) and for individual scene exemplars (Intraub, 1997). In addition, schema theories have been central in accounting for effects of scene knowledge on the perception of (for reviews, see Henderson, 1991; Hollingworth & Henderson, 1998) and memory for (Brewer & Treyens, 1981; Friedman, 1979) individual objects in scenes. The modal description of a scene schema is an abstract representation of a particular scene type (e.g., "kitchen") specifying the kinds of objects that are typically found in that scene (e.g., refrigerator, blender, toaster) and the typical spatial positions within the scene occupied by those objects (Mandler & Parker, 1976).

Although particular schema theories differ significantly in their claims about the influence of schemas on scene memory, two broad themes are consistently present: abstraction and distortion (for a general review of schema theory, see Alba & Hasher, 1983). Under schema theories, scene representations in memory are proposed to be highly abstracted and primarily conceptual in nature—that is, limited to the gist of the scene (Mandler & Ritchey, 1977; Potter et al., 2004). Scene details are initially activated when viewing a scene, but the details are quickly forgotten, leaving only the gist. The schema approach is in this respect quite similar to claims of abstract, gist-based representations in the change blindness literature (O'Regan, 1992; Rensink, 2000; Simons & Levin, 1997).

The evidence that scene representations preserve significant visual detail and are not limited to gist, has been reviewed earlier But whether one considers scene memory to be schematic or not depends on one's baseline comparison. If one compares the amount of detail retained from a scene against a representation of scene gist, then scene memory cannot be considered schematic. However, if one compares scene memory against the detail available in low-level sensory representations, then one could plausibly claim that scene memory is schematic. However, to be considered an example of schema abstraction, the loss of detail must be functionally related to the extraction of scene meaning. For example, if low-level sensory information was maintained long enough to extract the gist of the scene (i.e., identify it) and, as soon as the meaning of the scene was established, the sensory information was then discarded, the loss of sensory detail would certainly be a schematic operation, because it would be functionally related to the extraction of meaning. However, the decay of sensory information is unrelated to stimulus meaning. The loss of sensory information simply reflects the passive decay of neural activity in early visual regions of the brain (Chapter 2). Because the loss of sensory detail is entirely passive, it cannot be considered a schema abstraction operation.

The schema approach also holds that memory will be distorted based on the semantic relationship between the scene and individual objects in the scene. Semantically consistent objects (e.g., refrigerator in a kitchen) should be remembered frequently, as they will have pre-existing slots within the schema representation. Semantically inconsistent objects (e.g., a horse in a kitchen) should be remembered less frequently, as they do not fit within the currently active schema, and thus their memory representations are not supported by schematic structure. This process of normalization is a central feature of schema theory (Bartlett, 1932). Brewer and Treyens (1981) tested normalization processes in scene memory, having participants remember the objects present in a graduate student office, some of which were semantically consistent (desk) and some inconsistent (skull). On a free-recall test, participants were more likely to recall semantically consistent objects than inconsistent objects, potentially indicating normalization. However, Brewer and Treyens provided no control over guessing, and it is unclear whether participants actually remembered consistent objects more reliably or were simply biased to guess that consistent objects had been present.

Subsequent studies have found the reverse effect: better memory for semantically inconsistent objects in scenes (Friedman, 1979; Hollingworth & Henderson, 2000, 2003; Pedzek et al., 1989). To account for this type of result, Friedman modified the standard schema account to allow for accurate inconsistent object memory. In this view, inconsistent objects are stored as part of a "weird list," a list of scene elements that distinguish, episodically, the particular scene exemplar from other exemplars of that scene type. That is, inconsistent objects are stored robustly precisely because they *do not* fit within the scene schema. It is troubling when a theoretical approach can account for contradictory findings (i.e., normalization and the absence of normalization), and the explanatory power of any such theory is weakened in that event, which is one of the reasons that the influence of schema theory has waned over the last 20 years. In addition, the most common empirical finding—an inconsistent object memory advantage—need not be the result of structural effects in memory. In these studies, inconsistent objects were clearly anomalous during initial viewing, and the memory advantage for inconsistent objects could therefore reflect differences in initial encoding rather than differences in the organization of memory (Friedman, 1979; Gordon, 2004; Henderson, Weeks, & Hollingworth, 1999; Hollingworth & Henderson, 2000, 2003; Pedzek et al., 1989). In general, the absence of normalization in scene memory casts in doubt the claim that scene memory is schematic in the standard sense of that term.

A second type of visual memory effect attributed to scene schemas is the phenomenon of *boundary extension* (see Intraub, 1997 for a review). Boundary extension occurs when participants remember a scene as spatially extending beyond the actual boundaries in the image. In a boundary extension experiment, participants typically see a series of picture of scenes composed of a few objects (Gottesman & Intraub, 2002; Intraub & Richardson, 1989). At test, they are required to reconstruct the original image or judge whether a test image is the same as the original. Reconstructions tend to include a greater spatial expanse than the original, and images depicting a greater spatial expanse are judged to be the original images at rates higher than that for the actual original images.

Intraub and colleagues have interpreted boundary extension as reflecting the influence of schemas on scene memory (Intraub, 1997). Their view draws from Hochberg's idea of a perceptual schema, in which the visual system infers the continuation of spatial structure (such as surfaces) beyond what is presently visible, and uses this representation of large-scale spatial layout to knit together the disparate episodes of experience caused by changes in viewing direction and observer position. This proposal can be considered a version of schema theory, because it proposes that the inferred information is sketchy and incomplete. However, there has been no specification in the boundary extension literature of the precise properties of such a scene schema and how those properties might interact, mechanistically, with available visual information to produce the effect. Thus, "schema" is a descriptive term in this context. If one simply were to say that scene representations instantiate the continuation of spatial structure beyond the immediate field of view, it is not clear that appending the term "schema" to this account adds any explanatory power. In any case, the boundary extension phenomenon does represent a systematic distortion of scene memory, which stands in contrast to the typically accurate memory observed in other studies.

5.3.2.2 Object-to-scene binding

How are individual object representations structured to form a more comprehensive, episodic representation of a scene? With little existing evidence regarding the relationship between memory for individual objects and memory for complex scenes, Hollingworth (2006) tested the basic question of whether individual visual objects are represented episodically—as part of a larger representation of a scene—or independently of scene context. Prior research in the face recognition literature had indicated that objects in scenes might be stored independently of scene context. J. W. Tanaka and Farah (1993) had participants learn a series of face stimuli and a series of house stimuli. Memory for individual features of the faces (e.g., nose) or houses (e.g., door) was tested, with the target feature presented either within the original face or house context or in isolation. Memory for face features showed a significant whole-face advantage, suggesting that face features were stored as part of a larger representation of the face, but there was no whole-house advantage for house feature memory, suggesting that the features of a house were stored independently of each other.

As a direct test of possible object-to-scene binding, Hollingworth (2006) examined memory for the visual form of individual objects in scenes, manipulating the presence of scene context at test, similar to the method of J. W. Tanaka and Farah (1993). Participants viewed a scene for 20 s, followed by a 2AFC test. In the test, a target object and a modified version of that object (token substitution or in-depth rotation) were displayed. The test object alternatives were either embedded within the original scene context or presented in an otherwise empty field. Discrimination performance was reliably superior when the target object was tested within the original scene context. This whole-scene advantage demonstrates that visual object representations are stored as part of a larger scene representation (and that faces are not "special" in showing contextual superiority in memory for constituents parts). The whole-scene advantage was observed both when object memory was tested immediately after scene viewing and when memory was tested after a delay of approximately 30 min. Similar effects of context deletion have been observed using random arrays of natural objects (Hollingworth, 2007) and using simplified objects under brief presentation conditions that are likely tap VSTM (Jiang et al., 2000). Contextual structure appears to be a fundamental property of higher-level visual memory systems.

5.3.2.3 Spatial structure of scene memory

Given that local object information is stored as part of a larger scene representation, how is visual memory for objects structured within a scene? Hollingworth and Henderson (2002) proposed that larger-scale scene representations are formed through the binding of local object representations to positions in a spatial representation of the scene: As the eyes and attention are oriented within a scene, higher-level visual representations are generated for attended objects and are bound to scene positions, forming a set of object files (Henderson, 1994; Irwin & Zelinsky, 2002; Kahneman et al., 1992; Zelinsky & Loschky, 2005). Initial support for the spatial binding hypothesis comes from that fact that participants can reliably remember the binding of object identity and position within real-world scenes (Diwadkar & McNamara, 1997; Hollingworth, 2005a; Irwin & Zelinsky, 2002; Rieser, 1989; Shelton & McNamara, 2001;

Zelinsky & Loschky, 2005). To test whether visual memory for objects is indeed bound to particular scene locations, Hollingworth (2006; Hollingworth, 2007) manipulated object position in a scene memory study. As in previous studies, participants viewed a scene for 20 s, followed by a 2AFC or change detection test probing memory for the visual form of a single object. The test object was presented either at the original location in which it had appeared within the scene or at a different location within the scene (equally distant from scene center). Local contextual information around the target object was obscured in both conditions, so that the position manipulation was not confounded with changes in the local intersection of object and scene contours. Memory performance was superior when the target object maintained its original position within the scene, a *same-position advantage*. Thus, visual object representations are not only bound to scene context but are bound to particular locations within a spatially organized representation of the scene.

To determine which spatial properties of the scene serve to define object position, Hollingworth (2007) examined the effect of contextual manipulations on the magnitude of this same position advantage. The experiments depended on the following logic. If a particular change to the scene context disrupts information functional in defining target position, then the same position advantage should be reduced or eliminated when the context changes (Fig. 5–3). First, Hollingworth (2007) examined the effect of context deletion on the same position advantage. In the background-present condition, the scene background was present in the test image. In the background-absent condition, the target object was displayed in isolation. Target position (same/different) was manipulated independently of background presence. Consistent with prior experiments, there was a robust same-target-position advantage when the background was present. However, there was no same-target-position advantage when the background was absent, demonstrating that target position was defined relative to the particular scene context in which the target was originally viewed.[5]

Hollingworth (2007) further probed the nature of the spatial representation serving to define object position using random arrays of common objects that allowed spatial manipulations not possible with real-world scene stimuli. As with real-world scene stimuli, the same position advantage was eliminated with context deletion using random object arrays, thus demonstrating that object arrays engage functionally similar contextual mechanisms as real-world scenes.

---

5   The finding that spatial binding parameters are "re-set" with context deletion is similar to the finding that the marking of attended positions during visual search—generating inhibition of return—is "re-set" with the deletion of the search context (Klein and MacInnes, 1999; Müller and Von Mühlenen, 2000; Takeda and Yagi, 2000). These similar contextual sensitivity effects raise the possibility that the dynamic indexing of object locations (as in inhibition of return) and the binding of visual memory representations to scene locations (Hollingworth, 2007) depend on the same form of spatial representation (or at least that the visuo-spatial systems supporting the two have similar functional properties).

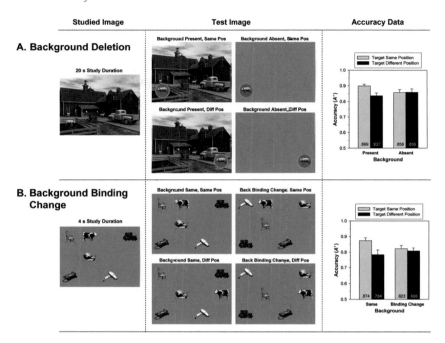

Figure 5–3. Illustration of contextual manipulations in Hollingworth (2007). (**A**) Background deletion. Participants saw an image of a natural scene for 20 s (*first column*), followed by a test scene in which the presence of the background scene and the position of the target object were independently manipulated (*second column*). The target was either same or mirror reversed, and the task was change detection. A change detection advantage was observed for same target position over different target position when the background was present at test. However, no same-position advantage occurred when the background was deleted at test. (**B**) Background binding change. Participants saw an image of an object array for 4 s (*first column*), followed by a test array in which the binding of contextual objects to locations and the position of the target object were independently manipulated (*second column*). Again, the task was mirror-reversal change detection. The same-target-position advantage was observed when the background bindings stayed the same, but no such advantage occurred when the binding of contextual objects to locations changed. Error bars are standard errors of the means.

Research by Jiang et al. (2000), in a paradigm examining VSTM, indicated that the primary spatial structure of visual memory representations is the global spatial configuration objects, with individual object representations bound to locations defined relative to array configuration. In Hollingworth (2007), the locations of contextual array objects were scrambled at test, disrupting global configuration. Again, target position was manipulated independently of background scrambling. Despite the fact that all the same objects were present at test as at study, the same position advantage was eliminated when the background objects were scrambled, supporting the Jiang et al. hypothesis.

However, spatial contextual representations preserve more than just the abstract configuration of occupied locations. Hollingworth (2007) used a background binding change manipulation to examine whether spatial contextual representations encode the binding of individual contextual objects to locations (Fig. 5–3). At test, the contextual objects either retained their original positions, or they all traded positions (background binding change). Background binding change preserved the abstract spatial configuration of occupied locations. Thus this manipulation should not have influenced the same-position advantage if abstract spatial configuration constitutes the context for object-position binding (Jiang et al., 2000). Yet, the same-position advantage was practically eliminated with background binding change, demonstrating that spatial contextual representations preserve the binding of contextual objects to locations (i.e., as a set of object files, Hollingworth & Henderson, 2002).

Finally, the spatial contextual representation serving to define object position is maintained in an array-relative reference frame. Translation of the contextual objects did not significantly disrupt the same-position advantage (Hollingworth, 2007). In the two critical conditions: (a) all objects including the target were translated (the array-relative position of the target stayed the same, but its absolute position changed); and (b) all objects except the target were translated (the array-relative position of the target changed, but its absolute position stayed the same). Change-detection performance was reliably higher in the former condition, demonstrating that the target's visual memory representation was bound to a location defined relative to the array configuration.

In summary, larger-scale scene memory appears to be constructed through the binding of local object representations to locations within a spatial representation of the scene layout (Hollingworth, 2007; Hollingworth & Henderson, 2002). This contextual representation is scene-specific, maintains the spatial configuration of object locations, preserves the binding of contextual objects to locations, and codes individual object position in array-relative coordinates. Note that there might be other forms of episodic structure in scene memory, such as direct object-to-object association, but such possibilities have yet to be explored.

5.3.2.3 Brain mechanisms of episodic scene memory

Thus far, we have reviewed behavioral evidence regarding the episodic structure of scene representations. A growing literature examines the brain mechanisms of scene perception and memory, and this work is bridging the gap between our understanding of human visual memory and the large animal literature on spatial memory and environmental representation.

Visual memory representations of structured scenes are primarily maintained in medial temporal brain regions forming the hippocampal complex (for reviews, see Burgess, Maguire, & O'Keefe, 2002; Epstein, 2005; see Chapter 7 of this volume for a comprehensive discussion). Parahippocampal cortex, particularly the parahippocampal gyrus, appears to play a central role in scene perception, recognition, and the viewpoint-dependent (Christou & Bulthoff, 1999; Diwadkar & McNamara, 1997; Simons & Wang, 1998) representation of environmental layout (Epstein, Graham, & Downing, 2003; Epstein & Kanwisher, 1998). The hippocampus proper constructs spatially structured representations of visual environments in an allocentric coordinate system that is suitable for large-scale navigation (Kumaran & Maguire, 2005; Maguire et al., 1998; O'Keefe & Nadel, 1978; Spiers, Burgess, Hartley, Vargha-Khadem, & O'Keefe, 2001).

Higher-level visual memory representations of discrete objects (such as those operational in VSTM and VLTM) are primarily maintained in ventral stream, inferotemporal (IT) brain regions (Logothetis & Sheinberg, 1996; K. Tanaka, 1996; Chapter 6; Chapter 8), coding object form in a manner that is abstracted away from the precise metric structure of early vision. An episodic representation of a visual scene, in which local object information is bound to scene locations, could be produced by simple associative links between scene-specific hippocampal/parahippocampal place codes and IT object representations.

This proposal draws from models of the hippocampus (generated primarily from rodent data) holding that the primary function of the hippocampus is to associate local events and stimuli with particular spatial locations in scene-specific maps (McNaughton et al., 1996; O'Keefe & Nadel, 1978; Redish, 2001; Rolls, 1996). In this view, medial temporal regions maintain multiple maps specific to particular environments and to task goals within those environments (Barnes, Suster, Shen, & McNaughton, 1997; Bostock, Muller, & Kubie, 1991). Hippocampal position representations coding a location within an environment are associated with visual codes for landmarks visible at that location, establishing an episodic environmental representation. If the animal returns to a location where visual landmark information was encoded, place codes are activated for that environmental position. This activation then provides a cue for retrieval of the landmark information associated with that location (Gallistel, 1990; McNaughton et al., 1996).

In rats, spatially selective hippocampal cells coding environmental locations ("place cells") represent the animal's physical location in the environment (O'Keefe & Nadel, 1978). In primates, however, hippocampal and parahippocampal place cells code environmental locations in term of gaze position (for a review, see Rolls, 1999). That is, spatially selective cells in the primate hippocampus and parahippocampal gyrus respond not when the monkey occupies a particular environmental location but when gaze is directed to a particular environmental location (Rolls, Robertson, & Georges-Francois, 1997). Rolls and colleagues have termed these cells *spatial view cells*. The response of spatial view cells generalizes over differences in the absolute position of the monkey in the environment and over differences in viewing direction (Georges-Francois, Rolls, & Robertson, 1999), demonstrating that the underlying spatial representation is allocentric. In addition, the response of some spatial view cells generalizes over changes in the visual surface features present at the fixated location (Robertson, Rolls, & Georges-Francois, 1998), suggesting that these cells code environmental positions rather than local visual features.

The relationship between place cells and gaze position in primates raises a possible means by which position and object information could be bound.

During the viewing of a scene, a spatial representation specific to the particular viewed scene is formed in medial temporal regions. Activation of position representations in the scene map is driven by gaze position; when a location is fixated, spatial view cells coding that scene position are activated. Simultaneously, fixation of the object at that location leads to selective activation of IT representations coding the visual form of that object (Rolls, Aggelopoulos, & Zheng, 2003; Sheinberg & Logothetis, 2001). Because object fixation leads to simultaneous activation of visual object and position codes, the binding of the two can be accomplished through autoassociative mechanisms that have been proposed to support episodic binding in the hippocampus (Marr, 1971; Treves & Rolls, 1994; Chapter 8 of this volume). In short, gaze fixation would establish the correspondence between visual object representations and spatial representations, forming the core of episodic scene memory. This view is broadly consistent with the idea that gaze fixation serves as an indexing mechanism in vision (Ballard et al., 1997).

Support for the general claim that medial temporal regions support object-position binding in scenes comes from evidence that lesions to the hippocampus (Crane & Milner, 2005; Hannula, Tranel, & Cohen, 2006; Olson, Page, Moore, Chatterjee, & Verfaellie, 2006; Parkinson, Murray, & Mishkin, 1988; Pigott & Milner, 1993), to hippocampal output pathways (Gaffan, 1994), and to parahippocampal cortex (Malkova & Mishkin, 2003) lead to specific deficits in learning of and memory for the positions of objects in scenes. In addition, medial temporal damage impairs the learning of associations between individual object locations and spatial context (Chun & Phelps, 1999; Chapter 7). Direct support for medial temporal coding of the association between place cell (spatial view) activity and object memory comes from evidence of a population of neurons that respond to particular combinations of fixated location and object (Rolls, Xiang, & Franco, 2005). In Rolls et al., monkeys were trained to learn both the visual form of objects and their computer screen positions. Neurons in the hippocampus and parahippocampal gyrus were approximately evenly divided between those responding to object form independently of location, those responding to fixated location independently of object form, and those responding to a particular combination of object form and location. Neurons of the last kind encode precisely the type of information necessary to generate spatially organized representations of complex, natural scenes.

5.4 CONCLUSION

When looking upon a natural scene, visual sensory representations are generated across the visual field. If the scene is removed or perceptual processing otherwise interrupted (e.g., across an eye movement), sensory persistence decays very quickly (Averbach & Coriell, 1961; Di Lollo, 1980; Sperling, 1960) and is not integrated from one view of the scene to the next (Henderson & Hollingworth, 2003b; Irwin et al., 1983). However, directing attention to an object allows the formation of a coherent visual representation (Treisman, 1988) and the consolidation of that representation into more stable VSTM

(Averbach & Coriell, 1961; Irwin, 1992; Schmidt et al., 2002), which maintains visual representations abstracted away from precise sensory information (Irwin, 1991; Phillips, 1974). After attention is withdrawn from an object, abstracted visual representations persist (Hollingworth, 2003; Hollingworth & Henderson, 2002), and they accumulate in memory as attention and the eyes are oriented from object-to-object within a scene, supported both by VSTM (for approximately the last two objects attended) and by VLTM (for objects attended earlier) (Hollingworth, 2004). Visual long-term memory then supports the retention of scores of individual object representations over relatively long periods of time (Hollingworth, 2004, 2005c), and LTM for the visual form of entire scenes is highly robust over retention intervals as long as weeks or years (Nickerson, 1968). Visual object representations are stored as part of a larger, episodic representation of a scene (Hollingworth, 2006), which binds objects to scene locations within a spatial–configural representation of that scene (Hollingworth, 2007). Such binding likely depends on medial temporal brain regions known to support episodic memory for complex environments (Burgess et al., 2002; O'Keefe & Nadel, 1978).

ACKNOWLEDGMENTS

Preparation of this chapter was supported by NIH grants R01EY017356 and R03MH65456.

REFERENCES

Aivar, M. P., Hayhoe, M. M., Chizk, C. L., and Mruczek, R. E. B. (2005). Spatial memory and saccadic targeting in a natural task. *Journal of Vision* 5:177–193.

Alba, J., and Hasher, L. (1983). Is memory schematic? *Psychological Bulletin* 93:203–231.

Allen, R. J., Baddeley, A. D., and Hitch, G. J. (2006). Is the binding of visual features in working memory resource-demanding? *Journal of Experimental Psychology-General* 135:298–313.

Angelone, B. L., Levin, D. T., and Simons, D. J. (2003). The relationship between change detection and recognition of centrally attended objects in motion pictures. *Perception* 32:947–962.

Averbach, E., and Coriell, A. S. (1961). Short-term memory in vision. *The Bell System Technical Journal* 40:309–328.

Ballard, D. H., Hayhoe, M. M., and Pelz, J. B. (1995). Memory representations in natural tasks. *Journal of Cognitive Neuroscience* 7:66–80.

Ballard, D. H., Hayhoe, M. M., Pook, P. K., and Rao, R. P. (1997). Deictic codes for the embodiment of cognition. *Behavioral and Brain Sciences* 20:723–767.

Barnes, C. A., Suster, M. S., Shen, J. M., and McNaughton, B. L. (1997). Multistability of cognitive maps in the hippocampus of old rats. *Nature* 388:272–275.

Bartlett, F. C. (1932). *Remembering: An Experimental and Social Study*. Cambridge: Cambridge University Press.

Becker, M. W., and Pashler, H. (2002). Volatile visual representations: Failing to detect changes in recently processed information. *Psychonomic Bulletin and Review* 9:744–750.

Biederman, I., Mezzanotte, R. J., and Rabinowitz, J. C. (1982). Scene Perception: Detecting and judging objects undergoing relational violations. *Cognitive Psychology* 14:143–177.

Bostock, E., Muller, R. U., and Kubie, J. L. (1991). Experience-dependent modifications of hippocampal place cell firing. *Hippocampus* 1:193–205.

Brewer, W. F., and Treyens, J. C. (1981). Role of schemata in memory for places. *Cognitive Psychology* 13:207–230.

Bridgeman, B., Hendry, D., and Stark, L. (1975). Failure to detect displacement of the visual world during saccadic eye movements. *Vision Research* 15:719–722.

Burgess, N., Maguire, E. A., and O'Keefe, J. (2002). The human hippocampus and spatial and episodic memory. *Neuron* 35:625–641.

Castelhano, M. S., and Henderson, J. M. (2005). Incidental visual memory for objects in scenes. *Visual Cognition* 12:1017–1040.

Christou, C. G., and Bulthoff, H. H. (1999). View dependence in scene recognition after active learning. *Memory and Cognition* 27:996–1007.

Chun, M. M. (2003). Scene perception and memory. *Psychology of Learning and Motivation* 42:79–108.

Chun, M. M., and Jiang, Y. H. (2003). Implicit, long-term spatial contextual memory. *Journal of Experimental Psychology: Learning Memory and Cognition* 29:224–234.

Chun, M. M., and Phelps, E. A. (1999). Memory deficits for implicit contextual information in amnesic patients with hippocampal damage. *Nature Neuroscience* 2:844–847.

Chun, M. M., and Potter, M. C. (1995). A two-stage model for multiple target detection in rapid serial visual presentation. *Journal of Experimental Psychology: Human Perception and Performance* 21:109–127.

Cohen, J. (2002). The grand grand illusion illusion. *Journal of Consciousness Studies* 9:141–157.

Coltheart, M. (1980). The persistences of vision. *Philosophical Transactions of the Royal Society of London Series B* 290:269–294.

Crane, J., and Milner, B. (2005). What went where?: Impaired object-location learning in patients with right hippocampal lesions. *Hippocampus* 15:216–231.

Davidson, M. L., Fox, M. J., and Dick, A. O. (1973). Effect of eye movements on backward masking and perceived location. *Perception and Psychophysics* 14:110–116.

Dennett, D. C. (1991). *Consciousness Explained*. Boston: Little, Brown.

Deubel, H., Schneider, W. X., and Bridgeman, B. (1996). Post-saccadic target blanking prevents saccadic suppression of image displacement. *Vision Research* 36:985–996.

Deubel, H., Wolf, W., and Hauske, G. (1982). Corrective saccades: Effect of shifting the saccade goal. *Vision Research* 22:353–364.

Di Lollo, V. (1980). Temporal integration in visual memory. *Journal of Experimental Psychology: General* 109:75–97.

Diwadkar, V. A., and McNamara, T. P. (1997). Viewpoint dependence in scene recognition. *Psychological Science* 8:302–307.

Droll, J. A., Hayhoe, M. M., Triesch, J., and Sullivan, B. T. (2005). Task demands control acquisition and storage of visual information. *Journal of Experimental Psychology: Human Perception and Performance* 31:1416–1438.

Epstein, R. (2005). The cortical basis of visual scene processing. *Visual Cognition* 12:954–978.

Epstein, R., Graham, K. S., and Downing, P. E. (2003). Viewpoint-specific scene representations in human parahippocampal cortex. *Neuron* 37:865–876.

Epstein, R., and Kanwisher, N. (1998). A cortical representation of the local visual environment. *Nature* 392:598–601.

Friedman, A. (1979). Framing pictures: The role of knowledge in automatized encoding and memory for gist. *Journal of Experimental Psychology: General* 108:316–355.

Gaffan, D. (1994). Scene-specific memory for objects: A model of episodic memory impairment in monkeys with fornix transection. *Journal of Cognitive Neuroscience* 6:305–320.

Gajewski, D. A., and Brockmole, J. R. (2006). Feature bindings endure without attention: Evidence from an explicit recall task. *Psychonomic Bulletin and Review* 13:581–587.

Gallistel, C. R. (1990). *The Organization of learning*. Cambridge, MA: MIT Press.

Georges-Francois, P., Rolls, E. T., and Robertson, R. G. (1999). Spatial view cells in the primate hippocampus: Allocentric view not head direction or eye position or place. *Cerebral Cortex* 9:197–212.

Gibson, J. J. (1979). *The Ecological Approach to Visual Perception*. Boston: Houghton Mifflin.

Gordon, R. D. (2004). Attentional allocation during the perception of scenes. *Journal of Experimental Psychology: Human Perception and Performance* 30:760–777.

Gottesman, C. V., and Intraub, H. (2002). Surface construal and the mental representation of scenes. *Journal of Experimental Psychology-Human Perception and Performance* 28:589–599.

Grimes, J. (1996). On the failure to detect changes in scenes across saccades. In *Perception: Vancouver Studies in Cognitive Science, Vol. 5*, ed. K. Akins, 89–110. Oxford, England: Oxford University Press.

Hannula, D. E., Tranel, D., and Cohen, N. J. (2006). The long and the short of it: Relational memory impairments in amnesia, even at short lags. *Journal of Neuroscience* 26:8352–8359.

Hayhoe, M. M. (2000). Vision using routines: A functional account of vision. *Visual Cognition* 7:43–64.

Hayhoe, M. M., Bensinger, D. G., and Ballard, D. H. (1998). Task constraints in visual working memory. *Vision Research* 38:125–137.

Hayhoe, M. M., Shrivastava, A., Mruczek, R., and Pelz, J. B. (2003). Visual memory and motor planning in a natural task. *Journal of Vision* 3:49–63.

Henderson, J. M. (1991). Object identification in context: The visual processing of natural scenes. *Canadian Journal of Psychology* 46:319–341.

Henderson, J. M. (1994). Two representational systems in dynamic visual identification. *Journal of Experimental Psychology: General* 123:410–426.

Henderson, J. M., and Hollingworth, A. (1999). The role of fixation position in detecting scene changes across saccades. *Psychological Science* 10:438–443.

Henderson, J. M., and Hollingworth, A. (2003a). Eye movements and visual memory: Detecting changes to saccade targets in scenes. *Perception and Psychophysics* 65:58–71.

Henderson, J. M., and Hollingworth, A. (2003b). Global transsaccadic change blindness during scene perception. *Psychological Science* 14:493–497.

Henderson, J. M., Weeks, P. A., and Hollingworth, A. (1999). The effects of semantic consistency on eye movements during complex scene viewing. *Journal of Experimental Psychology: Human Perception and Performance* 25:210–228.

Hoffman, J. E., and Subramaniam, B. (1995). The role of visual attention in saccadic eye movements. *Perception and Psychophysics* 57:787–795.

Hollingworth, A. (2003). Failures of retrieval and comparison constrain change detection in natural scenes. *Journal of Experimental Psychology: Human Perception and Performance* 29:388–403.

Hollingworth, A. (2004). Constructing visual representations of natural scenes: The roles of short- and long-term visual memory. *Journal of Experimental Psychology: Human Perception and Performance* 30:519–537.

Hollingworth, A. (2005a). Memory for object position in natural scenes. *Visual Cognition* 12:1003–1016.

Hollingworth, A. (2005b). *Preserved memory for scene brightness following an undetected change.* Annual Meeting of the Vision Sciences Society, Sarasota, FL.

Hollingworth, A. (2005c). The relationship between online visual representation of a scene and long-term scene memory. *Journal of Experimental Psychology: Learning, Memory, and Cognition* 31:396–411.

Hollingworth, A. (2006). Scene and position specificity in visual memory for objects. *Journal of Experimental Psychology: Learning, Memory, and Cognition* 32:58–69.

Hollingworth, A. (2007). Object-position binding in visual memory for natural scenes and object arrays. *Journal of Experimental Psychology: Human Perception and Performance* 33:31–47.

Hollingworth, A. (unpublished data). Memory for visual objects after an undetected change: Evidence against the overwriting hypothesis.

Hollingworth, A., and Henderson, J. M. (1998). Does consistent scene context facilitate object perception? *Journal of Experimental Psychology: General* 127:398–415.

Hollingworth, A., and Henderson, J. M. (2000). Semantic informativeness mediates the detection of changes in natural scenes. *Visual Cognition* 7:213–235.

Hollingworth, A., and Henderson, J. M. (2002). Accurate visual memory for previously attended objects in natural scenes. *Journal of Experimental Psychology: Human Perception and Performance* 28:113–136.

Hollingworth, A., and Henderson, J. M. (2003). Testing a conceptual locus for the inconsistent object change detection advantage in real-world scenes. *Memory and Cognition* 31:930–940.

Hollingworth, A., and Henderson, J. M. (2004). Sustained change blindness to incremental scene rotation: A dissociation between explicit change detection and visual memory. *Perception and Psychophysics* 66:800–807.

Hollingworth, A., Hyun, J. S., and Zhang, W. (2005). The role of visual short-term memory in empty cell localization. *Perception and Psychophysics* 67:1332–1343.

Hollingworth, A., Richard, A. M., & Luck, S. J. (2008). Understanding the function of visual short-term memory: Transsaccadic memory, object correspondence, and gaze correction. *Journal of Experimental Psychology: General, 137,* 163-181

Hollingworth, A., Schrock, G., and Henderson, J. M. (2001). Change detection in the flicker paradigm: The role of fixation position within the scene. *Memory and Cognition* 29:296–304.

Hollingworth, A., Williams, C. C., and Henderson, J. M. (2001). To see and remember: Visually specific information is retained in memory from previously attended objects in natural scenes. *Psychonomic Bulletin and Review* 8:761–768.

Intraub, H. (1997). The representation of visual scenes. *Trends in Cognitive Sciences* 1:217–222.

Intraub, H., and Richardson, M. (1989). Wide-Angle Memories of Close-up Scenes. *Journal of Experimental Psychology-Learning Memory and Cognition* 15:179–187.

Irwin, D. E. (1991). Information integration across saccadic eye movements. *Cognitive Psychology* 23:420–456.

Irwin, D. E. (1992). Memory for position and identity across eye movements. *Journal of Experimental Psychology: Learning, Memory, and Cognition* 18:307–317.

Irwin, D. E., and Andrews, R. (1996). Integration and accumulation of information across saccadic eye movements. In *Attention and Performance XVI: Information Integration in Perception and Communication*, eds. T. Inui and J. L. McClelland, 125–155. Cambridge, MA: MIT Press.

Irwin, D. E., Yantis, S., and Jonides, J. (1983). Evidence against visual integration across saccadic eye movements. *Perception and Psychophysics* 34:35–46.

Irwin, D. E., and Yeomans, J. M. (1986). Sensory registration and informational persistence. *Journal of Experimental Psychology: Human Perception and Performance* 12:343–360.

Irwin, D. E., and Zelinsky, G. J. (2002). Eye movements and scene perception: Memory for things observed. *Perception and Psychophysics* 64:882–895.

Jiang, Y. (2004). Time window from visual images to visual short-term memory: Consolidation or integration? *Experimental Psychology* 51:45–51.

Jiang, Y., Olson, I. R., and Chun, M. M. (2000). Organization of visual short-term memory. *Journal of Experimental Psychology: Learning, Memory, and Cognition* 26:683–702.

Johnson, J. S., Hollingworth, A., & Luck, S. J. (2008). The role of attention in the maintenance of feature bindings in visual short-term memory. *Journal of Experimental Psychology: Human Perception and Performance, 34*, 41-55. Jonides, J., Irwin, D. E., and Yantis, S. (1982). Integrating visual information from successive fixations. *Science* 215:192–194.

Kahneman, D., Treisman, A., and Gibbs, B. J. (1992). The reviewing of object files: Object-specific integration of information. *Cognitive Psychology* 24:175–219.

Kapoula, Z. (1985). Evidence for a range effect in the saccadic system. *Vision Research* 25:1155–1157.

Klein, R. M., and MacInnes, W. J. (1999). Inhibition of return is a foraging facilitator in visual search. *Psychological Science* 10:346–352.

Kumaran, D., and Maguire, E. A. (2005). The human hippocampus: Cognitive maps or relational memory? *Journal of Neuroscience* 25:7254–7259.

Land, M. F., and Hayhoe, M. (2001). In what ways do eye movements contribute to everyday activities? *Vision Research* 41:3559–3565.

Land, M. F., Mennie, N., and Rusted, J. (1999). Eye movements and the roles of vision in activities of daily living: Making a cup of tea. *Perception* 28:1311–1328.

Levin, D. T., and Simons, D. J. (1997). Failure to detect changes to attended objects in motion pictures. *Psychonomic Bulletin and Review* 4:501–506.

Levin, D. T., Simons, D. J., Angelone, B. L., and Chabris, C. F. (2002). Memory for centrally attended changing objects in an incidental real-world change detection paradigm. *British Journal of Psychology* 93:289–302.

Loftus, E. F., Miller, D. G., and Burns, H. J. (1978). Semantic integration of verbal information into a visual memory. *Journal of Experimental Psychology: Human Learning and Memory* 4:19–31.

Logothetis, N. K., and Sheinberg, D. L. (1996). Visual object recognition. *Annual Review of Neuroscience* 19:577–621.

Luck, S. J., and Vogel, E. K. (1997). The capacity of visual working memory for features and conjunctions. *Nature* 390:279–281.

Maguire, E. A., Burgess, N., Donnett, J. G., Frackowiak, R. S. J., Frith, C. D., and O'Keefe, J. (1998). Knowing where and getting there: A human navigation network. *Science* 280:921–924.

Malkova, L., and Mishkin, M. (2003). One-trial memory for object-place associations after separate lesions of hippocampus and posterior parahippocampal region in the monkey. *Journal of Neuroscience* 23:1956–1965.

Mandler, J. M., and Parker, R. E. (1976). Memory for descriptive and spatial information in complex pictures. *Journal of Experimental Psychology: Human Learning and Memory* 2:38–48.

Mandler, J. M., and Ritchey, G. H. (1977). Long-term memory for pictures. *Journal of Experimental Psychology: Human Learning and Memory* 3:386–396.

Marr, D. (1971). Simple memory: A theory for archicortex. *Philosophical Transactions of the Royal Society of London B* 262:23–81.

Matin, E. (1974). Saccadic suppression: A review and an analysis. *Psychological Bulletin* 81:899–917.

McCloskey, M., and Zaragoza, M. (1985). Misleading postevent information and memory for events: Arguments and evidence against memory impairment hypothesis. *Journal of Experimental Psychology: General* 114:1–16.

McConkie, G. W., and Currie, C. B. (1996). Visual stability across saccades while viewing complex pictures. *Journal of Experimental Psychology: Human Perception and Performance* 22:563–581.

McConkie GW & Rayner K (1975) The span of the effective stimulus during a fixation in reading, *Perception & Psychophysics*, 17, 578–86.

McNaughton, B. L., Barnes, C. A., Gerrard, J. L., Gothard, K., Jung, M. W., Knierim, J. J., et al. (1996). Deciphering the hippocampal polyglot: The hippocampus as a path integration system. *Journal of Experimental Biology* 199:173–185.

Mitroff, S. R., Simons, D. J., and Levin, D. T. (2004). Nothing compares 2 views: Change blindness can occur despite preserved access to the changed information. *Perception and Psychophysics* 66:1268–1281.

Müller, H. J., and Von Mühlenen, A. (2000). Probing distractor inhibition in visual search: Inhibition of return. *Journal of Experimental Psychology: Human Perception and Performance* 26:1591–1605.

Murdock, B. B. (1962). The serial position effect of free recall. *Journal of Experimental Psychology* 64:482–488.

Nelson, W. W., and Loftus, G. R. (1980). The functional visual field during picture viewing. *Journal of Experimental Psychology: Human Learning and Memory* 6:391–399.

Nickerson, R. S. (1965). Short-term memory for complex meaningful visual configurations: A demonstration of capacity. *Canadian Journal of Psychology* 19:155–160.

Nickerson, R. S. (1968). A note on long-term recognition memory for pictorial material. *Psychonomic Science* 11:58.

O'Keefe, J., and Nadel, L. (1978). *The Hippocampus as a Cognitive Map.* Oxford, U.K.: Clarendon.

O'Regan, J. K. (1992). Solving the "real" mysteries of visual perception: The world as an outside memory. *Canadian Journal of Psychology* 46:461–488.

O'Regan, J. K., Deubel, H., Clark, J. J., and Rensink, R. A. (2000). Picture changes during blinks: Looking without seeing and seeing without looking. *Visual Cognition* 7:191–211.

O'Regan, J. K., and Lévy-Schoen, A. (1983). Integrating visual information from successive fixations: Does trans-saccadic fusion exist? *Vision Research* 23:765–768.

O'Regan, J. K., and Noë, A. (2001). A sensorimotor account of vision and visual consciousness. *Behavioral and Brain Sciences* 24:939–1011.

Olson, I. R., Page, K., Moore, K. S., Chatterjee, A., and Verfaellie, M. (2006). Working memory for conjunctions relies on the medial temporal lobe. *Journal of Neuroscience* 26:4596–4601.

Palmer, S. E. (1999). *Vision Science: Photons to Phenomenology.* Cambridge, MA: MIT Press.

Parkinson, J. K., Murray, E. A., and Mishkin, M. (1988). A selective mnemonic role for the hippocampus in monkeys: Memory for the location of objects. *Journal of Neuroscience* 8:4159–4167.

Pashler, H. (1988). Familiarity and the detection of change in visual displays. *Perception and Psychophysics* 44:369–378.

Pedzek, K., Whetstone, T., Reynolds, K., Askari, N., and Dougherty, T. (1989). Memory for real-world scenes: The role of consistency with schema expectations. *Journal of Experimental Psychology: Learning, Memory, and Cognition* 15:587–595.

Phillips, W. A. (1974). On the distinction between sensory storage and short-term visual memory. *Perception and Psychophysics* 16:283–290.

Phillips, W. A., and Christie, D. F. M. (1977). Components of visual memory. *Quarterly Journal of Experimental Psychology* 29:117–133.

Pigott, S., and Milner, B. (1993). Memory for different aspects of complex visual scenes after unilateral temporal- or frontal-lobe resection. *Neuropsychologia* 31:1–15.

Potter, M. C., Staub, A., and O'Connor, D. H. (2004). Pictorial and conceptual representation of glimpsed pictures. *Journal of Experimental Psychology: Human Perception and Performance* 30:478–489.

Rayner, K., and Pollatsek, A. (1983). Is visual information integrated across saccades? *Perception and Psychophysics* 34:39–48.

Redish, A. D. (2001). The hippocampal debate: Are we asking the right questions? *Behavioural Brain Research* 127:81–98.

Rensink, R. A. (2000). The dynamic representation of scenes. *Visual Cognition* 7:17–42.

Rensink, R. A. (2002). Change detection. *Annual Review of Psychology* 53:245–277.

Rensink, R. A., O'Regan, J. K., and Clark, J. J. (1997). To see or not to see: The need for attention to perceive changes in scenes. *Psychological Science* 8:368–373.

Rieser, J. J. (1989). Access to knowledge of spatial structure at novel points of observation. *Journal of Experimental Psychology: Learning, Memory, and Cognition* 15:1157–1165.

Robertson, R. G., Rolls, E. T., and Georges-Francois, P. (1998). Spatial view cells in the primate hippocampus: Effects of removal of view details. *Journal of Neurophysiology* 79:1145–1156.

Rolls, E. T. (1996). A theory of hippocampal function in memory. *Hippocampus* 6:601–620.

Rolls, E. T. (1999). Spatial view cells and the representation of place in the primate hippocampus. *Hippocampus* 9:467–480.

Rolls, E. T., Aggelopoulos, N. C., and Zheng, F. S. (2003). The receptive fields of inferior temporal cortex neurons in natural scenes. *Journal of Neuroscience* 23:339–348.

Rolls, E. T., Robertson, R. G., and Georges-Francois, P. (1997). Spatial view cells in the primate hippocampus. *European Journal of Neuroscience* 9:1789–1794.

Rolls, E. T., Xiang, J. Z., and Franco, L. (2005). Object, space, and object-space representations in the primate hippocampus. *Journal of Neurophysiology* 94:833–844.

Ryan, J. D., Althoff, R. R., Whitlow, S., and Cohen, N. J. (2000). Amnesia is a deficit in relational memory. *Psychological Science* 8:368–373.

Schmidt, B. K., Vogel, E. K., Woodman, G. F., and Luck, S. J. (2002). Voluntary and automatic attentional control of visual working memory. *Perception and Psychophysics* 64:754–763.

Scholl, B. J. (2000). Attenuated change blindness for exogenously attended items in a flicker paradigm. *Visual Cognition* 7:377–396.

Sheinberg, D. L., and Logothetis, N. K. (2001). Noticing familiar objects in real world scenes: The role of temporal cortical neurons in natural vision. *Journal of Neuroscience* 21:1340–1350.

Shelton, A. L., and McNamara, T. P. (2001). Systems of spatial reference in human memory. *Cognitive Psychology* 43:274–310.

Shepard, R. N. (1967). Recognition memory for words, sentences, and pictures. *Journal of Verbal Learning and Verbal Behavior* 6:156–163.

Simons, D. J. (1996). In sight, out of mind: When object representations fail. *Psychological Science* 7:301–305.

Simons, D. J. (2000). Current approaches to change blindness. *Visual Cognition* 7:1–15.

Simons, D. J., Chabris, C. F., Schnur, T., and Levin, D. T. (2002). Evidence for preserved representations in change blindness. *Consciousness and Cognition* 11:78–97.

Simons, D. J., Franconeri, S. L., and Reimer, R. L. (2000). Change blindness in the absence of a visual disruption. *Perception* 29:1143–1154.

Simons, D. J., and Levin, D. T. (1997). Change blindness. *Trends in Cognitive Sciences* 1:261–267.

Simons, D. J., and Levin, D. T. (1998). Failure to detect changes to people during a real-world interaction. *Psychonomic Bulletin and Review* 5:644–649.

Simons, D. J., and Rensink, R. A. (2005). Change blindness: Past, present, and future. *Trends in Cognitive Sciences* 9:16–20.

Simons, D. J., and Wang, R. F. (1998). Perceiving real-world viewpoint changes. *Psychological Science* 9:315–320.

Sperling, G. (1960). The information available in brief visual presentations. *Psychological Monographs* 74;(11): Whole of No. 498.

Spiers, H. J., Burgess, N., Hartley, T., Vargha-Khadem, F., and O'Keefe, J. (2001). Bilateral hippocampal pathology impairs topographical and episodic memory but not visual pattern matching. *Hippocampus* 11:715–725.

Standing, L. (1973). Learning 10,000 pictures. *Quarterly Journal of Experimental Psychology* 25:207–222.

Standing, L., Conezio, J., and Haber, R. N. (1970). Perception and memory for pictures: Single-trial learning of 2500 visual stimuli. *Psychonomic Science* 19:73–74.

Takeda, Y., and Yagi, A. (2000). Inhibitory tagging in visual search can be found if search stimuli remain visible. *Perception and Psychophysics* 62:927–934.

Tanaka, J. W., and Farah, M. J. (1993). Parts and wholes in face recognition. *Quarterly Journal of Experimental Psychology*, 46A, 225–245.

Tanaka, K. (1996). Inferotemporal cortex and object vision. *Annual Review of Neuroscience* 19:109–139.

Thornton, I. M., and Fernandez-Duque, D. (2002). Converging evidence for the detection of change without awareness. In *The Brain's Eyes: Neurobiological and Clinical Aspects of Occulomotor Research*, eds. D. P. Munoz, W. Heide, R. Radach and J. Hyönä, 99–118). Amsterdam: Elsevier.

Treisman, A. (1988). Features and objects: The fourteenth Bartlett memorial lecture. *Quarterly Journal of Experimental Psychology* 40A:201–237.

Treisman, A., and Gelade, G. (1980). A feature-integration theory of attention. *Cognitive Psychology* 12:97–136.

Treves, A., and Rolls, E. T. (1994). Computational analysis of the role of the hippocampus in memory. *Hippocampus* 4:374–391.

Triesch, J., Ballard, D. H., Hayhoe, M. M., and Sullivan, B. T. (2003). What you see is what you need. *Journal of Vision* 3:86–94.

Varakin, D. A., Levin, D. T., and Collins, K. M. (2007). Both comparison and representation failures cause real-world change blindness. *Perception* 36:737–749.

Vogel, E. K., Woodman, G. E., and Luck, S. J. (2001). Storage of features, conjunctions, and objects in visual working memory. *Journal of Experimental Psychology: Human Perception and Performance* 27 92–114.

Wheeler, M. E., and Treisman, A. M. (2002). Binding in short-term visual memory. *Journal of Experimental Psychology: General* 131:4864.

Williams, C. C., Henderson, J. M., and Zacks, R. T. (2005). Incidental visual memory for targets and distractors in visual search. *Perception and Psychophysics* 67:816–827.

Yantis, S., and Jonides, J. (1984). Abrupt visual onsets and selective attention: Evidence from visual search. *Journal of Experimental Psychology: Human Perception and Performance* 10:601–621.

Yarbus, A. L. (1967). *Eye Movements and Vision*. New York: Plenum Press.

Zelinsky, G. J., and Loschky, L. C. (2005). Eye movements serialize memory for objects in scenes. *Perception and Psychophysics* 67:676–690.

Chapter 6

Visual Object Perception and Long-term Memory

Thomas J. Palmeri
Vanderbilt University

Michael J. Tarr
Brown University

> . . . they took twenty-seven eight-by-ten color glossy photographs with circles and arrows and a paragraph on the back of each one explaining what each one was to be used as evidence against us.
>
> —from *Alice's Restaurant,* by Arlo Guthrie

6.1 INTRODUCTION

The late cognitive psychologist and memory theorist, Robert G. Crowder (MJT's colleague for 6 years), was fond of saying "memory *is* perception." What he meant was that memory is not a box in which things—objects, meanings, etc.—are stored. To Bob, memory was intrinsic to and a consequence of information processing, whether it be perceptual, linguistic, or cognitive in nature. In this context, it seems natural that our chapter discusses both object perception and object memory. At the same time, we acknowledge that in classic information processing flowcharts, as well as in the organization of most introductory textbooks, object perception precedes sensory or iconic memory (Chapter 2), which precedes short-term or working memory (Chapter 3), which precedes long-term memory (e.g., Atkinson & Shiffrin, 1968). By such accounts, visual perception is a modular, encapsulated *input* system, whereas memory is a cognitive box in which you put information (c.f., Fodor, 1983). But, as we shall see, contemporary research has demonstrated far closer links between object perception and object memory than anticipated by classic approaches to perception and cognition (Palmeri & Gauthier, 2004). Indeed, we are of the same mind as Bob: Drawing a clear demarcation between perception and memory is misguided.

163

We begin with a discussion of how objects are perceived and come to be represented over experience. And we describe the perceptual nature of the particular information stored in long-term memory (LTM) that allows us to recognize, identify, categorize, and perform perceptual skills on visual objects. These topics forge natural links to other chapters in this volume. To what extent do visual working memory and LTM have similar representational formats (Chapter 3)? How closely tied is visual working memory to visual LTM (Chapter 3)? What are the relationships between objects and scenes (Chapter 5)? What are the relationships between visual memory for objects and mental imagery (Chapter 9)?

Two themes weave their way throughout this chapter. One theme concerns the role of abstraction in perception and memory. Our everyday experience suggests that familiar objects can be recognized effortlessly under dramatically different viewing conditions, including changes in viewing position, object pose, and object configuration. According to this intuition, vision abstracts an invariant object representation that is removed from the particulars of specific experiences with that object. Everyday experience also suggests that our conceptual knowledge about objects is abstract. According to this intuition, although our experiences are specific, our knowledge is abstracted from those experiences. The ability to abstract from particular experiences is clear and is a hallmark of human perception and cognition. But this ability to abstract does not necessarily imply that object representations and object knowledge are themselves abstract in nature or that these abstractions are themselves amodal (Barsalou, 1999; Barsalou, Simmons, Barbey, & Wilson, 2003).

The second theme is how to carve up perception and memory into functional systems. A basic modus operandi of cognitive science is to "carve things up at the joints" (c.f., Fodor, 1983). This issue emerges in discussions of how to parcelize working memory (Chapter 3). And, in the context of object perception and object memory, are there domain-specific, informationally encapsulated subsystems for recognizing certain kinds of objects, remembering certain qualities about objects, or performing certain kinds of tasks on objects (Fig. 6–1)? These questions are particularly germane when interrelating theory and behavior with evidence from neurophysiology, functional brain imaging, and neuropsychological studies (Chapters 8 and 9).

6.2 VISUAL OBJECT PERCEPTION

How do we know that an object is the same object we have seen before? Or, at least, that it is of the same kind we have seen before? At first pass, this appears to be a trivial problem. One of us (TJP) can remember a meeting many years ago with an Associate Dean soon after being hired to talk about future research plans. The Dean simply could not understand why studying how people recognize objects could ever be a viable research problem. What could be simpler, he said. You just open your eyes and you see what's there [or as Terry Pratchett said in *Men at Arms* (1993): "How? He recognized him, of course. That's how you know who people are. You look at them and you say . . . that's him.

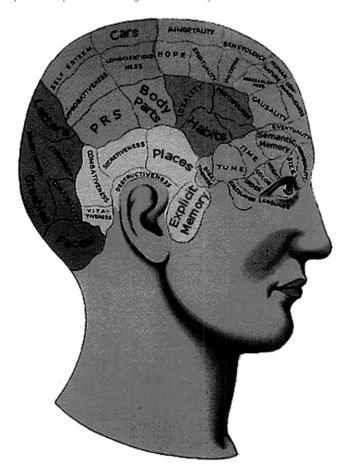

Figure 6–1. Phrenologists assumed that the mind was composed of numerous distinct innate faculties (secretiveness, benevolence, conjugality, self-esteem) and that each of these faculties had a unique location in the brain. Some contemporary accounts of brain organization localize function according to particular kinds of objects (faces, places, body parts) and particular kinds of memory (explicit memory, semantic memory, habits). Although some have rejected localization accounts entirely as a new form of phrenology (Uttal, 2001), we instead argue that localization of function should be characterized in terms of the representations and processes underlying the computational mechanisms of visual cognition.

That's called re-cog-nit-ion."]. That we all share such naïve intuitions belies the tremendous computational challenges facing our visual system with every glance of the world around us and ignores the fact that about one-half of our cortex is related to vision. The dynamic, ever-changing world conspires to present a dramatically different stimulus to our eyes even though the very same physical object may be present in front of us. Not only do we overcome such variation, but our perception of the world appears stable. Three-dimensional objects seem stable as we move around, as objects move around, and as the lighting changes (Fig. 6–2). But how does the visual system allow us to perceive this stability when the two-dimensional images falling on our retinae are changing so dramatically?

Answers to these questions are rooted in our visual memory for objects; that is, how they are represented with respect to such variation. This is true regardless of which form memory takes: I can ask you whether you saw this particular object recently (working memory), whether you have ever seen this object before (recognition memory), what category this object belongs to (classification), or to do something with an object (procedural task). All of these tasks require you to compare a representation of the perceived input with a representation encoded in memory. Classic approaches to cognitive science have often assumed that this comparison is amodal, and some contemporary approaches assume significant abstraction from any previous experience. Even so, understanding visual memory for objects requires understanding not only the representations and processes underlying those memories, but also understanding the inputs to memory—the perceptual representations. At the same time, more contemporary theories of visual memory assume that this comparison— the process of object recognition—is inherently perceptual. That is, visual memories for objects are part and parcel of the perception of those same objects, and object recognition is accomplished by comparing two *perceptual* representations.

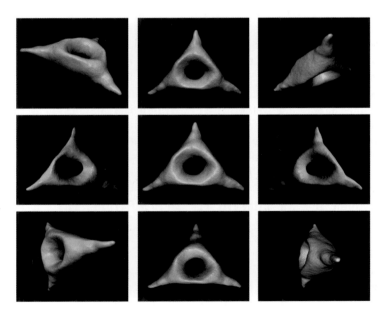

Figure 6–2. This figure illustrates the dramatic variability in viewed images of the same object when subjected to rotation along various axes and changes in lighting direction.

Under this view, the nature of the perceptual representations of objects created by the visual system place strong constraints on the nature of representations for objects in visual memory. Logically, memory representations abstracted from visual experience can be no less abstract than the visual representations derived from those visual experiences. In other words, if high-level visual representations have normalized away many of the perceptual details of visual experience, then memory representations will be void of those perceptual details as well. Of course, the converse need not be true: If visual representations retain some details, then memory representations might still be more abstract, and need not reflect those perceptual details. Such is the more standard view within both the cognitive and high-level vision communities (Biederman, 1987). In contrast, we propose that memory representations of objects do indeed retain perceptual details (see Chapter 5). And, in fact, many of those detailed memory representations are the very representations that underlie visual object perception itself.

6.3 THE PROBLEM

Very young children are fond of pointing to two similar objects and declaring "same thing!" So-called *basic-level* recognition involves categorizing visually similar yet distinct objects as members of the same class. Thus, one form of invariance requires our visual systems to perform a many-to-one mapping between individual exemplars and object categories. At the same time, individual exemplars of three-dimensional objects rarely appear the same from one moment to the next. Variation in the two-dimensional images falling on our retinae arises from almost any change in viewing conditions, including changes in position, object pose, lighting, or object configuration. We never really see the same object, or at least the same retinal image of an object, twice. This form of invariance requires our visual systems to perform a many-to-one mapping between individual *views* of objects and their unique identities.

Almost all solutions to the problem of vision begin by generally characterizing visual processing as a form of dimensionality reduction. The retinal representation has extremely high dimensionality in that each of the 120 million or so photoreceptors can independently encode a different (albeit highly local) aspect of the visual scene. The visual system transforms this high-dimensional stimulus representation into a low-dimensional representation (at least relative to the dimensionality of the retinal stimulation) that is used to recognize or categorize objects. Different theories propose different solutions to the problem of creating a low-dimensional object representation. Theories differ rather markedly in the form of visual representation and, in particular, how great a dimensionality reduction is assumed. In turn, such assumptions themselves are based on the assumptions each theory makes about the goals of vision.

6.3.1 Structural-description Theories

One early and influential class of models assumed that the fundamental goal of vision was to *reconstruct* the three-dimensional structure of objects and their spatial relationships (Marr & Nishihara, 1978). The appeal of such an approach is that many sources of variance are "partialed out" as a consequence of the reconstruction process. For example, different images arising from changes in lighting are mapped into a single shape, and different images arising from changes in viewpoint are mapped into a single three-dimensional object representation. This same reconstruction process achieves theoretically optimal dimensionality reduction: mapping the high-dimensional image array arriving at our eyes into a low-dimensional scene composed of objects and surfaces. One of the most intuitive proposals for constructing such representations, originally put forth by Marr and Nishihara (1978) and elaborated by Biederman (1987), assumes that every given object can be described in terms of generic three-dimensional components ("primitives") and their spatial relationships. The key idea is that the recovered three-dimensional *structural description* will be invariant over both class variation and viewing conditions, thereby directly addressing the twin challenges facing vision. That is, different views of an object *and* different exemplars within an object class will all map to the same configuration of three-dimensional primitives. This approach assumes the primary goal of vision is basic-level recognition without respect to image characteristics arising from lighting, viewpoint, and other variables. In this context, structural-description models—if achievable—are near-optimal.

Beyond the popularization of the study of object recognition, Biederman's contribution was to realize that structural-description models are far more likely to succeed if the mapping from images to primitives is precisely defined. Marr and Nishihara assumed an unrealized computational process that relied on dividing an object into parts, finding the major axis of each part, and, finally, deriving a cross-section capturing the three-dimensional appearance of a part with respect to its axis (although this is somewhat of an oversimplification, it serves to illustrate the basic principles of their theory). For, example, a three-dimensional cylinder might be described as a straight axis with a circular cross-section. This method for describing object parts leaves a great deal to the imagination: How are axes found, and how is the cross-section derived? How well does this description generalize from one exemplar to another? How consistent is this process over image variation? The concern is that, although the intent is dimensionality reduction, the actual mapping may be inefficient, with slight variations in axes or cross-sections leading to different representations.

To address such concerns, Biederman (1987) based his recognition-by-components (RBC) theory on a small set of *qualitative* three-dimensional primitives known as "Geons" (Fig. 6–3). Two innovations are included in RBC. First, primitives are recovered by attending to configurations of "viewpoint invariant properties" in the two-dimensional image. For example, a brick (one type of Geon) might be inferred when one encounters two sets of three parallel lines, several L junctions, several arrow junctions, and a Y junction (Fig. 6–4). Notice that this description avoids quantitative specifics about object parts: Many different brick-like parts from many different viewpoints will exhibit this configuration of image features and be reconstructed simply as a Geon brick in RBC's vocabulary (Fig. 6–4). Second, the entire repertoire of Geons numbers

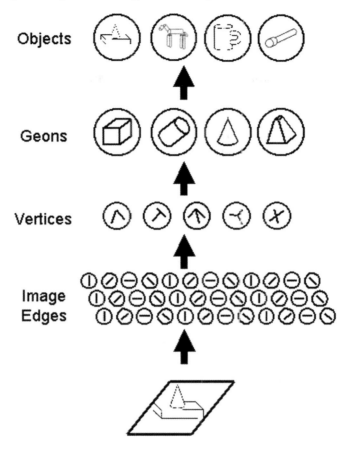

Figure 6–3. Recognition-by-components (Biederman, 1987; Hummel & Biederman, 1992) assumes that a retinal image is initially described in terms of its edges. A variety of nonaccidental primitive features are extracted from this edge description, such as L junctions, Y junctions, and other properties. Combinations of various viewpoint invariant primitives signal the presence of one of the small number of geometric icons (Geons). Viewpoint invariant object recognition involves recognizing the particular combination and relative configuration of the viewpoint-invariant Geon representations extracted from a complex object.

about 35 distinct primitives. Biederman's thesis is that any basic-level, visually defined object category may be uniquely represented by a small subset of these primitives in a particular spatial configuration. For example, a wide variety of birds are made up of roughly the same parts—head, body, wings, etc.—the assumption being that, across different birds (the exception being highly visually dissimilar birds such as penguins), the image projections of these parts will yield the same Geons in the same Geon configuration, that is, a single visual representation for many different birds. Thus, RBC provides a more satisfying

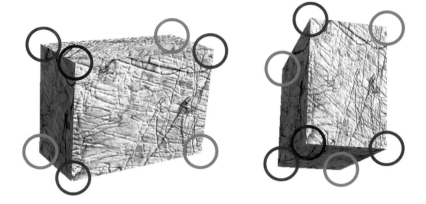

Figure 6–4. Illustration of various primitives that could be extracted from a three-dimensional brick as seen from two different viewpoints, including L junctions, arrow junctions, and Y junctions.

(less filling) approach to structural-description models: The inferential perception mechanisms for reconstruction are well-specified, and the mapping from high-to-low dimensionality is inherent in the end representation.

One of the most salient characteristics of structural-description models is their invariance over image variation. In particular, it is often assumed that changes in three-dimensional viewing position provide one of the strongest tests of theories of object recognition. Structural-description models, and RBC in particular, posit viewpoint invariance. That is, the same representation is derived, irrespective of prior experience, over a wide range of viewing conditions (although with opaque objects different configurations of Geons may be visible across large changes in viewpoint). The behavioral implication of this is that recognition performance should be independent of the particular viewpoint from which the object is seen (Biederman & Gerhardstein, 1993). This prediction is also consistent with our intuitions: Our recognition of familiar objects from unfamiliar viewpoints feels effortless.

At the same time, the prediction of viewpoint invariance seems at odds with the idea that we do remember a great deal of what we see, including the particular appearance of individual objects from specific vantage points. Indeed, a classic study in cognitive science demonstrated that our memories for objects are better at "canonical" viewpoints as compared to others (Palmer, Rosch, & Chase, 1981). If we have learned nothing over the past half century, it is that we should not always trust our conscious intuitions: What seems effortless may actually be an effortful, albeit unconscious, process. For the past 15 years or so, something of a cottage industry has arisen for testing these assumptions. More specifically, many different labs have attempted to devise psychophysical tests of the viewpoint-invariance assumption assessing, when, if ever, objects are recognized in a viewpoint-invariant manner (e.g., with equivalent error rates and response times for both familiar and unfamiliar views of an object (Bülthoff & Edelman, 1992; Humphrey & Khan, 1992; Jolicoeur, 1985; Lawson & Humphreys, 1996; Poggio & Edelman, 1990; Tarr, 1995; Tarr et al., 1998; Tarr & Pinker, 1989). The conclusion is . . . it depends. Certainly, there are limited conditions under which viewpoint invariance is achieved immediately (Biederman & Gerhardstein, 1993; Tarr & Bülthoff, 1998; Tarr, Kersten, & Bülthoff, 1998). However, the vast majority of the time, viewpoint invariance is only attainable with experience. More specifically, numerous studies have found that if observers learn to recognize novel objects from specific viewpoints, they are both faster and more accurate at recognizing these same objects from those familiar viewpoints relative to unfamiliar viewpoints (Bülthoff & Edelman, 1992; Tarr, 1995; Tarr & Pinker, 1989). Recognition performance at unfamiliar viewpoints is systematically related to those views that are familiar, with observers taking progressively more time and being progressively less accurate as the distance between the unfamiliar and the familiar increases. Consequently, viewpoint invariance seems to be achieved by learning about the appearance of objects from multiple viewpoints, not by deriving structural descriptions. Human object recognition seems to rely on multiple *views*, where each view encodes the appearance of an object under specific viewing conditions, including viewpoint, pose, configuration, and lighting (Tarr, Kersten, & Bülthoff, 1998), and a collection of such views constitutes the long-term visual representation of a given object.

6.3.2 Image-based Theories

Over the past decade, image-based theories have become popular as an alternative to structural-description models. These theories are based in part on the already-mentioned empirical findings regarding viewpoint invariance and in part on different assumptions regarding the goals of vision (Edelman, 1999; Shepard, 1994). Rather than assuming that we reconstruct the three-dimensional world, image-based approaches typically stress generalization from past to present experience (Shepard, 1994). Consider that we are highly unlikely to ever experience the same situation twice. Because similar objects often give rise to similar consequences, survival demands that we recognize these similarities (Shepard, 1987). One possible solution is for visual perception to create a faithful representation of each object that preserves its shape and three-dimensional structure (Marr, 1982). Similar objects should have similar or, as in the case of RBC, identical, mental representations. But an alternative solution is to create representations that preserve the similarity structure between objects without necessarily representing three-dimensional object structure explicitly (Edelman, 1997, 1999). As mentioned, image-based theories assume that objects are represented in terms of their similarity to collections of views that are instantiated in memory. Physically similar objects in the world, viewed under similar conditions, will all be similar to the same sets of views, allowing for generalization to occur, without any explicit representation of three-dimensional shape. At least for purposes of object recognition, representation of three-dimensional shape may not be necessary.

Particularly in the context of a volume on visual memory, we cannot under-state one fundamental difference between structural-description and image-based theories. Structural-description theories assume a fixed processing architecture and a fixed set of primitives that construct object representations, irrespective of visual experience; particular configurations of primitives (say Geons) must be learned in order to categorize birds from dogs, but the primi-tives themselves (say, Geons) are not shaped by experience. By contrast, image-based theories assume that visual experience plays a significant role in shaping our visual behavior throughout a lifetime. Stable object perception is achieved by deploying our astonishing capacities for remembering particular experi-ences with particular objects under particular viewing conditions. We do encode a great deal of what we see as it originally appears. Object perception *is* visual memory.

But if we represent three-dimensional objects as collections of specific views, how do we manage to attain view invariance? One clue may be found in the systematic pattern of performance seen for the recognition of familiar objects in unfamiliar viewpoints. According to one view (Tarr & Pinker, 1989), this pattern is a consequence of mental rotation (Shepard & Metzler, 1971) or a continuous alignment process (Ullman, 1989) to transform unfamiliar view-points to familiar views in visual memory, with familiar viewpoints being rec-ognized without the need for any transformation. The strongest evidence favoring this interpretation is the nearly identical linear reaction time pattern across viewpoint obtained for the same objects in naming and left- and right-handedness discrimination tasks (Tarr & Pinker, 1989). However, in an exam-ple of how neuroimaging can inform us regarding cognitive processes, Gauthier et al. (2002) found that entirely different brain systems exhibited viewpoint-dependent activity for recognition tasks and mental rotation tasks. Consistent with current thinking on the "division of labor" in the primate visual system (Goodale & Milner, 1992), the recognition of objects in unfamiliar viewpoints preferentially recruited the fusiform region along the ventral pathway, whereas handedness discriminations recruited the superior parietal lobe along the dorsal pathway (Gauthier et al., 2002). Thus, the computational mechanism underlying viewpoint-dependent recognition behavior seems to be based on "evidence accumulation" across neural subunits coding for different features of the object (e.g., Perret, Oram, & Ashbridge, 1998) and not, as suggested by Tarr and Pinker (1989), on the continuous transformation process of mental rota-tion (assumed to be isomorphic with physical rotations).

View invariance might be achieved by generalizing according to the similar-ity relationships between perceptual representations and stored views, without a need for any explicit image transformation (Poggio & Edelman, 1990; Riesenhuber & Poggio, 1999, 2002); see Figure 6–5 for one example. Indeed, the predictions of image-based models are consistent with the patterns of interpo-lation between learned views and limited extrapolation beyond learned views seen experimentally (Bülthoff & Edelman, 1992; Edelman & Bülthoff, 1992). One of the appealing aspects of using similarity as a means to invariance is that the same mechanisms can account for how we generalize across both viewing

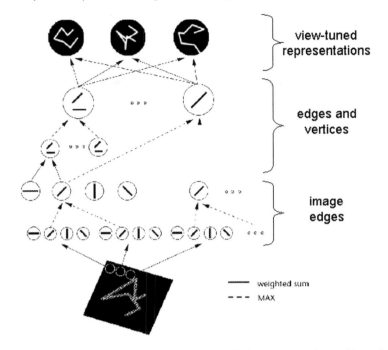

Figure 6–5. Sketch of one image-based model of object recognition. A hierarchy of representational layers consisting of weighted sum and max integration rules achieves representations that are scale- and translation-invariant. Objects are ultimately represented according to their similarity to learned view-tuned representations. Adapted with permission from Riesenhuber & Poggio, 1999, 2000.

and category variation. Specifically, invariance over viewing conditions can be achieved by encoding multiple views of *individual* objects. Invariance over object shape can be achieved by encoding multiple views of *multiple* objects. Both statements distill down to a memory-based explanation in which we remember a great deal about what we see. Thus, given a sufficient number of views per an object or class, viewpoint-invariant recognition is possible (Poggio & Edelman, 1990). Likewise, given a sufficient number of exemplars per a category, object categorization, even for new exemplars, is possible, and entirely novel objects can be represented in a distributed fashion according to their similarity to a relatively small number of views of known objects (Edelman, 1999).

At the same time, this memory-based account seems to miss a fundamental fact about human vision: We are incredibly good at generalizing from a *small number* of examples. Thus, exposure to a single view of an object or a single exemplar of a category is often sufficient to allow us to recognize that object across many different sources of variance, including identifying novel members of that category. Although some of this "heavy lifting" might be accomplished through view-based mechanisms, some forms of generalization also appear to require structural models (e.g., articulation; Barenholtz & Tarr, submitted). So, is the structural-description account right after all? In some sense yes.[1] An image-based account relying on *undifferentiated*, template-like representations would have difficulty generalizing across many types of image variation (Hummel, 1998). In contrast, structural-description models, including those proposed by Biederman and others, can readily generalize across both viewing conditions and members of a class. The caveat here is that this is true for *any* model relying on compositional structure, including models that use image-based features (e.g., Zhang & Cottrell, 2005); that is, any model that includes spatial relations between reusable features or parts (Bienenstock & Geman, 1995). Thus, the take-home message is not that structural-description models are right and image-based models are wrong (or vice versa), but, as discussed in the next section, elements of both approaches are likely be incorporated into a viable theory of object recognition (Barenholtz & Tarr, 2007). Structural-description models teach us that parts or features and their spatial relations are important. Image-based models teach us that specific visual memories are important. In combination, we can think of long-term visual memories as collections of spatially related image features that are matched to percepts on the basis of similarity within a low-dimensional (relative to images) image feature space (the nature of the features still being an open question). Dimensionality reduction is realized by moving from image pixels to image features and from a spatially undifferentiated image to spatial relations between features. At the same time, specificity is preserved in the spatial relations between features encoding local properties of the image. By preserving meaningful similarity relationships, yet reducing overall dimensionality, this architecture enables generalization from small numbers of examples. In contrast, a qualitative structural-description model (e.g., RBC) ignores meaningful similarity relationships by reducing dimensionality to the point at which many exemplars or many views are simply the *same* representation. Conversely, a template model breaks meaningful similarity relationships by preserving too much dimensionality to the point at which each exemplar or view is a *different* representation.

At this point, you might be asking, exactly how do you define "meaningful similarity"? Consider that a single exemplar has a similarity relationship with other members of the same category (which is why categories arise in the first place). Likewise, a single view has a similarity relationship with other views of the same object. These particular relationships are representationally meaningful and should be present in visual memory. Moreover, they do important work in explaining why, before we have learned many exemplars or views, we are able to recognize new instances of a category with few exemplars or familiar objects

---

1   Behavioral data on view specificity (e.g., Tarr et al., 1998) speaks to the nature of the features used in object representations, for example, arguing for image-based features rather than Geons. However, these same data are agnostic as to whether features participate in structural descriptions or only exist in more template-like forms.

in completely novel views. These generalization processes, unlike the invariance conferred by multiple instances in memory, take *more* time and produce *more* errors as the similarity between the known and the unknown decreases. In support of such representational assumptions, it is well established that objects learned at one view are more poorly and more slowly recognized at new views (Tarr, 1995; Tarr & Pinker, 1990) and that individual object-selective neurons tend to preferentially respond to specific object views (Logothetis & Pauls, 1995; Perrett et al., 1985). This sort of view-tuning may appear puzzling when considered at the single neuron level: If objects are represented by individual neurons tuned to specific views, how can any sort of invariance be achieved? The answer lies, of course, in considering populations of neurons as the actual neural code for objects. Individual neurons may code—from a familiar viewpoint—the complex features or parts of which objects are composed; that is, instantiating the representational architecture outlined earlier.

Consistent with this approach, Perrett et al. (1998) proposed that recognition then takes the form of an *accumulation of evidence* across all neurons selective for some aspect of a given object—a variation on classic stochastic accumulation-of-evidence models (Nosofsky & Palmeri, 1997; Ratcliff, 1978; Ratcliff & Smith, 2004; Smith, 2000; Smith & Ratcliff, 2004). Such models are achieving new prominence in explaining the neural bases of perceptual decision making across a variety of domains (Boucher, Palmeri, Logan, & Schall, 2007; Gold & Shadlen, 2001; Roitman & Shadlen, 2002; Schall, 2001, 2004). Critically, these models implement similarity relationships as a function of their pooled neural responses. For example, during recognition of a novel object view, the particular rate of accumulation will depend on the similarity between visible features in the present viewpoint and the view-specific features for which individual neurons are tuned (Perrett, Oram, & Ashbridge, 1998). Across a population of object-selective neurons, sufficient neural evidence (summed neural activity) will accumulate more slowly when the current appearance of an object is dissimilar from its learned appearance (Fig. 6–6). In contrast, when an object's appearance is close to a previously experienced view, evidence across the appropriate neural population will accumulate more rapidly. Thus, systematic behavioral changes in recognition performance with changes in viewpoint may be explained as a consequence of how similarity is computed between new object perceptual representations and their previously learned neural representations and how evidence is accumulated over time for a perceptual decision.

In these models, recognition amounts to reaching a threshold of sufficient evidence across a neural population. Unfamiliar views of objects will require more time to reach threshold, but will be successfully recognized given some similarity between an input and known viewpoints. Unfamiliar exemplars within a familiar class can likewise be recognized given some similarity (Tarr & Gauthier, 1998) with known exemplars from within that class. Consistent with the idea that view and category generalization rely on common mechanisms, one behavioral implication is that familiarity with individual objects should facilitate the viewpoint-dependent recognition of other, visually similar objects,

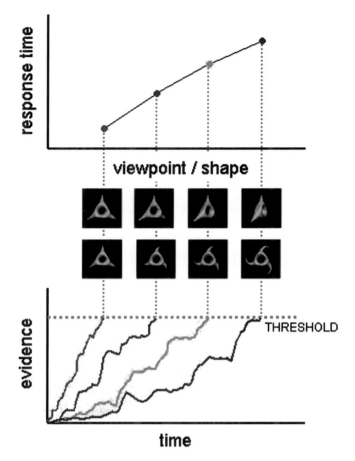

Figure 6–6. A broad class of models of perceptual decision making assume that evidence (*y-axis*) accumulates over time (*x-axis*). A response is made when an evidence threshold is reached (*bottom panel*). Response time is that time at which the threshold is reached (*top panel*). In the case of making a recognition or categorization decision, the rate of accumulation of evidence depends on the similarity between the perceived object and the stored memory representation of the object to be recognized or the class of objects to be categorized. Similarity can vary with either viewpoint or physical shape or both.

as borne out by several studies (Edelman, 1995, 1999; Tarr & Gauthier, 1998). Whether the same mechanism can account for all forms of object invariance remains unknown, although it seems possible that configuration and lighting variation present unique challenges that may require the inclusion of distinct forms of structural information (e.g., Bienenstock & Geman, 1995). Finally, as discussed later in this chapter, accumulation of evidence based on similarity to stored exemplars has also been proposed as a solution to the more general problem of categorization (Nosofsky & Palmeri, 1997). Thus, mechanisms based on similar (sic) computational principles seem to underlie many cognitive processes.

6.3.3 Hybrid Theories

As discussed earlier, one of the key differences between structural-description and image-based theories is the compositional nature of object representations. Under the cartoon view of the world, structural descriptions represent objects in terms of viewpoint-independent three-dimensional parts and their spatial relations (Biederman, 1987), and views represent objects in terms of a holistic image of the entire object (Edelman, 1997). However, both intuition and empirical evidence (Garner, 1974; Stankiewicz, 2002; Tversky, 1977) suggest that we represent complex objects in a compositional manner— objects are decomposable into parts. Yet these same intuitions and other empirical evidence (Hayward & Tarr, 1997; Tarr, Williams, Hayward, & Gauthier, 1998) suggest that these parts are not simple three-dimensional volumes. Is there a way to marry the best qualities of image-based theories with the compositional representations of structural-description theories?

One recent approach proposed by Ullman, Vidal-Naquet, and Sali (2002) measured mutual information between features and basic-level categories to discover the image features that were most informative for classification (see also Schyns & Rodet, 1997). They showed that features of "intermediate complexity" were best for basic-level classification. For faces, these features included what we would generally call the "parts" of a face such as the eyes or the nose; for cars, these included "parts" such as a wheel or the drivers' side window (Fig. 6–7).

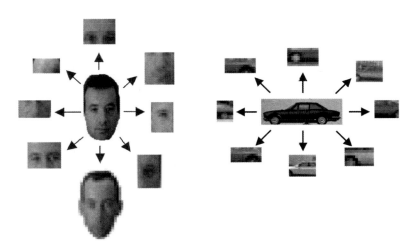

Figure 6–7. Image-based visual features of intermediate complexity maximize delivered information with respect to a basic-level category of objects. The figure shows examples of face fragments and car fragments. Zhang and Cottrell (2005) found somewhat larger and more complex image-based visual features for subordinate identification. Adapted with permission from Ullman, S., Vidal-Naquet, M., and Sali, E. (2002). Visual features of intermediate complexity and their use in classification. *Nature Neuroscience*, 5:682–687. Macmillan Publishers Ltd.

For other classes, "parts" are likely to include a wide variety of features, including, depending on the class, non–shape-based properties such as color or texture. Although there is as yet no direct evidence, it is tempting to speculate about the relationship of such "ad-hoc" features to the observed feature-selective responses of neurons in TEO (K. Tanaka, 1996, 2002). What is intriguing is that selective responses for individual neurons are elicited by somewhat odd patterns that do not correspond to what we might typically think of as distinct object parts (Fig. 6–8). Indeed, they appear to be ad-hoc and of intermediate complexity. This correspondence is less surprising if we consider that the features incorporated into the model proposed by Ullman et al. were found using an algorithm that operated on raw images without any intervention from a human teacher. These features emerged because they provided maximal information for the basic-level classification of those images. It is also important to emphasize that these are *viewpoint-dependent image-based features*, not anything like Geons or other volumetric primitives. Moreover, spatial relations between these parts are not explicitly encoded; rather, the local context is preserved for each image-based feature, and local features overlap, enabling an implicit representation of configural information.

To be clear, Ullman et al. (2002) proposed a solution to basic-level classification (classifying an object as a face or a car), not to more subordinate-level classification (classifying an object as Steve Luck or as a Porsche Boxster). Recently, Zhang and Cottrell (2005) extended the Ullman et al. approach to discover the image features possessing maximal informativeness for subordinate-level classification. What they found was that these image features were larger

Figure 6–8. Some examples of ad hoc "features" that are preferred by certain cells in IT cortex of macaque monkeys. Adapted from work by Keiji Tanaka and colleagues (e. g., K. Tanaka, 1996, 2002; see also http://www. brain. riken. go. jp/labs/cbms/tanaka. html).

and more complex than the features Ullman et al. reported for basic-level classification. For example, for face individuation, these features included an eye and a nose, or an eye with part of the nose and mouth. Thus, it is possible that accounting for configural/holistic effects, particularly as seen in face and expert-level object recognition, requires assembling *hierarchies* of features, not simply relating them in a single level of spatial relations (Gauthier & Tarr, 2002; Maurer, Grand, & Mondloch, 2002). Note that these maximally informative "parts" were still not the entire faces themselves. Thus, this approach to image-based representation is different from encoding complete views of objects for subordinate-level classification (Edelman, 1999). Here, incomplete yet complex image-based features were not only sufficient to successfully identify objects at the subordinate level, but provided the maximal information to support such classification.

As alluded to earlier, hybrid theories suggest a compositional aspect to the representation of objects in terms of ad-hoc features (parts). They also reflect the fact that we know more about objects than just their shape. We can remember an object's color, position, orientation, or size, and can use such dimensions to determine an object's identity or category if those dimensions prove diagnostic for those perceptual decisions (Kruschke, 1992; Naor-Raz, Tarr, & Kersten, 2003; Nosofsky, 1998). So, the perceptual representation of a complex object may consist of a collection of image-based parts, color, orientation, location, and other independent or semi-independent perceptual dimensions (Ashby & Townsend, 1986) and their spatial relations. Such information is recruited for a given task based on the difficulty of the discrimination at hand—that is, the degree to which particular features are stored or retrieved from working or long-term visual memory is modulated by task complexity, not object complexity per se.

Finally, many theories (and most experiments) of object recognition live in a world with just a single object at a time (but see Mozer, 1991; Mozer & Sitton, 1998). This assumption is typically justified by invoking early attentional proc-esses that select one object for high-level visual processing (Treisman & Gelade, 1980). Thus, the object perception problem is often reduced to the recognition of decontextualized, static objects. Yet, natural vision systems excel at dynamic scene recognition; that is, the invariant recognition of not only objects but their entire context as well as their actions. Indeed, it is probably not possible or desirable to completely separate the problems of object and scene recognition. All levels of object recognition seem contextualized. Recognizing an object part is dramatically facilitated by considering it in the context of the whole object (Tanaka & Farah, 1993). Scene recognition can be impossible without consid-ering constituent objects (but see Oliva, 2005), and object recognition itself is more effective if the nature of the scene has been established (Hollingworth, in press, 2006; Hollingworth & Henderson, 2002). Similarly, object recognition is enhanced by the inclusion of diagnostic dynamic information (Johanson, 1973; Vuong & Tarr, 2004). Thus, any architecture for object recognition and scene recognition should include dynamic information and processes that enable a compositional hierarchy of contexts to interact in a manner that aids interpretation.

6.3.4 Category-specific Visual Object Perception?

Although the question of invariance has often dominated thinking on visual object perception, recent neuroimaging results have focused on the perception and recognition of particular classes of object. One of the challenges to the human visual system is discriminating between objects at different levels of specificity, including, for some classes, individuals within a homogeneous set, the most salient example being face recognition. Following in the tradition of neuropsychology (Lissauer, 1890), the specific question addressed within this domain is often whether faces are "special" or not (Farah, Wilson, Drain, & Tanaka, 1998); that is, whether there exists a functional or neural module dedicated to face recognition. Although the form of this debate has varied, neuroimaging studies speak logically to the issue of neural modularity (Fodor, 1983) in that neuroimaging methods necessarily produce spatially localized neural responses associated with specific tasks—patterns that look temptingly like neural modules (recall Fig. 6–1). Of course, it is sometimes difficult to pin down what one means by a "module." Does module refer to an encapsulated cognitive function (which Fodor believed could only apply to perceptual systems, but others have extended to most cognitive abilities)? Or, does module refer to spatially localized brain regions that appear to subserve particular functions (independently of how such regions may interact with other regions)? Across multiple literatures, use of the term module is fast and loose, sometimes even to the point of absurdity (e.g., Fisher, Aron, & Brown, 2006; Beauregard & Paquette, 2006). Even worse, within the neuroimaging literature, there has been a tendency to associate functional localization with functional specialization, as if a localized peak of neural activity is equivalent to a discrete module dedicated to accomplishing a singular task.

With regard to a putative functional/neural module for face recognition, a large body of data show distinct regions of the visual system that appear to respond preferentially to faces. Neuroimaging studies using both positron emission tomography (Sergent, Ohta, & MacDonald, 1992) and functional magnetic resonance imaging (fMRI; Kanwisher, McDermott, & Chun, 1997; Puce, Allison, Gore, & McCarthy, 1995) reveal a small region in the fusiform gyrus of the ventral-temporal lobe that is more active when we view faces as compared to other objects. One interpretation of this finding is that this brain area, dubbed the "fusiform face area" or FFA (Kanwisher, McDermott, & Chun, 1997), is a face-specific neural module. That is, its function is to perceive or recognize faces and only faces. An alternative explanation is that this and other forms of putatively face-specific processing (e.g., Farah, 1990; Yin, 1969) are actually by-products of our extensive experience, which makes us face experts (Diamond & Carey, 1986). Thus, the recognition of individual faces exhibits qualities that should be true for any domain of visual expertise for a homogeneous object class. Faces are processed this way because of their social importance, but not as a result of anything intrinsic to them as visual objects.

Gauthier and colleagues (Gauthier & Brown, 2004) have explored these competing accounts using several different approaches. Experts have been created in the laboratory for novel objects called "Greebles" in order to measure the observed changes in behavioral (Gauthier & Tarr, 1997) and neural activity (Gauthier, Tarr, Anderson, Skudlarski, & Gore, 1999; Rossion et al., 2000) with expertise. Similar comparisons in both behavior and neural activity have been made between novices and real-world experts (Gauthier, Skudlarski, Gore, & Anderson, 2000; Righi & Tarr, 2004; Tanaka & Curran, 2001). Several findings speak directly to the question "Are faces special?" First, Greeble experts, but not Greeble novices, show behavioral effects—notably configural processing—that are often taken as markers for specialized face processing (Gauthier & Tarr, 1997; Gauthier, Williams, Tarr, & Tanaka, 1998). Second, Greeble experts, but not Greeble novices, show category-selectivity for Greebles in the right fusiform gyrus (Gauthier, Tarr, Anderson, Skudlarski, & Gore, 1999). Similarly, bird experts show category-selectivity for birds, but not cars, in the right fusiform, whereas car experts show category-selectivity for cars, but not birds (Gauthier, Skudlarski, Gore, & Anderson, 2000). Reinforcing the generality of this result, chess experts, but not chess novices, show category-selectivity in right fusiform for valid, but not invalid, chess game boards (Righi & Tarr, 2004). Third, across Greeble expertise training, subjects show a significant positive correlation between a behavioral measure of holistic processing (sensitivity to the presence of the correct parts for that object) and neural activity in the right fusiform (Gauthier & Tarr, 2002). Similarly, bird and car experts show a significant correlation between their relative expertise measured behaviorally (birds minus cars) and neural activity in the right fusiform (Gauthier, Skudlarski, Gore, & Anderson, 2000), and years of experience playing chess correlates significantly with localized fusiform responses (Righi & Tarr, 2004). Fourth, the N170 potential (as measured by event-related potentials) shows face-like modulation in both Greeble (Rossion et al., 2000) and bird or dog experts (Tanaka & Curran, 2001).

These and other findings (e.g., Gauthier, Curby, Skudlarski, & Epstein, in press; Tarr & Gauthier, 2000) suggest that putatively face-specific effects may be obtained with nonface objects, but only when subjects are experts for the nonface-object domain. Thus, the answer to the question "Are faces special?" is yes and no. There is no doubt that faces are special in terms of their centrality to social interaction. On the one hand, it could be that this social importance necessitates built-in special-purpose brain circuits devoted to face recognition. But on the other hand, it could be that social importance has more indirect effects in that people develop expertise with faces from the repeated interactions with faces and the demands for individual-level recognition of faces. Some data supporting the latter argument come from studies using both Greeble and extant experts in domains as diverse as cars, birds, and chess. Across these domains, we find a pattern of behavioral and neural effects consistent with those seen for face recognition. In particular, category-selective activation in the fusiform gyrus has, of late, been taken as the hallmark of face specificity. Gauthier, Tarr, and others see similar selectivity for many other object domains, particularly when subjects are experts. Of course, this analysis only addresses the question of spatial specialization: "Is a particular piece of neural real estate dedicated to face processing?" (unlikely given current data) and raises the more meaningful question "What are the computational principles underlying processing in this brain region?" (we don't know at present).

Recent arguments based on finer resolution imaging or other methods for assessing spatial overlap between selective regions in the fusiform for faces and nonface objects miss this point (see http://web.mit.edu/bcs/nklab/expertise. shtml). From a theoretical perspective, even if convincing evidence existed that the microstructure of the brain regions recruited by faces and nonface objects of expertise were non- or partially overlapping, this would not demonstrate that these regions were functionally distinct. Indeed, good evidence already suggests that category-selective regions for different object categories are not functionally separable and that the representations of faces and different objects are both distributed and overlapping (Haxby et al., 2001). Moreover, adjacent, overlapping regions in visual cortex often show selective tuning for particular stimulus properties, but common underlying computational principles—one example being orientation columns in V1 (Kamitani & Tong, 2005). From an empirical point of view, the two studies addressing the question of overlap both used stimuli that were outside of the domain of expertise being tested, for example, antique cars shown to modern car experts (Grill-Spector, Knouf, & Kanwisher, 2004; Rhodes, Byatt, Michie, & Puce, 2004). Thus, it is unlikely that any strong effect of expertise could have ever been obtained under these conditions, let alone evaluated in terms of its relationship to face processing.

6.4 VISUAL LONG-TERM MEMORY

What do we remember about objects, what do we know about objects, and what do we do with objects? According to classic cognitive theories, memory, knowledge, and skills are abstract. Memory is poor because only the gist, particularly the semantic content, is retained. Knowledge is abstract because knowledge representations—abstract rules, schemas, or prototypes—are abstracted from experience (see Chapter 5 for a discussion of memory for gist in scene memory). Cognitive skills generalize (the sine qua non of skilled behavior is generalization) because they are not tied to any specific instances of prior skilled action. But, alternatively, in much the same way that invariant visual object perception can arise from specific views of objects, abstract memory, knowledge, and skills can arise from specific perceptual experiences (Barsalou, 1999; Palmeri, Wong, & Gauthier, 2004). Much of visual perception is based on the context provided by visual memories. Much of visual cognition is similarly grounded.

Contemporary neuropsychological theories often posit different kinds of memory (with lots of circles and arrows)—declarative versus procedure, episodic versus semantic, perceptual versus habit, explicit versus implicit, and other such dichotomies—that are subserved by functionally independent systems (Fig. 6–9). As with the study of category-selectivity, neuropsychology and neuroimaging methods play naturally to this sort of (relatively simplistic) modular theorizing, providing evidence for system-specific, dedicated brain regions, each with a unique set of representational and processing assumptions.

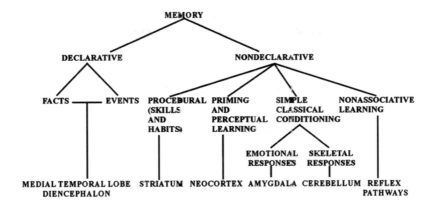

Figure 6–9. A well-known taxonomic hierarchy of long-term memory systems (from Squire, 2004). The taxonomy divides memory into conscious declarative (hippocampal-dependent) memory and unconscious nondeclarative (nonhippocampal-dependent) memory. There is little debate that particular brain structures are especially important for particular kinds of memory. Debate centers around whether those brain structures are important because those structures are the systems responsible for particular kinds of memory tasks or because those structures carry out processing that is especially important for certain kinds of memory tasks under certain conditions. Adapted with permission from Squire, L. R., & Zola, S. M. (1996). Structure and function of declarative and nondeclarative memory systems. *Proceedings of the National Academy of Sciences, USA.* 93, 13515–13522.

Much in the same way that functional specialization in visual cortex may be explained by alternative organizational principles, functional specialization for visual memory and learning may be organized around the kinds of representations and processes recruited by particular tasks and not around the tasks themselves (Palmeri & Flanery, 2002; Roediger, Buckner, & McDermott, 1999).

6.5 VISUAL MEMORY FOR OBJECTS

Our everyday experience leads us to the conclusion that our visual memory seems quite poor. Rare cases of eidetic memory aside (Luria, 1987), most people feel that they have great difficulty remembering visual details, even over relatively short periods of time. Supporting this intuition, some early experimental studies of long-term visual memory for objects and scenes suggested that people remember only the gist (e.g., Brewer & Treyens, 1981), but not the specific details (but see Shepard, 1967). This conclusion is reinforced by recent "change blindness" studies that suggest that we remember very little of what we see from one moment to the next (but see Hollingworth, in press; Rensink, O'Regan, & Clark, 1997; Simons & Rensink, 2005; see Chapter 5 of this volume for a detailed discussion of the change blindness literature and its theoretical implications).

Such limitations are especially apparent in eyewitness testimony, in which witnesses are notoriously bad at recognizing or recalling visual details, and their visual memories for events can be significantly influenced by nonvisual, interfering information (Loftus, 2004; Wells & Loftus, 2003; Wells & Olson, 2003). These and related results have led some researchers to conclude that memory for objects and scenes is not perceptual, but instead reflects a semantic recoding of perceptual information guided by abstract schematic knowledge (e.g., Fodor, 1975; Newell & Simon, 1972; see Barsalou, 1999). Indeed, the ability of people to form visual images has either been rejected outright or has been characterized as an epiphenomenon of cognitive processing in which images arise as a by-product of accessing inherently nonvisual memories (Anderson, 1978; Pylyshyn, 1973, 1981).

Happily, the field does lurch forward over time. Many contemporary memory models assume distinct episodic representations that can, in principle, retain detailed information about specific perceptual experiences (Hintzman, 1986; Logan, 1988; Nosofsky, 1991). Why, then, does memory often seem so poor? And why do we seem to remember only the gist and not the details? After all, memory performance should be related to how well information is encoded, stored, retrieved, and used (see Chapter 5). In principle, the visual detail of visual memories is constrained at the upper limit by the visual details provided by the perceptual system. Clearly, if some of the visual information is not processed during a perceptual episode, then that information cannot be encoded into an enduring memory representation to be retrieved later. Both visual attention and eye movements can conspire to render part of an object or scene invisible or poorly visible and, hence, absent from memory (Rensink, O'Regan, & Clark, 1997; Simons, 1996; Simons & Rensink, 2005). In addition, some visual information may be normalized or explained away (Kersten, Mamassian, & Yuille, 2004) during visual processing, rendering those visual details for all intents and purposes invisible to the perceiver. If it's not perceived, it can't be remembered. If it's perceived poorly, it can be remembered poorly at best.

At the same time, many theories of memory assume that some probability is associated with whether particular visual properties are encoded into memory, accurately or at all (Hintzman, 1986; Hintzman, 1988; Shiffrin & Steyvers, 1997). Thus, failures to remember can also arise from failures to encode. The ability to remember visual details is also limited by how well the information is retained in memory. Although some theories have attributed memory failures to factors other than memory storage (Gillund & Shiffrin, 1984), many theories also assume that memory traces can change rather dramatically because of decay (Hintzman, 1986) or some form of consolidation (McClelland, McNaughton, & O'Reilly, 1995; Shiffrin & Steyvers, 1997) over time. At one extreme, individual memory traces remain highly distinct from one another (Gillund & Shiffrin, 1984; Hintzman, 1986; Raaijmakers & Shiffrin, 1981), and storage failures are due to memory decay. At the other extreme, all memories share largely the same representational substrate, which results in similar memory representations becoming physically and informationally indiscriminable from one another (e.g., McClelland & Rumelhart, 1985). In this case, storage failures are due to interference from new memories. Both kinds of memory may exist, with the hippocampus and associated structures especially involved in distinct memories for particular visual episodes and cortical areas maintaining more generalized memories in a distributed fashion (e.g., O'Reilly & Norman, 2002).

Finally, failures of visual memory may also emerge due to failures of memory retrieval. Visual details may be visible, they may be successfully encoded into memory, and they may be retained in memory. But retrieval cues may be insufficient to retrieve the relevant visual memory representations. Retrieval failure is probably one of the primary reasons for memory failure. Consider that failing to provide the right retrieval cues is a failure to reinstantiate the context with which the memories were first encoded. Most explicit recognition or recall tasks do not ask subjects to report whether they have *ever* seen that object before. Rather, they typically require someone to say whether or not they saw a particular object during some initial encoding session—whether earlier that day, a week earlier, or a year earlier—while tested in the same context or a different context (Mensink & Raaijmakers, 1988; Shiffrin & Steyvers, 1997). Both external context cues (the room, the time, the experimenter, and the like) and internal context cues (associations with other studied items) are needed to discriminate old studied objects from new lures.

Apparent visual memory failures during retrieval can arise based on the way memory retrieval takes place. A large class of memory models assumes that explicitly recognizing an old object as one you have seen before could arise from retrieving a specific memory that matches the probe or from a global familiarity based on the match between a retrieval probe and all memory representations. According this view, we remember the gist not because it's the gist that is stored, but rather because a probe cue retrieves a number of matching memories that are combined together (Hintzman, 1988; Shiffrin & Steyvers, 1997). That is, seemingly abstract memories are produced online during the act of memory retrieval (Barsalou, 1990, 1999) because what is retrieved is a blend of memories. What is common between these memories is what we would typically call the "gist"—those visual properties present across many instances stored in memory.

6.5.1 Explicit Versus Implicit Visual Memory

If contemporary memory research has taught us one thing, it is that memory is far more than explicitly recognizing or recalling past experiences. With our every action, we reveal memory through our performance. Perhaps the most well-known experimental example of this is perceptual repetition priming. People are faster and more accurate at identifying a visual object they have seen before. Repetition priming is highly specific to perceptual details (e.g., see Schacter, Chiu, & Ochsner, 1993), it has been reported for delays of over a year in the absence of explicit recollection (Cave, 1997; Kolers, 1976), and it is normal in individuals with explicit memory deficits (e.g., Squire, 1992). Such results have led researchers to divide memory into functionally independent memory systems for explicit memory and implicit memory (Schacter & Tulving, 1994). For example, Tulving and Schacter (1990) proposed "Perceptual Representation Systems" that stored perceptual memories to support repetition priming. Primarily based on reports of various neuropsychological dissociations between memory tasks, the number of functionally independent memory systems has ballooned to include separate systems for episodic memory, semantic memory, habit learning, perceptual learning, conditioning, and host of other memory tasks (Schacter, 2000; Squire & Zola, 1996; Squire, 2004).

The multiple memory systems approach delineates the many different independent memory systems, often tying such systems to particular brain structures, and providing, perhaps, some rationale for why evolution could have favored these particular divisions and not others. However, specific versions of this approach typically omit much discussion regarding the specific mechanisms underlying the myriad component memory systems. How are memories encoded, how are they represented, and what processes can be brought to bear on them?

Interestingly, many of these weaknesses parallel those seen in modularist approaches to visual object recognition (Palmeri & Gauthier, 2004). For example, much in the same way that modularist approaches to visual perception assign independent systems to particular kinds of objects, multiple memory systems approaches assign independent systems to particular kinds of tasks without explaining how they accomplish said tasks. The hippocampus is for explicit declarative memory used to recognize or recall specific visual experiences. The basal ganglia is for learning skills that might associate an object with a well-learned response. Bits of visual cortex are for perceptual learning that leads to priming. Although at first approximations these assertions are indisputable based on the neuropsychological and brain imaging evidence, saying that the hippocampus is a necessary neural substrate for explicit declarative memory is different from saying that it creates explicit declarative memories and explicit declarative memories only (Squire, Stark, & Clark, 2004). Indeed, the hippocampus appears to be involved more generally in creating configural representations (Chun & Phelps, 1999; Cohen & Eichenbaum, 1993; Meeter, Myers, & Gluck, 2005) or consolidating memories in cortical representations (O'Reilly & Rudy, 2001). That is, its role in conscious declarative memory may be a useful by-product of its more general role in binding together cues from multiple modalities into a single representation. The importance of representations created by the hippocampus is clearly measured in explicit declarative memory tasks, such as recall or recognition. Thus, explicit declarative memory deficits are most conspicuous in amnesics with hippocampal damage. At the same time, the role of the hippocampus can also be gauged by performance in appropriately designed implicit memory tasks (see Chapter 7). Based on such evidence, contemporary theories of memory associate specific representations and process roles to a network of interdependent memory systems, rather than assuming separable systems that are tied to particular tasks (e.g., see Meeter, Myers, & Gluck, 2005).

Returning to perceptual repetition priming as an important example of implicit visual memory, what are some alternative explanations for enhanced object recognition as a result of prior perceptual experience? Tulving and Schacter (1990) proposed that priming was mediated by a perceptual representation system independent of the memory system that supports explicit declarative memory. Previous experiences are stored in this memory module in order to prime later experiences. Why? Priming has some adaptive value, so we should store perceptual memories for the purposes of enhancing perceptual performance at later encounters. Alternative theories do not place such a clear demarcation between memories underlying priming and memories used for other purposes. For example, Rouder, Ratcliff, and McKoon (2000) proposed that priming effects are a by-product of how view-based memories are used during normal object recognition. In their model, priming is caused by a bias to interpret perceptual information as supporting familiar objects, as opposed to unfamiliar objects. They instantiated this hypothesis by simply adding biases to Poggio and Edelman's (1990) simple view-based model of object recognition. The added biases simply reflect the learned likelihood of seeing a given object again, thereby causing known objects to be identified more quickly when they are seen again later. Adding this simple psychological mechanism accounts for perceptual priming without the need to posit any additional implicit memory system above and beyond the use of object representations already incorporated into almost all models of object recognition. Again, memory *is* perception.

Some more standard memory theories also posit that perceptual priming and other forms of implicit memory are a normal by-product of memory. In these models, a contrast is often drawn between the visual features of represented objects and the features associated with its context. That is, explicit memory tasks are contextualized judgments about whether a given object appeared at a particular location at a specific time, not whether that object has ever been seen before (Gillund & Shiffrin, 1984; Hintzman, 1988). Loss of this contextual information, or a failure to encode such information due to brain damage, would result in failures of explicit memory with preserved implicit memory. Moreover, a subset of these theories have hypothesized that, over time, memory traces can become decontextualized through memory consolidation (Shiffrin & Steyvers, 1997). Put another way, they are not transferred to a different memory store, but become dissociated from the context under which they were learned as a natural product of how memory storage works.

Consistent with a more integrated approach, a number of computational memory models make no clear demarcation between memories for general semantic knowledge, memories for particular experiences, and implicit memories. At the core, the same visual memories are used to recall, recognize, categorize, identify, or do things with objects (Logan, 2002; Nosofsky, 1992). For example, repetition priming may rely on the same memories that underlie cognitive skills (Logan, 1990). At first blush, single-system memory models of this sort may seem rather out of touch with contemporary cognitive neuroscience research on memory, in which the *desiderata* seems to be as many distinct systems as possible. Yet, a recent fMRI study supports the view that important aspects of perceptual priming and skill learning may share similar neural loci. Specifically, Dobbins et al. (Dobbins, Schnyer, Verfaellie, & Schacter, 2004) contrasted a perceptual locus for repetition priming with a high-level response learning locus for repetition priming. They found that prefrontal cortical activity tracked repetition priming behavior, not activity in visual cortex. Thus, as suggested by Rouder et al. (2000), repetition priming effects may not reflect the creation of new perceptual representations, or even the short-term tuning of perceptual representations, but may instead reflect a bias to do things with objects that we did with them before, and to do so more quickly (Logan, 1990).

Perceptual Categorization and Visual Knowledge of Objects

As discussed earlier, one hallmark of visual cognition is generalization. Even very young children seem to know when two visually similar but different objects are members of the same category. One solution to the problem of generalizing from specific experiences is to create knowledge representations that are themselves abstract generalizations. According to early theories, conceptual knowledge is organized into abstract semantic networks or conceptual hierarchies (Anderson, 1976; Collins & Quillian, 1969) that link one kind of thing with another kind of thing through propositional structures. Knowledge is stored efficiently, so that object properties that are true of a superordinate category of objects are only stored at the most general level (and are inherited as needed). Only properties that are unique to subordinate categories or specific individuals are encoded at lower levels of the conceptual hierarchy (Smith, Shoben, & Rips, 1974). In this way, what we know about objects is abstracted away from our perceptual experiences. As such, objects are categorized as different kinds of things using abstract logical rules (Ashby, Alfonso-Reese, Turken, & Waldron, 1998; Bruner, Goodnow, & Austin, 1956; Johansen & Palmeri, 2002; Nosofsky, Palmeri, & McKinley, 1994) or by comparing an object with an abstract prototype or schema (Lakoff, 1987; Minda & Smith, 2001; Posner & Keele, 1968; Rosch, 1975). That is, class invariance is achieved through representations that are invariant over members of that class.

A sharp distinction between memory for specific visual experiences and abstract visual knowledge is also manifest in the classic distinction between semantic and episodic memory (see Squire & Schacter, 2002; Tulving, 1985, 1993). Some memory researchers have argued that good computational reasons exist for keeping specific memories separate from abstract knowledge. After all, if all we have are specific memories for particular objects, how could we ever know anything general that was true about members of a class? And, if all we have is general knowledge, how could we ever know anything about specific objects?

This approach is generally similar to Biederman's (1987) theory in that RBC proposes that both view and class invariance are achieved by constructing representations—prototypes—that are themselves invariant over views and class exemplars. Interestingly, in the same way that theorists have argued that we do not have need for view- and/or class-invariant object representations to attain view and class invariant object recognition (Bülthoff & Edelman, 1992; Poggio & Edelman, 1990; Tarr & Pinker, 1989), we may not need class-invariant category representations to achieve a basic-level classification over object categories (Palmeri, 1999; see Palmeri & Gauthier, 2004).

To be clear, visual memories for specific experiences with objects can support *both* the recognition of particular objects and general knowledge about classes of objects. Direct abstraction is not needed. What matters is how specific exemplar memories are used relative to one another. As noted earlier, explicit recollection is typically a contextualized decision. Did you see this object on that occasion? Explicit recognition uses memory retrieval cues that contain both information about the object and its context. Explicit recall uses retrieval cues with context alone. Thus, any inability to reinstantiate the original context, to encode the context, or a loss of information about the context in memory will lead to degradation of explicit memory. In contrast, questions about visual knowledge are decontextualized. An object is a member of a particular category across most, if not all, contexts. And, an object is associated with other objects, has particular properties or elicits certain behaviors across many different contexts. Thus, explicit memory for objects requires the integrity of particular visual memories, whereas classification of objects or general knowledge of objects, including object recognition, can utilize a panoply of visual memories across a variety of visual contexts.

Two key properties of these memory models are: (a) retrieval is similarity-based, and (b) decisions are based on the retrieval of multiple visual memory traces. Additionally, LTM is probed with a retrieval cue tailored to the particular memory task. For example, the retrieval cue for a recognition memory task would include features of the object and features of the context, whereas the retrieval cue for a categorization task could often include features of the object only. Memory traces are activated according to the similarity between the retrieval cue and the trace (Gilund & Shiffrin, 1984; Hintzman, 1986; Nosofsky, 1992). Using a process of decisional selective attention, matches or mismatches of certain visual features may be weighed more heavily if they are particularly diagnostic for the decision being made (Kruschke, 1992; Lamberts, 1998, 2000; Logan, 2002; Nosofsky, 1984, 1986). Because retrieval is similarity-based, objects that have never been seen before can be falsely recognized as previously seen objects during recognition if they are similar to studied objects (Nosofsky, 1991). Similarly, objects that are prototypical will be quickly and accurately categorized as category members because they are similar to many other category examples, whether or not they have been studied before (Busemeyer, Dewey, & Medin, 1984; Hintzman, 1986; Shin & Nosofsky, 1992). Of course, the decision rules underlying categorization and recognition decisions are different. Recognition is an absolute judgment of whether an object is sufficiently similar to objects that have been studied before. If so, the object is recognized as old. Categorization is a relative judgment about an object's similarity to known categories. As such, although recognition and categorization may depend on the same underlying memories, recognition and categorization judgments need not be tightly correlated (Nosofsky, 1992). Thus, your ability or inability to recognize a familiar object does not predict whether you will be able to categorize it correctly. Critically, this stochastic independence between recognition and categorization does not imply that these two processes are based on different memory systems, rather it is equally probable that they are simply based on different decisions rules.

One challenge to this unified approach comes from reported neuropsychological dissociations between recognition and categorization (Squire & Zola, 1996). Specifically, amnesics can learn novel visual categories but are impaired (Knowlton & Squire, 1993) or at chance (Squire & Knowlton, 1995) at recognition. At first blush, this seems like clear evidence in support of functionally independent memory systems for visual recognition memory and visual categorization. However, simply by assuming that amnesics have poorly discriminated memories relative to normal controls, perhaps because of failures of the damaged hippocampus to create new configural representations or to consolidate memories into cortical areas, models assuming the same memories for categorization and recognition predict the observed dissociation a priori (Kinder & Shanks, 2001; Nosofsky & Zaki, 1998; Palmeri & Flanery, 2002). To elaborate, most categorization tasks require broad generalization from learned examples to test examples, whereas recognition requires fine discrimination between old and new test items. Recognition is influenced significantly more by degradation than categorization (Palmeri & Flanery, 2002). On top of this, many of the perceptual categorization tasks that have been used in the neuropsychological literature may not rely on long-term memories for trained category exemplars whatsoever. Specifically, a number of the categorization tests that have been used to assess long-term category memory can be performed just as well whether people have studied category exemplars or not (Palmeri & Flanery, 1999; Zaki & Nosofsky, 2001, 2004). When these methodological flaws are addressed, individuals with memory impairments may indeed learn novel categories less well than normal controls (Zaki, Nosofsky, Jessup, & Unversagt, 2003). Although it is possible that visual memories supporting recognition and visual memories supporting categorization are functionally independent of one another, a more computationally tractable solution is that the same visual memory representations underlie a variety of memory tasks, with the information requirements of the particular task modulating performance.

6.5.3 Levels of Categorization

Objects can be categorized at multiple levels of abstraction, from identifying unique individuals by name to grouping together dissimilar objects as the same kind of thing. Discriminating between highly similar objects for purposes of identification and generalizing across many different objects for purposes of categorization appear to be competing goals that require different kinds of visual representations (Biederman, 1987; Logothetis & Sheinberg, 1996;

Marr, 1982). In fact, some structural-description theories (e.g., Biederman, 1987) view basic-level classification as a primary goal of visual perception. In such theories, the structural descriptions for different members of the same basic-level category are the same. At the same time, visual memories of a qualitatively different sort are needed in order to discriminate similar objects for purposes of identification or more subordinate levels of classification (Biederman, 1987). Such is the logic often used in arguing for dissociations between face and nonface object recognition (e.g., Farah, Wilson, Drain, & Tanaka, 1998).

Along similar lines, evidence from speeded perceptual categorization tasks have been used as evidence that basic-level classification is a stage of processing that precedes more subordinate or superordinate classification because basic-level classification is significantly faster (Grill-Spector & Kanwisher, N., 2003; Jolicoeur, Gluck, & Kosslyn, 1984). Typically, the fastest categorization task is basic-level categorization and is termed the "entry level" (Jolicoeur, Gluck, & Kosslyn, 1984) into conceptual knowledge. However, the entry level for a given individual can vary greatly with experience (Johnson & Mervis, 1997; Tanaka & Taylor, 1991). At the same time, fastest does not mean first (Palmeri, Wong, & Gauthier, 2004). In fact, a number of computational models of object recognition and perceptual categorization make no clear demarcation between identifying unique objects and categorizing objects as members of a class (Nosofsky, 1992; Riesenhuber & Poggio, 1999, 2000; Tjan, 2001). Specifically, identification and categorization are both evidence-based perceptual decisions. Identification may require more perceptual processing (Lamberts, 2000), but prior categorization is not necessary. Thus, the same visual memories that support invariance across changes in the image, for example, as generated by rotations in depth, also support access to objects at multiple levels of categorization, for example, recognition memory, identification, and categorization (Edelman, 1999). What varies is not our memories, but how such memories are used to make perceptual decisions that change from one task to another (Palmeri & Gauthier, 2004) (Fig. 6–10).

It should be emphasized that invariant performance can emerge from memory representations that do not themselves embody that invariance. For instance, viewpoint-invariant object recognition is enabled by comparing percepts with views in memory. Class-invariant object recognition is enabled by comparing an object with category exemplars in memory. Beyond the point at which abstract memory representations are not needed, it behooves us to spell out the mechanisms by which said invariances are achieved. For example, do we remember *all* views of objects we encounter, or is generalization good enough to allow encoding of only salient (Tarr & Kriegman, 2001) or frequently experienced views (Blanz, Tarr, & Bülthoff, 1999; Palmer, Rosch, & Chase, 1981)? Similarly, are all exemplars of all categories encoded, or are there "key" exemplars that help to delineate a given category? Although precise estimates of the capacity of visual memory are impossible, a surprising amount of detailed perceptual information may be encoded into visual memory (Hollingworth, 2004, 2005; Standing, 1973). And such memories may persist and influence

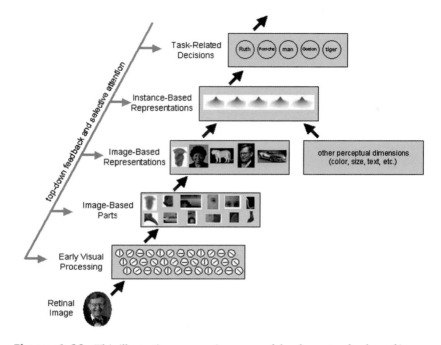

Figure 6–10. This illustration summarizes some of the elements of a class of image-based/instance-based/exemplar-based models of object recognition and perceptual categorization. Starting with the retinal image, a hierarchy of steps from low-level visual processing, to representations in terms of image-based parts (Ullman, Vidal-Naquet, & Sali, 2002), to representations of views and instances of objects (Riesenhuber & Poggio, 2000). The same representations of views and instances can be associated with perceptual decisions like a basic-level category (car or face), subordinate-level category (Honda Civic), or identity (Gordon Gee). An important component of many models is that selective attention can highlight aspects of a perceptual representation that are particularly diagnostic for a decision (e. g., Ahissar & Hochstein, 2004; Kruschke, 1992).

behavior for a long time period. One might argue that there is adaptive significance for the ability to encode a large amount of information in memory. This allows abstraction on-the-fly rather than requiring a prescient gatekeeper to decide what information might be necessary for survival at some later point in time (Barsalou, 1990). Along the same lines, instance-based models of object recognition and categorization have often been mathematically formalized, assuming that every view or every exemplar is stored in visual memory (Logan, 1988; Nosofsky, 1992). However, as discussed earlier, a more sparse encoding of views and exemplars that provides a nearly full but incomplete covering of the space of experienced instances supports recognition and categorization across changes in the image and exemplars within an object class (e.g., Bülthoff & Edelman, 1992; Rosseel, 2002). Moreover, detailed visual memories of specific perceptual experiences may support tasks beyond visual recognition and categorization. In particular, abstract conceptual knowledge that may appear amodal and abstracted from actual experience may in fact be grounded in perceptual knowledge (Barsalou, 1999; Martin, Ungerleider, & Haxby, 2000). In much the same way that abstractions of visual properties may be created on-the-fly, abstract conceptual properties may be "revealed" by mental simulations of perceptual knowledge (Barsalou, 1990).

Other isomorphisms seem to exist between visual and conceptual memories. For instance, in much the same way that evidence may differentially accumulate over time when recognizing particular views of an object (Perrett, Oram, & Ashbridge, 1998), evidence may differentially accumulate over time when categorizing different exemplars of a category. Nosofsky and Palmeri (1997) proposed a model of speeded categorization that combined representational elements of exemplar-based models of categorization and memory (Nosofsky, 1992), temporal assumptions of an instance-based model of automaticity (Logan, 1988), and stochastic evidence accumulation from random-walk models of perceptual decisions (Link, 1975; Luce, 1986; Ratcliff, 1978; Ratcliff & Rouder, 1998). In such models, the rate of accumulation depends on the similarity between the object to be categorized and the specific category exemplars in memory (Fig. 6–6). An object similar to many exemplars of a single category will be classified quickly and accurately. An object dissimilar to category exemplars will be classified more slowly, but perhaps accurately if only relatively similar to a single category. But an object similar to exemplars of different categories will be classified slowly and inaccurately because of the contradictory evidence.

6.5.4 Perceptual Expertise

Radiologists, ornithologists, firefighters, and other specialists are noted for their remarkable abilities at categorizing, identifying, and recognizing objects within their domain of expertise (Palmeri, Wong, & Gauthier, 2004). But understanding perceptual expertise is more than characterizing the behavior of individuals with idiosyncratic skills in highly specialized domains. Perceptual expertise may also explain some of the unique aspects of recognizing faces (Diamond & Carey, 1986; Gauthier & Tarr, 2002), words (McCandliss, Cohen, & Dehaene, 2003), and letters (McCandliss, Cohen, & Dehaene, 2003). The development of perceptual expertise involves a complex interplay of changes in visual perception, visual memory, visual categorization, and visual skills. Indeed, viewing perceptual expertise as the end-point of the normal learning trajectory, rather than an idiosyncratic skill, allows us to exploit studies of perceptual experts to understand the general principles as well as the limits of visual perception, memory, and learning.

Experts are fast (Tanaka & Taylor, 1991). They make fine perceptual discriminations and precise identifications with speeds that can astonish the novice observer. Experts also perceive differently within their domain of expertise (e.g., see Gauthier, Curran, Curby, & Collins, 2003; Goldstone, 2003; Myles-Worsley, Johnston, & Simons, 1988; Snowden, Davies, & Roling, 2000);

that is, "holistically" and more efficiently extracting discriminating information. What makes experts so fast? And what makes them apparently perceive objects in their domain so differently from novices? Have they developed qualitatively different ways of processing information? Have they created new ways of representing information? Or, have they discovered optimal ways of using the representations they had as novices (Gauthier, Tarr, Anderson, Skudlarski, & Gore, 1999; Joyce & Cottrell, 2004; Palmeri, Wong, & Gauthier, 2004)?

As discussed in the previous section, novices categorize objects fastest at a basic (Rosch, Mervis, Gray, Johnson, & Boyes-Braem, 1976) or entry level (Jolicoeur, Gluck, & Kosslyn, 1984). Expertise has been characterized as establishing a new entry level, such that objects are categorized as quickly at more subordinate levels (Johnson & Mervis, 1997; Tanaka & Taylor, 1991). But what does it mean to establish a new entry level? It could mean creating a new special-purpose module or perceptual routine (Jolicoeur, Gluck, & Kosslyn, 1984) for expert categorization at these subordinate levels. Positing the creation of such a module would indeed account for the automaticity, domain-specificity, and attentional inflexibility seen with perceptual experts, and it would link the development of perceptual expertise in novel domains with the purported modularity in domains such as face and letter recognition. Of course, this account begs questions of how a new module might be created, how this module might operate, and whether such a module is computationally necessary at all (Riesenhuber & Poggio, 1999, 2000; Tarr & Cheng, 2003). We have instead approached an understanding of the development of perceptual expertise by viewing it as the end-point of normal learning that underlies recognizing, categorizing, and remembering objects (Gauthier & Tarr, 2002; Joyce & Cottrell, 2004; Palmeri, Wong, & Gauthier, 2004), attempting to characterize the development of perceptual expertise within theories of normal object recognition, categorization, and memory.

An important step in becoming a perceptual expert is learning what aspects of an object class are relevant for a perceptual identification. This learning can get a head start when someone is given an explicit rule (Noelle & Cottrell, 1996). Such rules specify which features are important, explicitly guiding dimensional selective attention (Johansen & Palmeri, 2002), as well as how to combine this information to make a decision. Even when explicit rules are not provided, observers induce simple rules on their own (Ashby, Queller, & Berretty, 1999; Nosofsky & Palmeri, 1998; Nosofsky, Palmeri, & McKinley, 1994; Waldron & Ashby, 2001). But of course, in some domains, verbal labels cannot adequately convey the diagnostic perceptual qualities for the novice, making any explicit instruction a futile enterprise.

Moreover, the use of explicit rules does not seem to characterize expert behavior (Brooks, Norman, & Allen, 1991). Experts may or may not be able to articulate explicit rules to a novice—although in some cases they may simply "know" what things are and may be entirely unaware of whether there might exist a simple rule (Biederman & Shiffrar, 1987)—but they do not seem to use these rules, especially for making their rapid initial perceptual identifications. Perceptual experts make decisions automatically and implicitly. Taking the instance theory of automaticity as a theoretical starting point (Logan, 1988), we argue that this automaticity is largely grounded in the vast perceptual memories experts have acquired (Palmeri, 1997; Palmeri, Wong, & Gauthier, 2004). Experts are fast because memory retrieval is fast. Experts decisions are automatic because memory retrieval is automatic. Experts make difficult perceptual discriminations easily because they have performed similar perceptual discriminations before. Experts show relatively limited generalization because memory retrieval is based on perceptual similarity (Gauthier & Tarr, 1997; Palmeri, 1997; Tanaka, Curran, & Sheinberg, 2005). The development of expertise often entails a shift from rules to visual memories because memory retrieval becomes more efficient than rule use as perceptual memories are strengthened over learning (Johansen & Palmeri, 2002; Palmeri, 1997, 2001; Rickard, 1997).

These perceptual memories should not be confused with simple templates for several reasons. First, retrieval is similarity-based, allowing generalization to novel objects (Poggio & Bizzi, 2004; Shepard, 1987). Second, decisions are not based on retrieving a single perceptual memory, but on retrieving an ensemble of similar perceptual memories (Gauthier & Palmeri, 2002; Poggio & Bizzi, 2004). Third, retrieval of these perceptual memories is not based on raw similarity, but selective attention mechanisms serve to weight diagnostic dimensions over nondiagnostic dimensions in determining similarity (Kruschke, 1992; Lamberts, 1998; Nosofsky, 1984, 1986).

As stated earlier, initial stages of learning involve figuring out which parts of objects are more important than others for making perceptual identification and categorizations. Although this learning can get a boost from an explicit rule that might be supplied (Medin & Smith, 1981; Palmeri & Nosofsky, 1995), more fine-tuned learning involves more implicit trial-to-trial adjustment of selective attention to particular dimensions (Gauthier & Palmeri, 2002; Kruschke, 1992; Lee & Navarro, 2002; Nosofsky, Gluck, Palmeri, McKinley, & et al., 1994; Nosofsky & Kruschke, 1992). Indeed, learning to selectively attend to the right representations may characterize a significant amount of perceptual expertise and perceptual learning (Dosher & Lu, 1999; Petrov, Dosher, & Lu, 2005). Ahissar and Hochstein (2004) argued that "what typically limits naïve performance is the accessibility of task-relevant information rather than the absence of such information within neuronal representations." According to their theory, this selection process works from the top down, so that easy-to-learn problems are those that require selecting relatively high-level representations whereas difficult problems require selecting low-level representations. In this context, many classic category-learning problems are easy tasks (in that they can be learned in a few hundred training trials) because they require learning to selectively attend to highly salient parts or dimensions of an object. By contrast, many perceptual learning problems are hard tasks (in that they require many days of training) because they may require learning to selectively attend to visual processing channels early in the visual stream (Petrov, Dosher, & Lu). Although, selective attention mechanisms have been given a short shrift in some discussions of perceptual expertise and perceptual learning (Schyns, Goldstone, & Thibaut, 1998), they likely play a critical role, especially during initial learning (see also de Beeck, Wagemans, & Vogels, 2003; Palmeri, 1998; Petrov, Dosher, & Lu, 2005).

That said, the development of perceptual expertise requires creating new representations as well as selecting from existing representations. Of course, forming perceptual memories is creating new representations. The initial creation of these exemplar memories may be mediated by hippocampal areas thought to be involved in creating novel configural representations (Gluck, Meeter, & Myers, 2003; Meeter, Myers, & Gluck, 2005; O'Reilly & Norman, 2002). At the same time, exemplar memories may be insufficient to explain all of the perceptual effects manifest in perceptual experts (Palmeri & Gauthier, 2004; Palmeri, Wong, & Gauthier, 2004). Instead, an important aspect of the development of perceptual expertise may also involve the creation of new image-based part representations (Zhang & Cottrell, 2005). These image-based parts can support the perception, categorization, and memory for learned objects, but can also efficiently support perception and memory for new objects (Gauthier & Tarr, 2002). But creating a perceptual expert can take a long time (Gauthier, Williams, Tarr, & Tanaka, 1998). To the extent that this lower-level learning involves cortical updating, this learning will be far slower than the kind of rapid memory formation seen for particular exemplars. Mirroring the top-down progression for selective attention posited by Ahissar and Hochstein (2004), the creation of new representations likely takes place in a top-down manner, with exemplar memories being formed rapidly but image-based part memories taking more time. A critical aspect of learning probably involves creating the right perceptual building blocks, but arguably creating those building blocks may require a great deal of training (but cf. Schyns, Goldstone, & Thibaut, 1998).

6.6 CONCLUSION

Our goal in this chapter was to review and synthesize recent thinking in two domains: visual object perception and visual memory. For whatever reasons, as with much of the larger discipline of cognitive science, there has been a tendency toward compartmentalization. It is almost as if the field's conceptualization of the mind and brain as a collection of modular processing systems is reflected in how the field itself has become organized. Unfortunately, such divisions are often more matters of convenience (both in creating theory and in choosing our domains of study). As such, it is important to consider how nominally separable processes relate to one another. In the case of memory and object perception, this examination is more than cursory. We argue that memory and perception are intimately related and in essence two sides of the same coin. That is, memory arises as a consequence of object perception and, conversely, object recognition tasks are effectively memorial processes.

ACKNOWLEDGMENTS

This work was partially supported by a grant from the James S. McDonnell Foundation, NSF grant HSD-DHBS05, and by the Temporal Dynamics of Learning Center (NSF Science of Learning Center SBE-0542013).

REFERENCES

Ahissar, M., and Hochstein, S. (2004). The reverse hierarchy theory of visual perceptual learning. *Trends in Cognitive Sciences* 8:457–464.

Anderson, J. R. (1976). *Language, Memory, and Thought*. Hillsdale, NJ: Erlbaum.

Anderson, J. R. (1978). Arguments concerning representations for mental imagery. *Psychological Review* 85:249–277.

Ashby, F. G., Alfonso-Reese, L. A., Turken, A. U., and Waldron, E. M. (1998). A formal neuropsychological theory of multiple systems in category learning. *Psychological Review* 105:442–481.

Ashby, F. G., Queller, S., and Berretty, P. M. (1999). On the dominance of unidimensional rules in unsupervised categorization. *Perception and Psychophysics* 61:1178–1199.

Ashby, F. G., and Townsend, J. T. (1986). Varieties of perceptual independence. *Psychological Review* 93:154–179.

Atkinson, R. C., and Shiffrin, R. M. (1968). Human memory: A proposed system and its control processes. In *The Psychology of Learning and Memory, Vol. 2*, eds. K. W. Spence and J. T. Spence. New York: Academic Press.

Barsalou, L. W. (1990). On the indistinguishability of exemplar memory and abstraction in category representation. In *Content and Process Specificity in the Effects of Prior Experiences*, eds. T. K. Srull and R. S. Wyer, Jr., 61–88. Hillsdale, NJ: Lawrence Erlbaum.

Barsalou, L. W. (1999). Perceptual symbol systems. *Behavioral and Brain Sciences* 22:577–660.

Barsalou, L. W., Simmons, W. K., Barbey, A. K., and Wilson, C. D. (2003). Grounding conceptual knowledge in modality-specific systems. *Trends in Cognitive Sciences* 7:84–91.

Barenholtz, E., and Tarr, M. J. (2007). Reconsidering the role of structure in vision. In *Categories in Use. Series: The Psychology of Learning and Motivation*, Vol. 47, eds. A. Markman and B. Ross, 157–180. San Diego: Academic Press.

Barenholtz, E., and Tarr, M. J. (2006). Shape shifters: Visual judgment of similarity across shape transformations. *Journal of Vision*, 6, 606.

Beauregard, M., and Paquette, V. (2006). Neural correlates of a mystical experience in Carmelite nuns. *Neuroscience Letters* 405:186–190.

Biederman, I. (1987). Recognition-by-components: A theory of human image understanding. *Psychological Review* 94:115–147.

Biederman, I., and Gerhardstein, P. C. (1993). Recognizing depth-rotated objects: Evidence and conditions for three-dimensional viewpoint invariance. *Journal of Experimental Psychology: Human Perception and Performance* 19:1162–1182.

Biederman, I., and Shiffrar, M. M. (1987). Sexing day-old chicks: A case study and expert systems analysis of a difficult perceptual-learning task. *Journal of Experimental Psychology: Learning, Memory, and Cognition* 13:640–645.

Bienenstock, E., and Geman, S. (1995). Compositionality in Neural Systems. In *The Handbook of Brain Theory and Neural Networks*, ed. M. A. Arbib, 223–226. Cambridge, MA: MIT Press.

Blanz, V., Tarr, M. J., and Bülthoff, H. H. (1999). What object attributes determine canonical views? *Perception* 28 575–600.

Boucher, L., Palmeri, T. J., Logan, G. D., and Schall, J. D. (2007). Interactive race model of countermanding saccades. *Psychological Review*, 114, 376–397.

Brewer, W. F., and Treyens, J. C. (1981). Role of schemata in memory for places. *Cognitive Psychology* 13:207–230.

Brooks, L. R., Norman, G. R., and Allen, S. W. (1991). Role of specific similarity in a medical diagnostic task. *Journal of Experimental Psychology: General* 120:278–287.

Bruner, J. S., Goodnow, J. J., and Austin, G. A. (1956). *A Study of Thinking*. Oxford, England: Wiley.

Bülthoff, H. H., and Edelman, S. (1992). Psychophysical support for a two-dimensional view interpolation theory of object recognition. *Proceedings of the National Academy of Sciences* 89:60–64.

Busemeyer, J. R., Dewey, G. I., and Medin, D. L. (1984). Evaluation of exemplar-based generalization and the abstraction of categorical information. *Journal of Experimental Psychology: Learning, Memory, and Cognition* 10:638–648.

Cave, C. B. (1997). Very long-lasting priming in picture naming. *Psychological Science* 8:322–325.

Chun, M. M., and Phelps, E. A. (1999). Memory deficits for implicit contextual information in amnesic subjects with hippocampal damage. *Nature Neuroscience* 2:844–847.

Cohen, N.J., Eichenbaum, H. (1993). *Memory, Amnesia, and the Hippocampal System*. Cambridge, MIT Press.

Collins, A. M., and Quillian, M. R. (1969). Retrieval time from semantic memory. *Journal of Verbal Learning and Verbal Behavior* 8:240–247.

de Beeck, H. O., Wagemans, J., and Vogels, R. (2003). The effect of category learning on the representation of shape: Dimensions can be biased but not differentiated. *Journal of Experimental Psychology: General* 132:491–511.

Diamond, R., and Carey, S. (1986). Why faces are and are not special: An effect of expertise. *Journal of Experimental Psychology: General* 115:107–117.

Dobbins, I. G., Schnyer, D. M., Verfaellie, M., and Schacter, D. L. (2004). Cortical activity reductions during repetition priming can result from rapid response learning. *Nature* 428:316–319.

Dosher, B. A., and Lu, Z. L. (1999). Mechanisms of perceptual learning. *Vision Research* 39:3197–3221.

Edelman, S. (1995). Representation, similarity, and the chorus of prototypes. *Minds and Machines* 5:45–68.

Edelman, S. (1997). Computational theories of object recognition. *Trends in Cognitive Science* 1:296–304.

Edelman, S. (1999). *Representation and Recognition in Vision*. Cambridge, MA: MIT Press.

Edelman, S., and Bülthoff, H. H. (1992). Orientation dependence in the recognition of familiar and novel views of three-dimensional objects. *Vision Research* 32:2385–2400.

Farah, M. J. (1990). *Visual Agnosia: Disorders of Object Recognition and What They Tell Us about Normal Vision*. Cambridge, MA: MIT Press.

Farah, M. J., Wilson, K. D., Drain, M., and Tanaka, J. N. (1998). What is "special" about face perception? *Psychological Review* 105:482–498.

Fisher, H. E., Aron, A., and Brown, L. L. (2006). Romantic love: A mammalian brain system for mate choice. *Philosophical Transactions of the Royal Society of London. B: Biological Sciences* 361:2173–2186.

Fodor, J. A. (1975). *The Language of Thought*. Cambridge, MA: Harvard University Press.

Fodor, J. A. (1983). *Modularity of Mind*. Cambridge, MA: MIT Press.

Garner, W. R. (1974). *The Processing of Information and Structure*. Potomac, MD: Erlbaum.

Gauthier, I., and Brown, D. D. (2004). The Perceptual Expertise Network: Innovation on collaboration [Electronic Version]. *APA Online: Psychological Science Agenda* from http://www.apa.org/science/psa/sb-gauthier.html.

Gauthier, I., Curby, K. M., Skudlarski, P., and Epstein, R. A. (in press). Individual differences in FFA activity suggest independent processing at different spatial scales. *Cognitive and Affective Behavioral Neuroscience.*

Gauthier, I., Curran, T., Curby, K. M., and Collins, D. (2003). Perceptual interference supports a non-modular account of face processing. *Nature Neuroscience* 6:428–432.

Gauthier, I., Hayward, W. G., Tarr, M. J., Anderson, A. W., Skudlarski, P., and Gore, J. C. (2002). BOLD activity during mental rotation and viewpoint-dependent object recognition. *Neuron* 34:161–171.

Gauthier, I., and Palmeri, T. J. (2002). Visual neurons: Categorization-based selectivity. *Current Biology* 12:R282–284.

Gauthier, I., Skudlarski, P., Gore, J. C., and Anderson, A. W. (2000). Expertise for cars and birds recruits brain areas involved in face recognition. *Nature Neuroscience* 3:191–197.

Gauthier, I., and Tarr, M. J. (1997). Becoming a "greeble" expert: Exploring mechanisms for face recognition. *Vision Research* 37:1673–1682.

Gauthier, I., and Tarr, M. J. (2002). Unraveling mechanisms for expert object recognition: Bridging brain activity and behavior. *Journal of Experimental Psychology: Human Perception and Performance* 28:431–446.

Gauthier, I., Tarr, M. J., Anderson, A. W., Skudlarski, P., and Gore, J. C. (1999). Activation of the middle fusiform "face area" increases with expertise in recognizing novel objects. *Nature Neuroscience* 2:568–573.

Gauthier, I., Williams, P., Tarr, M. J., and Tanaka, J. (1998). Training "greeble" experts: A framework for studying expert object recognition processes. *Vision Research* 38:2401–2428.

Gillund, G., and Shiffrin, R. M. (1984). A retrieval model for both recognition and recall. *Psychological Review* 91:1–67.

Gluck, M. A., Meeter, M., and Myers, C. E. (2003). Computational models of the hippocampal region: Linking incremental learning and episodic memory. *Trends in Cognitive Sciences* 7:269–276.

Gold, J. I., and Shadlen, M. N. (2001). Neural computations that underlie decisions about sensory stimuli. *Trends in Cognitive Sciences* 5:10–16.

Goldstone, R. L. (2003). Learning to perceive while perceiving to learn. In *Perceptual Organization in Vision: Behavioral and Neural Perspectives*, eds. R. Kimchi, M. Behrmann and C. R. Olson, 233–280. Mahwah, NJ: Lawrence Erlbaum Associates.

Goodale, M. A., and Milner, A. D. (1992). Separate visual pathways for perception and action. *Trends in Neurosciences* 15:20–25.

Grill-Spector, K., Kanwisher, N. (2003). Visual recognition: As soon as you know it is there, you know what it is. *Psychological Science* 16:152–160.

Grill-Spector, K., Knouf, N., and Kanwisher, N. (2004). The fusiform face area subserves face perception, not generic within-category identification. *Nature Neuroscience* 7(5):555–562.

Haxby, J. V., Gobbini, M. I., Furey, M. L., Ishai, A., Schouten, J. L., and Pietrini, P. (2001). Distributed and overlapping representations of faces and objects in ventral temporal cortex. *Science* 293:2425–2430.

Hayward, W. G., and Tarr, M. J. (1997). Testing conditions for viewpoint invariance in object recognition. *Journal of Experimental Psychology: Human Perception and Performance* 23:1511–1521.

Hintzman, D. L. (1986). "Schema abstraction" in a multiple-trace memory model. *Psychological Review* 93:411–428.

Hintzman, D. L. (1988). Judgments of frequency and recognition memory in a multiple-trace memory model. *Psychological Review* 95:528–551.

Hollingworth, A. (2004). Constructing visual representations of natural scenes: The roles of short- and long-term visual memory. *Journal of Experimental Psychology: Human Perception and Performance* 30:519–537.

Hollingworth, A. (2005). The relationship between online visual representation of a scene and long-term scene memory. *Journal of Experimental Psychology: Learning, Memory, and Cognition* 31:396–411.

Hollingworth, A. (2006). Scene and position specificity in visual memory for objects. *Journal of Experimental Psychology: Learning, Memory, and Cognition* 32:58–69.

Hollingworth, A. (in press). Visual memory for natural scenes: Evidence from change detection and visual search. *Visual Cognition: Special Issue on Visual Search and Attention.*

Hollingworth, A., and Henderson, J. M. (2002). Accurate visual memory for previously attended objects in natural scenes. *Journal of Experimental Psychology: Human Perception and Performance* 28:113–136.

Hummel, J. E. (1998). Where view-based theories break down: The role of structure in shape perception and object recognition. In *Cognitive Dynamics: Conceptual Change in Humans and Machines*, eds. E. Dietrich and A. Markman. Cambridge, MA: MIT Press.

Hummel, J. E., and Biederman, I. (1992). Dynamic binding in a neural network for shape recognition. *Psychological Review* 99(3):480–517.

Humphrey, G. K., and Khan, S. C. (1992). Recognizing novel views of three-dimensional objects. *Canadian Journal of Psychology* 46:170–190.

Johansen, M. K., and Palmeri, T. J. (2002). Are there representational shifts during category learning? *Cognitive Psychology* 45:482–553.

Johanson, G. (1973). Visual perception of biological motion and a model for its analysis. *Perception and Psychophysics* 14:201–211.

Johnson, K. E., and Mervis, C. B. (1997). Effects of varying levels of expertise on the basic level of categorization. *Journal of Experimental Psychology: General* 126:248–277.

Jolicoeur, P. (1985). The time to name disoriented natural objects. *Memory and Cognition* 13:289–303.

Jolicoeur, P., Gluck, M. A., and Kosslyn, S. M. (1984). Pictures and names: Making the connection. *Cognitive Psychology,* 16, 243–275.

Joyce, C., and Cottrell, G. W. (2004). *Solving the visual expertise mystery.* Paper presented at the Proceedings of the Eighth Neural Computation and Psychology Workshop.

Kamitani, Y., and Tong, F. (2005). Decoding the visual and subjective contents of the human brain. *Nature Neuroscience* 8:679–685.

Kanwisher, N., McDermott, J., and Chun, M. M. (1997). The fusiform face area: A module in human extrastriate cortex specialized for face perception. *Journal of Neuroscience* 17:4302–4311.

Kersten, D., Mamassian, P., and Yuille, A. (2004). Object perception as Bayesian inference. *Annual Review of Psychology* 55:271–304.

Kinder, A., and Shanks, D. R. (2001). Amnesia and the declarative/nondeclarative distinction: A recurrent network model of classification, recognition, and repetition priming. *Journal of Cognitive Neuroscience* 13:648–669.

Knowlton, B., and Squire, L. R. (1993). The learning of categories: Parallel brain systems for item memory and category knowledge. *Science* 262:1747–1749.

Kolers, P. A. (1976). Reading a year later. *Journal of Experimental Psychology: Human Learning and Memory* 2:554–565.

Kruschke, J. K. (1992). ALCOVE: An exemplar-based connectionist model of category learning. *Psychological Review* 99:22–44.

Lakoff, G. (1987). *Women, Fire, and Dangerous Things: What Categories Reveal about the Mind*. Chicago: University of Chicago Press.

Lamberts, K. (1998). The time course of categorization. *Journal of Experimental Psychology: Learning, Memory, and Cognition* 24:695–711.

Lamberts, K. (2000). Information-accumulation theory of speeded categorization. *Psychological Review* 107:227–260.

Lawson, R., and Humphreys, G. W. (1996). View specificity in object processing: Evidence from picture matching. *Journal of Experimental Psychology: Human Perception and Performance* 22:395–416.

Lee, M. D., and Navarro, D. J. (2002). Extending the ALCOVE model of category learning to featural stimulus domains. *Psychonomic Bulletin and Review* 9:43–58.

Link, S. W. (1975). The relative judgment theory of two choice response time. *Journal of Mathematical Psychology* 12:114–135.

Lissauer, H. (1890). Ein fall von seelenblindheit nebst einem Beitrage zur Theori derselben. *Archiv fur Psychiatrie und Nervenkrankheiten* 21:222–270.

Loftus, E. F. (2004). Memories of things unseen. *Current Directions in Psychological Science* 13:145–147.

Logan, G. D. (1988). Toward an instance theory of automatization. *Psychological Review* 95(4):492–527.

Logan, G. D. (1990). Repetition priming and automaticity: Common underlying mechanisms? *Cognitive Psychology* 22:1–35.

Logan, G. D. (2002). An instance theory of attention and memory. *Psychological Review* 109:376–400.

Logothetis, N. K., and Pauls, J. (1995). Psychophysical and physiological evidence for viewer-centered object representations in the primate. *Cerebral Cortex* 5:270–288.

Logothetis, N. K., and Sheinberg, D. L. (1996). Visual object recognition. *Annual Review of Neuroscience* 19:577–621.

Luce, R. D. (1986). *Response Times: Their Role in Inferring Elementary Mental Organization*. New York: Oxford University Press.

Luria, A. R. (1987). *The Mind of a Mnemonist*. Cambridge, MA: Harvard.

Marr, D. (1982). *Vision: A Computational Investigation into the Human Representation and Processing of Visual Information*. San Francisco: Freeman.

Marr, D., and Nishihara, H. K. (1978). Representation and recognition of the spatial organization of three-dimensional shapes. *Proceedings of the Royal Society of London. Series B, Biological Sciences* 200:269–294.

Martin, A., Ungerleider, L. G., and Haxby, J. V. (2000). Category specificity and the brain: The sensory/motor model of semantic representations of objects. In *The New Cognitive Neurosciences*, ed. M. S. Gazzaniga. Cambridge: MIT Press.

Maurer, D., Grand, R. L., and Mondloch, C. J. (2002). The many faces of configural processing. *Trends in Cognitive Science* 6:255–260.

McCandliss, B. D., Cohen, L., and Dehaene, S. (2003). The visual word form area: Expertise for reading in the fusiform gyrus. *Trends in Cognitive Sciences* 7:293–299.

McClelland, J. L., McNaughton, B. L., and O'Reilly, R. C. (1995). Why there are complementary learning systems in the hippocampus and neocortex: Insights from the successes and failures of connectionist models of learning and memory. *Psychological Review* 102:419–457.

McClelland, J. L., and Rumelhart, D. E. (1985). Distributed memory and the representation of general and specific information. *Journal of Experimental Psychology: General* 114:159–188.

Medin, D. L., and Smith, E. E. (1981). Strategies and classification learning. *Journal of Experimental Psychology: Human Learning and Memory* 7:241–253.

Meeter, M., Myers, C. E., and Gluck, M. A. (2005). Integrating Incremental Learning and Episodic Memory Models of the Hippocampal Region. *Psychological Review* 112:560–585.

Mensink, G. J., and Raaijmakers, J. G. (1988). A model for interference and forgetting. *Psychological Review* 95:434–455.

Minda, J. P., and Smith, J. D. (2001). Prototypes in category learning: The effects of category size, category structure, and stimulus complexity. *Journal of Experimental Psychology: Learning, Memory, and Cognition* 27:775–799.

Mozer, M. C. (1991). *The Perception of Multiple Objects: A Connectionist Approach.* Cambridge, MA: MIT Press.

Mozer, M. C., and Sitton, M. (1998). Computational modeling of spatial attention. In *Attention*, ed. H. Pashler, 341–393). Hove, England: Psychology Press.

Myles-Worsley, M., Johnston, W. A., and Simons, M. A. (1988). The Influence of Expertise on X-Ray Image Processing. *Journal of Experimental Psychology: Learning, Memory, and Cognition* 14:553–557.

Naor-Raz, G., Tarr, M. J., and Kersten, D. (2003). Is color an intrinsic property of object representation? *Perception* 32:667–680.

Newell, A., and Simon, H. A. (1972). *Human Problem Solving.* Upper Saddle River, NJ: Prentice-Hall.

Noelle, D. C., and Cottrell, G. W. (1996). *Modeling interference effects in instructed category learning.* Paper presented at the 18th Annual Conference Of The Cognitive Science Society, La Jolla, CA.

Nosofsky, R. M. (1984). Choice, similarity, and the context theory of classification. *Journal of Experimental Psychology: Learning, Memory, and Cognition* 10:104–114.

Nosofsky, R. M. (1986). Attention, similarity, and the identification-categorization relationship. *Journal of Experimental Psychology: General* 115:39–61.

Nosofsky, R. M. (1991). Tests of an exemplar model for relating perceptual classification and recognition memory. *Journal of Experimental Psychology: Human Perception and Performance* 17:3–27.

Nosofsky, R. M. (1992). Exemplar-based approach to relating categorization, identification, and recognition. In *Multidimensional Models of Perception and Cognition*, ed. F. G. Ashby, 363–393. Hillsdale, NJ: Lawrence Erlbaum Associates.

Nosofsky, R. M. (1998). Optimal performance and exemplar models of classification. In *Rational Models of Cognition*, eds. M. Oaksford and N. Chater, 218–247. New York: Oxford University Press.

Nosofsky, R. M., Gluck, M. A., Palmeri, T. J., McKinley, S. C., et al. (1994). Comparing models of rule-based classification learning: A replication and extension of Shepard, Hovland, and Jenkins (1961). *Memory and Cognition* 22:352–369.

Nosofsky, R. M., and Kruschke, J. K. (1992). Investigations of an exemplar-based connectionist model of category learning. In *The Psychology of Learning and Motivation Vol. 28*, ed. D. L. Medin, 207–250). San Diego: Academic Press.

Nosofsky, R. M., and Palmeri, T. J. (1997). An exemplar-based random walk model of speeded classification. *Psychological Review* 104:266–300.

Nosofsky, R. M., and Palmeri, T. J. (1998). A rule-plus-exception model for classifying objects in continuous-dimension spaces. *Psychonomic Bulletin and Review* 5:345–369.

Nosofsky, R. M., Palmeri, T. J., and McKinley, S. C. (1994) Rule-plus-exception model of classification learning. *Psychological Review* 101:53–79.

Nosofsky, R. M., and Zaki, S. (1998). Dissociations between categorization and recognition in amnesic and normal individuals: An exemplar-based interpretation. *Psychological Science* 9:247–255.

O'Reilly, R. C., and Norman, K. A. (2002). Hippocampal and neocortical contributions to memory: Advances in the complementary learning systems framework. *Trends in Cognitive Sciences* 6:505–510.

O'Reilly, R. C., and Rudy, J. W. (2001). Conjunctive representations in learning and memory: Principles of cortical and hippocampal function. *Psychological Review* 108:311–345.

Oliva, A. (2005). Gist of a Scene. In *Neurobiology of Attention*, eds. L. Itti, G. Rees and J. Tsotsos, 251–256. San Diego: Academic Press.

Palmer, S., Rosch, E., and Chase, P. (1981). Canonical perspective and the perception of objects. In *Attention and Performance IX*, eds. J. Long and A. Baddeley, 135–151). Hillsdale, NJ: Lawrence Erlbaum.

Palmeri, T. J. (1997). Exemplar similarity and the development of automaticity. *Journal of Experimental Psychology: Learning, Memory, and Cognition* 23:324–354.

Palmeri, T. J. (1998). Formal models and feature creation. *Behavioral and Brain Sciences* 21:33–34.

Palmeri, T. J. (1999). Learning categories at different hierarchical levels: A comparison of category learning models. *Psychonomic Bulletin and Review* 6:495–503.

Palmeri, T. J. (2001). The time course of perceptual categorization. In *Similarity and Categorization*, eds. U. Hahn and M. Ramscar, 193–224. New York: Oxford University Press.

Palmeri, T. J., and Flanery, M. A. (1999). Learning about categories in the absence of training: Profound amnesia and the relationship between perceptual categorization and recognition memory. *Psychological Science* 10:526–530.

Palmeri, T. J., and Flanery, M. A. (2002). Memory systems and perceptual categorization. In *The Psychology of Learning and Motivation Vol. 41*, ed. B. H. Ross, 141–189. San Diego: Academic Press.

Palmeri, T. J., and Gauthier, I. (2004). Visual object understanding. *Nature Reviews Neuroscience* 5:291–303.

Palmeri, T. J., and Nosofsky, R. M. (1995). Recognition memory for exceptions to the category rule. *Journal of Experimental Psychology: Learning, Memory, and Cognition* 21:548–568.

Palmeri, T. J., Wong, A. C. N., and Gauthier, I. (2004). Computational approaches to the development of perceptual expertise. *Trends in Cognitive Sciences* 8:378–386.

Perrett, D. I., Oram, M. W., and Ashbridge, E. (1998). Evidence accumulation in cell populations responsive to faces: An account of generalisation of recognition without mental transformations. *Cognition* 67:111–145.

Perrett, D. I., Smith, P. A., Potter, D. D., Mistlin, A. J., Head, A. S., Milner, A. D., et al. (1985). Visual cells in the temporal cortex sensitive to face view and gaze direction. *Proceedings of the Royal Society of London. Series B, Biological Sciences* 223(1232):293–317.

Petrov, A. A., Dosher, B. A., and Lu, Z. L. (2005). The dynamics of perceptual learning: An incremental reweighting model. *Psychological Review* 112:715–743.

Poggio, T., and Bizzi, E. (2004). Generalization in vision and motor control. *Nature* 431:768–774.

Poggio, T., and Edelman, S. (1990). A network that learns to recognize three-dimensional objects. *Nature* 343:263–266.

Posner, M. I., and Keele, S. W. (1968). On the genesis of abstract ideas. *Journal of Experimental Psychology* 77:353–363.

Pratchett, T. (1993). *Men at Arms*: New York: Harper Collins.

Puce, A., Allison, T., Gore, J. C., McCarthy, G. (1995). Face-sensitive regions in human extrastriate cortex studied by functional MRI. *Journal of Neurophysiology* 74:1192–1200.

Pylyshyn, Z. W. (1973). What the mind's eye tells the mind's brain: A critique of mental imagery. *Psychological Bulletin* 80:1–24.

Pylyshyn, Z. W. (1981). The imagery debate: Analogue media versus tacit knowledge. *Psychological Review* 88:16–45.

Raaijmakers, J. G., and Shiffrin, R. M. (1981). Search of associative memory. *Psychological Review* 88:93–134.

Ratcliff, R. (1978). A theory of memory retrieval. *Psychological Review* 85:59–108.

Ratcliff, R., and Rouder, J. N. (1998). Modeling response times for two-choice decisions. *Psychological Science* 9:347–356.

Ratcliff, R., and Smith, P. L. (2004). A comparison of sequential sampling models for two-choice reaction time. *Psychological Review* 111:333–367.

Rensink, R. A., O'Regan, J. K., and Clark, J. J. (1997). To see or not to see: The need for attention to perceive changes in scenes. *Psychological Science* 8:368–373.

Rhodes, G., Byatt, G., Michie, P. T., and Puce, A. (2004). Is the fusiform face area specialized for faces, individuation, or expert individuation? *Journal of Cognitive Neuroscience* 16:189–203.

Rickard, T. C. (1997). Bending the power law: A CMPL theory of strategy shifts and the automatization of cognitive skills. *Journal of Experimental Psychology: General* 126:288–311.

Riesenhuber, M., and Poggio, T. (1999). Hierarchical models of object recognition in cortex. *Nature Neuroscience* 2:1019–1025.

Riesenhuber, M., and Poggio, T. (2000). Models of object recognition. *Nature Neuroscience* 3(Suppl):1199–1204.

Riesenhuber, M., and Poggio, T. (2002). Neural mechanisms of object recognition. *Current Opinion in Neurobiology* 12:162–168.

Righi, G., and Tarr, M. J. (2004). Are chess experts any different from face, bird, or Greeble experts? *Journal of Vision* 4:504.

Roediger, H. L., III, Buckner, R. L., and McDermott, K. B. (1999). Components of processing. In *Memory: Systems, Process, or Function?* eds. J. K. Foster and M. Jelici, 31–65. Oxford, England: Oxford University Press.

Roltman, J. D., and Shadlen, M. D. (2002). Response of neurons in the lateral intraparietal area during a combined visual discrimination reaction time task. *Journal of Neuroscience* 22:9475–9489.

Rosch, E. (1975). Cognitive representations of semantic categories. *Journal of Experimental Psychology: General* 104:192–233.

Rosch, E., Mervis, C. B., Gray, W. D., Johnson, D. M., and Boyes-Braem, P. (1976). Basic objects in natural categories. *Cognitive Psychology* 8:382–439.

Rosseel, Y. (2002). Mixture models of categorization. *Journal of Mathematical Psychology* 46:178–210.

Rossion, B., Gauthier, I., Tarr, M. J., Despland, P., Bruyer, R., Linotte, S., et al. (2000). The N170 occipito-temporal component is delayed and enhanced to inverted faces but not to inverted objects: An electrophysiological account of face-specific processes in the human brain. *Neuroreport* 11(1):69–74.

Rouder, J. N., Ratcliff, R., and McKoon, G. (2000). A neural network model of implicit memory for object recognition. *Psychological Science* 11:13–19.

Schacter, D. L. (2000). Memory: Memory systems. In *Encyclopedia of Psychology Vol. 5*, ed. A. E. Kazdin, 169–172. Washington, DC: American Psychological Association.

Schacter, D. L., Chiu, C.-Y. P., and Ochsner, K. N. (1993). Implicit memory: A selective review. *Annual Review of Neuroscience* 16:153–182.

Schacter, D. L., and Tulving, E. (1994). *Memory Systems*. MIT Press.

Schall, J. D. (2001). Neural Basis of Deciding, Choosing, and Acting. *Nature Reviews Neuroscience* 2:33–42.

Schall, J. D. (2004). On building a bridge between brain and behaviour. *Annual Review of Psychology* 55:23–50.

Schyns, P. G., Goldstone, R. L., and Thibaut, J.-P. (1998). The development of features in object concepts. *Behavioral and Brain Sciences* 21:1–54.

Schyns, P. G., and Rodet, L. (1997). Categorization creates functional features. *Journal of Experimental Psychology: Learning, Memory, and Cognition* 23:681–696.

Sergent, J., Ohta, S., and MacDonald, B. (1992). Functional neuroanatomy of face and object processing. A positron emission tomography study. *Brain* 115(1):15–36.

Shepard, R. N. (1967). Recognition memory for words, sentences, and pictures. *Journal of Verbal Learning and Verbal Behavior* 6:156–163.

Shepard, R. N. (1987). Toward a universal law of generalization for psychological science. *Science* 237:1317–1323.

Shepard, R. N. (1994). Perceptual-cognitive universals as reflections of the world. *Psychonomic Bulletin and Review* 1:2–28.

Shepard, R. N., and Metzler, J. (1971). Mental rotation of three-dimensional objects. *Science* 171:701–703.

Shiffrin, R. M., Steyvers, M. (1997). A model for recognition memory: REM: Retrieving effectively from memory. *Psychonomic Bulletin and Review* 4:145–166.

Shin, H. J., and Nosofsky, R. M. (1992). Similarity-scaling studies of dot-pattern classification and recognition. *Journal of Experimental Psychology: General* 121:278–304.

Simons, D. J. (1996). In sight, out of mind: When object representations fail. *Psychological Science* 7:301–305.

Simons, D. J., and Rensink, R. A. (2005). Change blindness: Past, present, and future. *Trends in Cognitive Sciences* 9:16–20.

Smith, E. E., Shoben, E. J., and Rips, L. J. (1974). Structure and process in semantic memory: A featural model for semantic decisions. *Psychological Review* 81:214–241.

Smith, P. L. (2000). Stochastic dynamic models of response time and accuracy: A foundational primer. *Journal of Mathematical Psychology* 44:408–463.

Smith, P. L., and Ratcliff, R. (2004). Psychology and neurobiology of simple decisions. *Trends in Neurosciences* 27:161–168.

Snowden, P. T., Davies, I. R. L., and Roling, P. (2000). Perceptual learning of the detection of features in X-ray images: A functional role for improvements in adults' visual sensitivity? *Journal of Experimental Psychology: Human Perception and Performance* 26:379–390.

Squire, L. R. (1992). Memory and the hippocampus: A synthesis from findings with rats, monkeys, and humans. *Psychological Review* 99:195–231.

Squire, L. R. (2004). Memory systems of the brain: A brief history and current perspective. *Neurobiology of Learning and Memory* 82:171–177.

Squire, L. R., and Knowlton, B. (1995). Learning about categories in the absence of memory. *Proceedings of the National Academy of Sciences* 92:12470–12474.

Squire, L. R., and Schacter, D. L. (2002). *Neuropsychology of memory (3rd ed.)*. New York, NY: Guilford Press.

Squire, L. R., Stark, C. E. L., and Clark, R. E. (2004). The medial temporal lobe. *Annual Review of Neuroscience* 27:279–306.

Squire, L. R., and Zola, S. M. (1996). Structure and Function of declarative and nondeclarative memory systems. *Proceedings of the National Academy of Sciences* 93:13515–13522.

Standing, L. (1973). Learning 10,000 pictures. *Quarterly Journal of Experimental Psychology* 25:207–222.

Stankiewicz, B. J. (2002). Empirical evidence for independent dimensions in the visual representation of three-dimensional shape. *Journal of Experimental Psychology: Human Perception and Performance* 28:913–932.

Tanaka, J. W., and Curran, T. (2001). A neural basis for expert object recognition. *Psychological Science* 12:43–47.

Tanaka, J. W., Curran, T., and Sheinberg, D. L. (2005). The training and transfer of real world perceptual expertise. *Psychological Science* 16(2):145–151.

Tanaka, J. W., and Farah, M. J. (1993). Parts and wholes in face recognition. *Quarterly Journal of Experimental Psychology* 46A:225–245.

Tanaka, J. W., and Taylor, M. (1991). Object categories and expertise: Is the basic level in the eye of the beholder? *Cognitive Psychology* 23:457–482.

Tanaka, K. (1996). Inferotemporal cortex and object vision. *Annual Review of Neuroscience* 19:109–139.

Tanaka, K. (2002). Neuronal representation of object images and effects of learning. In *Perceptual Learning*, eds. M. Fahle and T. Poggio, 67–82. Cambridge, MA: MIT Press.

Tarr, M. J. (1995). Rotating objects to recognize them: A case study on the role of viewpoint dependency in the recognition of three-dimensional objects. *Psychonomic Bulletin and Review* 2:55–82.

Tarr, M. J., and Bülthoff, H. H. (1998). Image-based object recognition in man, monkey, and machine. *Cognition* 67:1–20.

Tarr, M. J., and Cheng, Y. D. (2003). Learning to see faces and objects. *Trends in Cognitive Science* 7:23–30.

Tarr, M. J., and Gauthier, I. (1998). Do viewpoint-dependent mechanisms generalize across members of a class? *Cognition* 67:73–110.

Tarr, M. J., and Gauthier, I. (2000). FFA: A flexible fusiform area for subordinate-level visual processing automatized by expertise. *Nature Neuroscience* 3:764–769.

Tarr, M. J., Kersten, D., and Bülthoff, H. H. (1998). Why the visual recognition system might encode the effects of illumination. *Vision Research* 38:2259–2275.

Tarr, M. J., and Kriegman, D. J. (2001). What defines a view? *Vision Research* 41:1981–2004.

Tarr, M. J., and Pinker, S. (1989). Mental rotation and orientation-dependence in shape recognition. *Cognitive Psychology* 21:233–282.

Tarr, M. J., and Pinker, S. (1990). When does human object recognition use a viewer-centered reference frame? *Psychological Science* 1:253–256.

Tarr, M. J., Williams, P., Hayward, W. G., and Gauthier, I. (1998). Three-dimensional object recognition is viewpoint dependent. *Nature Neuroscience* 1:275–277.

Tjan, B. (2001). Adaptive object representation with hierarchiacally-distributed memory sites. *Advances in Neural Information Processing Systems* 13:66–72.

Treisman, A. M., and Gelade, G. (1980). A feature-integration theory of attention. *Cognitive Psychology* 12:97–136.

Tulving, E. (1985). How many memory systems are there? *American Psychologist* 40:385–398.

Tulving, E. (1993). What is episodic memory? *Current Directions in Psychological Science* 2:67–70.

Tulving, E., and Schacter, D. L. (1990). Priming and human memory systems. *Science* 247:301–306.

Tversky, A. (1977). Features of similarity. *Psychological Review* 84:327–352.

Ullman, S. (1989). Aligning pictorial descriptions: An approach to object recognition. *Cognition* 32:193–254.

Ullman, S., Vidal-Naquet, M., and Sali, E. (2002). Visual features of intermediate complexity and their use in classification. *Nature Neuroscience* 5:682–687.

Vuong, Q. C., and Tarr, M. J. (2004). Rotation direction affects object recognition. *Vision Research* 44:1717–1730.

Waldron, E. M., and Ashby, F. G. (2001). The effects of concurrent task interference on category learning: Evidence for multiple category learning systems. *Psychonomic Bulletin and Review* 8:168–176.

Wells, G. L., and Loftus, E. F. (2003). Eyewitness memory for people and events. In *Handbook of Psychology: Forensic Psychology, Vol. 11*, ed. A. M. Goldstein, 149–160. Hoboken, NJ: John Wiley and Sons, Inc.

Wells, G. L., and Olson, E. A. (2003). Eyewitness testimony. *Annual Review of Psychology* 54:277–295.

Yin, R. K. (1969). Looking at upside-down faces. *Journal of Experimental Psychology* 81:141–145.

Zaki, S. R., and Nosofsky, R. M. (2001). A single-system interpretation of dissociations between recognition and categorization in a task involving object-like stimuli. *Cognitive, Affective and Behavioral Neuroscience* 1:344–359.

Zaki, S. R., and Nosofsky, R. M. (2004). False prototype enhancement effects in dot pattern categorization. *Memory and Cognition* 32:390–398.

Zaki, S. R., Nosofsky, R. M., Jessup, N. M., and Unversagt, F. W. (2003). Categorization and recognition performance of a memory-impaired group: Evidence for single-system models. *Journal of the International Neuropsychological Society* 9:394–406.

Zhang, L., and Cottrell, G. W. (2005). Holistic processing develops because it is good. In *Proceedings of the 27th Annual Cognitive Science Conference*, eds. B. G. Bara, L. Barsalou and M. Bucciareli. Mahwah: Lawrence Erlbaum.

Chapter 7

Associative Learning Mechanisms in Vision

Marvin M. Chun and Nicholas B. Turk-Browne
Yale University

Visual objects and events do not occur in isolation, but rather within a rich context of other objects and events. Such context is almost always present in everyday vision, and, in the laboratory, has been shown to facilitate the deployment of eye movements (Loftus & Mackworth, 1978; Mackworth & Morandi, 1967; Torralba, Oliva, Castelhano, & Henderson, 2006), object identification (Boyce & Pollatsek, 1992; Boyce, Pollatsek, & Rayner, 1989), and visual search (Chun, 2000). For example, the context of a kitchen enhances recognition of a bread box, but not a drum (Palmer, 1975), and a football player is more accurately recognized on a football field than in church (Fig. 7–1; Davenport & Potter, 2004). How and when does context get associated with objects?

First, it is worth noting that distribution of objects in space and time in the visual environment is not random. Although visual cognition typically focuses on the processing of objects in isolation, the visual environment is rife with information about the relationships between objects. In fact, a visual scene can be defined as "a semantically coherent view of a real-world environment comprising background elements and multiple discrete objects arranged in a spatially licensed manner" (Henderson & Hollingworth, 1999, p. 244). In scenes, objects and events tend to covary with each other, and this statistical structure is invariant over time (Chun, 2000; Fiser & Aslin, 2001, 2002). Thus, if perceptual processes are sensitive to this structure, the complexity of processing can be reduced by improving the predictability of information (Gibson, 1963; Gibson, 1966a, 1966b).

What is lacking in theories of vision is a systematic way to characterize the structure of the visual environment. Is there a grammar for vision that can describe where and when objects should appear relative to each other, just as grammar in language dictates how words can be strung together? Although such a descriptive grammar for vision may not exist, there can be little doubt that rich associations exist between object identities distributed in space and time.

Figure 7–1. Scene context effects. In Davenport and Potter (2004), foreground objects (football player and priest, in these examples) were identified more accurately when presented in congruent background contexts (**A**), than in incongruent background contexts (**B**). Reprinted with permission from Davenport, J. L., & Potter, M. C. (2004). Scene consistency in object and background perception. *Psychological Science*, 15(8), 559–564. Blackwell Publishers.

These associative relations may be the syntax for vision—a tool for describing how objects co-occur—which can be exploited to facilitate visual processing. Indeed, the visual system seems designed to encode the associations between objects, and the capacity for such associative learning is prevalent throughout the brain.

In the first part of this chapter, we will review behavioral evidence of associative learning in vision. First, we will consider which types of associations can be learned, and then we will explore the properties and constraints of the mechanisms involved in such learning. We will also discuss how visual processing can be facilitated by knowledge of associative relationships between objects. The second part of the chapter consists of an analysis of the neural mechanisms that support visual associative learning.

7.1 TYPES OF RELATIONAL (ASSOCIATIVE) MEMORY

The visual environment contains a rich mosaic of associations acquired through repeated experience with objects and their contexts. Contextual information comes in a variety of flavors, such as *where* an object is located in space relative to other objects, *which* objects tend to co-occur, and *when* an object appears in time relative to preceding and subsequent objects. How this information is encoded into memory is the domain of associative learning. Specifically, across multiple experiences, associations are formed between those aspects of context that are predictive of a particular location, object identity, or temporal occurrence. These associations are not passive traces of past experience. Rather, they bias and facilitate future visual processing, helping to anticipate where and when to look, and what to expect.

In everyday vision, the spatial, object, and temporal dimensions of context are all mutually present. This is perhaps most obvious in the case of visual scanning. During scanning, gaze shifts force the visual input to be distributed across time. Each new fixation provides input from a specific location, conveying information about one or more objects. This is also true in the case of visual search while fixated. Covert attention can prioritize objects or locations (and in either case, the other may come along for free). Moreover, according to spotlight and other capacity-limited models of attention (e.g., Posner, Snyder, & Davidson, 1980), not all locations or objects can be sampled in parallel, such that visual input is distributed through time. Thus, in both of these common forms of visual processing, all types of context are simultaneously present.

Many laboratory studies have explored the spatial, object, and temporal aspects of context in relative isolation. It is especially useful to do so when trying to understand the underlying neural mechanisms, since different neural subsystems are specialized for certain types of information. Most of the studies discussed in the next section employ novel or otherwise artificial stimuli to afford greater experimental control and to reduce the influence of prior knowledge on the formation of new associations. Importantly, the insights gained from these artificial displays seem to scale-up to more naturalistic stimuli and situations.

7.1.1 Spatial Associations

Objects and object parts do not appear in random locations, but rather in systematic locations relative to the locations of other parts and objects. As Biederman famously pointed out, one does not experience sofas floating in the sky or fire hydrants on top of mailboxes. Accordingly, observers have greater difficulty recognizing objects that are presented out-of-place (Biederman, Mezzanotte, & Rabinowitz, 1982). However, these context effects may reflect a bias in reporting incongruent information rather than a problem in perception per se (Hollingworth & Henderson, 1998). As a different example, object parts such as the eyes, nose, and mouth always occur in a well-determined spatial relation to each other. Disruption of this configuration, by inverting the face for example, severely impairs face processing and recognition (e.g., Maurer, Grand, & Mondloch, 2002). Spatial associations are even more critical for recognition when an object or part is ambiguous on its own (e.g., Bar & Ullman, 1995). For example, a blurred-out face elicits face-specific neural activity only when placed atop a body (Cox, Meyers, & Sinha, 2004). In the sections below, we will first discuss how such spatial associations are learned, and then focus on an important way in which these associations facilitate visual processing.

7.1.1.1 Spatial statistical learning

At any given moment, we are bombarded with input from the entire visual field. How does the mind segment this input into spatial associations? It turns out that we are remarkably sensitive to statistical regularities between the relative locations of objects. A compelling demonstration of spatial associative learning employed novel shape displays similar to Figure 7–2A (Fiser & Aslin, 2001). Unknown to the observers, the distribution of shapes in the display was not random. Instead, the displays were structured, such that pairs of shapes (base pairs) occurred in fixed spatial relations (Figure 7–2B). Each display consisted of three base pairs (six shapes), and observers viewed series of displays generated from these base pairs. Importantly, the paired shapes were never presented in isolation; rather, they were always bordered by other nonpaired shapes. Thus, to learn the base pairs, observers had to represent the higher covariance between the paired shapes relative to the other adjacent, unpaired shapes. Observers were exposed to several samples of these displays. Afterwards, to test for statistical learning, observers were required to choose the more

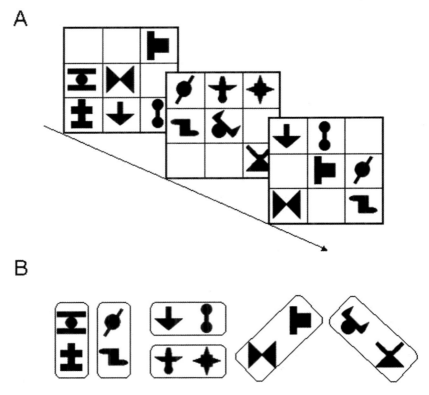

Figure 7–2. Spatial statistical learning. (**A**) In Fiser and Aslin (2001), observers were presented with grids of shapes during a passive viewing training phase. (**B**) Each grid was constructed from three "base pairs" — two shapes that always appeared together and in the same spatial layout. However, because the base pairs appeared adjacent to each other, they could only be segmented by relying on higher-order statistics between the shape elements. Adapted with permission from Fiser, J., & Aslin, R. N. (2001). Unsupervised statistical learning of higher-order spatial structures from visual scenes. *Psychological Science*, 12(6), 499–504. Blackwell Publishers.

familiar of two pairs: One was always a base pair from the first phase, and the other was a new pairing of two old shapes (foil pair). All individual shapes were old, so any familiarity with the base pair must be attributed to spatial association learning. Observers demonstrated remarkably high familiarity with the base pairs.

What information is being extracted in this situation? The most basic statistic that could allow observers to discriminate between the base and foil pairs is joint probability; that is, the relative frequency of co-occurrence. However, in the experiment, the base pairs could also be distinguished based on conditional probability: Given the location of the first shape in a pair, what's the likelihood that a different shape will appear in a certain adjacent location? To explore which statistical information is being extracted in this situation, Fiser and Aslin (2001) conducted another experiment in which joint probability was controlled, and test items could be distinguished only on the basis of conditional probability. Observers showed sensitivity to the conditional structure of the spatial grids. Further research has suggested that much of statistical learning is the extraction of conditional probabilities (e.g. Fiser & Aslin, 2002, 2005). Such data support the idea that statistical learning mechanisms may provide predictive information in everyday vision.

Most studies of statistical learning have relied on familiarity ratings at the end of the experiment to measure learning. Familiarity tests, however, may not be the best way to assess two important facets of statistical learning. First, to the degree that statistical learning is a form of implicit learning (Perruchet & Pacton, 2006), explicit familiarity judgments may not fully capture the extent of implicit knowledge. Second, testing learning in an offline manner at the end of an experiment could obscure learning-related changes in behavior that might otherwise have been observed online. Motivated by these issues, some studies have employed implicit (e.g., Turk-Browne, Jungé, & Scholl, 2005) and online (e.g., Hunt & Aslin, 2001) measures of statistical learning. Next, we explore a parallel literature on contextual influences in visual search that fully employs online, implicit measures.

7.1.1.2 Spatial contextual cuing

Studies of spatial statistical learning demonstrate that adult and infant observers have a remarkable ability to segment the visual world into meaningful spatial groups and to associate the items within these groups. But how does such learned knowledge affect visual behavior? The most basic answer is that spatial associations guide where we look. This guidance is necessary to ensure that we prioritize the most salient regions of space. At a traffic intersection, for example, regions of focus should include traffic lights and signs, crosswalks, and the other roads feeding into the intersection. Spatial associations help to filter out stimuli that are intrinsically salient, but in the wrong location. For example, even if a green neon advertisement is flashing in the background, it is critical to focus instead on the red traffic light. Extensive driving experience allows drivers to rapidly orient to and detect information important for driving safely. More generally, spatial context learning is adaptive because major landmarks and the configurations of various objects in the environment are mostly stable over time, providing useful cues for navigation and orienting. In addition to guiding eye movements, spatial associations can also guide covert attention in visual search tasks. Continuing the automotive theme, consider the instrumentation panel on your car's dashboard. You don't give second thought about where to find the fuel gauge or odometer. The relevant information appears in a fixed location relative to the stable context of the display. Regularities in how information appears relative to the context provide a useful cue for where to attend and look.

To study these intuitions in the laboratory, Chun and Jiang (1998) asked observers to search for a rotated T target amongst rotated L distractors, arrayed in displays as shown in Figure 7–3A. Observers were required to determine whether the T was rotated 90 degrees to the left or 90 degrees to the right. Response time was measured to assess the efficiency of search. Because T's and L's look similar, this type of difficult search task requires careful scanning; The target must be correctly localized with focused spatial attention in order to identify its orientation. The effects of context were tested by simply repeating a set of visual search displays across trials (old condition). These trials were randomly intermixed with trials containing newly generated visual search displays (new condition). In the old condition, the target appeared in a fixed location relative to the configuration of distractors. If observers learned these repeated spatial contexts, attention could be guided to the embedded target location on

A

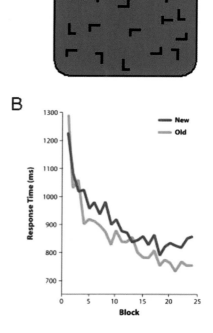

Figure 7–3. Spatial contextual cuing. (**A**) In the standard contextual cuing task (e. g., Chun & Jiang, 1998), observers search for a rotated T target among L distractors, and judge whether the target is rotated to the left or right. Response time is measured as an index of search efficiency. (**B**) Typical results from a contextual cuing task (from Chun & Jiang, 2003). When the configuration of distractors is repeated across many trials, and consistently paired with a target location (old condition), response times are faster than when the distractor and target locations are randomized (new condition). This difference provides evidence that observers can learn the association between spatial configurations and target locations. Adapted with permission from Chun, M. M., & Jiang, Y. (2003). Implicit, long-term spatial contextual memory. *Journal of Experimental Psychology: Learning Memory and Cognition,* 29, 224–234. American Psychological Association.

subsequent trials. In other words, search should become faster and faster as the old displays are repeated, relative to the new displays in which the context was uninformative. The comparison to new displays is essential because search performance also improves for targets in new displays because of perceptual learning of targets and distractors, and because of practice effects in generating responses to detected targets. This latter form of learning is noncontextual (procedural), while the additional benefit for old displays relative to new displays reflects associative/contextual learning.

Typical results are shown in Figure 7–3B (Chun & Jiang, 2003). Search was faster for targets appearing in old displays than in new displays. This indicates that the context of the target facilitated search for the target by cuing visual attention to the target location. Critically, this cuing effect—known as *contextual cuing*—is a spatial effect because the configuration of distractors did not predict the identity of the target, just its location. In other words, the context predicted where the target could be found, but not what it was. Likewise, contextual cuing is typically not sensitive to distractor identities, encoding just their locations and configurations (Chun & Jiang, 1998; but see Jiang & Song, 2005). We'll consider specific examples of identity cuing in the object association section later in the chapter.

It typically takes about five repetitions of each display (one epoch) for learning of the displays to facilitate search. Interestingly, observers do not usually become aware that some displays repeated or that spatial context is predictive of target location. Such explicit knowledge is formally tested by having observers discriminate old from new displays at the end of the session, and by having them try to guess the target location given an old display in which the target has been replaced by a distractor (Chun & Jiang, 2003). The dissociation between facilitated response times and explicit knowledge suggests that the learning underlying contextual cuing is implicit. Moreover, such knowledge is of high capacity and durable: Observers can implicitly learn dozens and dozens of different layouts while retaining immediate contextual cuing benefits even after a 1-week delay between sessions (Chun & Jiang, 2003; Jiang, Song, & Rigas, 2005).

Given this robust phenomenon of contextual cuing, one may ask whether all information in the background provides equally potent context. In the spatial contextual cuing task, it turns out that there are some constraints on which spatial information can facilitate search. Olson and Chun (2002) discovered that only a portion of each display is associated with a target location. In their study, one side of each display was repeated over multiple trials while the other side changed randomly from trial to trial. Thus, for each old display, half of the display was predictive and the other half was not, and the target could appear on either side. Contextual cuing for targets appearing within the predictive local context was as strong as when the entire display was repeated, suggesting that local context is sufficient; an equally predictive context on the opposite side of the display from the target did not produce contextual cuing. In fact, even a set of only three items around the target within the same screen quadrant was sufficient to elicit contextual cuing (Brady & Chun, 2007; see also Jiang & Wagner, 2004). Together, these results indicate that, in visual search tasks using dense displays, spatial contextual cuing is locally restricted to the region around the target.

The fact that spatial contextual cuing is driven by local items has several implications. First, this provides useful constraints on learning. Because there is so much information to encode in any background context, the complexity of the associative learning mechanism underlying contextual cuing is reduced by restricting the input. Second, the fact that contextual cuing is driven by local rather than global context sets a limit on how much guidance to expect from predictive spatial contexts in visual search. If predictive global context was implicitly recognized as soon as the display appears, then the associated target should be detected immediately, as would be the case if, for example, the target were a unique, brightly colored, blinking item. However, contextual cueing does not reach such levels of efficiency; the benefit is intermediate between perfect guidance and no guidance (Chun & Jiang, 1998; Kunar, Flusberg, Horowitz, & Wolfe, in press). Because predictive context is local, it cannot guide search to an embedded target until the relevant local cluster of items (e.g., quadrant of a display) is reached during scanning of the display. Computer simulations accurately predict how much guidance in search one should observe given the spatially constrained nature of contextual cuing (Brady & Chun, 2007).

Contextual cuing provides evidence of spatial associative learning and shows how such learning can benefit performance. But, how exactly do contextual associations facilitate search? We had proposed that context guides "attention" based on the assumption that the allocation of attention to a target precedes any action directed towards it; that is, faster responses reflect faster allocation of attention to the target location. However, prior studies did not directly demonstrate that the target location is more quickly attended. Moreover, it remains possible that contextual cuing reflects prioritization of the target location at a postselection stage—that is, in visual short-term memory or response selection (Kunar et al., 2007)—rather than prioritized selection of the item at the target location per se.

Support for the claim that contextual cuing reflects prioritized sampling of the target location comes from eye movement data, electrophysiological evidence, and functional magnetic resonance imaging (fMRI) studies. For example, fewer saccades are needed to acquire a target appearing in an old display compared to a new display (Peterson & Kramer, 2001a), and the first saccade in a natural scene is most often directed at the probable location of a target (Eckstein, Drescher, & Shimozaki, 2006). Similar results have been observed in monkeys making eye movements to targets embedded in natural-scene backgrounds (Sheinberg & Logothetis, 1998). Interestingly, such contextual cuing of eye movements may even override the powerful pull of salient visual events such as abrupt onsets (Peterson & Kramer, 2001b).

As more direct evidence, event-related potential and fMRI studies have demonstrated that attention is cued by contextual memory. The scalp-recorded N2pc component is a well-validated electrophysiological marker of the focusing of attention (Luck, Girelli, McDermott, & Ford, 1997). If contextual cuing increases the probability that attention is oriented to a target more quickly on repeated trials, then one should predict an increase in the amplitude of the N2pc waveform. Supporting this prediction, Johnson, Woodman, Braun, & Luck (2007) discovered that the N2pc amplitude was greater for repeated arrays than for novel arrays beginning at a latency of about 175 ms. This finding provides direct evidence that contextual cuing leads to greater early allocation of attention to the target. A separate fMRI study compared visually driven search and memory driven search. In visually driven search, observers were explicitly instructed to orient visual attention to a target location. In memory-driven search, observers learned to orient to a target location based on its associations with a background scene. Frontoparietal regions of the brain important for attentional orienting were commonly activated in both visually driven and memory-driven tasks (Summerfield, Lepsien, Gitelman, Mesulam, & Nobre, 2006). All of these results support a guided attention account of contextual cuing.

Although most of the laboratory studies just discussed employ highly artificial or abstracted displays, contextual cuing also operates in more natural displays. For example, contextual cuing is robust in three-dimensional displays (Kawahara, 2003) or pseudo-naturalistic displays with three-dimensional perspective (Chun & Jiang, 2003). Further, the arbitrary location of a target letter can be associated with the layout of a real-world scene (Brockmole & Henderson, 2006). Such scene-based contextual cuing shows some differences compared to contextual cuing in tasks using arbitrary stimuli. For example, observers became explicitly aware of the scene–target associations, and the degree of learning was sensitive to the semantic cohesiveness of the scene. It may be impossible to eliminate the influence of semantic knowledge in processing real-world scenes (and this is part of the motivation for using artificial displays), but such influences should still be considered contextual (Bar, 2004). For example, targets are identified in real-world scenes more quickly when their location is semantically consistent with the scene (Neider & Zelinsky, 2006).

Interestingly, unlike traditional demonstrations of contextual cuing, target locations get associated with global information in natural scenes (Brockmole, Castelhano, & Henderson, 2006): Learning of context transfers across local but not global relational changes. Given that contextual cuing in natural scenes varies as a function of semantic cohesiveness (Brockmole & Henderson, 2006), observers may be learning an association between the target location and a more holistic semantic representation of the scene, even if the identity of the target is semantically unrelated. Thus, local changes within a given semantic context will not affect the expression of learning, whereas global changes to the semantics of a scene might. Such an account is consistent with the fact that the parahippocampal place area (PPA), a region of ventral visual cortex selective for natural scenes, is more sensitive to global layout than to object configurations (Epstein & Kanwisher, 1998a). Moreover, processing in nearby parahippocampal cortex may serve as a semantic frame for object recognition (Bar, 2004) and, more specifically, may be directly involved in binding objects to background scenes (Goh et al., 2004). Thus, contextual cuing in natural scenes may reflect simpler associations between holistic scene representations and target locations, rather than between configurations of distractor and target locations. Such reliance on global features is a key component of a very promising computational model that can produce contextual guidance of eye movements and attention in real-world scenes (Torralba et al., 2006). This elegant and sophisticated model combines bottom-up saliency, scene context, and top-down mechanisms to predict image regions that are likely to be fixated during natural search tasks.

7.1.1.3 Links between spatial statistical learning and contextual cuing

In many ways, contextual cuing can be considered a special case of spatial statistical learning: Observers extract statistical relationships between the configuration of distractors and the target location. In other ways, the two phenomena are different. One superficial difference is that contextual cuing per se reflects the expression of learned associations; thus, the progression of learning can be easily tracked online, unlike most studies of statistical learning (cf. Hunt & Aslin, 2001). A more profound difference is the conscious accessibility of the learned associations: Most studies of statistical learning have relied on explicit familiarity tests to assess learning (cf. Turk-Browne et al., 2005), whereas, in the case of contextual cuing, such tests fail to elicit evidence of learning (e.g., Chun & Jiang, 1998, 2003). Therefore, to the degree that contextual cuing reflects statistical learning, familiarity may not be the most informative measure of statistical learning.

Another important consideration is the distinction between association and segmentation. The result of statistical learning could simply be a set of associations between elements, where the strength varies as a function of the statistical properties of the input. Performance on the familiarity test would then reflect the relatively stronger associations between the elements that had been grouped versus ungrouped. Another possibility, however, is that statistical learning results in segmented units or chunks: "words" in auditory statistical learning (e.g., Saffran, 2001) and "objects" in visual statistical learning (e.g., Fiser & Aslin, 2005). According to this view, the boundaries between chunks may be determined by statistical computations (or independently; see Perruchet & Pacton, 2006), and test performance may reflect the strength of the chunk's memory trace per se rather than the strength of the associations between constituent elements. Chunking does not seem to apply well to contextual cuing, however, since there is little information to be segmented in any given display; observers may instead learn associations between the target location and individual distractor locations (Jiang & Wagner, 2004).

7.1.1.4 Global spatial context

Thus far, we have focused on context defined as the distribution of objects in space. However, spatial context can also be defined at a stage prior to object individuation. For example, the semantic category of a scene can be determined from low spatial frequencies (e.g., Schyns & Oliva, 1994), the distribution of colors (Goffaux et al., 2005), and the distribution of orientations (McCotter, Gosselin, Sowden, & Schyns, 2005). Attention can then be guided efficiently to the most salient locations in a scene by combining this global semantic information with bottom-up local salience (e.g., Torralba et al., 2006). One advantage of this global property approach is that individual objects do not need to be segmented and identified. This does not rule out a contribution of individual object recognition to context effects, however. Both global scene-based and individual object–based forms of spatial context information can be integrated in a single model of visual recognition. Low spatial frequencies and spatial layout information in a scene may help activate a semantic frame and identify a range of possible interpretations of a target object, whereas high spatial frequencies may be contrasted with the possible interpretations and constrained by the semantic frame (Bar, 2004; Chun, 2003). Such approaches suggest that visual processing is most efficient when it takes advantage of statistical structure at multiple spatial scales and levels of complexity.

7.1.2 Object Associations

Although context specifies where things can be found, it can also specify what kinds of things should be expected. Objects that tend to covary in the environment can become associated independent of their spatial relations. For example, when looking at an office desk, one does not expect to see lawnmowers or rakes, but rather paper and pencils, even if their precise locations change from day to day. In this section, we explore how the covariance between objects (independent of spatial location) can be learned, and how this knowledge can be exploited to facilitate object recognition.

7.1.2.1 Object contextual cuing

The learning and expression of object covariance has been investigated using a modified contextual cuing paradigm (Fig. 7–4). Observers were presented with arrays of novel shapes containing a single target shape that was symmetric around the vertical axis and several distractor shapes that were symmetric around nonvertical axes (Chun & Jiang, 1999). Observers were instructed to search for the vertically symmetric object as quickly and as accurately as possible. By defining the search target according to symmetry, novel shape targets could be specified without labeling or showing the actual shape. As soon as observers detected the target, they pressed a key and response time was recorded. The array of novel shapes was then replaced with an array of probe letters, each appearing in a location previously occupied by a novel shape. Observers entered the probe letter that appeared in the same location as the target shape. This non-speeded probe task ensured that the target was localized correctly.

As in the spatial contextual cuing task described in the previous section, two conditions were present. In the old condition, the target shape was always paired with a fixed set of distractor shapes from block to block. In the new condition, the target shape and distractor sets were uncorrelated: The assignment of distractor shapes to a particular trial was randomized independently of the target shape. In other words, the target and distractor shapes consistently mapped in the old condition but, in the new condition, the mapping between target and distractor shapes was variable (Schneider & Shiffrin, 1977; Shiffrin

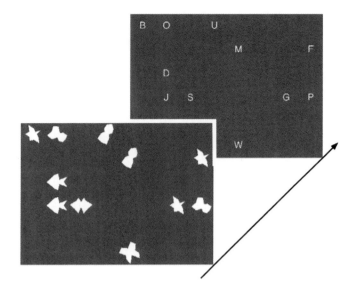

Figure 7–4. Object contextual cuing. In a variant of the contextual cuing task, observers search for the shape with vertical symmetry among non-symmetrical distractors (Chun & Jiang, 1999). To verify that the target shape was correctly localized, observers then respond by pressing the letter in the target location. In the old condition, the symmetrical target shape is consistently paired with a particular set of distractor shapes. In the new condition, the target shape is paired with a random assortment of distractor shapes from trial to trial. Critically, the distractor and target locations are completely randomized for each trial, eliminating the possibility of spatial associative learning. Visual search eventually becomes faster in the old condition than in the new condition. This difference provides evidence that the target and distractor shapes in the old condition have been associated. Reprinted with permission from Chun, M. M., & Jiang, Y. (1999). Top-down attentional guidance based on implicit learning of visual covariation. *Psychological Science*, 10, 360–365. Blackwell Publishers.

& Schneider, 1977). All target shapes and distractor sets were repeated an equal number of times in both conditions, ruling out perceptual learning of individual shapes as a contributing factor in performance. Critically, the location of the target and distractors in a given display were fully randomized from trial to trial. Thus, any differences in performance between old and new conditions must be attributed to the covariance or consistent mapping between target and distractor sets, divorced from spatial structure (later, in the section on cross-dimensional learning, we'll discuss a study in which both object and spatial statistical structure were simultaneously present).

Observers demonstrated robust object contextual cuing: On trials where the target probe letter was correctly identified, target detection was faster in old displays than new displays. This reveals that we are sensitive to the covariance of objects in the visual environment in spite of (or because of; Endo & Takeda,

2004) spatial variability, and that learned object–object associations can facilitate recognition of search targets in context. Like spatial contextual cuing, such associative learning produces implicit knowledge: Observers performed at chance when attempting to discriminate between old and new displays.

The wealth of research on spatial contextual cuing raises many questions that have yet to be answered about the nature of object contextual cuing. For example, how do the distractor shape identities get associated with the target identities? Specifically, individual shapes may become associated in pairs, and thus, the serial processing of distractors associated with the target shape will increasingly activate the target representation. However, the distractor shapes could also become associated together in a set, which, in turn, would become associated with the target identity; from work on consistent versus variable mapping (Schneider & Shiffrin, 1977; Shiffrin & Schneider, 1977), we know that identity set effects are powerful in visual learning and search.

Finally, it is interesting to consider how the attentional guidance in spatial contextual cuing might relate to the facilitation observed here. Specifically, because the target and distractor locations were randomized, the effect cannot be spatial. How can knowing the identity of the target facilitate search through a series of spatial locations? In serial searches, object contextual cuing may reflect facilitation at either (or both) selection and identification stages. In other words, the target location may be selected more quickly because previously processed distractors would set up an attentional set for the target identity. Additionally, the distractors may not affect the speed with which the target location is selected, but rather, the speed with which the target is identified after selection. According to this view, the distractors may associatively prime the identity of the target, facilitating the decision of whether the selected shape has vertical symmetry.

7.1.2.2 Spatial specificity of learning

Spatial and object contextual cuing tasks were purposefully designed to test for the formation of one specific type of knowledge without influence from the other. In the case of spatial contextual cuing, observers can only learn spatial associations: Only the spatial configuration of distractors is predictive (distractors are homogenous L shapes), and only the target location can be predicted (target identity is chosen randomly). Conversely, in object contextual cuing, observers can only learn object associations: Only the set of distractor identities is predictive (distractor locations are randomized), and only the target identity can be predicted (the target location is randomized). Such restricted tasks were deliberately constructed to isolate specific mechanisms, but may never be fully dissociable in other situations.

For example, both sources of structure are present in spatial statistical learning tasks. In other words, in the study of Fiser and Aslin (2001) discussed earlier, observers could have learned two things about the base shape pairs: (a) that the two shapes are associated in a particular spatial configuration, or (b) that the two shapes are simply associated (with no spatial specificity). Their study was unable to distinguish between the two possibilities because the pairs were always tested in their original configuration. However, if spatial and object learning can be separated, do associations learned in one dimension generalize to the other?

A recent study demonstrates that spatial statistical learning can result in object associations (Turk-Browne & Scholl, in press). In this study, observers were exposed to the training displays from Fiser and Aslin (2001), but statistical learning was tested in a different way. Observers performed target detection in rapid sequences of shapes presented one-at-a-time in a single location. Detection was facilitated when the target shape was preceded by the shape with which it was spatially associated during learning. Because no spatial structure was present at test, these results suggest that observers were able to abstract object associations in the presence of spatial structure.

Future research could explore the situations under which spatial associations between objects can be abstracted to pure object associations. As demonstrated by object contextual cuing, variability in spatial configurations can encourage learning of object–object associations (see also Endo & Takeda, 2004). Another important factor may be the nature of the task during learning. In contextual cuing, observers are actively engaged in visual search through space; in typical spatial statistical learning tasks, observers passively view displays without a spatial task.

7.1.2.3 Learning within objects

While we have thus far focused on learning of associations between objects, a wealth of information also exists about covariance between object parts (used loosely for both surface and shape features). Much like spatial and object context, feature associations can affect object recognition. For example, it takes longer to name the color of a purple banana than a yellow banana (Naor-Raz, Tarr, & Kersten, 2003), purportedly because the banana shape is associated with the color yellow, which causes Stroop-like interference. The strength of an association between shape and color within an object is governed by color-*diagnosticity*, that is, the variability of the mapping of a particular color to a particular shape (Tanaka & Presnell, 1999). For example, objects with high diagnosticity (e.g., fire engines) are more quickly recognized when presented in color, whereas objects with low diagnosticity (e.g., chairs) are just as quickly recognized without color. These results suggest that colors become associated with shapes because they co-occur in the environment. In turn, such covariation between surface features may help define the objects over which other forms of associative learning operate (Turk-Browne, Isola, Scholl, & Treat, 2008).

In addition to surface features, two or more shape features may themselves become associated into objects on the basis of co-occurrence (Fiser & Aslin, 2005), and grouping cues can further help shape features become associated with each other (Baker, Olson, & Behrmann, 2004). The result of learning within objects may be the attentional prioritization of other regions of the object (Egly, Driver, & Rafal, 1994; Shomstein & Yantis, 2002), analogous to the guidance of attention between objects.

7.1.3 Temporal Associations

In a static snapshot, spatial configurations and object identities provide rich context for visual search and recognition. However, this context can change from moment to moment for several reasons. First, the visual environment itself is highly dynamic; in order to perceive the world with some continuity, we must be able to recognize objects over time and transformations. Second, the visual input received from our eyes is dynamic even when the world is static. We constantly move our eyes and head to sample new regions of space, and such movements cause massive shifts in retinal input. The visual system is remarkably good at compensating for such shifts, helping to maintain a stable percept (this compensation can be subverted by directly moving the eyeball with a finger). Third, because of the capacity limitations of spatial attention and visual short-term memory, we must iteratively sample the visual environment. This serial processing ensures that some spatial and object associations in the environment will be distributed across mental time. Finally, events can unfold over time in predictable ways. This rich temporal structure may guide our expectations for what will happen from one moment to the next. We will consider how observers can learn regularities in how objects move in a later section on spatiotemporal learning. In this section, we will focus on how context distributed in time is learned, and how such context can help predict upcoming events.

7.1.3.1 Temporal statistical learning

As discussed earlier, the distribution of objects in space is often continuous: Objects are associated into groups, but these groups are not necessarily spatially segregated. Rather, we can learn to segment or chunk the visual world into meaningful units via spatial statistical learning. Similarly, visual processing is continuous in time: The focus of attention changes from object to object as we navigate through the visual environment. Embedded within this continuous stream are two types of structure: (a) reliable and ordered sequences of input, or "events" (Zacks & Tversky, 2001) and (b) associations between objects that tend to co-occur in the environment and thus are more likely to be processed in temporal proximity. The ability to extract and represent both kinds of temporal structure is another form of statistical learning and, much like spatial statistical learning, seems to be governed by the conditional probabilities of (now temporally) adjacent items.

To study temporal statistical learning, Fiser and Aslin (2002) presented short animations of simple shapes appearing one at a time (Fig. 7–5A). Unknown to observers, the stream contained very regular patterns. Specifically, the shapes were assigned into groups of three that always appeared in the same order (Fig. 7–5B). The stream was constructed by randomly sequencing these "triplets," such that the transitional probabilities between shapes within a triplet was very high, whereas the transitional probability between shapes at the triplet boundaries was very low. Importantly, the stream was continuous, thus providing no temporal cues to the boundaries between triplets. Learning was

A

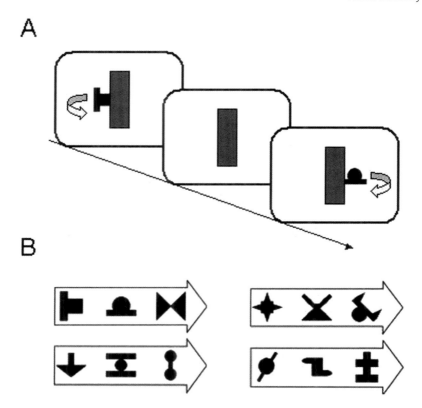

B

Figure 7–5. Temporal statistical learning. (**A**) In Fiser and Aslin (2002), observers watched a stream of shapes appearing one at a time from behind an occluder. (**B**) The stream of shapes was constructed from subsequences of three shapes that always appeared in succession. Observers learned these subsequences, but because the stream was continuous (and thus the boundaries between subsequences were unmarked), they were required to rely on higher-order statistics between the shape elements. Adapted with permission from Fiser, J., & Aslin, R. N. (2002). Statistical learning of higher-order temporal structure from visual shape sequences. *Journal of Experimental Psychology: Learning Memory and Cognition*, 28(3), 458–467, Figures 2 and 3. American Psychological Association.

tested by having observers repeatedly judge whether the triplets or new combinations of the same shapes were more familiar. Because only familiar shapes were used, the two alternatives could only be distinguished based on the relatively higher transitional probabilities within the triplets. Observers demonstrated a robust familiarity preference for the old sequences, suggesting that they had learned the triplet structure of the stream. This segmentation may reflect sensitivity not only to the high transitional probabilities between shapes within a triplet, but the high variability of the transitions at the triplet boundaries. Interestingly, high variability alone may also serve to define boundaries between events in natural vision, even without other cues (Avrahami & Kareev, 1994).

Sensitivity to temporal structure may be domain general. Specifically, one of the most prominent demonstrations of temporal statistical learning was in the domain of language acquisition (Saffran, Aslin, & Newport, 1996). In that study, 8-month-old infants were presented with streams of syllable triplets and, after 2 min, could distinguish between repeated and novel sequences. Such learning may provide an especially useful mechanism for word segmentation, since normal speech is undifferentiated (Saffran, 2001). However, as in the case of spatial statistical learning, observers may not, in fact, be extracting temporal sequences per se (Turk-Browne & Scholl, in press). After being exposed to a stream of triplets (as in Fiser & Aslin, 2002), observers could recognize the triplets in static spatial displays that were presented for only 150 ms. This suggests that, although the processing of objects may be distributed across time, these regularities are represented as simple object associations. Of course, representations may also exist that possess temporal order; such specificity would be critical for language learning, where words are not simply a collection of syllables, but possess a particular ordering.

7.1.3.2 Temporal contextual cuing

These studies of temporal statistical learning rely on familiarity tests after the fact. How does knowledge of temporal sequences affect performance? In another variant of contextual cuing (Olson & Chun, 2001), observers were presented with sequences of letters. The letter identities appeared in either a fixed sequence or a random sequence. The task involved detecting a prespecified target letter as quickly as possible. When the target letter was preceded by a repeated (and hence, predictive) sequence of letter identities, observers were quicker to respond than when it was preceded by a random sequence. This demonstrates sensitivity to the temporal structure of events, such that prior processing can facilitate future recognition. Similar facilitation effects have been observed as a result of temporal statistical learning (Turk-Browne et al., 2005) and appear to grow when additional context is added. Independent of object identity, observers are also sensitive to the timing or rhythm of sequences. Target detection is faster when the target appears at a time that can be predicted by the onset times of the preceding items (Olson & Chun, 2001; see also Shin & Ivry, 2002).

7.1.3.3 Other (more abstract) types of temporal associative learning

Although we are focusing here on visual temporal context, the topic of sequence learning more generally has a long and important history. Much of this research began as an exploration of the distributional properties of language (Harris, 1955). Subsequent research explored the mechanisms of grammar learning, specifically, how experience with a set of exemplars can produce knowledge of the artificial grammar from which they were generated (Reber, 1967). More recently, research has been focused on how sequences of manual responses can be learned (serial reaction time learning; Nissen & Bullemer, 1987). The degree to which the mechanisms involved in these forms of learning apply to visual associative learning remains an open and interesting question. For example, similar constraints apply to serial reaction time and statistical learning: Selective attention is necessary, but learning can occur without intent or awareness, and even during secondary tasks (Jiménez & Méndez, 1999; Turk-Browne et al., 2005). On the other hand, serial reaction time learning and spatial contextual cuing may rely on different neural mechanisms. For example, contextual cuing is spared in healthy aging, whereas sequence learning can be impaired in the same subjects (Howard, Dennis, Howard, Yankovich, and Vaidya, 2004).

7.1.4 Cross-dimensional Associations

As discussed earlier, the isolation of spatial, object, and temporal aspects of context is theoretically useful, but one must also characterize the wealth of learning that occurs between these dimensions. In everyday vision, these three facets of context are not only simultaneously present, but are often inextricably linked. Thus, we review here some examples of how learning operates over multidimensional or *spatiotemporal* objects.

7.1.4.1 Spatial–temporal learning

Regularities exist in how objects change over time. For example, in many team sports such as basketball, football, and soccer, one must be sensitive to how other players move around the field. These movements are not random but are also not necessarily instructed. Skilled players are able to sense these patterns, which can in turn allow them to anticipate and exploit how a play will evolve. The best players are those with "field sense," which refers to the ability to make an optimal play based on the global state of how players are moving about. To mimic this situation in the lab, one study asked observers to search for a target that moved around the computer screen amid a set of moving distractors (Chun & Jiang, 1999). All of the objects moved along independent trajectories, with the constraint that they could not run into each other. To study the effects of dynamic context, the target motion trajectories in the old condition were consistently paired with their own sets of distractor motion trajectories. In other words, the entire dynamic vignette was repeated from block to block. In the new condition, the target and distractor motion trajectories were randomized from block to block. Observers were faster to detect the target in the old condition, indicating that they implicitly learned the dynamic contexts that were predictive of the target motion trajectory. This is analogous to how patterns in player movements on a ball field may allow an experienced eye to predict how events will unfold. The associative learning of motion trajectories may be analogous to the learning of object associations; like objects, brief reliable motions are a basic unit of perception (Cavanagh, Labianca, & Thornton, 2001).

Not only can we learn patterns of object motion, we can also learn patterns of where and when different objects will appear during dynamic events. To test this kind of learning in the laboratory, observers can be presented with a series of objects appearing one at a time in a very regular sequence of spatial locations. In traditional serial reaction time tasks (e.g., Nissen & Bullemer, 1987), observers press a different response key for each of the possible locations, and response times decrease as the sequence is repeated. However, because the spatial sequence and the response sequence are perfectly correlated in this design, it is unclear whether the learning is spatial rather than response-driven.

To convincingly demonstrate learning of spatial sequences, Mayr (1996; see also Willingham, Nissen, & Bullemer, 1989) employed a different task. Instead of responding to the spatial location, observers responded to the identity of each object as it appeared in different locations. In addition to the spatial sequence, the object identities formed their own sequence. The two sequences were uncorrelated, such that any effects of spatial sequence learning could be decoupled from response demands. Spatial sequence learning was demonstrated in a test block in which the sequence of spatial locations was scrambled and responses became slower; critically, because the identity sequence was preserved, this effect could not be attributed to response learning. As in the learning of spatial configurations, knowledge of the spatial sequences was implicit (Mayr, 1996). Subsequent research has demonstrated that static spatial configurations, in addition to spatial sequences, can be used to predict the location of a target that has yet to appear in the display—for example, the location of a visual search target on the next trial (Ono, Jiang, & Kawahara, 2005). All of these results reveal that we are remarkably sensitive to spatial statistical structure, whether conveyed in static or dynamic displays.

7.1.4.2 Spatial–object learning

We have seen how context distributed in time can facilitate target detection in space. Other examples demonstrate how information in two dimensions can get associated. As discussed earlier, spatial contextual cuing is a special situation, since the identities of the distractors are completely uninformative (beyond simply identifying them as distractors), and only the location of the target can be predicted. In this situation, observers can only learn associations between the spatial locations of the distractors and the target. In the visual environment, however, spatial configurations are often only as good as the objects they contain: The context of three objects arranged in a triangular configuration is not especially useful for finding a person's mouth without knowing that these three objects are two eyes and a nose. Similarly in the laboratory, spatial contextual cuing can be attenuated when the distractor identities are altered, but the distractor locations are preserved (Jiang & Leung, 2005). This is not to say that spatial configurations alone provide no benefit, but rather that attaching diagnostic identity information can enhance learning and its subsequent expression.

To explore how the conjunction of spatial and object identity information affects search, Endo and Takeda (2004) employed another variant of the contextual cuing paradigm. Observers were presented with an array of outlined shapes, and were required to detect the shape whose contour was closed; the open-contour shapes served as distractors. Critically, each of the repeated target

A

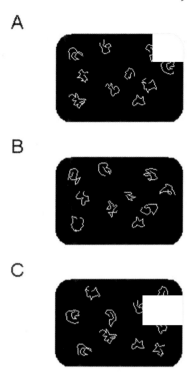

Figure 7–6. Multidimensional contextual cuing. In Endo and Takeda (2004), observers performed a visual search task for the line drawing with the closed contour among distractors with open contours. In one experiment, the configuration of shapes was repeated during training, and, at test, observers search for the target in either (**A**) the original display (combined repetition), (**B**) a repetition of the configuration with new shapes (configuration repetition), or (**C**) a repetition of the shapes in a new spatial configuration (identity repetition). Only the combined and configuration repetitions facilitated visual search, suggesting that completely redundant identity information is discarded in contextual cuing. In another experiment in which identity repetitions were included in training (and thus, spatial configuration was not always reliable), all three types of repetition facilitated visual search at test.

and distractor locations was consistently mapped to a unique shape (Fig. 7–6A; *combined repetition*). Thus, both spatial configuration and distractor identity sets could predict both target location and target identity. In a test block, either the spatial configuration was left intact and the distractor identities randomized (Fig. 7–6B; *configuration repetition*), or the set of distractor identities was maintained and the locations randomized (Fig. 7–6C; *identity repetition*). Interestingly, the combined and configuration repetition facilitated target detection relative to a new configuration of shapes and locations, but the identity repetition did not. When all three types of old displays (combined, configuration, and identity repetition) were intermixed throughout training, rather than just being presented in the test block, target detection was facilitated by all three types of repetition. This surprising reversal suggests that, during visual search, completely redundant object context is not learned. Finally, in a different experiment in which spatial configuration predicted target identity and distractor identities predicted target location (the two untested combinations from Chun & Jiang, 1998, 1999), only the latter type of association was learned. Thus, regardless of the type of context, associations with target location are most beneficial during visual search.

Similar mechanisms may serve to associate objects and their most common spatial locations in a scene (Hollingworth, 2005). To explore this *object-in-place* learning, researchers can test how memory for individual objects depends on whether they are presented in their original scene locations at test. For example, in one study (Hollingworth, 2006b), observers viewed a naturalistic scene for several seconds, and then completed a memory test. They were presented with one of the original objects from the scene and a modified version of the same object (rotated in depth, or a different exemplar of the same object type), and were required to determine which alternative was the original. Critically, although all test items were superimposed on the original background scene, the two alternatives were either presented in the same spatial location as the original, or in a new spatial location. Object memory—as defined by the accuracy of choosing the original object—was better when the alternatives were presented in the original location than in the new location, suggesting that the object's identity had been bound to that location.

Subsequent research has demonstrated that this form of learning is not strictly spatial; rather, it is relative to the configuration of the other objects in the display: Object memory is preserved in a new location if the configuration of the other objects is likewise translated (Hollingworth, 2007). Moreover, although such relational learning can improve explicit object recognition, it can also be observed using implicit eye movement measures. For example, when an object in a learned scene moves to a new location (thus violating the relational structure of the scene), it receives a disproportionate amount of viewing (e.g., Ryan, Althoff, Whitlow, & Cohen, 2000; Ryan, Leung, Turk-Browne, & Hasher, 2007). In fact, this increased sampling often only occurs when observers lack explicit awareness of the relational manipulation itself (Ryan et al., 2000).

NEURAL MECHANISMS FOR VISUAL ASSOCIATIVE LEARNING

Our review thus far describes the many rich ways in which the visual system encodes associations between objects and object parts across both space and time. The neural mechanisms that support such powerful learning are complex, yet great progress has been made toward understanding this highly adaptive and important function.

All brain systems are plastic (Gaffan, 2002). From the earliest stages of cortical processing in striate cortex to high-level representations in medial temporal and frontal cortices, such plasticity optimizes visual processing for features, objects, and scenes. This section will consider how visual associations may be encoded in the brain, which may eventually help us understand the organization of visual knowledge. We will first discuss basic principles for how visual associations can be represented in local neuronal circuitry. Then, we will discuss the neural substrates of visual associative learning at a systems level, describing how different structures in the brain may encode different types of visual associations. Specifically, we will focus on the medial temporal lobe system (MTL), which plays a central role in visual associative learning, but is still the subject of active debate about the specific functions of the different subregions, including the hippocampus, parahippocampal cortex, and perirhinal cortex.

7.2.1 Basic Mechanisms for Associative Learning

Miyashita and colleagues conducted classic studies to demonstrate how visual associations are encoded in temporal cortex (Miyashita, 1988; Sakai & Miyashita, 1991). In the first phase, they trained monkeys on visual shapes that were novel, avoiding contamination from preexisting associations that exist for familiar shapes. With such training, individual neurons in inferotemporal (IT) cortex become shape-selective (Kobatake, Wang, & Tanaka, 1998; Logothetis, Pauls, & Poggio, 1995; Mishkin, 1982). Inferotemporal cortex is the final stage of the ventral processing stream devoted to object vision, and it is where visual long-term representations are stored (Miyashita, 1993). Then, going beyond exhibiting such selectivity for individual trained stimuli, they demonstrated that IT neurons can also associate these geometrically unrelated items through co-occurrence over time (Miyashita, 1988; Sakai & Miyashita, 1991). In other words, if a neuron shows a good response to stimulus A, then it can also become responsive to other different-looking stimuli that appeared close in time to stimulus A during training. In theory, such mechanisms of associative learning in shape-selective neurons should not only allow for object-to-object priming between associated items, but also for the integration of different views of the same object (Logothetis & Pauls, 1995; Logothetis et al., 1995). More specifically in perirhinal cortex, a region in anterior medial IT cortex, Erickson and Desimone (1999) demonstrated that perirhinal neurons responded more similarly to associated stimuli, and significant activity occurred during the delay period between a predictor stimulus and its associated stimulus appearing after the delay.

Given such basic mechanisms of associative learning, one can ask about the functional organization of visual long-term memory. Cognitive models suggest that semantically related items should have strong, "close" connections, whereas unrelated items should have weaker, more "distant" connections. In the case of visual learning, this literally seems to be true. Erickson, Jagadeesh, and Desimone (2000) recorded from pairs of neurons in perirhinal cortex of macaques while the monkeys viewed series of complex visual images. When the stimuli were novel, neuronal responses for pairs of nearby neurons and far-apart neurons were uncorrelated. However, even after just 1 day of experience, the response preferences of nearby neurons became more similar, suggesting that learning induces the development of clusters with similar stimulus preferences. This finding is consistent with similar results obtained for simpler objects in more posterior regions of IT cortex (Gawne, Kjaer, Hertz, & Richmond, 1996; Gochin, Colombo, Dorfman, Gerstein, & Gross, 1994; Tanaka, 1996). Such evidence for local clustering makes it interesting to consider whether different temporal lobe brain regions may contain functional subdivisions at a more global level.

7.2.2 Basic Global Organization

The MTL system is critical for long-term storage of information. Key brain structures that we will focus on here include the hippocampus, parahippocampal cortex, and perirhinal cortex. Beyond the MTL proper, retrosplenial cortex appears to play a role in visual long-term associative memory as well.

A fundamental question is whether these diverse components of the MTL operate in a unitary manner or whether multiple functional subdivisions exist. Converging evidence suggests some degree of functional specialization. For example, the hippocampus is important for spatial processing, whereas perirhinal cortex is involved in object processing (for a review, see Murray, Graham, & Gaffan, 2005). Yet, it remains controversial whether hippocampal function should be segregated from other MTL structures using dichotomies such as associative versus nonassociative memory, declarative versus nondeclarative memory, explicit versus implicit memory, episodic versus semantic memory, and recollection versus familiarity (Squire, Stark, & Clark, 2004).

7.2.2.1 Hippocampus

The hippocampus performs a central function in associative and contextual learning. Contextual learning requires the binding of multiple cues. Thus, it can also be described as configural, spatioconfigural, or relational learning (Cohen & Eichenbaum, 1993; Hirsh, 1974; Johnson & Chalfonte, 1994; Kim & Fanselow, 1992; Moscovitch, 1994; Nadel & Moscovitch, 1997; O'Keefe & Nadel, 1978; Sutherland & Rudy, 1989). The Morris Water Maze task has been extensively studied to reveal the importance of the hippocampus in spatial contextual learning (Morris, Garrud, Rawlins, & O'Keefe, 1982). When rats are placed in a tank of opaque water, they can adeptly navigate to a hidden platform based on spatial cues provided by the room context. However, when the hippocampus is damaged, they lose the ability to perform this navigation task. Contextual fear conditioning is another popular measure of hippocampus-dependent configural learning (Kim & Fanselow, 1992; Phillips & LeDoux, 1992). When rats receive an aversive, electric shock in a cage, they become conditioned to associate the shock with the cage. When placed in the same cage after conditioning, they exhibit a fear-related freezing response. However, such fear conditioning is abolished with hippocampal ablation.

These findings suggest that the hippocampus and associated MTL structures should be important for visual context learning. As discussed earlier, one straightforward way to study visual context learning is to measure how subjects learn the positions of objects within scenes (Hollingworth, 2006a, 2006b). Gaffan, Murray, and colleagues demonstrated that hippocampus, perirhinal, and fornix lesions significantly impaired the ability to locate visual target shapes on complex backgrounds (Gaffan, 1994; Gaffan & Parker, 1996; Murray, Baxter, & Gaffan, 1998). Furthermore, electrophysiological recordings provide direct evidence that hippocampal neurons change their response properties during a learning task that required associating target locations with background scenes (Wirth et al., 2003). In human subjects tested with fMRI, an elegant study showed that the hippocampus and parahippocampal regions were sensitive to the bindings of objects with their backgrounds showing fMRI adaptation only when the object–background pairings were repeated (Goh et al., 2004).

Neuropsychological studies provide further insight into the role of the hippocampus in contextual learning. Patients with hippocampal and extended MTL damage exhibited impairments in the spatial contextual cueing task described earlier (Chun & Phelps, 1999). Contextual cueing can also be disrupted with neuropharmacological manipulations such as midazolam, which produces transient amnesia (Park, Quinlan, Thornton, & Reder, 2004). Importantly, the contextual learning in both of these two studies was implicit in all observers. Hence, these findings must be explained in terms of impaired spatial context learning rather than impaired conscious, explicit memory, which is also dependent on the hippocampus and MTL system (Squire, 1992).

However, the role of the hippocampus in implicit spatial associative learning is controversial. Manns and Squire (2001) compared contextual cueing in amnesic patients with restricted hippocampal damage and amnesic patients with more extended MTL damage. Only patients with extended MTL damage showed no spatial contextual cuing; patients with focal damage to the hippocampus (average 30% atrophy) showed normal contextual cuing effects. Because hippocampal damage was not complete in these patients, however, there remains some ambiguity about how these findings should be interpreted. Nevertheless, the patients were amnesic for declarative memory tasks, suggesting that the damage was consequential, and thus the dissociation between focal hippocampal and extended MTL damage deserves careful attention. Needless to say, human patient lesions are not precise enough to resolve refined questions of functional specialization.

Animal lesion studies and human brain imaging evidence using implicit tasks may provide further insight. For example, a brain imaging study revealed increased hippocampal and parahippocampal activation in tasks that required associating face stimuli and house stimuli, compared to single-item learning (Henke, Buck, Weber, & Wieser, 1997). Another study demonstrated hippocampal and parahippocampal involvement during associative encoding of line drawings of unrelated objects, for example, a picture of a monkey holding an umbrella (Rombouts et al., 1997). Thus, the hippocampus and posterior parahippocampal gyrus are involved in both the encoding and retrieval of novel picture pairs. Even for implicit contextual cueing tasks, fMRI reveals significant hippocampal activation (Greene et al., 2007). Although neuroimaging studies do not establish the necessity of a brain region for a given function, converging evidence from both human and animal models suggest that the hippocampus is important for both explicit and implicit learning of visual associations.

7.2.2.2 Parahippocampal cortex

The ability to perceive and represent one's local visual environment from scene information is fundamental for navigation and other visual behaviors. Thus, it is not surprising that dedicated neural machinery is specialized for processing scene information in medial temporal cortex (Aguirre, Detre, Alsop, & D'Esposito, 1996; Aguirre, Zarahn, & D'Esposito, 1998; Epstein, Harris, Stanley, & Kanwisher, 1999; Epstein & Kanwisher, 1998a, 1998b). Termed the PPA, this region shows higher fMRI activation to scenes and three-dimensional spatial layouts than to faces, single objects, objects in arrays without three-dimensional layout information, or scrambled scene stimuli. Figure 7–7 shows individual PPA regions of five subjects tested in our lab. A robust PPA can be localized in

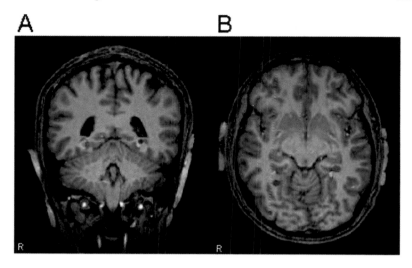

Figure 7–7. Bilateral parahippocampal place area (PPA) of five typical observers (in different colors) in coronal (**A**) and oblique axial (**B**) views. Regions-of-interest were defined as a 4-mm sphere surrounding the voxel on the collateral sulcus/parahippocampal gyrus showing the greatest difference between the hemodynamic response to scenes and faces.

almost all observers in both hemispheres, and the precise anatomical location is remarkably consistent across individuals.

It is quite interesting that the PPA is more responsive to spatial structure than to component objects per se. This is relevant because encoding spatial information requires configural, associative encoding, as shown earlier for the hippocampus. The PPA's sensitivity to spatial structure can be seen most clearly in Figure 7–8, which shows how this region responds to various types of stimuli (Epstein & Kanwisher, 1998a). Although the PPA response was most robust to scenes that contain rich structure, such as outdoor or indoor naturalistic scenes, it was also robust to even an empty room that did not contain any objects. Notably, the empty room response was higher than to a two-dimensional picture of furniture from a room on a blank background that lacked three-dimensional layout information.

However, the PPA does exhibit a significant response to objects as well, even when presented in isolation. The parahippocampal region is large in anatomical extent, beyond what is localized in the scene–object comparison used to define the PPA, and it is significantly involved in a wide variety of episodic memory tasks (Brewer, Zhao, Desmond, Glover, & Gabrieli, 1998; Turk-Browne, Yi, & Chun, 2006; Wagner et al., 1998). Thus, beyond the PPA's role in encoding spatial layout, we will review next how object associations are encoded in parahippocampal cortex.

One line of work provides clear evidence that the parahippocampal region is important for object contextual memory. Bar and Aminoff (2003) asked subjects to simply name a visually presented object on each trial. They compared

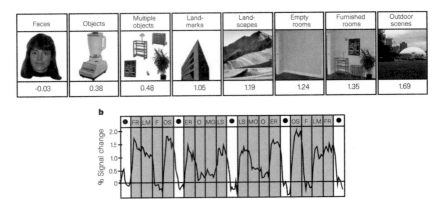

Figure 7–8. Example functional magnetic resonance imaging (fMRI) responses in the parahippocampal place area (PPA) to eight different stimulus types. Reprinted with permission from Epstein, R., & Kanwisher, N. (1998). A cortical representation of the local visual environment. *Nature*, 392(6676), 598–601. Macmillan Publishers Ltd.

cortical processing for two different sets of objects. Objects with strong contextual associations (strong CA objects) were rated to have strong associations with specific contexts, such as a shopping cart for supermarkets or microscopes for labs. In contrast, weak CA objects did not have such strong associations because they could occur in a wider variety of situations, such as a rope or a camera. The clever hypothesis was that pictures of strong CA objects should activate additional information associated with corresponding contexts, whereas weak CA objects should not elicit such contextual information. In other words, strong CA objects should trigger more activity in those brain regions that store or process visual contextual knowledge. Functional magnetic resonance imaging revealed two main sites of stronger activation for strong CA objects relative to weak CA objects. The first and largest focus was in the posterior part of the parahippocampal cortex, and the anatomical coordinates of this region (Talairach -24, -41, -4) overlap with those previously reported for the PPA. Another major region of activation was in the retrosplenial cortex, which is involved in episodic memory tasks and spatial navigation; retrosplenial function will be discussed in more detail in the next section.

Parahippocampal cortex and retrosplenial cortex are active to both spatial and nonspatial contexts. Interestingly, some gradation of spatial processing occurred in the parahippocampal gyrus, with stronger effects of spatial context along the posterior section and stronger effects of nonspatial context in the anterior section (Bar & Aminoff, 2003). The posterior end showed stronger overlap with the PPA (Epstein & Kanwisher, 1998a). This posterior–anterior axis of spatial specificity was confirmed even more directly in a nice study that directly compared spatial associations and nonspatial associations (Aminoff, Gronau, & Bar, 2006). Parahippocampal cortex was involved for both types of associative encoding, but nonspatial associations were mainly encoded in anterior parahippocampal cortex, whereas spatial associations were represented in posterior parahippocampal cortex. Interestingly, only the latter posterior regions involved in spatial context learning overlapped with the PPA, defined by comparing scenes versus faces and scrambled scenes.

7.2.2.3 Retrosplenial cortex

In addition to the parahippocampal cortex, retrosplenial cortex is important for contextual associations, scene representation, and navigation (Aguirre & D'Esposito, 1999; Bar, 2004). Retrosplenial cortex runs as an arch around the splenium of the corpus callosum, encompassing the isthmus of the cingulate gyrus (Maguire, 2001). Navigation tasks represent an especially challenging function that requires the ability to associate and sequence disparate views and locations. Neuroimaging studies also point to a role for the retrosplenial cortex in spatial navigation tasks such as navigating through a virtual-reality maze (Aguirre et al., 1996) or when London taxi drivers were asked to recall complex routes around the city (Maguire, Frackowiak, & Frith, 1997). Beyond explicit navigation tasks, the role of retrosplenial cortex in associative processing is reinforced by several neuroimaging studies showing its involvement in episodic memory tasks (Andreasen et al., 1995; Fink et al., 1996; Wiggs, Weisberg, & Martin, 1999). Accordingly, retrosplenial damage produces general memory problems (Valenstein et al., 1987). Some interesting lateralization in function also appears to occur: Left retrosplenial cortex is more involved in general aspects of episodic memory, whereas right retrosplenial cortex is more involved in topographical orientation and spatial navigation (Maguire, 2001).

Interesting functional differences are apparent with parahippocampal cortex. Damage to retrosplenial cortex impairs the ability to orient oneself or navigate around the environment, even while the ability to identify scenes or landmarks remains intact (Maguire, 2001; Takahashi, Kawamura, Shiota, Kasahata, & Hirayama, 1997). In contrast, damage to parahippocampal cortex compromises the basic ability to identify scenes that lack individual distinctiveness (Mendez & Cherrier, 2003). Thus, the neuropsychological evidence suggests that parahippocampal and retrosplenial cortex may play different roles in scene perception and memory.

Epstein and Higgins (2007) raised an interesting proposal to understand the functional differences between parahippocampal and retrosplenial cortex. They proposed that parahippocampal cortex is involved in identifying specific locations from the geometry and spatial cues in scenes, whereas the retrosplenial cortex plays a more integrative role in associating the scene with other related scenes to form a global topographic representation useful for directional navigation. In support of this hypothesis, they found that, compared to parahippocampal responses, retrosplenial activity was relatively weak when spatial scenes were merely viewed, but much stronger when task cues required subjects to retrieve information about the larger environment surrounding the scenes. In further support of an integrative function, responses in retrosplenial cortex, relative to parahippocampal cortex, are independent of exact physical properties (Bar & Aminoff, 2003).

Extending these ideas further, preliminary work in our lab explored the hypothesis that scene representations should be more viewpoint-invariant in retrosplenial cortex than in parahippocampal cortex (Park & Chun, under revision). Subjects were presented with three panoramic views of the same scene; each view overlapped with its adjacent view by only 30% of the image area. A viewpoint-dependent response would treat these three views as different from each other, whereas a viewpoint-independent response would treat these three views as similar to each other. Similarity can be measured by the fact that neural responses and corresponding fMRI signals are lower for sequences of similar-looking images than for different-looking images. In parahippocampal cortex, fMRI responses were similar for panoramic images as for sequences of novel images, suggesting that the panoramic images were treated as different from each other; that is, the responses were viewpoint-dependent. In contrast, responses to panoramic images were lower than to novel images in retrosplenial cortex, suggesting that these were treated as the "same," in support of a more integrative, viewpoint-invariant representation of the scenes from which the panoramic views were drawn. Future work will further clarify the differences and interactions between parahippocampal and retrosplenial processing.

7.2.2.4 Perirhinal cortex

Perirhinal cortex, which is located at the ventromedial aspect of the primate temporal lobe, is important for both the perception and memory of objects (Gaffan & Parker, 1996; Murray & Bussey, 1999). Perirhinal cortex is well suited to associate features of objects or objects with other objects, as it receives diffuse projections from inferotemporal cortex area TE (Saleem & Tanaka, 1996; Suzuki & Amaral, 1994). Murray and Richmond (2001) have summarized several functions of the perirhinal cortex.

First, perirhinal cortex is involved in object memory. Activity in perirhinal cortex neurons reflect long-term familiarity of visual images, as overall neuronal firing rate is higher to familiar relative to novel images (Holscher, Rolls, & Xiang, 2003). Also, ablation of perirhinal cortex impairs the ability to match an object with a target object presented previously (Buffalo et al., 1999; Meunier, Bachevalier, Mishkin, & Murray, 1993).

Second, perirhinal cortex is important for perception as well as memory. Perceptual factors can be tested by requiring observers to discriminate objects under various challenges, such as visual degradation or visual transformations. For example, recognition of complex objects is commonly viewpoint-dependent; that is, it becomes more difficult as the test object is rotated away from the original viewing angle. Monkeys with perirhinal damage have greater difficulty matching the same object presented in different viewing orientations (Buckley & Gaffan, 1998b), although human subjects with perirhinal damage do not show such impairments relative to control subjects with intact perirhinal cortex. Although perirhinal damage does not always produce impairments in difficult perceptual discriminations (Stark & Squire, 2000), it does seem to be important for difficult, ambiguous discriminations of complex objects; that is, when objects cannot be distinguished based on unique visual features alone

(Buckley, Booth, Rolls, & Gaffan, 2001; Lee et al., 2005; but see Levy, Shrager, & Squire, 2005).

Third, perirhinal cortex associates objects with other objects. Learning visual paired associates is impaired by perirhinal and entorhinal lesions (Buckley & Gaffan, 1998a; Higuchi & Miyashita, 1996; Miyashita, Okuno, Tokuyama, Ihara, & Nakajima, 1996; Murray, Gaffan, & Mishkin, 1993). Furthermore, brain-derived neurotrophic factor, which is involved in activity-dependent neural reorganization, is upregulated in perirhinal cortex during pair-associate learning (Tokuyama, Okuno, Hashimoto, Xin Li, & Miyashita, 2000). Perirhinal cortex also associates information about trial sequences. Monkeys readily learn visual cues that indicate progress toward a trial in which juice reward would be provided, but lesions to rhinal cortex impaired this ability to learn the predictive visual cues (Liu, Murray, & Richmond, 2000). Recent work is starting to distinguish whether perirhinal cortex is important for encoding, retrieval, or both stages of associative memory. An fMRI study suggests that perirhinal cortex is only active during encoding, but not retrieval of novel picture pairs, in contrast to the activation of hippocampus and parahippocampal gyrus areas in both encoding and retrieval (Pihlajamaki et al., 2003).

7.3 CONCLUSION

Visual objects and events always appear in a rich context of other objects and events, distributed over space and time. Statistical regularities occur in how objects appear with each other, and the brain has evolved exquisite mechanisms to encode such regularities, both within its local circuitry and at the systems level. Understanding these associative learning mechanisms will allow us to characterize the nature of visual knowledge and representation. As we aimed to highlight here, the effort to understand visual associative learning will require the continued development of innovative behavioral tasks, integrative theory, as well as advanced neuroscientific methods and techniques.

REFERENCES

Aguirre, G. K., and D'Esposito, M. (1999). Topographical disorientation: A synthesis and taxonomy. *Brain* 122(Pt 9):1613–1628.

Aguirre, G. K., Detre, J. A., Alsop, D. C., and D'Esposito, M. (1996). The parahippocampus subserves topographical learning in man. *Cerebral Cortex* 6(6):823–829.

Aguirre, G. K., Zarahn, E., and D'Esposito, M. (1998). Neural components of topographical representation. *Proceedings of the National Academy of Sciences of the United States of America* 95(3):839–846.

Aminoff, E., Gronau, N., and Bar, M. (2006). The parahippocampal cortex mediates spatial and nonspatial associations. *Cerebral Cortex* 17(7):1493–1503.

Andreasen, N. C., O'Leary, D. S., Cizadlo, T., Arndt, S., Rezai, K., Watkins, G. L., et al. (1995). Remembering the past: Two facets of episodic memory explored with positron emission tomography. *American Journal of Psychiatry* 152(11):1576–1585.

Avrahami, J., and Kareev, Y. (1994). The emergence of events. *Cognition* 53(3):239–261.

Baker, C. I., Olson, C. R., and Behrmann, M. (2004). Role of attention and perceptual grouping in visual statistical learning. *Psychological Science* 15(7):460–466.

Bar, M. (2004). Visual objects in context. *Nat Rev Neurosc* 5(8):617–629.

Bar, M., and Aminoff, E. (2003). Cortical analysis of visual context. *Neuron* 38(2):347–358.

Bar, M., and Ullman, S. (1995). *Spatial context in recognition*. Paper presented at the ARVO, Fort Lauderdale, FL.

Biederman, I., Mezzanotte, R. J., and Rabinowitz, J. C. (1982). Scene perception: Detecting and judging objects undergoing relational violations. *Cognitive Psychology* 14(2):143–177.

Boyce, S. J., and Pollatsek, A. (1992). Identification of objects in scenes: The role of scene background in object naming. *Journal of Experimental Psychology: Learning, Memory, and Cognition* 18:531–543.

Boyce, S. J., Pollatsek, A., and Rayner, K. (1989). Effect of background information on object identification. *Journal of Experimental Psychology: Human Perception and Performance* 15:556–566.

Brady, T. F., and Chun, M. M. (2007). Spatial constraints on learning in visual search: Modeling contextual cuing. *Journal of Experimental Psychology: Human Perception and Performance* 33:798–815.

Brewer, J. B., Zhao, Z., Desmond, J. E., Glover, G. H., and Gabrieli, J. D. (1998). Making memories: Brain activity that predicts how well visual experience will be remembered [see comments]. *Science* 281(5380):1185–1187.

Brockmole, J. R., Castelhano, M. S., and Henderson, J. M. (2006). Contextual cueing in naturalistic scenes: Global and local contexts. *Journal of Experimental Psychology. Learning Memory and Cognition* 32(4):699–706.

Brockmole, J. R., and Henderson, J. M. (2006). Using real-world scenes as contextual cues for search. *Visual Cognition* 13:99–108.

Buckley, M. J., Booth, M. C., Rolls, E. T., and Gaffan, D. (2001). Selective perceptual impairments after perirhinal cortex ablation. *Journal of Neuroscience* 21(24):9824–9836.

Buckley, M. J., and Gaffan, D. (1998a). Perirhinal cortex ablation impairs configural learning and paired-associate learning equally. *Neuropsychologia* 36(6):535–546.

Buckley, M. J., and Gaffan, D. (1998b). Perirhinal cortex ablation impairs visual object identification. *Journal of Neuroscience* 18(6):2268–2275.

Buffalo, E. A., Ramus, S. J., Clark, R. E., Teng, E., Squire, L. R., and Zola, S. M. (1999). Dissociation between the effects of damage to perirhinal cortex and area te. *Learning and Memory* 6(6):572–599.

Cavanagh, P., Labianca, A. T., and Thornton, I. M. (2001). Attention-based visual routines: Sprites. *Cognition* 80(1–2):47–60.

Chun, M. M. (2000). Contextual cueing of visual attention. *Trends in Cognitive Science* 4(5):170–178.

Chun, M. M. (2003). Scene perception and memory. In *Psychology of Learning and Motivation: Advances in Research and Theory: Cognitive Vision Vol. 42*, eds. D. Irwin and B. Ross, 79–108. San Diego: Academic Press.

Chun, M. M., and Jiang, Y. (1998). Contextual cueing: Implicit learning and memory of visual context guides spatial attention. *Cognitive Psychology* 36:28–71.

Chun, M. M., and Jiang, Y. (1999). Top-down attentional guidance based on implicit learning of visual covariation. *Psychological Science* 10:360–365.

Chun, M. M., and Jiang, Y. (2003). Implicit, long-term spatial contextual memory. *Journal of Experimental Psychology: Learning Memory and Cognition* 29:224–234.

Chun, M. M., and Phelps, E. A. (1999). Memory deficits for implicit contextual information in amnesic subjects with hippocampal damage. *Nature Neuroscience* 2(9):844–847.

Cohen, N. J., and Eichenbaum, H. (1993). *Memory Amnesia and the Hippocampal System*. Cambridge, MA: MIT Press.

Cox, D., Meyers, E., and Sinha, P. (2004). Contextually evoked object-specific responses in human visual cortex. *Science* 304(5667):115–117.

Davenport, J. L., and Potter, M. C. (2004). Scene consistency in object and background perception. *Psychological Science* 15(8):559–564.

Eckstein, M. P., Drescher, B. A., and Shimozaki, S. S. (2006). Attentional cues in real scenes, saccadic targeting, and bayesian priors. *Psychological Science* 17(11): 973–980.

Egly, R., Driver, J., and Rafal, R. D. (1994). Shifting visual attention between objects and locations: Evidence from normal and parietal lesion subjects. *Journal of Experimental Psychology: General* 123(2):161–177.

Endo, N., and Takeda, Y. (2004). Selective learning of spatial configuration and object identity in visual search. *Perception and Psychophysics* 66(2):293–302.

Epstein, R., Harris, A., Stanley, D., and Kanwisher, N. (1999). The parahippocampal place area: Recognition, navigation, or encoding? *Neuron* 23(1):115–125.

Epstein, R., and Kanwisher, N. (1998a). A cortical representation of the local visual environment. *Nature* 392(6676):598–601.

Epstein, R., and Kanwisher, N. (1998b). The parahippocampal place area: A cortical representation of the local visual environment. *Journal of Cognitive Neuroscience*, 20–20.

Epstein, R. A., and Higgins, J. S. (2007). Differential parahippocampal and retrosplenial involvement in three types of visual scene recognition. *Cerebral Cortex* 17(7):1680–1693.

Erickson, C. A., and Desimone, R. (1999). Responses of macaque perirhinal neurons during and after visual stimulus association learning. *Journal of Neuroscience* 19(23):10404–10416.

Erickson, C. A., Jagadeesh, B., and Desimone, R. (2000). Clustering of perirhinal neurons with similar properties following visual experience in adult monkeys. *Nature Neuroscience* 3(11):1143–1148.

Fink, G. R., Markowitsch, H. J., Reinkemeier, M., Bruckbauer, T., Kessler, J., and Heiss, W. D. (1996). Cerebral representation of one's own past: Neural networks involved in autobiographical memory. *Journal of Neuroscience* 16(13):4275–4282.

Fiser, J., and Aslin, R. N. (2001). Unsupervised statistical learning of higher-order spatial structures from visual scenes. *Psychological Science* 12(6):499–504.

Fiser, J., and Aslin, R. N. (2002). Statistical learning of higher-order temporal structure from visual shape sequences. *Journal of Experimental Psycholog. Learning Memory and Cognition* 28(3):458–467.

Fiser, J., and Aslin, R. N. (2005). Encoding multielement scenes: Statistical learning of visual feature hierarchies. *Journal of Experimental Psychology: General* 134(4):521–537.

Gaffan, D. (1994). Scene-specific memory for objects: A model of episodic memory impairment in monkeys with fornix transection. *Journal of Cognitive Neuroscience* 6:305–320.

Gaffan, D. (2002). Against memory systems. *Philosophical Transactions of the Royal Society of London. Series B: Biological Sciences* 357(1424):1111–1121.

Gaffan, D., and Parker, A. (1996). Interaction of perirhinal cortex with the fornix-fimbria: Memory for objects and "object-in-place" memory. *Journal of Neuroscience* 16:5864–5869.

Gawne, T. J., Kjaer, T. W., Hertz, J. A., and Richmond, B. J. (1996). Adjacent visual cortical complex cells share about 20% of their stimulus-related information. *Cerebral Cortex* 6(3):482–489.

Gibson, E. J. (1963). Perceptual learning. *Annual Review of Psychology* 14:29–56.

Gibson, E. J. (1966a). *Perceptual development and the reduction of uncertainty*. Paper presented at the Proceedings of the 18th International Congress of Psychology, Moscow.

Gibson, J. J. (1966b). *The Senses Considered as Perceptual Systems*. Boston: Houghton Mifflin.

Gochin, P. M., Colombo, M., Dorfman, G. A., Gerstein, G. L., and Gross, C. G. (1994). Neural ensemble coding in inferior temporal cortex. *Journal of Neurophysiology* 71(6):2325–2337.

Goffaux, V., Jacques, C., Mouraux, A., Oliva, A., Schyns, P. G., and Rossion, B. (2005). Diagnostic colours contribute to the early stages of scene categorization: Behavioural and neurophysiological evidence. *Visual Cognition* 12(6):878–892.

Goh, J. O., Siong, S. C., Park, D., Gutchess, A., Hebrank, A., and Chee, M. W. (2004). Cortical areas involved in object, background, and object-background processing revealed with functional magnetic resonance adaptation. *Journal of Neuroscience* 24(45):10223–10228.

Greene, A.J., Gross, W.L., Elsinger, C.L., Rao, S.M. (2007). Hippocampal differentiation without recognition: An fMRI analysis of the contextual cueing task. *Learning & Memory*, 14, 548-553.

Harris, Z. (1955). From phoneme to morpheme. *Language: Journal of the Linguistic Society of America* 31:190–222.

Henderson, J. M., and Hollingworth, A. (1999). High-level scene perception. *Annual Review of Psychology* 50:243–271.

Henke, K., Buck, A., Weber, B., and Wieser, H. G. (1997). Human hippocampus establishes associations in memory. *Hippocampus* 7(3):249–256.

Higuchi, S., and Miyashita, Y. (1996). Formation of mnemonic neuronal responses to visual paired associates in inferotemporal cortex is impaired by perirhinal and entorhinal lesions. *Proceedings of the National Academy of Sciences of the United States of America* 93(2):739–743.

Hirsh, R. (1974). The hippocampus and contextual retrieval of information from memory: A theory. *Behavioral Biology* 12(4):421–444.

Hollingworth, A. (2005). Memory for object position in natural scenes. *Visual Cognition* 12(6):1003–1016.

Hollingworth, A. (2006a). Memory for object position in natural scenes. *Visual Cognition* 12:1003–1016.

Hollingworth, A. (2006b). Scene and position specificity in visual memory for objects. *Journal of Experimental Psychology. Learning Memory and Cognition* 32(1):58–69.

Hollingworth, A. (2007). Object-position binding in visual memory for natural scenes and object arrays. *Journal of Experimental Psychology: Human Perception and Performance* 33, 31–47.

Hollingworth, A., and Henderson, J. M. (1998). Does consistent scene context facilitate object perception? *Journal of Experimental Psychology: General* 127:398–415.

Holscher, C., Rolls, E. T., and Xiang, J. (2003). Perirhinal cortex neuronal activity related to long-term familiarity memory in the macaque. *European Journal of Neuroscience* 18(7):2037–2046.

Howard, J. H., Jr., Dennis, N. A., Howard, D.V., Yankovich, H., and Vaidya, C. J. (2004). Implicit spatial contextual learning in healthy aging. *Neuropsychology* 18:124–134.

Hunt, R. H., and Aslin, R. N. (2001). Statistical learning in a serial reaction time task: Access to separable statistical cues by individual learners. *Journal of Experimental Psychology: General* 130(4):658–680.

Jiang, Y., and Leung, A. W. (2005). Implicit learning of ignored visual context. *Psychonomic Bulletin and Review* 12:100–106.

Jiang, Y., and Song, J-H (2005). Hyper-specificity in visual implicit learning: Learning of spatial layout is contingent on item identity. *Journal of Experimental Psychology: Human Perception and Performance* 31(6):1439–1448.

Jiang, Y., Song, J-H, and Rigas, A (2005). High-capacity spatial contextual memory. *Psychonomic Bulletin and Review* 12(3):524–529.

Jiang, Y., and Wagner, L. C. (2004). What is learned in spatial contextual cueing: Configuration or individual locations? *Perception and Psychophysics* 66:454–463.

Jiménez, L., and Méndez, C. (1999). Which attention is needed for implicit sequence learning? *Journal of Experimental Psychology: Learning Memory and Cognition* 25:236–259.

Johnson, J. S., Woodman, G. F., Braun, E., and Luck, S. J. (2007). Implicit memory influences the allocation of attention in visual cortex. *Psychonomic Bulletin and Review* 14:834–837.

Johnson, M. K., and Chalfonte, B. L. (1994). Binding complex memories: The role of reactivation and the hippocampus. In *Memory Systems*, eds. D. L. Schacter and E. Tulving, 311–350. Cambridge, MA: MIT Press.

Kawahara, J. (2003). Contextual cueing in 3-D layouts defined by binocular disparity. *Visual Cognition* 10:837–852.

Kim, J. J., and Fanselow, M. S. (1992). Modality-specific retrograde amnesia of fear. *Science* 256(5057):675–677.

Kobatake, E., Wang, G., and Tanaka, K. (1998). Effects of shape-discrimination training on the selectivity of inferotemporal cells in adult monkeys. *Journal of Neurophysiology* 80(1):324–330.

Kunar, M. A., Flusberg, S., Horowitz, T. S., and Wolfe, J. M. (in press). Does contextual cueing guide the deployment of attention. *Journal of Experimental Psychology: Human Perception and Performance* 33:816–828.

Lee, A. C., Bussey, T. J., Murray, E. A., Saksida, L. M., Epstein, R. A., Kapur, N., et al. (2005). Perceptual deficits in amnesia: Challenging the medial temporal lobe 'mnemonic' view. *Neuropsychologia* 43(1):1–11.

Levy, D. A., Shrager, Y., and Squire, L. R. (2005). Intact visual discrimination of complex and feature-ambiguous stimuli in the absence of perirhinal cortex. *Learning and Memory* 12(1):61–66.

Liu, Z., Murray, E. A., and Richmond, B. J. (2000). Learning motivational significance of visual cues for reward schedules requires rhinal cortex. *Nature Neuroscience* 3(12):1307–1315.

Loftus, G. R., and Mackworth, N. H. (1978). Cognitive determinants of fixation location during picture viewing. *Journal of Experimental Psychology: Human Perception and Performance* 4:565–572.

Logothetis, N. K., and Pauls, J. (1995). Psychophysical and physiological evidence for viewer-centered object representations in the primate. *Cerebral Cortex* 5(3): 270–288.

Logothetis, N. K., Pauls, J., and Poggio, T. (1995). Shape representation in the inferior temporal cortex of monkeys. *Current Biology* 5(5):552–563.

Luck, S. J., Girelli, M., McDermott, M. T., and Ford, M. A. (1997). Bridging the gap between monkey neurophysiology and human perception: An ambiguity resolution theory of visual selective attention. *Cognitive Psychology* 33:64–87.

Mackworth, N. H., and Morandi, A. J. (1967). The gaze selects informative details within pictures. *Perception and Psychophysics* 2:547–552.

Maguire, E. A. (2001). The retrosplenial contribution to human navigation: A review of lesion and neuroimaging findings. *Scandinavian Journal of Psychology* 42(3):225–238.

Maguire, E. A., Frackowiak, R. S., and Frith, C. D. (1997). Recalling routes around London: Activation of the right hippocampus in taxi drivers. *Journal of Neuroscience* 17(18):7103–7110.

Manns, J., and Squire, L. R. (2001). Perceptual learning, awareness, and the hippocampus. *Hippocampus* 11:776–782.

Maurer, D., Grand, R. L., and Mondloch, C. J. (2002). The many faces of configural processing. *Trends in Cognitive Sciences* 6(6):255–260.

Mayr, U. (1996). Spatial attention and implicit sequence learning: Evidence for independent learning of spatial and nonspatial sequences. *Journal of Experimental Psychology: Learning Memory and Cognition* 22(2):350–364.

McCotter, M., Gosselin, F., Sowden, P., and Schyns, P. (2005). The use of visual information in natural scenes. *Visual Cognition* 12(6):938–953.

Mendez, M. F., and Cherrier, M. M. (2003). Agnosia for scenes in topographagnosia. *Neuropsychologia* 41(10):1387–1395.

Meunier, M., Bachevalier, J., Mishkin, M., and Murray, E. A. (1993). Effects on visual recognition of combined and separate ablations of the entorhinal and perirhinal cortex in rhesus monkeys. *Journal of Neuroscience* 13(12):5418–5432.

Mishkin, M. (1982). A memory system in the monkey. *Philosophical Transactions of the Royal Society of London. Series B: Biological Sciences* 298(1089):83–95.

Miyashita, Y. (1988). Neuronal correlate of visual associative long-term memory in the primate temporal cortex. *Nature* 335(6193):817–820.

Miyashita, Y. (1993). Inferior temporal cortex: Where visual perception meets memory. *Annual Review of Neuroscience* 16:245–263.

Miyashita, Y., Okuno, H., Tokuyama, W., Ihara, T., and Nakajima, K. (1996). Feedback signal from medial temporal lobe mediates visual associate mnemonic codes of inferotemporal neurons. *Cognitive Brain Research* 5:81–86.

Morris, R. G., Garrud, P., Rawlins, J. N., and O'Keefe, J. (1982). Place navigation impaired in rats with hippocampal lesions. *Nature* 297(5868):681–683.

Moscovitch, M. (1994). Memory and working with memory: Evaluation of a component process model and comparisons with other models. In *Memory Systems*, eds. D. L. Schacter and E. Tulving, 269–310. Cambridge, MA: MIT Press.

Murray, E. A., Baxter, M. G., and Gaffan, D. (1998). Monkeys with rhinal cortex damage or neurotoxic hippocampal lesions are impaired on spatial scene learning and object reversals. *Behavioral Neuroscience* 112(6):1291–1303.

Murray, E. A., and Bussey, T. J. (1999). Perceptual-mnemonic functions of the perirhinal cortex. *Trends in Cognitive Sciences* 3:142–151.

Murray, E. A., Gaffan, D., and Mishkin, M. (1993). Neural substrates of visual stimulus-stimulus association in rhesus monkeys. *Journal of Neuroscience* 13(10):4549–4561.

Murray, E. A., Graham, K. S., and Gaffan, D. (2005). Perirhinal cortex and its neighbours in the medial temporal lobe: Contributions to memory and perception.

Quarterly Journal of Experimental Psychology. B Comparative and Physiological Psychology 58(3–4):378–396.

Murray, E. A., and Richmond, B. J. (2001). Role of perirhinal cortex in object perception, memory, and associations. *Current Opinion in Neurobiology* 11(2):188–193.

Nadel, L., and Moscovitch, M. (1997). Memory consolidation, retrograde amnesia and the hippocampal complex. *Current Opinion in Neurobiology* 7(2):217–227.

Naor-Raz, G., Tarr, M. J., and Kersten, D. (2003). Is color an intrinsic property of object representation? *Perception* 32(6):667–680.

Neider, M. B., and Zelinsky, G. J. (2006). Scene context guides eye movements during visual search. *Vision Research* 46(5):614–621.

Nissen, M. J., and Bullemer, P. (1987). Attentional requirements of learning: Evidence from performance measures. *Cognitive Psychology* 19:1–32.

O'Keefe, J., and Nadel, L. (1978). *The Hippocampus as a Cognitive Map*. Oxford: Clarendon Press.

Olson, I. R., and Chun, M. M. (2001). Temporal contextual cueing of visual attention. *Journal of Experimental Psychology: Learning Memory and Cognition* 27:1299–1313.

Olson, I. R., and Chun, M. M. (2002). Perceptual constraints on implicit learning of spatial context. *Visual Cognition* 9:273–302.

Ono, F., Jiang, Y., and Kawahara, J. (2005). Intertrial temporal contextual cuing: Association across successive visual search trials guides spatial attention. *Journal of Experimental Psychology: Human Perception and Performance* 31:703–712.

Palmer, S. E. (1975). The effects of contextual scenes on the identification of objects. *Memory and Cognition* 3:519–526.

Park, H., Quinlan, J., Thornton, E., and Reder, L. M. (2004). The effect of midazolam on visual search: Implications for understanding amnesia. *Proceedings of the National Academy of Sciences of the United States of America* 101(51):17879–17883.

Park, S., and Chun, M. M. (under revision). Different roles of the parahippocampal place area (PPA) and retrosplenial cortex (RSC) in panoramic scene perception.

Perruchet, P., and Pacton, S. (2006). Implicit learning and statistical learning: One phenomenon, two approaches. *Trends in Cognitive Sciences* 10(5):233–238.

Peterson, M. S., and Kramer, A. F. (2001a). Attentional guidance of the eyes by contextual information and abrupt onsets. *Perception and Psychophysics* 63(7):1239–1249.

Peterson, M. S., and Kramer, A. F. (2001b). Contextual cueing reduces interference from task-irrelevant onset distractors. *Visual Cognition* 8:843–859.

Phillips, R. G., and LeDoux, J. E. (1992). Differential contribution of amygdala and hippocampus to cued and contextual fear conditioning. *Behavioral Neuroscience* 106(2):274–285.

Pihlajamaki, M., Tanila, H., Hanninen, T., Kononen, M., Mikkonen, M., Jalkanen, V., et al. (2003). Encoding of novel picture pairs activates the perirhinal cortex: An fMRI study. *Hippocampus* 13(1):67–80.

Posner, M. I., Snyder, C. R. R. and Davidson, B. J. (1980). Attention and the detection of signals. *Journal of Experimental Psychology: General* 109:160–174.

Reber, A. S. (1967). Implicit learning of artificial grammars. *Journal of Verbal Learning and Verbal Behavior* 6:855–863.

Rombouts, S. A., Machielsen, W. C., Witter, M. P., Barkhof, F., Lindeboom, J., and Scheltens, P. (1997). Visual association encoding activates the medial temporal lobe: A functional magnetic resonance imaging study. *Hippocampus* 7(6):594–601.

Ryan, J. D., Althoff, R. R., Whitlow, S., and Cohen, N. J. (2000). Amnesia is a deficit in relational memory. *Psychological Science* 11(6):454–461.

Ryan, J. D., Leung, G., Turk-Browne, N. B., and Hasher, L. (2007). Assessment of age-related changes in inhibition and binding using eye movement monitoring. *Psychology and Aging* 22:239–250.

Saffran, J. R. (2001). Words in a sea of sounds: The output of infant statistical learning. *Cognition* 81(2):149–169.

Saffran, J. R., Aslin, R. N., and Newport, E. L. (1996). Statistical learning by 8–month-old infants [see comments]. *Science* 274(5294):1926–1928.

Sakai, K., and Miyashita, Y. (1991). Neural organization for the long-term memory of paired associates [see comments]. *Nature* 354(6349):152–155.

Saleem, K. S., and Tanaka, K. (1996). Divergent projections from the anterior inferotemporal area te to the perirhinal and entorhinal cortices in the macaque monkey. *Journal of Neuroscience* 16(15):4757–4775.

Schneider, W., and Shiffrin, R. M. (1977). Controlled and automatic human information processing: I. Detection, search and attention. *Psychological Review* 84(1):1–66.

Schyns, P. G., and Oliva, A. (1994). From blobs to boundary edges: Evidence for time and spatial scale dependent scene recognition. *Psychological Science* 5:195–200.

Sheinberg, D. L., and Logothetis, N. K. (1998). Implicit memory for scenes guides visual exploration in monkey. *Society for Neuroscience Abstracts* 24(2):1506.

Shiffrin, R. M., and Schneider, W. (1977). Controlled and automatic human information processing: II. Perceptual learning, automatic attending and a general theory. *Psychological Review* 84(2):127–190.

Shin, J. C., and Ivry, R. B. (2002). Concurrent learning of temporal and spatial sequences. *Journal of Experimental Psychology. Learning Memory and Cognition* 28(3):445–457.

Shomstein, S., and Yantis, S. (2002). Object-based attention: Sensory modulation or priority setting. *Perception and Psychophysics* 64(1):41–51.

Squire, L. R. (1992). Declarative and nondeclarative memory: Multiple brain systems supporting learning and memory. *Journal of Cognitive Neuroscience* 99:195–231.

Squire, L. R., Stark, C. E., and Clark, R. E. (2004). The medial temporal lobe. *Annual Review of Neuroscience* 27:279–306.

Stark, C. E., and Squire, L. R. (2000). Intact visual perceptual discrimination in humans in the absence of perirhinal cortex. *Learning and Memory* 7(5):273–278.

Summerfield, J. J., Lepsien, J., Gitelman, D. R., Mesulam, M. M., and Nobre, A. C. (2006). Orienting attention based on long-term memory experience. *Neuron* 49(6):905–916.

Sutherland, R. J., and Rudy, J. W. (1989). Configural association theory: The role of the hippocampal formation in learning, memory, and amnesia. *Psychobiology* 17:129–144.

Suzuki, W. A., and Amaral, D. G. (1994). Perirhinal and parahippocampal cortices of the macaque monkey: Cortical afferents. *Journal of Comparative Neurology* 350(4):497–533.

Takahashi, N., Kawamura, M., Shiota, J., Kasahata, N., and Hirayama, K. (1997). Pure topographic disorientation due to right retrosplenial lesion. *Neurology* 49(2):464–469.

Tanaka, J. W., and Presnell, L. M. (1999). Color diagnosticity in object recognition. *Perception and Psychophysics* 61(6):1140–1153.

Tanaka, K. (1996). Inferotemporal cortex and object vision. *Annual Review of Neuroscience* 19:109–139.

Tokuyama, W., Okuno, H., Hashimoto, T., Xin Li, Y., and Miyashita, Y. (2000). BDNF upregulation during declarative memory formation in monkey inferior temporal cortex. *Nature Neuroscience* 3(1):1134–1142.

Torralba, A., Oliva, A., Castelhano, M. S., and Henderson, J. M. (2006). Contextual guidance of eye movements and attention in real-world scenes: The role of global features in object search. *Psychological Review* 113(4):766–786.

Turk-Browne, N. B., Isola, P. J., Scholl, B. J., and Treat, T. A. (2008). Multidimensional visual statistical learning. *Journal of Experimental Psychology: Learning Memory and Cognition* 24(2):399–407.

Turk-Browne, N. B., Jungé, J., and Scholl, B. J. (2005). The automaticity of visual statistical learning. *Journal of Experimental Psychology: General* 134(4):552–564.

Turk-Browne, N. B., and Scholl, B. J. (in press). Flexible visual learning: Transfer across space and time. *Journal of Experimental Psychology: Human Perception and Performance.*

Turk-Browne, N. B., Yi, D.-J., and Chun, M. M. (2006). Linking implicit and explicit memory: Common encoding factors and shared representations. *Neuron* 49:917–927.

Valenstein, E., Bowers, D., Verfaellie, M., Heilman, K. M., Day, A., and Watson, R. T. (1987). Retrosplenial amnesia. *Brain* 110(6):1631–1645.

Wagner, A. D., Schacter, D. L., Rotte, M., Koutstaal, W., Maril, A., Dale, A. M., et al. (1998). Building memories: Remembering and forgetting of verbal experiences as predicted by brain activity. *Science* 281(5380):1188–1191.

Wiggs, C. L., Weisberg, J., and Martin, A. (1999). Neural correlates of semantic and episodic memory retrieval. *Neuropsychologia* 37(1):103–118.

Willingham, D. B., Nissen, M. J., and Bullemer, P. (1989). On the development of procedural knowledge. *Journal of Experimental Psychology: Learning Memory and Cognition* 15(6):1047–1060.

Wirth, S., Yanike, M., Frank, L. M., Smith, A. C., Brown, E. N., and Suzuki, W. A. (2003). Single neurons in the monkey hippocampus and learning of new associations. *Science* 300(5625):1578–1581.

Zacks, J. M., and Tversky, B. (2001). Event structure in perception and conception. *Psychological Bulletin* 127(1):3–21.

Chapter 8

Neural Mechanisms of Visual Memory:
A Neurocomputational Perspective

Gustavo Deco
Institució Catalana de Recerca i Estudis Avançats (ICREA)
Universitat Pompeu Fabra, Barcelona, Spain

Edmund T. Rolls
University of Oxford, England

A number of cognitive neuroscience studies have shown that the prefrontal cortex (PFC) is involved in at least some types of working memory functions (Fuster, 2000; Goldman-Rakic, 1995; Goldman-Rakic, 1996; Goel & Grafman, 1995). Working memory refers to an active system for maintaining and manipulating information in mind during a short period of time (in the order of seconds) (Baddeley, 1986). Neurophysiological recording studies reveal high spiking rates in prefrontal neurons during the execution of working memory tasks (Funahashi, Bruce, & Goldman-Rakic, 1989; Funahashi, Chafee, & Goldman-Rakic, 1993; Fuster & Alexander, 1971; Kubota & Niki, 1971). Functional brain imaging studies confirm activation of prefrontal cortical areas during working memory processing (Adcock, Constable, Gore, & Goldman-Rakic, 2000; Courtney, Ungerleider, Keil, & Haxby, 1997; Ungerleider, Courtney, & Haxby, 1998; Zarahn, Aguirre, & D'Esposito, 1997). Prefrontal lesions in humans (Goldman-Rakic, 1987; Milner, 1963) and monkeys (Butters & Pandya, 1969; Levy & Goldman-Rakic, 1999) result in severe deficits in tasks demanding short-term memory (STM) processing.

Neurodynamics helps us to understand the underlying mechanisms that implement the working memory–related activity observed in the primate PFC. In this chapter, we will review the application of these techniques for the analysis of experimental measurements gained at different levels [single-cell, functional magnetic resonance imaging (fMRI)] of the prefrontal and inferior temporal (IT) visual cortex that result in a better understanding of the neural mechanisms of visual memory.

We will also consider the mechanisms that enable the IT visual cortex to set up view-invariant representations of objects, which is a process that involves not just storing information in a long-term form of memory, but also building suitable object representations to be stored.

8.1 GENERAL MECHANISMS OF TEMPORARY AND LONG-TERM STORAGE IN NEURAL CIRCUITS

A STM can be maintained during a delay period of up to many seconds by using ongoing firing of a subset of neurons in an autoassociation or attractor network, which has associatively modified synapses in the recurrent collateral connections between the neurons. Long-term representations of objects can be built and stored in competitive networks by long-term synaptic potentiation (LTP). The properties of these two types of network are described briefly here—with fuller descriptions provided by Hertz, Krogh, and Palmer (1991), Rolls and Treves (1998), and Rolls and Deco (2002)—and we make the important point that the PFC is used for a STM that can be maintained when posterior perceptual areas, such as the IT visual cortex, have to be involved in representing each incoming visual stimulus and so cannot maintain a STM across intervening stimuli (Rolls, 2008).

8.1.1 Reverberation/Recurrence

Single-neuron recordings from the monkey PFC have studied working memory–related activity in the framework of delayed-response tasks (tasks that introduce a delay period between the presentation of a relevant stimulus and a motor response period). Consequently, the animal must retain the memory of the visual stimulus (identity or location) during the delay period to correctly respond in the subsequent choice period after the delay. Neurons in the PFC show a selectively enhanced activity throughout the delay period (Funahashi et al., 1989; Funahashi et al., 1993; Fuster & Alexander, 1971; Kubota & Niki, 1971; Miller, Erickson, & Desimone, 1996; Rainer, Rao, & Miller, 1999). This STM-related persistent activity during the delay period could be sustained by assuming an underlying substrate of excitatory synaptic loops (Amit, 1995; Goldman-Rakic, 1995; Hebb, 1949; Lorente de No, 1933) that generate reverberations.

The main type of network that can maintain the firing of neurons during a delay period is an *autoassociation* or *attractor network* (Amit, 1995; Hopfield, 1982). The architecture of an attractor network is illustrated in Figure 8–1, which shows attractor networks in both the IT visual cortex and the PFC. An attractor network stores a set of memory patterns in the recurrent synaptic connections between the excitatory neurons (pyramidal cells). Each memory pattern is represented by a subset of the neurons firing. Associative synaptic modification (implemented by a process such as LTP) increases the strength of

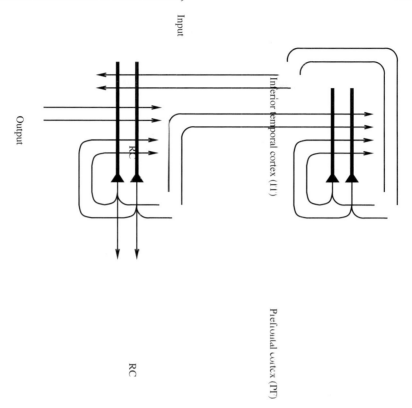

Figure 8–1. A short-term memory (STM) autoassociation (attractor) network in the PFC could hold active a working memory representation by maintaining its firing in an attractor state. The prefrontal module would be loaded with the to-be-remembered stimulus by the posterior module (in the temporal or parietal cortex), in which the incoming stimuli are represented. Back projections from the prefrontal cortex (PFC) STM module to the posterior module would enable the working memory to be unloaded, to (for example) influence ongoing perception and attention. The pyramidal cells are indicated by triangles, with a dendrite (*thick line*) indicated above the cell body and an axon (*thin line*) leaving the base of the cell body. Synapses occur where the axons cross dendrites. RC, recurrent collateral connections. After Rolls and Deco, 2002.

the connections between the coactive neurons that represent each memory pattern. After learning one or more patterns, the network can be triggered with any one of the memory cue patterns, and it can maintain that pattern of neuronal firings in a stable "attractor" state even when the cue is removed (Amit, 1995; Hertz et al., 1991; Hopfield, 1982; Rolls and Deco, 2002; Rolls and Treves, 1998). In this way, long-term memories that are created by means of synaptic modification can be activated to produce short-term memories (see Chapter 3 for a discussion of the relationship between short- and long-term visual memories).

8.1.1.1 Prefrontal cortex short-term memory networks and their relation to temporal and parietal perceptual networks

In the IT visual cortex, neuronal firing may be maintained after the end of a stimulus for a few hundred milliseconds even when the monkey is not performing a memory task (Desimone, 1996; Rolls & Tovee, 1994; Rolls, Tovee, & Panzeri, 1999; Rolls, Tovee, Purcell, Stewart, & Azzopardi, 1994). In more ventral temporal cortical areas, such as the entorhinal cortex, the firing may be maintained for longer periods in delayed match-to-sample tasks (Suzuki, Miller, & Desimone, 1997) and in the PFC for even tens of seconds (Fuster, 1997; Fuster, 2000). In the dorsolateral and inferior convexity PFC, the firing of the neurons may be related to the memory of spatial responses, objects (Goldman-Rakic, 1996; Wilson, O'Sclaidhe, & Goldman-Rakic, 1993b), or both (Rao, Rainer, & Miller, 1997), and in the principal sulcus/arcuate sulcus region to the memory of places for eye movements (Funahashi et al., 1989).

For the STM to be maintained during periods in which new stimuli are to be perceived, separate networks must exist for the perceptual and STM functions. The computational reason for this is that a STM attractor network can keep only one STM pattern active at a time by continual firing, and so a perceptual region such as the IT visual cortex cannot simultaneously hold active a previous STM and also respond to a new perceptual input. The STM network needed to bridge intervening stimuli must therefore be kept separate from the perceptual networks needed to respond to each new input. Indeed, two coupled networks, one in the IT visual cortex for perceptual functions and another in the PFC for maintaining the STM during intervening stimuli, provide a precise model of the interaction of perceptual and STM systems (Renart, Moreno, Rocha, Parga, & Rolls, 2001; Renart, Parga, & Rolls, 2000; Rolls & Deco, 2002; Rolls, 2008) (see Fig. 8–1).

In particular, this model shows how a PFC attractor (autoassociation) network could be triggered by a sample visual stimulus represented in the IT visual cortex in a delayed match-to-sample task and could keep this attractor active during a memory interval in which intervening stimuli are shown. Then, when the sample stimulus reappears in the task as a match stimulus, the IT cortex module shows a large response to the match stimulus, because it is activated both by the visual incoming match stimulus and by the consistent back-projected memory of the sample stimulus still being represented in the PFC memory module (see Fig. 8–1). This computational model makes it clear that, for ongoing perception to occur unhindered implemented by posterior cortex (parietal and temporal lobe) networks, there must be a separate set of modules that is capable of maintaining a representation over intervening stimuli. This is the fundamental understanding offered for the evolution and functions of the dorsolateral PFC, and it is this ability to provide multiple, separate, short-term attractor memories that we suggest provides (Rolls & Deco, 2002) the basis for its functions in attention, decision making, and planning (Rolls, 2008).

Renart, Parga, and Rolls (2000) and Renart, Moreno, Rocha, Parga, and Rolls (2001) performed analyses and simulations that showed that, for working memory to be implemented in this way, the connections between the perceptual and the STM modules (see Fig. 8–1) must be relatively weak. As a starting point, they used the neurophysiological data showing that, in delayed match-to-sample tasks with intervening stimuli, the neuronal activity in the IT visual cortex is driven by each new incoming visual stimulus (Miller & Desimone, 1994; Miller, Li, & Desimone, 1993), whereas in the PFC, neurons start to fire when the sample stimulus is shown and continue the firing that represents the sample stimulus even when the potential match stimuli are being shown (Miller, Erickson, & Desimone, 1996). The architecture studied by Renart, Parga, and Rolls (2000) and Renart, Moreno, Rocha, Parga, and Rolls (2001) was as shown in Figure 8–1, with both the intramodular (recurrent collateral) and the intermodular (forward IT to PF, and backward PF to IT) connections trained on the set of patterns with an associative synaptic modification rule. A crucial parameter is the strength of the intermodular connections, g, which indicates the relative strength of the intermodular to the intramodular connections. [This parameter measures effectively the relative strengths of the currents injected into the neurons by the intermodular relative to the intramodular connections; the importance of setting this parameter to relatively weak values for useful interactions between coupled attractor networks was highlighted by Renart, Parga, & Rolls (1999b) and Renart, Parga, & Rolls (1999a), as shown in Rolls & Deco (2002).] The patterns themselves were sets of random numbers, and the simulation utilized a dynamical approach with neurons with continuous (hyperbolic tangent) activation functions (Amit & Tsodyks, 1991; Kuhn, 1990; Kuhn, Bos, & van Hemmen, 1991; Shiino & Fukai, 1990). The external current injected into IT by the incoming visual stimuli was sufficiently strong to trigger the IT module into a state representing the incoming stimulus. When the sample was shown, the initially silent PF module was triggered into activity by the weak ($g > 0.002$) intermodular connections. The PF module remained firing to the sample stimulus even when IT was responding to potential match stimuli later in the trial, provided that g was less than 0.024, because then the intramodular recurrent connections could dominate the firing (Fig. 8–2).

If g was higher than this, then the PF module was pushed out of the attractor state produced by the sample stimulus. The IT module responded to each incoming potentially matching stimulus provided that g was not greater than approximately 0.024. Moreover, this value of g was sufficiently large that a larger response of the IT module was found when the stimulus matched the sample stimulus (the match enhancement effect found neurophysiologically, and a mechanism by which the matching stimulus can be identified). This simple model thus shows that the operation of the PFC in STM tasks such as delayed match-to-sample with intervening stimuli, and its relation to posterior perceptual networks, can be understood by the interaction of two weakly coupled attractor networks, as shown in Figures 8–1 and 8–2.

8.1.1.2 Short-term memory modelled at the integrate-and-fire level

To model the dynamics of the system, integrate-and-fire models take into account the membrane and synaptic time constants and conductances, and

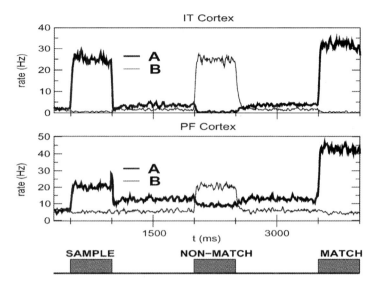

Figure 8–2. Interaction between the prefrontal cortex (PF) and the inferior temporal cortex (IT) in a delayed match-to-sample task with intervening stimuli using the architecture illustrated in Figure 8–1. *Above*: Activity in the IT attractor module. *Below*: Activity in the PF attractor module. Thick lines show the firing rates of the set of neurons with activity selective for the Sample stimulus (which is also shown as the Match stimulus, and is labelled A). Thin lines show the activity of neurons with activity selective for the Non-Match stimulus, which is shown as an intervening stimulus between the Sample and Match stimulus and is labelled B. A trial is illustrated in which A is the Sample (and Match) stimulus. The PFC module is pushed into an attractor state for the sample stimulus by the IT activity induced by the sample stimulus. Because of the weak coupling to the PF module from the IT module, the PF module remains in this Sample-related attractor state during the delay periods, even while the IT module is responding to the Non-Match stimulus. The PF module remains in its Sample-related state even during the Non-Match stimulus because, once a module is in an attractor state, it is relatively stable. When the Sample stimulus reappears as the Match stimulus, the PF module shows higher Sample stimulus–related firing, because the incoming input from IT is now adding to the activity in the PF attractor network. This in turn also produces a match enhancement effect in the IT neurons with Sample stimulus–related selectivity, because the back-projected activity from the PF module matches the incoming activity to the IT module. Adapted with permission from Renart, A., Parga, N. and., and Rolls, E. T. (2000). A recurrent model of the interaction between the prefrontal cortex and inferior temporal cortex in delay memory tasks. In *Advances in Neural Information Processing Systems, Vol. 12*, eds. S. Solla, T. Leen and K. -R. Mueller 171–177. Cambridge MA: MIT Press; and Renart, A., Moreno, R., Rocha, J., Parga, N., and Rolls, E. T. (2001). A model of the IT-PF network in object working memory which includes balanced persistent activity and tuned inhibition. *Neurocomputing* 38–40:1525–1531.

they simulate the firing time of each neuron, so that the spiking activity in the model can be compared with that actually recorded from neurons. Brunel and Wang (2001) [see also Compte, Brunel, Goldman-Rakic, & Wang (2000)] introduced a very elegant and thorough theoretical model of the neurodynamic mechanisms underlying working memory neural activity in a single-attractor network that reproduces the neurophysiological observations from behaving monkeys. Global inhibition between the neurons [implemented in the brain by inhibitory γ aminobutyric acid (GABA)ergic interneurons] is necessary to prevent runaway neuronal activity and to maintain the selectivity of the firing state for one of the patterns (Brunel & Wang, 2001; Goldman-Rakic, 1995; Kawaguchi, 1997). To help maintain the stability of this dynamical feedback system (including reducing oscillations), the inhibition should be at least partly shunting or divisive (implemented by GABAergic synapses close to the cell body; Battaglia & Treves, 1998; Rolls & Treves, 1998), and connections between the inhibitory neurons are useful (Brunel & Wang, 2001; Camperi & Wang, 1998; Compte et al., 2000). In fact, synaptic inhibition seems to be critical for shaping the selectivity of mnemonic neural activity in a working memory network (Brunel & Wang, 2001; Camperi & Wang, 1998; Compte et al., 2000; Goldman-Rakic, 1995; Rao, Williams, & Goldman-Rakic, 1999). Brunel and Wang (2001) investigated also the effect of external distracting inputs and neuromodulation on the memory-related persistent activity and have shown that recurrence is dominated by inhibition, although persistent activity is generated through recurrent excitation in populations or "pools" of excitatory neurons. In some of the work described here, we have built on this formalization, extending it to deal with multiple, hierarchically organized systems of attractor networks, so that we can account for interactions between the PFC and posterior perceptual areas and for how STM is involved in attention and decision-making.

8.1.2 Synaptic Modification (LTP) in Competitive Networks to Build Perceptual Representations

Competitive neural networks learn to categorize input pattern vectors. Each category of inputs activates a different output neuron or set of output neurons. The categories formed are based on similarities between the input vectors. Similar (i.e., correlated) input vectors activate the same output neuron(s). In that the learning is based on similarities in the input space and no external teacher forces classification, this is an unsupervised network. The term *categorization* is used to refer to the process of placing vectors into categories based on their similarity.

The categorization produced by competitive nets is of great potential importance in perceptual systems, including the whole of the visual cortical processing hierarchies (Rolls & Deco, 2002). Each category formed reflects a set or cluster of active inputs x_j that occur together. (The index j specifies which input to a neuron i is considered.) This cluster of coactive inputs can be thought of as a feature, and the competitive network can be described as building feature analyzers, in which a feature can now be defined as a correlated set of inputs.

During learning, a competitive network gradually discovers these features in the input space, and the process of finding these features without a teacher is referred to as *self-organization*.

The basic architecture of a competitive network is shown in Figure 8–3. It is a one-layer network with a set of inputs that make modifiable excitatory synapses w_{ij} with the output neurons. The output cells compete with each other (for example by lateral inhibition implemented by inhibitory interneurons) in such a way that the most strongly activated neuron or neurons win the competition and are left firing strongly. The synaptic weights, w_{ij}, are initialized to random values before learning starts. If some of the synapses are missing—that is, if randomly diluted connectivity occurs—it is not a problem for such networks, and it can even help them.

The basic algorithm for a competitive net is as follows:

1. Apply an input vector x of firing rates x_j and calculate the activation h_i of each neuron

$$h_i = \sum_j x_j w_{ij} \qquad {}^\star(1)$$

where the sum is over the C input axons, indexed by j. (It is useful to normalize the length of each input vector x. In the brain, a scaling effect is likely to be achieved both by feedforward inhibition and by

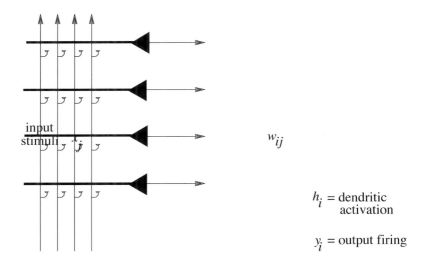

responses

Figure 8–3. The architecture of a competitive network.

feedback inhibition among the set of input cells (in a preceding network) that give rise to the axons conveying x.)

The output firing y_i^1 is a function of the activation of the neuron:

$$y_i = f(h_i). \qquad *(2)$$

The function f can be linear, sigmoid, monotonically increasing, etc.

2. Allow competitive interaction between the output neurons by a mechanism such as lateral or mutual inhibition (possibly with self-excitation) to produce a contrast-enhanced version of the firing rate vector:

$$y_i = g(y_i^1). \quad *(3)$$

Function g is typically a nonlinear operation and, in its most extreme form, may be a winner-take-all function, in which (after the competition) one neuron may be "on" and the others "off," or a sparse set of output neurons may be left firing. [In a dynamical implementation, y_i^1 would not be separately computed, and the steps from the activation to the competitive interaction between the neurons would involve inhibitory interneurons and continuous dynamics, as described by Rolls and Deco (2002).]

3. Apply an associative Hebb-like learning rule to increase the strengths of the active synapses onto neurons with high firing rates:

$$\delta w_{ij} = \alpha y_i x_j. \qquad *(4)$$

4. Normalize the length of the synaptic weight vector on each dendrite to prevent the same few neurons always winning the competition:

$$\sum_j (w_{ij})^2 = 1. \qquad *(5)$$

A less efficient alternative is to scale the sum of the weights to a constant (e.g., 1.0). An approximation to steps 3 and 4 could be realized by synaptic modification that included LTP and long-term depression (LTD), which depended on the existing strength of a synapse:

$$\delta w_{ij} = \alpha y_i (x_j - w_{ij}). \qquad *(6)$$

5. Repeat steps 1–4 for each different input stimulus x, in random sequence, a number of times. We show in the section on Visual Working Memory, Cognitive Flexibility, and Attention how this competitive learning algorithm can be modified to help build invariant representations of objects.

8.2 NEURAL MECHANISMS OF VISUAL WORKING MEMORY IN THE PREFRONTAL CORTEX

Two different models of the topographical and functional organization of the PFC have been proposed [see Miller (2000) for a review]: (a) an organization with separate regions for object ("what") and spatial ("where") STM-related information processing (i.e., organization-by-stimulus domain) and (b) a functional organization in which different processes, such as the maintenance of STM and item manipulation, are separately represented (i.e., organization-by-process).

The first hypothesis—organization-by-stimulus domain—proposes that visual working memory is organized into two networks within the PFC, with spatial working memory supported by the dorsolateral PFC in the neighborhood of the principal sulcus [Brodmann's area (BA) 46/9 in the middle frontal gyrus (MFG)], and object working memory supported by the ventrolateral PFC on the lateral convexity [BA 45 in the inferior frontal gyrus (IFG)]. Event-related fMRI studies in humans (Leung, Gore, & Goldman-Rakic, 2002) and single-cell data in primates (Goldman-Rakic, 1987; Wilson, O'Scalaidhe, & Goldman-Rakic, 1993a) lend support to this topographical organization-by-stimulus domain hypothesis and to the proposal that the active maintenance of behaviorally relevant information (object-based "what" or spatially based "where" information) can be construed as the main contribution of the PFC to working memory. Moreover, this anatomical segregation of the processing of "what" and "where" information in the ventrolateral versus dorsolateral PFC can be thought of as a prolongation into the PFC of the "what"/"where" segregation of the ventral/dorsal streams of the posterior (occipital, temporal, and parietal) visual cortex (Ungerleider & Mishkin, 1982).

The second hypothesis addressing the function of PFC—organization-by-process—proposes a hierarchical organization of the PFC by which nonmnemonic higher-order functions (e.g., manipulation of items in memory) are ascribed to dorsolateral prefrontal areas, and STM maintenance functions are ascribed to inferior prefrontal areas (D'Esposito et al., 1998; Owen et al., 1999; Petrides, 1994). Among the investigations used to support this second hypothesis are event-related fMRI studies (Postle & D'Esposito, 1999; Postle & D'Esposito, 2000) employing a "what-then-where" design (i.e., a subject has to make an object- and spatial-delayed response within the same trial) that failed to find evidence for anatomical segregation of spatial and object visual working memory in the PFC of humans. Neuronal recordings from nonhuman primate PFC have also been analyzed while monkeys perform a delay task with a "what-then-where" design (Rao et al., 1997). In this task, a sample object was briefly presented on the screen. After a first delay ("What"-delay), two test objects were briefly presented at two of four possible extrafoveal locations. One of the test objects matched the sample; the other was a nonmatch. After a second delay ("Where"-delay), the monkey had to respond with a saccade to the remembered location of the match. Rao et al. (1997) found neurons that showed not only either object-tuned ("what") or location-tuned ("where") delay activity in the task, but also a large percentage of neurons (52%) showing *both* "what" and "where" tuning. Taken together, these results imply that the topographical organization of the PFC in the context of working memory is still uncertain.

We have suggested previously that questions like those associated with the topographical organization of the PFC can be better addressed if different kinds of cognitive neuroscience data, taken at different levels, are unified and integrated via a computational neuroscience approach (Horwitz, Friston, & Taylor, 2000; Horwitz, Tagamers, & McIntosh, 1999; Rolls & Deco, 2002; Rolls & Treves, 1998). A test of whether one's understanding is correct is to simulate the processing and show whether the simulation can perform the tasks under study and whether the simulated data have values close to those obtained experimentally. The computational neuroscience approach leads to detailed neurally based hypotheses about how the processing is performed and to precise and quantitative tests of these hypotheses, as described next. Specifically, we will describe how a specific model can explain single-unit and fMRI data from the "what-then-where" task.

8.2.1 Neurodynamic Model of the Prefrontal Cortex

We begin by describing the basic neuronal units (Brunel & Wang, 2001) comprising the excitatory and inhibitory neurons of our models of PFC (Deco & Rolls, 2003; Deco, Rolls, & Horwitz, 2004). The basic circuit is an integrate-and-fire model that consists of the cell membrane capacitance C_m in parallel with the cell membrane resistance R_m driven by a synaptic current (producing an excitatory or inhibitory postsynaptic potential, EPSP or IPSP, respectively). If the voltage across the capacitor reaches a threshold θ, the circuit is shunted and a δ-pulse (spike) is generated and transmitted to other neurons. We use biologically realistic parameters. We assume for both kinds of neuron a resting potential $V_L = -70$ mV, a firing threshold $\theta = -50$ mV, and a reset potential $V_{reset} = -55$ mV. The membrane capacitance C_m is 0.5 nF for the excitatory pyramidal neurons and 0.2 nF for the inhibitory interneurons. The membrane leak conductance g_m is 25 nS for pyramidal cells, and, 20 nS for interneurons. The refractory period τ_{ref} is 2 ms for pyramidal cells and 1 ms for interneurons. More specifically, the subthreshold membrane potential $V(t)$ of each neuron evolves according to the following equation:

$$C_m \frac{dV(t)}{dt} = -g_m(V(t) - V_L) - I_{syn}(t) \quad *(7)$$

where $I_{syn}(t)$ is the total synaptic current flow into the cell.

The synaptic current flows into the cells are mediated by three different families of receptors. The total synaptic current is given by the sum of glutamatergic excitatory components [N-methyl-D-aspartic (NMDA) and α-amino-3-hydroxy-5-methyl-4-isoxazole propionic acid (AMPA) and inhibitory components (GABA, I_G)]. We consider that external excitatory contributions are produced through AMPA receptors (I_{Ae}), whereas the excitatory recurrent synapses are produced through AMPA and NMDA receptors (I_{Ar} and I_{Nr}). [The NMDA receptors require special implementation because of their voltage-dependent nonlinearity and the important contribution they make to neural computation because of this and because of their long time constant (Brunel &Wang, 2001; Rolls & Deco, 2002).] The total synaptic current is therefore given by:

$$I_{syn}(t) = I_{Ae}(t) + I_{Ar}(t) + I_{Nr}(t) + I_{G}(t) \qquad *(8)$$

where

$$I_{Ae}(t) = g_{Ae}(V(t) - V_{E}) \sum_{j=1}^{N_{EXT}} s_{j}^{Ae}(t) \qquad *(9)$$

$$I_{Ae}(t) = g_{Ar}(V(t) - V_{E}) \sum_{j=1}^{N_{E}} w_{j} s_{j}^{Av}(t) \qquad *(10)$$

$$I_{Nr}(t) = \frac{g_{N}(V(t) - V_{E})}{\left(1 + C_{Mg} e^{\left(\frac{-0.062 V(t)}{3.57}\right)}\right)} \sum_{j=1}^{N_{E}} w_{j} s_{j}^{N}(t) \qquad *(11)$$

$$I_{G}(t) = g_{G}(V(t) - V_{I}) \sum_{j=1}^{N_{I}} s_{j}^{G}(t) \qquad *(12)$$

In the preceding equations, $V_{E} = 0$ mV and $V_{I} = -70$ mV. The fractions of open channels s are given by:

$$\frac{ds_{j}^{Ae}(t)}{dt} = -\frac{s_{j}^{Ae}(t)}{\tau_{AMPA}} + \sum_{k} \delta(t - t_{j}^{k}) \qquad *(13)$$

$$\frac{ds_{j}^{Ar}(t)}{dt} = -\frac{s_{j}^{Ar}(t)}{\tau_{AMPA}} + \sum_{k} \delta(t - t_{j}^{k}) \qquad *(14)$$

$$\frac{ds_{j}^{N}(t)}{dt} = -\frac{s_{j}^{N}(t)}{\tau_{N,d}} + \alpha x_{j}(t)(1 - s_{j}^{N}(t)) \qquad *(15)$$

$$\frac{dx_{j}(t)}{dt} = -\frac{x_{j}(t)}{\tau_{N,r}} + \sum_{k} \delta(t - t_{j}^{k}) \qquad *(16)$$

$$\frac{ds_{j}^{G}(t)}{dt} = -\frac{s_{j}^{G}(t)}{\tau_{G}} + \sum_{k} \delta(t - t_{j}^{k}) \qquad *(17)$$

where the sums over k represent a sum over spikes emitted by presynaptic neuron j at time t_j^k. The value of $\alpha = 0.5$ ms^{-1}.

The values of the conductances (in nS) for pyramidal neurons were: $g_{Ae} = 2.08$, $g_{Ar} = 0.052$, $g_N = 0.164$, and $g_G = 0.67$; and for interneurons: $g_{Ae} = 1.62$, $g_{Ar} = 0.0405$, $g_N = 0.129$, and $g_G = 0.49$. We consider that the NMDA currents have a voltage dependence controlled by the extracellular magnesium concentration, [Mg^{++}] = 1 mM. We neglect the rise time of both AMPA and GABA synaptic currents, because they are typically extremely short (<1 ms). The rise time constant for NMDA synapses is $\tau_{N,r} = 2$ ms. The decay time constant for AMPA synapses is $\tau_{AMPA} = 2$ ms, for NMDA synapses $\tau_{N,d} = 100$ ms, and for GABA synapses $\tau_G = 10$ ms.

Figure 8–4 shows schematically the synaptic structure assumed in the prefrontal cortical network we use to simulate the "what-then-where" experimental design (Deco et al., 2004). The network is composed of N_E (excitatory) pyramidal cells and N_I inhibitory interneurons. In our simulations, we use $N_E = 1600$ and $N_I = 400$. The neurons are fully connected. Different populations or pools of neurons exist in the prefrontal cortical network. Each pool of excitatory cells contains fN_E neurons, where f, the fraction of the neurons in any one pool, was set to be 0.05. There are four subtypes of excitatory pools, namely: object-tuned ("what" pools), space-tuned ("where" pools), object-and-space–tuned ("what-and-where" pools), and nonselective. Object pools are feature-specific. The spatial pools are location-specific and encode the spatial position of a stimulus. The integrated object-and-space–tuned pools encode both specific feature and location information. The remaining excitatory neurons are in a nonselective pool. All the inhibitory neurons are clustered into a common inhibitory pool, so that global competition occurs throughout the network.

Assuming Hebbian learning, neurons within a specific excitatory pool are mutually coupled with a strong weight, $w_s = 2.1$. Neurons in the inhibitory pool are mutually connected with an intermediate weight, $w = 1$. They are also connected with all excitatory neurons with the same intermediate weight, $w = 1$. The connection strength between two neurons in two different specific excitatory pools is weak and given by $w_w = 1 - 2f(w_s - 1)/(1-2f)(= 0.8778)$ unless otherwise specified. Neurons in a specific excitatory pool are connected to neurons in the nonselective pool with a feedforward synaptic weight, $w = 1$ and a feedback synaptic connection of weight w_w. The connections between the different pools are set up so that specific integrated "what-and-where" pools are connected with the corresponding specific "what"-tuned pools and "where"-tuned pools, as if they were associatively (Hebb) learned based on the activity of individual pools while the different tasks are being performed. The forward connections (input to integrated "what-and-where" pools) are $w_f = 1.65$. The corresponding feedback synaptic connections are symmetric.

Each neuron (pyramidal cells and interneurons) receives $N_{ext} = 800$ excitatory AMPA synaptic connections from outside the network. These connections provide three different types of external interactions: (a) a background noise due to the spontaneous firing activity of neurons outside the network,

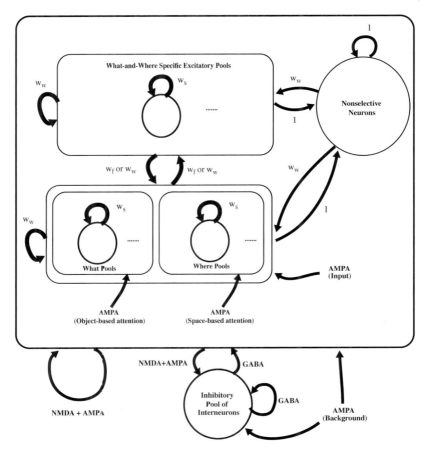

Figure 8–4. Prefrontal cortex module. Topographic what/where organization. Adapted with permission from Deco, G., Rolls, E. T. and., and Horwitz, B. (2004). "'What'" and "'where'" in visual working memory: A computational neurodynamic perspective for integrating fMRI and single-neuron data. *Journal of Cognitive Neuroscience* 16:683–701.

(b) a sensory-related input, and (c) an attentional bias that specifies the task ("what" or "where" delayed response). The external inputs are given by a Poisson train of spikes. We assume that Poisson spikes arrive at each external synapse with a rate of 3 Hz, consistent with the spontaneous activity observed in the cerebral cortex. The sensory input is encoded by increasing the external input Poisson rate v_{ext} to $v_{ext} + \lambda_{input}$ to the neurons in the appropriate specific sensory pools. We used $\lambda_{input} = 85$ Hz. Finally, the attentional biasing specification of the task (i.e., which dimension is relevant) is modelled by assuming that each neuron in each of the pools associated with the relevant stimulus domain (object or space) receives external Poisson spikes with an increased rate from v_{ext} to $v_{ext} + \lambda_{att}$ throughout the trial. We use $\lambda_{att} = 85$ Hz.

We simulate the temporal evolution of fMRI signals (i.e., event-related) by convolving the total synaptic activity with the standard hemodynamic response function $h(t)$ (Glover, 1999):

$$S_{fMRI}(t) = \int_0^\infty h(t - t') I_{syn}(t') dt'$$

where

$$h(t) = t^{n_1} e^{-t/t_1} / c_1 - a_2 t^{n_2} e^{-t/t_2} / c_2$$

$$c_i = max(t^{n_i} e^{-t\backslash t_1})$$

In our simulation (Deco et al., 2004), we calculated numerically the convolution by sampling the total synaptic activity every 0.1 seconds and introducing a cut-off at a delay of 25 seconds. The parameters utilized for the hemodynamic standard response function $h(t)$ were taken from the paper by Glover (1999), and were: $n_1 = 6.0$, $t_1 = 0.9s$, $n_2 = 12.0$, $t_2 = 0.9s$, and $a_2 = 0.2$.

8.2.2 Electrophysiological Single-cell Recordings

In this subsection, we present a theoretical analysis of neuronal activity in the primate PFC underlying the execution of a "what-then-where" working memory task (Deco et al., 2004). The neuronal recordings of Rao et al. (1997) demonstrated the existence of neurons showing domain-specific-sensitivity; that is, object-tuned activity in the "what" delay and location-tuned activity in the "where" delay, but they found also a large proportion of neurons showing integrated "what-and-where"–tuned activity during both "what" and "where" delays. During each trial of their experiment, while the monkey maintained fixation on a center spot, a sample object was briefly presented on the screen. After a first delay ("What"-delay), two test objects were briefly presented at two of four possible extrafoveal locations. One of the test objects matched the sample; the other was a nonmatch. After a second delay ("Where"-delay), the monkey had to respond with a saccade to the remembered location of the match.

We performed (Deco et al., 2004) numerical simulations of the experiment of Rao et al. (1997), and we evaluated in the model the neural spiking activity of specific pools. The simulation starts with a pre-cue period of 1000 ms. A target stimulus with a feature characteristic F_i and at a location S_j is presented next during the first cue period of 1500 ms. After the first cue period, the stimulus is removed, and only the feature characteristics of the target object have to be encoded and retained during a "what"-delay period of 6500 ms. We modelled the attentional "what" bias by assuming that all feature-specific pools receive Poisson spikes with an increased rate ($v_{ext} + \lambda_{att}$). This is followed by a second cue period of 1500 ms, during which a matched object reappeared at another new location, different from the one originally cued during the first cue period. After that, only the location of the matched target has to be encoded, and the feature information can be ignored during this second "where"-delay period of 6500 ms. Again, we modelled the attentional "where" bias by assuming that all location-specific pools receive Poisson spikes with an increased rate $(v_{ext} + \lambda_{att})$. This second delay is followed by a period of 1500 ms, in which the final probe is presented and a response has to be elicited.

Figure 8–5 plots the response of a single prefrontal neuron showing object-tuned activity in the first "what" delay and location-tuned activity during the second "where" delay (left and central panel). The right panel shows object and location information during the second "where" delay. [Contrast these plots with the very similar experimental results shown in Figure 3 of Rao et al. (1997).] For the generation of the simulations presented in Figure 8–5, we plot the averaged pool activity of the different integrated "what-and-where" pools. As found in the neurophysiological experiments, cuing a good location with a good object elicited more activity than cuing a good location with a poor object. A poor location elicited less activity than a good location, regardless of which object cued it. These specific global attractors corresponding to a specific stimulus-domain–attention condition, incorporate several single pool attractors, from the group of sensory pools (object or space specific) and from the group of integrated "what-and-where" pools. The cue stimulus, and the biasing attentional top-down information applied to the sensory neurons, drive the system into the corresponding global attractor according to the biased competition mechanism. The numerical simulations show that the assumed microcircuits in the PFC are consistent with the empirical neurophysiological measurements of Rao et al. (1997) and therefore offer a concrete computational account of the organization of the PFC using an extended stimulus-domain–specific implementation that combines sensory pools with "what"-specific and "where"-specific tuning with other neurons that respond to combinations of "what-and-where" information.

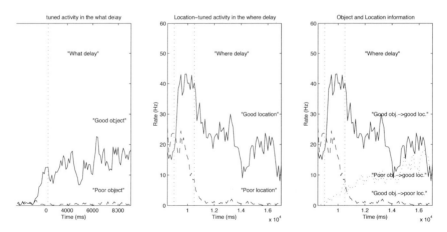

Figure 8–5. Simulations of "what-then-where" delay task. Adapted with permission from Deco, G., Rolls, E. T. and., and Horwitz, B. (2004). "'What'" and "'where'" in visual working memory: A computational neurodynamic perspective for integrating fMRI and single-neuron data. *Journal of Cognitive Neuroscience* 16:683–701.

8.2.3 Event-related Functional Magnetic Resonance Imaging Data: "What-Then-Where"

The work of Postle and D'Esposito (2000) presents an event-related fMRI design with which the authors investigated the macroscopic organization of the PFC. They used the "what-then-where" and "where-then-what" behavioral task. We ran our model for the setup of Postle and D'Esposito (2000) and simulated the temporal evolution of the fMRI signal (Deco et al., 2004). We found that the experimentally observed event-related fMRI data could be obtained only if we assumed that the network associated with the dorsolateral PFC had a higher level of inhibition than the network associated with the ventrolateral PFC. The level of inhibition was increased by multiplying the maximal GABA conductivity constants by a factor of 1.05. By altering this level of inhibition, we could simulate the different time courses of the fMRI signal in the ventrolateral and dorsolateral PFC, as shown in Figure 8–6.

Figures 8–6A and 8–6B present the simulated fMRI signal for both conditions and for both ventrolateral PFC (low inhibition, A) and dorsolateral PFC (high inhibition, B). The simulations produced results very similar to those of Postle and D'Esposito (2000), as shown by Deco et al. (2004). No difference is macroscopically detected between the "what-then-where" and "where-then-what" conditions for the ventrolateral network model with low inhibition or for the dorsolateral network model with high inhibition. However, this fact does not mean that both ventrolateral and dorsolateral dynamic behaviors are identical during both "what-then-where" and "where-then-what" conditions, because the underlying microscopic (neuron-level) activity is different. The spatiotemporal spiking activity shows that, at the microscopic level that possesses "what"-, "where"-, and "what-and-where"–specific neurons, strong differences are evident in the evolution and structure of the successively elicited attractors for each temporal period. That is, each attractor ("what" versus "where") has activity at the appropriate time and in the appropriate delay period, even though this is not evident in the fMRI signal simulated by Deco et al. (2004), or recorded by Postle and D'Esposito (2000). This detailed microscopic structure is lost at the macroscopic level of coarser spatial and temporal resolution measured by MRI. In fact, during the STM delay period associated with a "what" or "where" task, only the neurons representing the feature characteristics or spatial location of the cue maintain persistent activity and build up a stable global attractor in the network that maintains the firing during the delay period. These specific global attractors, corresponding to a specific stimulus-domain–attention condition, incorporate several single-pool attractors, from the group of sensory pools (object- or space-specific) and from the group of integrated "what-and-where" pools. The cue stimulus, and the biasing attentional top-down information applied to the sensory neurons, drive the system into the corresponding global attractor according to the biased competition mechanism (Deco & Rolls, 2005a; Reynolds & Desimone, 1999; Rolls & Deco, 2002).

Thus, an important conclusion of this study was that the different fMRI signals recorded from the dorsolateral and ventrolateral PFC could be reproduced

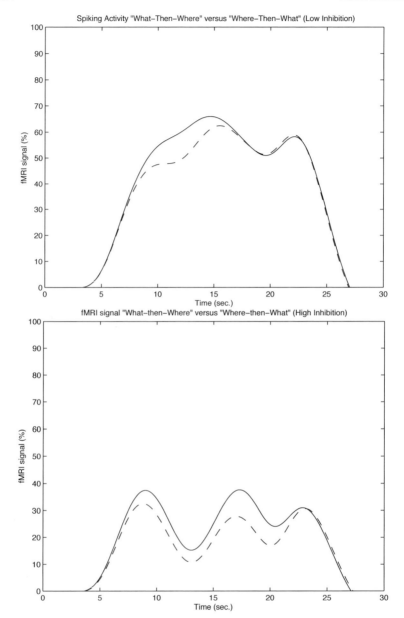

Figure 8–6. "What-then-where" delay task. **A** and **B** show simulations of the event-related fMRI experiment of Postle and D'Esposito (2000) by Deco, Rolls, and Horwitz (2004). The solid line shows the "where-then-what" condition, and the dashed line the "what-then-where" condition. The first stimulus of duration 1. 5 s was shown at 1 s followed by a 6. 5-second delay period, and the second stimulus of duration 1. 5 s was shown at 8 s followed by a 6. 5-second delay period.

in the simulation by assuming higher inhibition in the dorsolateral than vent-rolateral PFC (Deco et al., 2004).

8.3 VISUAL WORKING MEMORY, COGNITIVE FLEXIBILITY, AND ATTENTION

Asaad, Rainer, and Miller (2000) investigated the functions of the PFC in working memory by analyzing neuronal activity when a monkey performs two different working memory tasks using the same stimuli and responses. In a *conditional object-response (associative) task* with a delay, the monkey was shown one of two stimulus objects (O1 or O2; i.e., object 1 or object 2) and, after a delay, had to make either a rightward or leftward oculomotor saccade response depending on which stimulus was shown. In a *delayed spatial-response task*, the same stimuli were used, but the rule required was different; namely, to respond after the delay towards the left or right location where the stimulus object had been shown (Asaad et al., 2000). The main motivation for such stud-ies was the fact that, for real-world behavior, the mapping between a stimulus and a response is typically more complicated than a one-to-one mapping. The same stimulus can lead to different behaviors depending on the situation, or the same behavior may be elicited by different cuing stimuli. In the perform-ance of these tasks, populations of neurons have been described that respond in the delay period to the stimulus object, the stimulus position (*sensory pools*), to combinations of the response and the stimulus object or position (*interme-diate pools*), and to the response required (left or right; *premotor pools*). Their results demonstrated that the information represented by neurons in the lateral PFC of primates is not limited to discrete sensory events or motor responses, but instead that the behavioral context in which the animals were engaged had a decisive influence on the activity of some of the neurons. In particular, the combination neurons in the intermediate pools are task-dependent. As described later, these PFC neurons provide a neural substrate for responding appropriately on the basis of an abstract rule or context.

8.3.1 Neurodynamics of Task-dependent Memory

Figure 8–7 shows schematically the synaptic structure assumed in the prefron-tal cortical network. The network is composed of N_E (excitatory) pyramidal cells and N_I inhibitory interneurons. In our simulations, we use $N_E = 1600$ and $N_I = 400$. The neurons are fully connected. Different populations or pools of neurons exist in the prefrontal cortical network. Each pool of excitatory cells contains fN_E neurons, where f is the fraction of the neurons in any one pool was set to be 0.05. There are four types of excitatory pool; namely, sensory, task or rule-specific, premotor, and nonselective. The sensory pools encode informa-tion about objects, or spatial location. The premotor pools encode the motor response (in our case, the leftward or rightward oculomotor saccade). The intermediate pools are task-specific and perform the mapping between the sensory stimuli and the required motor response. The intermediate pools

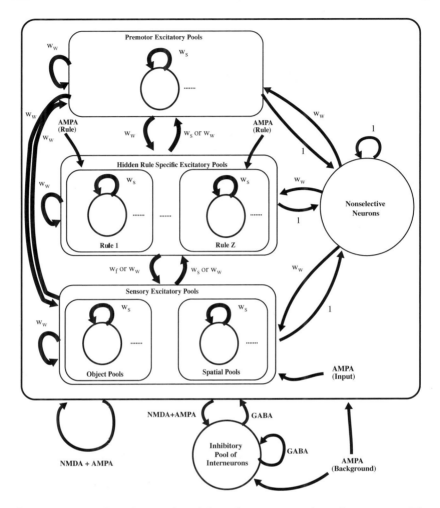

Figure 8–7. Prefrontal cortical module. Rule- or context-dependent memory. The neurons in the intermediate or hidden pool respond to different combinations of the stimuli (including the object shown or its spatial position) and the response required. The neurons in the intermediate pool receive a rule-dependent biasing input to enable them to operate as a biased competition network. Adapted with permission from Deco, G. and., and Rolls, E. T. (2003). Attention and working memory: A dynamical model of neuronal activity in the prefrontal cortex. *European Journal of Neuroscience* 18:2374–2390.

respond to combinations of the sensory stimuli and the response required; for example, to object 1 requiring a left oculomotor saccade. The intermediate pools receive an external biasing input that reflects the current rule (e.g., on this trial, when object 1 is shown, make the left response after the delay period). The remaining excitatory neurons do not have specific sensory, response, or biasing inputs and are in a nonselective pool. All the inhibitory neurons are clustered into a common inhibitory pool, so that global competition occurs throughout the network.

We assume that the synaptic coupling strengths between any two neurons in the network are established by Hebbian learning. As a consequence of this, neurons within a specific excitatory pool are mutually coupled with a strong weight, $w_s = 2.1$. Neurons in the inhibitory pool are mutually connected with an intermediate weight, $w = 1$. They are also connected with all excitatory neurons with the same intermediate weight, $w = 1$. The connection strength between two neurons in two different specific excitatory pools is weak and given by $w_w = 1 - 2f(w_s - 1)/(1 - 2f)(= 0.8778)$ unless otherwise specified. Neurons in a specific excitatory pool are connected to neurons in the nonselective pool with a feedforward synaptic weight, $w = 1$ and a feedback synaptic connection of weight w_w. The connections between the different pools are set up to achieve the required mapping from the sensory input pools thorough the intermediate pools to the premotor pools, assuming Hebbian learning based on the activity of individual pools while the different tasks are being performed. The forward connections (input to intermediate to output pools) are $w_s = 2.1$. The corresponding feedback synaptic connections are slightly weaker ($wf = 1.7$ for the feedback synapses between rule-specific and sensory pools, and w_w for the feedback synapses between the premotor and rule-specific pools).

Each neuron (pyramidal cells and interneurons) receives $N_{ext} = 800$ excitatory AMPA synaptic connections from outside the network. These connections provide three different type of external interactions: (a) a background noise due to the spontaneous firing activity of neurons outside the network, (b) a sensory-related input, and (c) a rule or context-related bias input that specifies the task. The external inputs are given by a Poisson train of spikes. To model the background spontaneous activity of neurons in the network (Brunel & Wang, 2001), we assume that Poisson spikes arrive at each external synapse with a rate of $v_{ext} = 3$ Hz, consistent with the spontaneous activity observed in the cerebral cortex. The sensory input is encoded by increasing the external input Poisson rate v_{ext} to $v_{ext} + \lambda_{input}$ to the neurons in the appropriate, specific sensory pools. We used $\lambda_{input} = 100$ Hz. Finally, the biasing specification of the context (i.e., which rule is active) is modelled by assuming that each neuron in each of the pools in the group of intermediate pools associated with the active task receives external Poisson spikes with an increased rate from v_{ext} to $v_{ext} + \lambda_{rule}$ throughout the trial. We use $\lambda_{rule} = 120$ Hz. This external, top-down, rule-specific input probably comes from the external prefrontal neurons that directly encode abstract rules (Wallis, Anderson, & Miller, 2001), which in turn are influenced by the reward system (in the orbitofrontal cortex and amygdala) to enable the correct rule to be selected during, for example, reversal when the task contingencies change (Deco & Rolls, 2005b). During the last 100 ms of the response period, the external rate to all neurons is increased by a factor 1.5, to take into account the increase in afferent inputs due to behavioral responses and reward signals (Brunel & Wang, 2001).

We consider now theoretical analyses of the single-cell recordings of PFC neurons by Asaad et al. (2000), in which monkeys were trained to perform either an object-response task with a delay or a delayed spatial response task. The conditional object-response task with a delay is defined by the association of the identity of an object (O1 or O2) with a saccade response (L or R), independently of the location of the cue object. On the other hand, the spatially delayed response task required the monkey to make a saccade (L or R) response after a delay toward the location at which the cue object was presented (S1 or S2). Under this second condition, the monkey had to ignore the feature characteristics of the object and allocate its attention and memory to process the spatial location of the stimulus. Asaad et al. (2000) found some neurons that responded to the objects (O1 or O2), some to the locations of the object (S1 or S2), and other neurons that only responded in the relevant task and to a combination of the stimulus and required response. For example, some of these combination neurons responded only in the delayed object-response task (e.g., to O1-L or O2-R), and others only in the delayed spatial-response task (to S1-L or S2-R). Other neurons responded to the motor response required, L versus R.

We performed numerical simulations of the experiment of Asaad et al. (2000) by means of a prefrontal cortical architecture that includes two premotor pools of response neurons, one corresponding with leftward saccade responses (L) and the other corresponding to rightward saccade responses (R); four sensory pools (two object-selective neuronal pools, one corresponding to object O1 and the other corresponding to object O2; and two pools with selectivity for the spatial location of the stimulus, one corresponding to location S1 and the other corresponding to the location S2); and four intermediate neuronal pools, one for each of the four possible stimulus–response combinations. The intermediate pools are considered as being in two groups, one for the object-response associative task, and the other for the delayed spatial-response task. Figure 8–8 plots the temporal evolution of the averaged population activity for three neural pools, namely the premotor pool L, the intermediate spatial pool S1-L, and the intermediate associative pool O1-L. Cue, response, and selective context-specific associative activity is explicitly maintained during the STM-related delay period by the recurrent connections. As in Figure 8–5, the left panel corresponds to the delayed spatial response condition and the right panel to the conditional object–response associative task condition. Each graph shows two curves corresponding to the two possible response directions (blue corresponds to L and red to R). The first row shows activity in the premotor pool L, which was response direction–selective in both tasks. The second row shows activity in the intermediate spatial pool S1-L, which was response direction–selective (to the L, blue curve) in only the delayed spatial-response task. The third row shows activity in the intermediate associative pool O1-L, which was direction-selective in only the conditional object–place associative task. All three types of neurons found experimentally by Asaad et al. (2000) can be identified with pools in our prefrontal network.

Figure 8–9 plots the rastergrams of randomly selected neurons for each pool in the network. The spatiotemporal spiking activity shows that, during the STM delay period, only the relevant sensory cue, associated future oculomotor response, and intermediate neurons maintain persistent activity and build up a stable global attractor in the network. The underlying biased competition mechanisms are very explicit in this experiment. Note that neurons in pools for

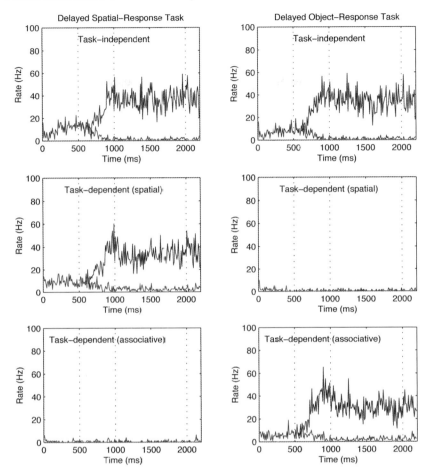

Figure 8–8. Simulation results corresponding to the experimental paradigm of Asaad et al. (2000) in a delayed spatial-response task and in a delayed object-response task. Adapted with permission from Deco, G. and., and Rolls, E. T. (2003). Attention and working memory: A dynamical model of neuronal activity in the prefrontal cortex. *European Journal of Neuroscience* 18:2374–2390.

the irrelevant input sensory dimension (location for the object–response associative task, and object for the delayed spatial-response task) are inhibited during the sensory cue period and are not sustained during the delay STM period. Given the rule context, only the relevant single-pool attractors that are suitable for the cue-response mapping survive the competition and are persistently maintained with high firing activity during the short-term memory delay period.

This suppression effect has been recently observed by recording the activity of prefrontal neurons in monkeys carrying out a focused attention task

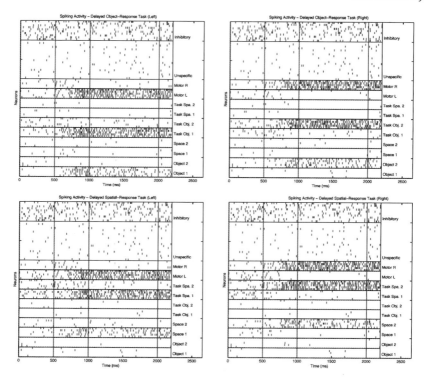

Figure 8–9. Rastergrams for pools in the PFC network in a delayed spatial-response task and in a delayed object-response task. Some neurons respond to the objects (O1 or O2), some to the positions of the objects (Space 1 or Space 2), some to combinations of the task and the object or its spatial position, and some to the motor response (R versus L). Each vertical line shows a spike of a neuron, and each row is for a different neuron. Adapted with permission from Deco, G. and., and Rolls, E. T. (2003). Attention and working memory: A dynamical model of neuronal activity in the prefrontal cortex. *European Journal of Neuroscience* 18:2374–2390.

(Everling, Tinsley, Gaffan, & Duncan, 2002). In their spatial cuing task, they observed strong filtering of the PFC response to unattended targets. These attentional modulation effects are well-known in posterior areas of the visual system (Chelazzi, 1998).

Our computational simulations (Deco & Rolls, 2003; Rolls & Deco, 2002) suggest that, in the PFC, filtering of ignored inputs may reach a level commensurate with the strong, global effects of selective attention in human behavior, and that this selection in the PFC is the basis of the attentional modulation found in more posterior sensory cortical areas, implemented through back-projections from the PFC to the more posterior cortical areas.

This model thus shows how a rule or context input can influence decision making by biasing competition in a hierarchical network that thus implements a flexible mapping from input stimuli to motor outputs (Deco & Rolls, 2003;

Rolls & Deco, 2002). The model also shows how the same network can implement a STM, and indeed, how the competition required for the biased competition selection process can be implemented in an attractor network that itself requires inhibition implemented through the inhibitory neurons.

8.4 OBJECT REPETITION/ADAPTATION EFFECTS

Some IT cortex neurons may be involved in a short-term recency memory for whether a particular familiar visual stimulus (such as a face) has been seen recently. The evidence for this is that some of these neurons respond differently to recently seen stimuli in short-term visual memory tasks (Baylis & Rolls, 1987; Miller & Desimone, 1994; Xiang & Brown, 1998). In the IT visual cortex proper, neurons respond more to novel than to familiar stimuli, but treat the stimuli as novel if more than one other stimulus intervenes between the first (novel) and second (familiar) presentations of a particular stimulus (Baylis & Rolls, 1987). More ventrally, in what is contained by or close to the perirhinal cortex, these memory spans may hold for several intervening stimuli in the same task (Xiang & Brown, 1998). This type of memory may be implemented by synaptic adaptation effects

Some neurons in these areas respond more when a sample stimulus reappears in a delayed match-to-sample task with intervening stimuli (Miller & Desimone, 1994), and the basis for this using a STM implemented in the PFC was described earlier, in the section on general mechanisms of temporary and long-term storage in neural circuits.

Some neurons in the more ventral (perirhinal) cortical area respond during the delay in a match-to-sample task with a delay between the sample stimulus and the to-be-matched stimulus (Miyashita, 1993; Renart, Parga, & Rolls, 2000). Other neurons respond more to the sample than to the match stimulus (Suzuki, 1999), and these neurons in the perirhinal cortex are actively involved in these STM processes in that they reset their responsiveness at the start of each new trial, even if the sample stimulus at the start of a trial has been seen recently (Hölscher & Rolls, 2002).

Some perirhinal cortex neurons reflect a very long-term familiarity memory in that their responses gradually increase over 400 presentations of a visual stimulus seen during a period of 1 week (Hölscher, Rolls, & Xiang, 2003; Rolls, Franco, & Stringer, 2005). This type of long-term familiarity memory could be useful in the recognition of other members of a social group, home territory, and belongings.

8.5 LONG-TERM VISUAL MEMORY IN INFERIOR TEMPORAL CORTEX

Some neurons in the IT visual cortex encode objects and faces and, in this sense, provide a long-term visual memory for faces and objects. The neurons provide a perceptual representation, which is a type of long-term memory (LTM) representation of an object or face. Some of these neurons have invariant representations; thus, neurons in receiving areas that learn about the associations of these objects or faces automatically generalize their learning to different views of the objects or faces. The encoding of information in IT cortex, and the way in which the invariant representations are built by learning, are considered in this section and are covered in more detail elsewhere (Rolls, 2000; Rolls, 2007; Rolls & Deco, 2002; Rolls & Deco, 2006; Rolls & Stringer, 2006; Rolls 2008).

8.5.1 Nature of Neural Coding in Inferior Temporal Cortex, Including Viewpoint Invariance

While recording in the temporal lobe cortical visual areas of macaques, Charles Gross and colleagues found some neurons that appeared to respond best to complex visual stimuli, such as faces (Bruce, Desimone, & Gross, 1981; Desimone, 1991; Desimone & Gross, 1979; Rolls, 2007). It was soon found that although some of these neurons could respond to parts of faces, other neurons required several parts of the face to be present in the correct spatial arrangement, and that many of these neurons did not just respond to any face that was shown, but responded differently to different faces (Desimone, Albright, Gross, & Bruce, 1984; Gross, Desimone, Albright, & Schwartz, 1985; Perrett, Rolls, & Caan, 1982; Rolls, 1984). By responding differently to different faces, these neurons potentially encode information useful for identifying individual faces. Some specialization of function exists for different temporal cortical visual areas (Baylis, Rolls, & Leonard, 1987; Rolls, 2007).

The representation of faces and objects by IT neurons is distributed in that each neuron typically responds to a number of stimuli in a set of stimuli, with each neuron having a different profile of responses to each stimulus (Baylis, Rolls, & Leonard, 1985; Rolls, Treves, Tovee, & Panzeri, 1997b). The distributed nature of the representation can be further understood by the finding that the firing rate probability distribution of single neurons, when a wide range of natural visual stimuli are being viewed, is approximately exponentially distributed, with rather few stimuli producing high firing rates and increasingly large numbers of stimuli producing lower and lower firing rates (Baddeley et al., 1997; Franco, Rolls, Aggelopoulos, & Jerez, 2007; Rolls & Tovee, 1995; Treves, Panzeri, Rolls, Booth, & Wakeman, 1999).

At the neuronal population level, it has been shown that the information about which face or object has been shown increases approximately linearly with the number of neurons (up to approximately 20 neurons), indicating that the neurons convey almost independent information in their firing rates (Abbott, Rolls, & Tovee, 1996; Booth & Rolls, 1998; Rolls, Treves, & Tovee, 1997a). Moreover, almost all (95%) of the information is present in the firing rates, with little additional information present in any stimulus-dependent synchrony that may be present between the spiking of simultaneously recorded neurons (Franco, Rolls, Aggelopoulos, & Treves, 2004; Rolls, Franco, Aggelopoulos, & Reece, 2003b; Rolls, Aggelopoulos, Franco, & Treves, 2004), even when multiple objects must be discriminated in complex natural scenes (Aggelopoulos, Franco, & Rolls, 2005).

One of the major computational problems solved by the visual system is the building of a representation of visual information that allows recognition to occur relatively independently of size, contrast, spatial frequency, position on the retina, angle of view, and the like (Rolls, 2007; Rolls & Deco, 2002; Rolls & Stringer, 2006) (see also Chapter 6 of this volume). This is required, so that if the receiving regions—such as amygdala, orbitofrontal cortex, and hippocampus— learn about one view, position, or size of the object, the organism generalizes correctly to other positions, views, and sizes of the object (Rolls, 2005). Some single neurons in the IT cortex show invariant representations for all these types of transformation (Booth & Rolls, 1998; Hasselmo, Rolls, Baylis, & Nalwa, 1989; Rolls & Baylis, 1986; Rolls, Baylis, & Leonard, 1985; Tovee, Rolls, & Azzopardi, 1994). Moreover, these neurons give reliable outputs about the objects to which they respond even when the objects are presented in complex natural scenes (Rolls, Aggelopoulos, & Zheng, 2003a; Rolls & Deco, 2006). Neurons with invariant responses have also been found in the human medial temporal lobe regions such as the hippocampus (Quiroga, Reddy, Kreiman, Koch, & Fried, 2005).

The way in which these invariant representations of objects and faces are built into LTM representations are considered next (cf., Rolls, 2000; Rolls & Deco, 2002; Rolls & Stringer, 2006; Rolls & Stringer, 2007; Rolls 2008).

Cortical visual processing for object recognition is considered to be organized as a set of hierarchically connected cortical regions consisting at least of V1, V2, V4, posterior IT cortex (TEO), IT cortex (e.g., TE3, TEa, and TEm), and anterior temporal cortical areas (e.g., TE2 and TE1). Each small part of a region converges upon the succeeding region (or layer in the hierarchy) in such a way that the receptive field sizes of neurons (e.g., 1 degree near the fovea in V1) become larger by a factor of approximately 2.5 with each succeeding stage (and the typical parafoveal receptive field sizes found would not be inconsistent with the calculated approximations of, say, 8 degrees in V4, 20 degrees in TEO, and 50 degrees in the IT cortex; Boussaoud & Ungerleider, 1991) (see Fig. 8–10).

Such zones of convergence would overlap continuously with each other (see Fig. 8–10). This connectivity would be part of the architecture by which translation-invariant representations are computed.

Each layer is considered to act partly as a set of local, self-organizing, competitive neuronal networks with overlapping inputs. These competitive nets operate (a) by a single set of forward inputs leading to (typically nonlinear; e.g., sigmoid) activation of output neurons; (b) through competition between the output neurons, mediated by a set of feedback-inhibitory interneurons that receive from many of the principal (in the cortex, pyramidal) cells in the net and project back (via inhibitory interneurons) to many of the principal cells, thus serving to decrease the firing rates of the less active neurons relative to the rates of the more active neurons; and (c) through synaptic modification by a modified Hebb rule, such that synapses to strongly activated output neurons from active input axons strengthen, and those from inactive input axons weaken. A biologically plausible form of this learning rule that operates well in such networks is:

$$\delta w_{ij} = \alpha y_i (x_j - w_{ij}) \qquad *(18)$$

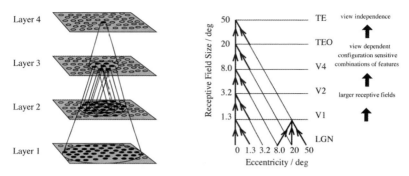

Figure 8–10. Convergence in the visual system. *Right*, as it occurs in the brain. *Left*, as implemented in VisNet. Convergence through the network is designed to provide fourth-layer neurons with information from across the entire input retina. V1, visual cortex area V1; TEO, posterior IT cortex; TE, IT cortex.

where α is a learning rate constant, and x_j and w_{ij} are in appropriate units. Such competitive networks operate to detect correlations between the activity of the input neurons and to allocate output neurons to respond to each cluster of such correlated inputs. These networks thus act as categorizers. In relation to visual information processing, they would remove redundancy from the input representation and would develop low-entropy representations of the information (cf., Barlow, 1985; Barlow, Kaushal, & Mitchison, 1989). Such competitive nets are biologically plausible, in that they utilize Hebb-modifiable forward excitatory connections, with competitive inhibition mediated by cortical inhibitory neurons.

The competitive scheme would not result in the formation of "winner-take-all" or "grandmother" cells, but would instead result in a small ensemble of active neurons representing each input (Rolls, 1989a; Rolls, 1989b; Rolls & Treves, 1998). The scheme has advantages in that the output neurons learn better to distribute themselves between the input patterns (cf. Bennett, 1990) and in that the sparse representations formed have utility in maximizing the number of memories that can be stored when, toward the end of the visual system, the visual representation of objects is interfaced to associative memory (Rolls, 1989a; Rolls, 1989b; Rolls & Treves, 1998; Rolls 2008).

Translation invariance would be computed in such a system by utilizing competitive learning to detect regularities in inputs when real objects are translated in the physical world. The hypothesis is that, because objects have continuous properties in space and time in the world, an object at one place on the retina might activate feature analyzers at the next stage of cortical processing. Then, when the object was translated to a nearby position (and because this would occur within a short period; e.g., 0.5 s), the membrane of the postsynaptic neuron would still be in its Hebb-modifiable state (caused for example by calcium entry as a result of the voltage-dependent activation of NMDA receptors). Thus, the presynaptic afferents activated with the object in its new position would become strengthened on the still-activated postsynaptic neuron. It is suggested that the short temporal window (e.g., 0.5 s) of Hebb-modifiability helps neurons to learn the statistics of objects moving in the physical world and, at the same time, form different representations of different feature combinations or objects, as these are physically discontinuous and present less regular correlations to the visual system. Foldiak (1991) has proposed computing an average activation of the postsynaptic neuron to assist with the same problem. One idea here is that the temporal properties of the biologically implemented learning mechanism are such that it is well suited to detecting the relevant continuities in the world of real objects. Another suggestion is that a memory trace for what has been seen in the last 300 ms appears to be implemented by a mechanism as simple as continued firing of IT neurons after the stimulus has disappeared (Rolls et al., 1994; Rolls et al., 1999; Rolls & Tovee, 1994).

It is also suggested that other invariances—for example size, spatial frequency, and rotation invariance—could be learned by a comparable process. It is suggested that this process takes place at each stage of the multiple-layer cortical processing hierarchy, so that invariances are learned first over small regions of space and then over successively larger regions. This limits the size of the connection space within which correlations must be sought.

Increasing complexity of representations could also be built in such a multiple-layer hierarchy by similar mechanisms. At each stage or layer, the self-organizing competitive nets would result in combinations of inputs becoming the effective stimuli for neurons. To avoid the combinatorial explosion, it is proposed (following Feldman, 1985), that low-order combinations of inputs would be learned by each neuron. (Each input would not be represented by activity in a single input axon, but instead by activity in a set of active input axons.) Evidence consistent with this suggestion that neurons are responding to combinations of a few variables represented at the preceding stage of cortical processing is that some neurons in V1 respond to combinations of bars or edges; neurons V2 and V4 respond to end-stopped lines, to tongues flanked by inhibitory subregions, or to combinations of colors; neurons in posterior IT cortex respond to stimuli that may require two or more simple features to be present (Tanaka, Saito, Fukada, & Moriya, 1990); and, in the temporal cortical face processing areas, neurons respond to images that require the presence of several features in a face (such as eyes, hair, and mouth) in order to respond (Perrett, Rolls, & Caan, 1982; Yamane, Kaji, & Kawano, 1988). It is an important part of this suggestion that some local spatial information would be inherent in the features being combined. For example, cells might not respond to the combination of an edge and a small circle unless they were in the correct spatial relationship to each other. [This is in fact consistent with the data of Tanaka, Saito, Fukada and Moriya (1990), and with our data on face neurons, in that some faces neurons require the face features to be in the correct spatial configuration and not jumbled, Rolls, Tovee, Purcell, Stewart and Azzopardi (1994).] The local spatial information in the features being combined would ensure that the representation at the next level would contain some information about the (local) arrangement of features. Further low-order combinations of such neurons at the next stage would include sufficient local spatial information, so that an arbitrary spatial arrangement of the same features would not activate the same neuron. This is the proposed, and limited, solution that this mechanism would provide for the feature binding problem (Elliffe, Rolls, & Stringer, 2002; Malsburg, 1990). By this stage of processing, a view-dependent representation of objects suitable for view-dependent processes, such as behavioral responses to face expression and gesture, would be available.

It is suggested that view-independent representations could be formed by the same type of computation, operating to combine a limited set of views of objects. The plausibility of providing view-independent recognition of objects by combining a set of different views of objects has been proposed by a number of investigators (Koenderink & Van Doorn, 1979; Logothetis, Pauls, Bulthoff, & Poggio, 1994; Poggio & Edelman, 1990; Ullman, 1996). Consistent with the suggestion that the view-independent representations are formed by combining view-dependent representations in the primate visual system is the fact that, in the temporal cortical areas, neurons with view-independent representations of faces are present in the same cortical areas as neurons with view-dependent representations (from which the view-independent neurons could receive inputs) (Booth & Rolls, 1998; Hasselmo, Rolls, Baylis, & Nalwa, 1989; Perrett, et al., 1985). This solution to "object-based" representations is very different from that traditionally proposed for artificial vision systems, in which the coordinates of objects in three-dimensional space are stored in a database, and general-purpose algorithms operate on these to perform transforms such as translation, rotation, and scale change within three-dimensional space (for review, see Rolls & Deco, 2002). In the present, much more limited but more biologically plausible scheme, the representation would be suitable for recognition of an object and for linking associative memories to objects, but would be less suitable for making actions in three-dimensional space to particular parts of, or inside, objects, as the three-dimensional coordinates of each part of the object would not be explicitly available. It is therefore proposed that visual fixation is used to locate in foveal vision part of an object to which movements must be made, and that local disparity and other measurements of depth then provide sufficient information for the motor system to make actions relative to the small part of space in which a local, view-dependent representation of depth would be provided (cf. Ballard, 1990).

The computational processes proposed here operate by an unsupervised learning mechanism, which utilizes statistical regularities in the physical environment to enable representations to be built. In some cases, it may be advantageous to utilize some form of mild teaching input to the visual system, to enable it to learn—for example—that rather similar visual inputs have very different consequences in the world, so that different representations of them should be built. In other cases, it might be helpful to bring representations together, if they have identical consequences, to use storage capacity efficiently. It is proposed elsewhere (Rolls, 1989a; Rolls, 1989b; Rolls & Treves, 1998) that the back-projections from each adjacent cortical region in the hierarchy (and from amygdala and hippocampus to higher regions of the visual system) play such a role by providing guidance to those competitive networks suggested earlier to be important in each cortical area. This guidance, and also the capability for recall, are, it is suggested, implemented by Hebb-modifiable connections from the back-projecting neurons to the principal (pyramidal) neurons of the competitive networks in the preceding stages (Rolls, 1989a; Rolls, 1989b; Rolls & Treves, 1998).

These hypotheses have been explored in a four-layer competitive network with convergence from stage to stage, local lateral inhibition within a stage, and training by a trace learning rule. The trace update rule used in the baseline simulations of VisNet (Wallis & Rolls, 1997) is equivalent to Foldiak's, used in the context of translation invariance. The rule can be summarized as follows:

$$\delta w_j = \alpha \bar{y}^\tau x_j \qquad *(19)$$

where

$$\bar{y}^\tau = (1-\eta)y^\tau + \eta \bar{y}^{\tau-1} \qquad *(20)$$

and

x_j: j^{th} input to the neuron.

$\bar{y}^\tau$: Trace value of the output of the neuron at time step τ.
w_j: Synaptic weight between j^{th} input and the neuron.
y: Output from the neuron.
β: Learning rate. Annealed between unity and zero.
η: Trace value. The optimal value varies with presentation sequence length.

It has been shown that the network can compute translation-, size-, and view- invariant representations, and modifications to the learning rules have been introduced and explored (Rolls & Deco, 2002; Rolls & Milward, 2000; Rolls & Stringer, 2001; Wallis and Rolls, 1997). It has been shown that feature binding can be implemented in the architecture by allowing competitive learning in the early layers to form neurons that respond to combinations of features in particular spatial relationships (Elliffe, Rolls, & Stringer, 2002). It has been shown that, after training, the network can recognize objects in cluttered environments and with partially occluded stimuli (Stringer & Rolls, 2000), and can learn three-dimensional perspectival transforms of three-dimensional objects (Stringer & Rolls, 2002). The network, by incorporating a greater magnification factor for the fovea, can account for the effects of foveal dominance in complex scenes (Deco & Rolls, 2004; Trappenberg, Rolls, & Stringer, 2002) and, by introducing back-projections, can account for top-down attentional effects (Deco & Rolls, 2004). VisNet thus provides a biologically plausible model of invariant object recognition and the LTM representations that implement this.

A related approach to invariant object recognition is described by Riesenhuber and Poggio (1999b) and builds on the hypothesis that invariances such as scale, rotation, and even view, could be built into a feature hierarchy system, as suggested by Rolls (1992). The approach of Riesenhuber and Poggio (1999b) (see also Riesenhuber & Poggio, 1999a; Riesenhuber & Poggio, 2000) is a feature hierarchy approach that uses alternate "simple cell" (S) and "complex cell" (C) layers in a way analogous to Fukushima (1980). The function of each S cell layer is to build more complicated features from the inputs, and it works by template matching. The function of each C cell layer is to provide some translation invariance over the features discovered in the preceding simple cell layer (as in Fukushima, 1980), and it operates by performing a MAX function on the inputs. The nonlinear MAX function makes a complex cell respond only to whatever is the highest activity input being received, and is part of the process by which invariance is achieved according to this proposal. This C layer process involves "implicitly scanning over afferents of the same type differing in the parameter of the transformation to which responses should be invariant (for instance, feature size for scale invariance), and then selecting the best-matching afferent" (Riesenhuber & Poggio, 1999b). Brain mechanisms by which this computation could be set up are not part of the scheme; the model does not self-organize by training and so does not yet provide a biologically plausible model of invariant object recognition and the LTM representations that implement this.

8.5.2 Object Training Studies

To investigate the idea that visual experience might guide the formation of the responsiveness of neurons, so that they provide an economical and ensemble-encoded representation of items actually present in the environment, the responses of IT cortex face-selective neurons have been analyzed while a set of new faces were shown. Using monkeys as subjects, some of the neurons studied in this way altered the relative degree to which they responded to the different members of the set of novel faces over the first few (1–2) presentations of the set (Rolls, Baylis, Hasselmo, & Nalwa, 1989). If, in a different experiment, a single novel face was introduced when the responses of a neuron to a set of familiar faces were being recorded, the responses to the set of familiar faces were not disrupted, whereas the responses to the novel face became stable within a few presentations. Alteration of the tuning of individual neurons in this way may result in a good discrimination over the population as a whole of the faces known to the monkey. This evidence is consistent with the categorization being performed by self-organizing competitive neuronal networks, as described in earlier and elsewhere (Rolls & Treves, 1998).

Further evidence that these neurons can learn new representations very rapidly comes from an experiment in which binarized black-and-white (two-tone) images of faces that blended with the background were used. These did not activate face-selective neurons. Full gray-scale images of the same photographs were then shown for ten 0.5-second presentations. In a number of cases, if the neuron happened to be responsive to that face, when the binarized version of the same face was shown next, the neurons responded to it (Tovee, Rolls, & Ramachandran, 1996). This is a direct parallel to the same phenomenon observed psychophysically and provides dramatic evidence that these neurons are influenced by only a very few seconds (in this case 5 s) of experience with a visual stimulus. We have shown a neural correlate of this effect using similar stimuli and a similar paradigm in a positron emission tomography (PET) neuroimaging study in humans, with a region showing an effect of the learning found for faces in the right temporal lobe and for objects in the left temporal lobe (Dolan et al., 1997).

The responses of IT neurons become tuned to relevant features in a task in which macaques must classify visual stimuli (Bakers, Behrmann, & Olson, 2002; Sigala, 2004; Sigala, Gabbiani, & Logothetis. 2002; Sigala & Logothetis, 2002). Inferior temporal cortex neurons in macaques (Kayaert, Biederman, & Vogels, 2005) and medial temporal lobe neurons in humans can reflect perceptual categories (Kreiman, Koch, & Freid, 2000). A number of different types of feedback process are involved in such tasks (Tarr & Cheng, 2003), and this feedback must be able to influence IT cortex neuronal responses, perhaps by utilizing back-projection effects in competitive networks (Rolls & Deco, 2002; Rolls & Treves, 1998) from areas directly influenced by outcomes (Rolls, 2005).

8.6 PERCEPTUAL PLASTICITY: LEARNING TO ATTEND

In a recently performed neurophysiological experiment (Sigala & Logothetis, 2002), the activity level of single IT cortex neurons of awake, behaving monkeys engaged in a visual categorization task was recorded to measure how the IT representation of the visual stimuli is affected by the learned categorization. In this experiment, monkeys learned to categorize a set of images (schematic face and fish stimuli) into two categories, each associated with one lever (left or right) that the monkeys had to pull when the corresponding stimulus was presented. The schematic images were characterized by a set of a few features, each varying in a discrete set of values. For the faces, each of the four features could take three discrete values: high, medium, or low. Only two features, referred to as *diagnostic*, were informative for solving the categorization task; that is, the two categories could be linearly separated along the two diagnostic features in the stimulus space. The other two features, referred to as *nondiagnostic*, gave no information about the stimulus-associated category and were irrelevant for the task.

After training, the number of presented stimuli was enlarged by choosing different test exemplars in the stimulus space. The experimental results (Sigala & Logothetis, 2002) represent the averaged activity of all visually responsive neurons measured in IT (a total of 96 units) after the monkey had learned to categorize the presented stimuli. For each neuron, the responses were sorted by the presented stimulus feature values and averaged over many trials. The resulting average activity levels reflect which feature values excite a given neuron most and least, respectively. The population average activation trace over all responsive neurons was then calculated by grouping all best and worst responses for each of the stimulus features, respectively. The results showed an enhancement in neuronal tuning for the values of the diagnostic features. Responses to nondiagnostic features, in contrast, were poorly tuned. Hence IT activity not only encodes the presence and properties of visual stimuli, but also becomes tuned to their behavioral relevance.

The relevance to behavior of different features of the presented stimuli is determined through the consequences—receiving reward or not—of the selected action. The monkey learns to associate specific values of the diagnostic features with the corresponding category by evaluating the received reward.

As reviewed in the earlier section on prefrontal cortex short-term memory networks and their relation to temporal and parietal perceptual networks, the IT visual cortex and PFC are two interconnected cortical areas thought to be involved in the performance of visual tasks, such as visual recognition, categorization, and memory, although the contribution of each of these two areas for visual processing is not fully understood. In this context, recent studies have suggested that the PFC is mainly associated with cognitive processing (such as categorization), whereas the IT cortex is more associated with feature processing (Freedman, Riesenhuber, Poggio, & Miller, 2003). Further, top-down signals from PFC to IT are thought to partially determine IT neuronal responses (Freedman et al., 2003; Freedman, Riesenhuber, Poggio, & Miller, 2001; Tomita, Ohbayashi, Nakahara, Hasegawa, & Miyashita, 1999). Taking into account all these findings on perceptual learning, higher visual processing, and the tuning of IT neurons during the categorization task (Sigala & Logothetis, 2002), Szabo, Almeida, Deco, and Stetter (2005a) hypothesize that the enhancement of selectivity for the levels of the diagnostic features of IT neurons might emerge through a higher-level cognitive feedback, possibly from the PFC, where the previously learned categories could be encoded.

To test this hypothesis and account for the experimental results, Szabo, Deco, Fusi, Del Giudice, Mattia, and Stetter (2005b) proposed a neurodynamic computational two-layer model in the framework of biased competition and cooperation. The first layer corresponds to a part of IT and is organized into populations of neurons that receive feature-specific inputs. The second layer corresponds to a region in PFC where the categories of the stimuli are supposedly encoded. In the IT layer of the model, cooperation takes place between specific populations, implemented by uniform lateral connectivity. They encode the same type of stimulus and are differentiated only by their specific preferences for the feature values of the stimuli. The neural activity of the PFC model layer is designed to reflect the category to which the presented stimulus corresponds. Competition is implemented between the category-encoding populations. The network is trained using a simple reward-based Hebbian algorithm. After successful learning, as a stimulus is presented to the trained network, the sensory inputs (coming from lower visual processing areas) activate the IT neurons and are propagated through feedforward connections to PFC. This bottom-up input from IT biases the competition between the category encoding populations. The winning category expresses the monkey's decision and influences the activity of the neurons in the IT layer such that they become selective for some of the presented features.

In conclusion, based on these simulation results, we find that the described effect could result from reward-based Hebbian learning that robustly modifies the connections between the feature encoding layer (IT) and the category encoding layer (PFC) to a setting in which the neurons activated by the level of a feature that determines the categorization required are strongly connected to the associated category and weakly connected to the other category; the neurons that receive inputs specific for a task-irrelevant feature are connected to the category neurons with an average weight not significantly changed during training. This structure of the interlayer connectivity seems to be a stable fixed-point of this learning dynamics and is able to reproduce the experimental data by achieving high selectivity of the IT neurons for the diagnostic features and low selectivity for the nondiagnostic feature. By setting all weights equal, so that no structure exists in the interlayer connectivity, the network could not reproduce the enhancement in selectivity for the diagnostic features.

CONCLUSION

In this chapter, we have reviewed experimental and computational approaches to the functions of the IT visual cortex and the PFC in learning visual representations, in visual memory, in visual attention, in switching between tasks, and in the use of visual stimuli based on a STM for which rule is currently active.

REFERENCES

Abbott, L. F., Rolls, E. T., and Tovee, M. J. (1996). Representational capacity of face coding in monkeys. *Cerebral Cortex* 6:498–505.

Adcock, R., Constable, R., Gore, J., and Goldman-Rakic, P. (2000). Functional neuroanatomy of executive processes involved in dual-task performance. *Proceedings of the National Academy of Science* 97:3567–3572.

Aggelopoulos, N. C., Franco, L., and Rolls, E. T. (2005). Object perception in natural scenes: Encoding by inferior temporal cortex simultaneously recorded neurons. *Journal of Neurophysiology* 93:1342–1357.

Amit, D. (1995). Model of global spontaneous activity and local structured activity during delay periods in the cerebral cortex. *Behavioral Brain Science* 18:617.

Amit, D., and Tsodyks, M. (1991). Quantitative study of attractor neural network retrieving at low spike rates: I. Substrate spikes, rates and neuronal gain. *Network* 2:259–273.

Asaad, W. F., Rainer, G., and Miller, E. K. (2000). Task-specific neural activity in the primate prefrontal cortex. *Journal of Neurophysiology* 84:451–459.

Baddeley, A. (1986). *Working memory*, Oxford University Press, New York.

Baddeley, R. J., Abbott, L. F., Booth, M. J. A., Sengpiel, F., Freeman, T., Wakeman, E. A., and Rolls, E. T. (1997). Responses of neurons in primary and inferior temporal visual cortices to natural scenes. *Proceedings of the Royal Society B* 264:1775–1783.

Bakers, C. I., Behrmann, M., and Olson, C. R. (2002). Impact of learning on representation of parts and wholes in monkey inferotemporal cortex. *Nature Neuroscience* 5:1210–1216.

Ballard, D. H. (1990). Animate vision uses object-centred reference frames. In *Advanced Neural Computers*, ed. R. Eckmiller, 229–236. Amsterdam: North-Holland.

Barlow, H. B. (1985). Cerebral cortex as model builder. In *Models of the Visual Cortex*, eds. D. Rose and V. Dobson, 37–46. Chichester, U.K.: Wiley.

Barlow, H. B., Kaushal, T., and Mitchison, G. (1989). Finding minimum entropy codes. *Neural Computation* 1:421–423

Battaglia, F., and Treves, A. (1998). Stable and rapid recurrent processing in realistic autoassociative memories. *Neural Computation* 10:431–450.

Baylis, G. C., and Rolls, E. T. (1987). Responses of neurons in the inferior temporal cortex in short term and serial recognition memory tasks. *Experimental Brain Research* 65:614–622.

Baylis, G. C., Rolls, E. T., and Leonard, C. M. (1985). Selectivity between faces in the responses of a population of neurons in the cortex in the superior temporal sulcus of the monkey. *Brain Research* 342:91–102.

Baylis, G C., Rolls, E. T., and Leonard, C. M. (1987). Functional subdivisions of temporal lobe neocortex. *Journal of Neuroscience* 7:330–342.

Bennett, A. (1990). Large competitive networks. *Network* 1:449–462.

Booth, M. C. A., and Rolls, E. T. (1998). View-invariant representations of familiar objects by neurons in the inferior temporal visual cortex. *Cerebral Cortex* 8:510–523.

Boussaoud, D. D. R., and Ungerleider, L. G. (1991). Visual topography of area TEO in the macaque. *Journal of Comparative Neurology* 306:554–575.

Bruce, C., Desimone, R., and Gross, C. G. (1981). Visual properties of neurons in a polysensory area in superior temporal sulcus of the macaque. *Journal of Neurophysiology* 46:369–384.

Brunel, N., and Wang, X. (2001). Effects of neuromodulation in a cortical networks model of object working memory dominated by recurrent inhibition. *Journal of Computational Neuroscience* 11:63–85.

Butters, N., and Pandya, D. (1969). Retention of delayed-alternation: Effect of selective lesions of sulcus principalis. *Science* 165:1271–1273.

Camperi, M., and Wang, X. (1998). A model of visuospatial short-term memory in prefrontal cortex: Recurrent network and cellular bistability. *Journal of Computational Neuroscience* 5:383–405.

Chelazzi, L. (1998). Serial attention mechanisms in visual search: A critical look at the evidence. *Psychological Research* 62:, 195–219.

Compte, A., Brunel, N., Goldman-Rakic, P., and Wang, X. (2000). Synaptic mechanisms and network dynamics underlying spatial working memory in a cortical network model. *Cerebral Cortex* 10:910–923.

Courtney, S., Ungerleider, L., Keil, K., and Haxby, J. (1997). Transient and sustained activity in a distributed neural system for human working memory. *Nature* 386:608–611.

Deco, G., and Rolls, E. T. (2003). Attention and working memory: A dynamical model of neuronal activity in the prefrontal cortex. *European Journal of Neuroscience* 18:2374–2390.

Deco, G., and Rolls, E. T. (2004). A neurodynamical cortical model of visual attention and invariant object recognition. *Vision Research* 44:621–644.

Deco, G., and Rolls, E. T. (2005a). Attention, short term memory, and action selection: A unifying theory. *Progress in Neurobiology* 76:236–256.

Deco, G., and Rolls, E. T. (2005b). Synaptic and spiking dynamics underlying reward reversal in the orbitofrontal cortex. *Cerebral Cortex* 15:15–30.

Deco, G., Rolls, E. T., and Horwitz, B. (2004). "What" and "where" in visual working memory: A computational neurodynamical perspective for integrating fMRI and single-neuron data. *Journal of Cognitive Neuroscience* 16:683–701.

Desimone, R. (1991). Face-selective cells in the temporal cortex of monkeys. *Journal of Cognitive Neuroscience* 3:1–8.

Desimone, R. (1996). Neural mechanisms for visual memory and their role in attention. *Proceedings of the National Academy of Sciences USA* 93:13494–13499.

Desimone, R., Albright, T. D., Gross, C. G and Bruce, C. (1984). Stimulus-selective properties of inferior temporal neurons in the macaque. *Journal of Neuroscience* 4:2051–2062.

Desimone, R., and Gross, C. G. (1979). Visual areas in the temporal lobe of the macaque. *Brain Research* 178:363–380.

D'Esposito, M., Aguirre, G K., Zarahn, E., Ballard, D., Shin, R. K., and Lease, J. (1998). Functional MRI studies of spatial and nonspatial working memory. *Cognitive Brain Research* 7:1–13.

Dolan, R. J., Fink, G. R., Rolls, E. T., Booth, M., Holmes, A., Frackowiak, R. S. J., and Friston, K. J. (1997). How the brain learns to see objects and faces in an impoverished context. *Nature* 389:596–99.

Elliffe, M. C. M., Rolls, E. T., and Stringer, S. M. (2002). Invariant recognition of feature combinations in the visual system. *Biological Cybernetics* 86:59–71.

Everling, S., Tinsley, C., Gaffan, D., and Duncan, J. (2002). Filtering of neural signals by focused attention in the monkey prefrontal cortex. *Nature Neuroscience* 5:671–676.

Feldman, J. A. (1985). Four frames suffice: A provisional model of vision and space. *Behavioural Brain Sciences* 8:265–289.

Foldiak, P. (1991). Learning invariance from transformation sequences. *Neural Computation* 3:193–199.

Franco, L., Rolls, E. T., Aggelopoulos, N. C., and Jerez, J. M. (2007). Neuronal selectivity, population sparseness, and ergodicity in the inferior temporal visual cortex. *Biology and Cybernetics* 96(6):547–560.

Franco, L., Rolls, E. T., Aggelopoulos, N. C., and Treves, A. (2004). The use of decoding to analyze the contribution to the information of the correlations between the firing of simultaneously recorded neurons. *Experimental Brain Research* 155:370–384.

Freedman, D. J., Riesenhuber, M., Poggio, T., and Miller, E. K. (2001). Categorical representation of visual stimuli in the primate prefrontal cortex. *Science* 291:312–316.

Freedman, D. J., Riesenhuber, M., Poggio, T., and Miller, E. K. (2003). A comparison of primate prefrontal and inferior temporal cortices during visual categorisation. *Journal of Neuroscience* 23:5235–5246.

Fukushima, K. (1980). Neocognitron: A self-organizing neural network model for a mechanism of pattern recognition unaffected by shift in position. *Biological Cybernetics* 36:193–202.

Funahashi, S., Bruce, C., and Goldman-Rakic, P. (1989). Mnemonic coding of visual space in the monkey's dorsolateral prefrontal cortex. *Journal of Neurophysiology* 61:331–349.

Funahashi, S., Chafee, M., and Goldman-Rakic, P. (1993). Prefrontal neural activity in rhesus monkeys performing a delayed anti-saccade task. *Nature* 365:753–756.

Fuster, J. (1997). *The Prefrontal Cortex*, 3rd ed. New York: Raven Press.

Fuster, J. (2000). Executive frontal functions. *Experimental Brain Research* 133:66–70.

Fuster, J., and Alexander, G. (1971). Neuron activity related to short-term memory. *Science* 173:652–654.

Glover, G. H. (1999). Deconvolution of impulse response in event-related BOLD fMRI. *NeuroImage* 9:416–29.

Goel, V., and Grafman, J. (1995). Are the frontal lobes implicated in "planning" functions? Interpreting data from the Tower of Hanoi. *Neuropsychologia* 33:632–642.

Goldman-Rakic, P. (1987). Circuitry of primate prefrontal cortex and regulation of behavior by representational memory. In *Handbook of Physiology: The Nervous System*, eds. F. Plum and V. Mountcastle, 373–417. Bethesda, MD: American Physiological Society.

Goldman-Rakic, P. (1995). Cellular basis of working memory. *Neuron* 14:477–485.

Goldman-Rakic, P. (1996). Regional and cellular fractionation of working memory. *Proceedings of the National Academy of Science* 93:13473–13480.

Gross, C. G., Desimone, R., Albright, T. D., and Schwartz, E. L. (1985). Inferior temporal cortex and pattern recognition. *Experimental Brain Research* 11(Suppl):179–201.

Hasselmo, M. E., Rolls, E. T., Baylis, G C., and Nalwa, V. (1989). Object-centered encoding by face-selective neurons in the cortex in the superior temporal sulcus of the monkey. *Experimental Brain Research* 75:417–429.

Hebb, D. (1949). *The Organization of Behavior:- A Neurophysiological Theory*. New York: Wiley.

Hertz, J., Krogh, A., and Palmer, R. G. (1991). *Introduction to the Theory of Neural Computation*. Wokingham, U.K.: Addison Wesley.

Hölscher, C., and Rolls, E. T. (2002). Perirhinal cortex neuronal activity is actively related to working memory in the macaque. *Neural Plasticity* 9:41–51.

Hölscher, C., Rolls, E. T., and Xiang, J. Z. (2003). Perirhinal cortex neuronal activity related to long term familiarity memory in the macaque, *European Journal of Neuroscience* 18:2037–2046.

Hopfield, J. J. (1982). Neural networks and physical systems with emergent collective computational abilities. *Proceedings of the National Academy of Sciences, USA* 79:2554—2558.

Horwitz, B., Friston, K. J., and Taylor, J. G. (2000). Neural modeling and functional brain imaging: An overview. *Neural Networks* 13:829–846.

Horwitz, B., Tagamets, M.-A., and McIntosh, A. R. (1999). Neural modeling, functional brain imaging, and cognition. *Trends in Cognitive Sciences* 3:85–122.

Kawaguchi, Y. (1997). Selective cholinergic modulation of cortical GABAergic cell subtypes. *Journal of Neurophysiology* 78:1743–1747.

Kayaert, G., Biederman, I., and Vogels, R. (2005). Representation of regular and irregular shapes in macaque inferotemporal cortex. *Cerebral Cortex* 15:1308–1321.

Koenderink, J. J., and Van Doorn, A. J. (1979). The internal representation of solid shape with respect to vision. *Biological Cybernetics* 32:211–217.

Koch, C., and Freid, I. (2000). Category-specific visual responses of single neurons in the human temporal lobe. *Nature Neuroscience* 3:946–953.

Kubota, K., and Niki, H. (1971). Prefrontal cortical unit activity and delayed alternation performance in monkeys. *Journal of Neurophysiology* 34:337–347.

Kuhn, R. (1990). Statistical mechanics of neural networks near saturation. In *Statistical Mechanics of Neural Networks*, ed. L. Garrido. Berlin: Springer–Verlag.

Kuhn, R., Bos, S., and van Hemmen, J. L. (1991). Statistical mechanics for networks of graded response neurons. *Physical Review A* 243:2084–2087.

Leung, H., Gore, J., and Goldman-Rakic, P. (2002). Sustained mnemonic response in the human middle frontal gyrus during on-line storage of spatial memoranda. *Journal of Cognitive Neuroscience* 14:659–671.

Levy, R., and Goldman-Rakic, P. (1999). Executive frontal functions. *Journal of Neuroscience* 19:5149–5158.

Logothetis, N. K., Pauls, J., Bulthoff, H. H., and Poggio, T. (1994). View-dependent object recognition by monkeys. *Current Biology* 4:401–414.

Lorente de No, R. (1933). Vestibulo-ocular reflex arc. *Archives of Neurology Psychiatry* 30:245–291.

Malsburg, C. V. D. (1990). A neural architecture for the representation of scenes. *Brain Organization and Memory: Cells, Systems and Circuits*, eds. J. L. McGaugh, N. M. Weinberger, and G. Lynch, 356–372. New York: Oxford University Press.

Miller, E., Erickson, C., and Desimone, R. (1996). Neural mechanisms of visual working memory in prefrontal cortex of the macaque. *Journal of Neuroscience* 16:5154–5167.

Miller, E. K. (2000). The prefrontal cortex and cognitive control. *Nature Reviews Neuroscience* 1:59–65.

Miller, E. K., and Desimone, R. (1994). Parallel neuronal mechanisms for short-term memory. *Science* 263:520–522.

Miller, E. K., Li, L., and Desimone, R. (1993). Activity of neurons in anterior inferior temporal cortex during a short-term memory task. *Journal of Neuroscience* 13:1460–1478.

Milner, B. (1963). Effects of different brain lesions on card sorting. *Archives of Neurology* 9:100–110.

Miyashita, Y. (1993). Inferior temporal cortex: Where visual perception meets memory. *Annual Review of Neuroscience* 16:245–263.

Owen, A. M., Herrod, N. J., Menon, D. K., Clark, C. J., Downey, S. P. M. J., Carpenter, T. A., Minhas, P. S., Turkheimer, F. E., Williams, E. J., Robbins, T. W., Sahakian, B. J., Petrides, M., and Pickard, J. (1999). Redefining the functional organization of working memory processes within human lateral prefrontal cortex. *European Journal of Neuroscience* 11:567–574.

Perrett, D. I., Rolls, E. T., and Caan, W. (1982). Visual neurons responsive to faces in the monkey temporal cortex. *Experimental Brain Research* 47:329–342.

Perrett, D. I., Smith, P. A. J., Potter, D. D., Mistlin, A. J. Head, A. S., Milner, D., and Jeeves, M. A. (1985). Visual cells in temporal cortex sensitive to face view and gaze direction. *Proceedings of the Royal Society B* 223:293–317.

Petrides, M. (1994). Frontal lobes and behaviour. *Current Opinion in Neurobiology* 4:207–211.

Poggio, T., and Edelman, S. (1990). A network that learns to recognize three-dimensional objects. *Nature* 343:263–266.

Postle, B. R., and D'Esposito, M. (1999). "What" - then - "Where" in visual working memory: An event-related fMRI study. *Journal of Cognitive Neuroscience* 11:585–597.

Postle, B. R., and D'Esposito, M. (2000). Evaluating models of the topographical organization of working memory function in frontal cortex with event-related fMRI, *Psychobiology* 28:132–145.

Quiroga, R. Q., Reddy, L., Kreiman, G., Koch, C., and Fried, I. (2005). Invariant visual representation by single neurons in the human brain. *Nature* 453:1102–1107.

Rainer, G., Rao, S., and Miller, E. (1999). Prospective coding for objects in primate prefrontal cortex. *Journal of Neuroscience* 16:5493–5505.

Rao, S., Rainer, G., and Miller, E. (1997). Integration of what and where in the primate prefrontal cortex. *Science* 276:821–824.

Rao, S., Williams, G., and Goldman-Rakic, P. (1999). Isodirectional tuning of adjacent interneurons and pyramidal cells during working memory: Evidence for microcolumnar organization in PFC. *Journal of Neurophysiology* 81:1903–1916.

Renart, A., Moreno, R., Rocha, J., Parga, N., and Rolls, E. T. (2001). A model of the IT-PF network in object working memory which includes balanced persistent activity and tuned inhibition. *Neurocomputing* 38–40:1525–1531.

Renart, A., Parga, N., and Rolls, E. T. (1999a). Associative memory properties of multiple cortical modules. *Network* 10:237–255.

Renart, A., Parga, N., and Rolls, E. T. (1999b). Backprojections in the cerebral cortex: Implications for memory storage. *Neural Computation* 11:1349–1388.

Renart, A., Parga, N., and Rolls, E. T. (2000). A recurrent model of the interaction between the prefrontal cortex and inferior temporal cortex in delay memory tasks, In *Advances in Neural Information Processing Systems, Vol. 12*, eds. S. Solla, T. Leen and K.-R. Mueller, 171–177. Cambridge MA: MIT Press.

Reynolds, J., and Desimone, R. (1999). The role of neural mechanisms of attention in solving the binding problem. *Neuron* 24:19–29.

Riesenhuber, M., and Poggio, T. (1999a). Are cortical models really bound by the "binding problem"?. *Neuron* 24:87–93.

Riesenhuber, M., and Poggio, T. (1999b). Hierarchical models of object recognition in cortex. *Nature Neuroscience* 2:1019–1025.

Riesenhuber, M., and Poggio, T. (2000). Models of object recognition. *Nature Neuroscience Supplement* 3:1199–1204.

Rolls, E. T. (1984). Neurons in the cortex of the temporal lobe and in the amygdala of the monkey with responses selective for faces. *Human Neurobiology* 3:209–222.

Rolls, E. T. (1989a). Functions of neuronal networks in the hippocampus and neocortex in memory. In *Neural Models of Plasticity: Experimental and Theoretical Approaches*, eds. J. Byrne and W. Berry. Academic Press, San Diego: Academic Press.

Rolls, E. T. (1989b). The representation and storage of information in neuronal networks in the primate cerebral cortex and hippocampus. In *The Computing Neuron*, eds. R. Durbin, C. Miall, and G. Mitchison, 125–159. Wokingham U.K.: Addison-Wesley.

Rolls, E. T. (1992). Neurophysiological mechanisms underlying face processing within and beyond the temporal cortical visual areas. *Philosophical Transactions of the Royal Society* 335:11–21.

Rolls, E. T. (2000). Functions of the primate temporal lobe cortical visual areas in invariant visual object and face recognition. *Neuron* 27:205–218.

Rolls, E. T. (2005). *Emotion Explained*. Oxford University Press, Oxford.

Rolls, E. T. (2007). The representation of information about faces in the temporal and frontal lobes of primates including humans. *Neuropsychologia* 45:124–143.

Rolls, E. T. (2008). *Memory, Attention, and Decision-Making: A Unifying Computational Neuroscience Approach*. Oxford University Press, Oxford.

Rolls, E. T., Aggelopoulos, N. C., Franco, L., and Treves, A. (2004). Information encoding in the inferior temporal visual cortex: Contributions of the firing rates and the correlations between the firing of neurons. *Biological Cybernetics* 90:19–32.

Rolls, E. T., Aggelopoulos, N. C., and Zheng, F. (2003a). The receptive fields of inferior temporal cortex neurons in natural scenes. *Journal of Neuroscience* 23:339–348.

Rolls, E. T., and Baylis, G. C. (1986). Size and contrast have only small effects on the responses to faces of neurons in the cortex of the superior temporal sulcus of the monkey. *Experimental Brain Research* 65:38–48.

Rolls, E. T., Baylis, G. C., Hasselmo, M., and Nalwa, V. (1989). The representation of information in the temporal lobe visual cortical areas of macaque monkeys. In *Seeing Contour and Colour*, eds. J. Kulikowski, C. Dickinson, and I. Murray. Oxford, U.K.: Pergamon.

Rolls, E. T., Baylis, G. C., and Leonard, C. M. (1985). Role of low and high spatial frequencies in the face-selective responses of neurons in the cortex in the superior temporal sulcus. *Vision Research* 25:1021–1035.

Rolls, E. T., and Deco, G. (2002). *Computational Neuroscience of Vision*. Oxford: Oxford University Press.

Rolls, E. T., and Deco, G (2006). Attention in natural scenes: Neurophysiological and computational bases. *Neural Networks*, 19:1383–1394.

Rolls, E. T., Franco, L., Aggelopoulos, N. C., and Reece, S. (2003b). An information theoretic approach to the contributions of the firing rates and the correlations between the firing of neurons. *Journal of Neurophysiology* 89:2810–2822.

Rolls, E. T., Franco, L., and Stringer, S. M. (2005). The perirhinal cortex and long-term familiarity memory, *Quarterly Journal of Experimental Psychology B* 58:234–245.

Rolls, E. T., and Milward, T. (2000). A model of invariant object recognition in the visual system: Learning rules, activation functions, lateral inhibition, and information-based performance measures. *Neural Computation* 12:2547–2572.

Rolls, E. T., and Stringer, S. M. (2001). Invariant object recognition in the visual system with error correction and temporal difference learning. *Network Computation in Neural Systems* 12:111–129.

Rolls, E. T., and Stringer, S. M. (2006). Invariant visual object recognition: A model, with lighting invariance. *Journal of Physiology - Paris* 100:43–62.

Rolls, E. T., and Stringer, S. M. (2007). Invariant global motion recognition in the dorsal visual system: A unifying theory. *Neural Computation* 19:139–169.

Rolls, E. T., and Tovee, M. J. (1994). Processing speed in the cerebral cortex and the neurophysiology of visual masking. *Proceedings of the Royal Society B* 257:9–15.

Rolls, E. T., and Tovee, M. J. (1995). Sparseness of the neuronal representation of stimuli in the primate temporal visual cortex. *Journal of Neurophysiology* 73:713–726.

Rolls, E. T., Tovee, M. J., and Panzeri, S. (1999). The neurophysiology of backward visual masking: Information analysis. *Journal of Cognitive Neuroscience* 11:335–346.

Rolls, E. T., Tovee, M. J., Purcell, D. G., Stewart, A. L., and Azzopardi, P (1994). The responses of neurons in the temporal cortex of primates, and face identification and detection. *Experimental Brain Research* 101:474–484.

Rolls, E. T., and Treves, A. (1998). *Neural Networks and Brain Function*. Oxford: Oxford University Press.

Rolls, E. T., Treves, A., and Tovee, M. J. (1997a). The representational capacity of the distributed encoding of information provided by populations of neurons in the primate temporal visual cortex. *Experimental Brain Research* 114:149–162.

Rolls, E. T., Treves, A., Tovee, M., and Panzeri, S. (1997b). Information in the neuronal representation of individual stimuli in the primate temporal visual cortex. *Journal of Computational Neuroscience* 4:309–333.

Shiino, M., and Fukai, T. (1990). Replica-symmetric theory of the nonlinear analogue neural networks. *Journal of Physics A: Mathematical and General* 23:L1009–L1017.

Sigala, N. (2004). Visual categorisation and the inferior temporal cortex. *Behavioural Brain Research* 149:1–7.

Sigala, N., Gabbiani, F., and Logothetis, N. K. (2002). Visual categorisation and object representation in monkeys and humans. *Journal of Cognitive Neuroscience* 14:187–198.

Sigala, N., and Logothetis, N. K. (2002). Visual categorisation shapes feature selectivity in the primate temporal cortex. *Nature* 415:318–320.

Stringer, S. M., and Rolls, E. T. (2000). Position invariant recognition in the visual system with cluttered environments. *Neural Networks* 13:305–315.

Stringer, S. M., and Rolls, E. T. (2002). Invariant object recognition in the visual system with novel views of 3D objects. *Neural Computation* 14:2585–2596.

Suzuki, W. A. (1999). The long and the short of it: Memory signals in the medial temporal lobe. *Neuron* 24:295–298.

Suzuki, W. A., Miller, E. K., and Desimone, R. (1997). Object and place memory in the macaque entorhinal cortex. *Journal of Neurophysiology* 78:1062–1081.

Szabo, M., Almeida, R., Deco, G., and Stetter, M. (2005a). A neuronal model for the shaping of feature selectivity in IT by visual categorization. *Neuro computing* 65–66:195–201.

Szabo, M., Deco, G., Fusi, S., Del Giudice, P., Mattia, M., and Stetter, M. (2006)(2005b). Learning to attend: Modelling the shaping of selectivity in infero-temporal cortex in a categorization task. *Biology and Cybernetics* 94(5):351–365.

Tanaka, K., Saito, C., Fukada, Y., and Moriya, M. (1990). Integration of form, texture, and color information in the inferotemporal cortex of the macaque. In *Vision, Memory and the Temporal Lobe*, eds. E. Iwai and M. Mishkin, 101–109. New York: Elsevier.

Tarr, M. J., and Cheng, Y D. (2003). Learning to see faces and objects. *Trends in Cognitive Sciences* 7:23–29.

Tomita, H., Ohbayashi, M., Nakahara, K., Hasegawa, I., and Miyashita, Y. (1999). Top-down signal from prefrontal cortex in executive control of memory retrieval. *Nature* 401:699–703.

Tovee, M. J., Rolls, E. T., and Azzopardi, P. (1994). Translation invariance and the responses of neurons in the temporal visual cortical areas of primates. *Journal of Neurophysiology* 72:1049–1060.

Tovee, M. J., Rolls, E. T., and Ramachandran, V. S. (1996). Rapid visual learning in neurones of the primate temporal visual cortex. *NeuroReport* 7:2757–2760.

Trappenberg, T. P., Rolls, E. T., and Stringer, S. M. (2002). Effective size of receptive fields of inferior temporal visual cortex neurons in natural scenes. In *Advances in Neural Information Processing Systems, Vol. 14*, eds. T. G. Dietterich, S. Becker and Z. Gharamani, 293–300. Cambridge MA: MIT Press.

Treves, A., Panzeri, S., Rolls, E. T., Booth, M., and Wakeman, E. A. (1999). Firing rate distributions and efficiency of information transmission of inferior temporal cortex neurons to natural visual stimuli. *Neural Computation* 11:611–641.

Ullman, S. (1996). *High-Level Vision. Object Recognition and Visual Cognition.* Cambridge MA: Bradford/MIT Press.

Ungerleider, L., Courtney, S., and Haxby, J. (1998). A neural system for human visual working memory. *Proceedings of the National Academy of Science* 95:883–890.

Ungerleider, L. G., and Mishkin, M. (1982). Two cortical visual systems. In *Analysis of Visual Behavior*, ed. D. J. Ingle, 549–586. Cambridge MA: MIT Press.

Wallis, G. and Rolls, E. T. (1997). Invariant face and object recognition in the visual system. *Progress in Neurobiology* 51:167–194.

Wallis, J., Anderson, K., and Miller, E. (2001). Single neurons in prefrontal cortex encode abstract rules. *Nature* 411:953–956.

Wilson, F. A. W., O'Scalaidhe, S. P., and Goldman-Rakic, P. S. (1993a). Dissociation of object and spatial processing domains in primate prefrontal cortex. *Science* 260:1955–1958.

Wilson, F., O'Sclaidhe, S., and Goldman-Rakic, P. (1993b). Dissociation of object and spatial processing domains in primate prefrontal cortex. *Science* 260:1955–1958.

Xiang, J. Z., and Brown, M. W. (1998). Differential neuronal encoding of novelty, familiarity and recency in regions of the anterior temporal lobe. *Neuropharmacology* 37:657–676.

Yamane, S., Kaji, S., and Kawano, K. (1988). What facial features activate face neurons in the inferotemporal cortex of the monkey?. *Experimental Brain Research* 73:209–214.

Zarahn, E., Aguirre, G., and D'Esposito, M. (1997). A trial-based experimental design for fMRI. *Neuroimage* 6:75–144.

Chapter 9

The Retrieval and Manipulation of Visual Memories: Evidence from Neuropsychology

M. Jane Riddoch and Glyn W. Humphreys
University of Birmingham

This chapter is concerned with neuropsychological disorders of visual short-term memory (VSTM) and the importance of these disorders for theories of VSTM. Following the neuropsychological literature, but unlike many of the other chapters in the volume, we stress the role of VSTM not only in "bottom-up" processes (forming a memory for new material from the environment) but also in "top-down" processing, as when we form visual images from material from long-term memory (LTM). Our suggestion here is that, just as VSTM is involved when we need to remember new visual input, so visual imagery recruits VSTM, which then serves as a medium for retrieving stored visual memories. Hence, the same processes (and brain regions) that play a part in typical laboratory studies of VSTM using relatively simple visual displays (say, for memorizing some colored shapes) may also be involved when people make judgments about the visual characteristics of objects retrieved from LTM (say, to judge whether a fly is larger than an ant). The involvement of common representations in bottom-up (typical, lab-based VSTM tasks) and top-down (imagery-based) processing is indicated by co-occurring dissociations in patients, in which, for example, an impairment in LTM for a stimulus can be shown to affect the ability to hold a visual memory of that stimulus from a picture. At the end of the chapter, we discuss the neuropsychological data in relation to convergent evidence from studies of normal individuals (e.g., using brain imaging), and we present a framework for conceptualizing the role of VSTM in both bottom-up and top-down modes of operation. For now, we will use a common term (*VSTM*) to refer to the memory system supporting visual representations derived from new stimuli and representations derived from LTM. We then highlight all cases in which the evidence indicates an overlap between VSTM formed to perceptual input and VSTM serving the retrieval of visual information from LTM

8.1 THE FRACTIONATION OF SHORT-TERM MEMORY

The initial conceptions of short-term memory (STM), appearing at the start of modern-day cognitive psychology, stressed the verbal nature of temporary memory processes. Thus, studies demonstrating effects of variables, such as the phonological similarity of items held in STM (Conrad, 1964), were interpreted as defining the nature of the underlying representations. Neuropsychological studies provided an important input into this debate, particularly the finding that damage to left temporoparietal regions gave rise to poor STM for verbal material without necessarily disrupting LTM (see Vallar & Shallice, 1990). This suggested a difference between long- and short-term memory storage that has remained current to this day. Interestingly, the data collected with these patients also pointed to a dissociation between different forms of STM. For example, although the patients' memory span for auditorily presented items could be markedly impaired (e.g., as measured in auditory digit span), visual span for the same material was characteristically better (Vallar & Shallice, 1990). In addition, performance on tests of spatial working memory (e.g., in the Corsi blocks task[1]) could be spared. The neuropsychological data indicated that STM was unlikely to be a unitary whole and unlikely to be based purely on verbal/phonological representations of stimuli. Rather, distinct STM representations may exist for different modalities of input, for visual as well as for auditory/verbal STM (see Chapter 3 for additional discussion of dissociations among memory systems).

Distinctions between different modalities of memory remain in today's theories of STM representation, especially those derived from the *working memory* framework proposed by Baddeley and colleagues (Baddeley, 1986). According to this framework, STM is built from a series of components including visuo-spatial and phonological *slave systems*, an *episodic buffer* that helps to bind temporary representations together, and a central executive component needed to coordinate information across the different memory formats (Baddeley, 2000). Logie (1995, 2003) has further argued that visuo-spatial working memory can be subdivided into two components: the visual cache and the inner scribe. The visual cache is held to store information about specific visual properties of an image, such as the form and color of any shapes, whereas the inner scribe is involved in representing information about the spatial and movement-related properties of stimuli. Since the inner scribe is inherently concerned with manipulating visual information, it is difficult to separate the role of this specific component from executive control processes, which are also held to be responsible for switching between representations.

---

1   In the Corsi block task, the experimenter points to blocks in a random spatial array in a particular order. The task of the observer is to reproduce the experimenter's pointing actions in the correct spatial order.

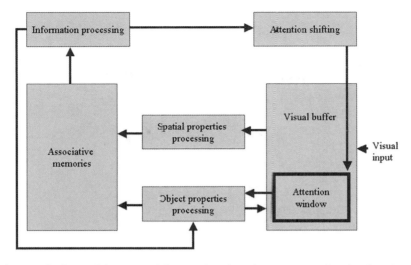

Figure 9–1. Model proposed by Kosslyn (2005) to account for the functional processes underlying visual short-term memory.

A yet more elaborated view of the functional processes underlying visual STM (VSTM), and relevant to neuropsychological cases, is offered by Kosslyn (2005). This is illustrated in Figure 9–1.

According to this model, the visual buffer serves as a temporary interface between the processing of sensory representations from the environment and associative representations in LTM. The buffer is thus involved both when visual information must be encoded and maintained in STM, and when information is retrieved from LTM for visualization (e.g., to support performance in visual imagery tasks). This visualization process would be required whenever the information required for the judgment is not an explicit attribute in LTM, but must be derived from a retrieved visual representation of the object—examples being when we are asked to judge whether a fly is larger than an ant, or whether an animal has a relatively large tail, since information about the precise relative sizes of the different stimuli, or the relative sizes of parts, is unlikely to be specified in the long-term representations of many stimuli.[2] Kosslyn and colleagues link the visual buffer to areas of primary visual cortex (Brodmann areas 17 and 18; see Kosslyn & Thompson, 2003), suggesting that these regions of early visual cortex are necessarily recruited when high-resolution, detailed visual representations must be formed/maintained for the task. Information in this visual buffer is made available through a window of spatial attention, which feeds activity in an attended region of space through to higher-level processes concerned with image interpretation and recognition (*object processing properties,*

---

2 An exception to the argument about judgments of the relative sizes of parts may be with Indian or African elephants, where knowledge about the relative sizes of their ears is likely to be a defining piece of knowledge in LTM!

taking place at higher levels of ventral visual cortex). In addition, separate spatial operations are conducted on attended representations in the visual buffer, involving interactions with the parietal lobe (*spatial processing properties*). Kosslyn also posits an *information processing* module, perhaps akin to the executive components of Baddeley's (1986) working memory model, which is involved in problem solving and selecting the appropriate visual (object property processing) or spatial (spatial property processing) routine to use for a given task. According to this model, the information processing component is also involved in directing shifts of spatial attention to different regions in the visual buffer (through the attention switching component).

In interpreting Kosslyn's model, it is tempting to think of the visual buffer as a kind of "picture in the head," held within retinotopically coded units in early visual areas. We might then think that these units are subsequently interpreted through higher-level object- and spatial-properties processing routines. As we go on to elaborate, we believe this is an incorrect view of VSTM, emphasizing essentially a static view of the representations involved; in contrast to this, we will argue that VSTM is a dynamic process, taking place across distributed neural areas and modulated by interactions between perception and long-term associative memory. Nevertheless, the model (Fig. 9–1) is useful because it makes important distinctions that serve to direct our analysis of VSTM; hence, we will use this model as a guide for our review of neuropsychological disorders of VSTM. One important aspect of the model is that it posits that VSTM involves common processes, whether accessed in a bottom-up (from visual input) or top-down manner (e.g., from LTM). Furthermore, these common processes depend on the activation of regions of early visual cortex. On the other hand, distinct operations are proposed in order to manipulate the short-term representations, with procedures dependent on object properties (shape, size, color) being separable from those concerned with retrieving and manipulating the spatial properties of stimuli (see further discussion of this issue in Chapters 3 and 8 of this volume). Also other neural regions (e.g., regions of the temporal lobe concerned with long-term associative memories, frontal lobe structures concerned with selecting appropriate processing operations) should be involved in supporting short-term visual memory but they themselves are not the site of the memory representations themselves.

From this framework, we can derive various predictions concerning neuropsychological disorders of VSTM. One is that common problems should occur in VSTM, whether the memory processes are "driven" from imagery or perception. It follows that impairments in visual perception should be accompanied by disorders in VSTM, since an overlap occurs in the representations supporting memory and perception within the earliest levels of visual cortex. This is considered in the next section, on Perception and Memory. A second prediction is that some dissociations may occur between patients according to the underlying processing operation required in the task (particularly, a dissociation should occur between object processing and spatial processing of memory representations). A third is that impairments to higher-level regions of cortex (particularly temporal, frontal, and parietal structures) may affect various aspects of VSTM performance, but not the basic maintenance of the memory representations themselves. These two predictions are reviewed in the section on Objects and Space. Having considered the predictions from the framework in Figure 9–1, in the section on Distributed Dynamics of Visual Short-term Memory, we consider an alternative account of VSTM in an attempt to reconcile the neuropsychological results. In this alternative account, we propose that VSTM itself may be distributed, with separate processes (and neural regions) maintaining different visual properties of stimuli (their color, shape, location, and so forth).

8.2 PERCEPTION AND MEMORY

8.2.1 Visual Memory Deficits Following Lesions of the Primary Visual Cortex

One clear prediction from the framework presented in Figure 9–1 is that, if the site of the visual buffer is in primary visual cortex, then patients who are cortically blind due to damage to primary occipital cortex should not be able to experience visual images (Kosslyn, 2005). One particularly strong way to assess visual memory representations in cases with occipital lesions is to use hemianopic patients, in whom any impairment may be restricted to one visual field, with the other field serving as a control to rule out effects such as whether the patient has appropriate long-term knowledge or adopts appropriate strategies for the task (Butter et al., 1997). Butter et al. used a modified version of an image scanning task devised by Finke and Pinker (1982). A case series of hemianopic patients were presented with a brief random dot pattern display. On a subsequent page in the test booklet, an arrow was presented and patients had to indicate whether it was pointing to the location of a dot in the previously presented display. A number of control tasks were also presented. The perceptual control was identical to the memory condition except that dots and arrow were presented simultaneously. An *arrow control task* was included, in which the task was to determine whether successively presented arrows shared the same orientation or not, as well as a *dot control task*, in which the task was to determine whether successively presented arrays of dots occupied the same spatial locations or not. In the experimental condition stressing visual memory, the subjects performed worse when the arrow pointed to the contralesional field relative to the ipsilesional field. These effects were not apparent in the control tasks. Butter et al. state that the results are not due to the patients having neglect of their contralesional space (cf. Heilman, 1979). No neglect was shown on screening tasks, or on the dot control task. Instead, Butter et al. conclude that patients with unilateral occipital damage demonstrate a VSTM deficit in the field contralateral to the lesion, and that these data support the hypothesis that the primary visual cortex is needed for the VSTM representations supporting the imagery task. A similar argument was made by Farah, Soso, and Dasheiff (1992), who provided evidence that, in hemianopia, images were reduced to about half the size found in normal participants. Moreover, this size reduction was apparent only along the horizontal but not the vertical meridian, matching the loss of field following a unilateral lesion. Converging evidence from normal participants comes from studies using transcranial magnetic stimulation (TMS) to alter activation in primary visual cortex. Kosslyn et al. (1999) for example, found equivalent disruption from repetitive TMS applied to occipital cortex to judgments made either viewing a visual pattern or when maintaining it in memory. They concluded that common representations in primary visual cortex were involved in both the perceptual and memory versions of the task.

In contrast to these arguments, other authors are skeptical about the relationships between damage to primary occipital cortex and visual imagery (e.g., Bartolomeo, 2002). Goldenberg, Mullbacher, and Nowak (1995) for example, reported a patient who suffered cortical blindness following occlusion of the basilar artery and was initially unable to detect light from dark (although there was a pupillary reaction to light). On first examination, no visually evoked responses could be evoked with either checkerboard or flash stimulation. However, these effects were only apparent in the acute stage of her pathology, and 2 months following her stroke, sight was regained in the right lower visual field. On assessment during the acute phase, the patient claimed that she was able to see some objects. In some instances, this was cued by a characteristic sound (e.g., keys clinking, scissors cutting) when she claimed that she was actually perceiving the object. Goldenberg et al. describe this as the "synaesthetic translation of acoustic perceptions into mental visual images" (p. 1380). However, whether imagery was truly involved here is not compelling. On tasks putatively requiring imagery for stimuli (e.g., verifying sentences specifying the shape or color of objects, verifying the shapes of letters), this same patient performed at the bottom of the control range, suggesting that performance was not completely spared. Moreover, it is unclear whether the sentence verification tasks in particular required the creation of STM representations or whether questions could be answered using more general semantic knowledge. Care must be taken to ensure that specific visual representations are required for the performance of such tasks. In addition, Goldenberg et al.'s patient had some preserved areas of occipital cortex, including the occipital tip of the left calcarine lip. In opposition to Goldenberg et al.'s case, Policardi et al. (1996) report a patient with damage to calcarine and associative occipital cortex, who failed across a range of visual imagery tests (including imagery for color and for the shapes of well-known objects). Policardi et al.'s patient did perform reasonably well when questioned about the functional properties of objects (e.g., do apples grow on trees?), so the problem on imagery tasks could not be attributed to a general loss of knowledge about objects. These authors propose that patients with relatively better imagery than perception, following damage to primary visual cortex, may be depending on islets of preserved neurons within the affected area. It may be easier for patients to recruit these spared islets when forming their own images, since the images may be shifted to the spared cortical regions.

Perhaps the strongest evidence for a dissociation between perception and imagery following damage to primary occipital cortex comes from Chattergee and Southwood (1995). They describe three cases of cortical blindness, all having damage to Brodmann area 17. All three patients were unable to identify visually presented shapes or colors but they performed at variable levels on a reasonably large range of imagery tasks. One patient, however, performed at a level matching the best controls, across a range of tasks probing imagery for shape and color, and for letters and faces, as well as for objects. To maintain the account proposed by Kosslyn (2005, Fig. 9-1), we would need to attribute the impressive level of performance on imagery tasks in this case to some functional preservation of visual cortex (there was little evidence for this in behavioral measures, although the patient reported being able sometimes to distinguish light from dark). Unfortunately, as things stand, we cannot be sure on this point, and such patients need to be assessed using functional imaging procedures to provide a definitive answer.

8.2.2 Effects of Damage to Higher-level Ventral Cortex

8.2.2.1 Dissociations between high-level perception and imagery: impaired perception and spared imagery

If patients have damage not to primary visual cortex itself but to higher-level regions involved in perceptual organization and object recognition, the framework in Figure 9–1 predicts that an overlap still should occur between performances on perceptual and imagery tasks, because similar object processing routines should mediate performance in both types of task. Against this, however, are a number of reports of patients with relatively preserved imagery along with impaired perceptual processing of objects. We focus here on six cases in which imagery has been assessed in reasonable detail.

1. CK (Behrmann, Moscovitch, & Winocur, 1994) sustained a head injury in 1988. Scans performed in 1991 and 1992 showed no focal mass or abnormality, but there was a suggestion of bilateral thinning of the occipital lobes. CK was impaired at visual recognition of both real objects and line drawings (performing more poorly with line drawings). Letter and word recognition were also severely impaired. Unusually, his poor recognition performance did not extend to faces. In contrast to his poor performance at object and letter recognition tasks, imagery for objects and letters appeared to be spared. CK was able to report the colors of objects from LTM, he knew whether animals had large tails or ears, and he showed intact imagery for letter shapes, including being able manipulate letters to create new forms in his "mind's eye."[3] A clear contrast was noted between CK's performance on imagery versions of tasks and on the same tasks performed on visually presented stimuli. For example, he performed at ceiling on

---

3 For example, take the letter H, drop the right vertical line and add horizontal lines to the top and bottom. What is the new letter? (Answer = E.)

size judgment tasks in an imagery version, but at chance with a perceptual version. His drawing from memory was also preserved.

2. DF (Servos & Goodale, 1995; Servos, Goodale, & Humphrey, 1993) suffered brain damage as a result of carbon monoxide poisoning, affecting the ventral portion of the lateral occipital region (areas 18 and 19), while area 17 was largely spared. Like CK, DF performed better at naming of real objects (70% correct) versus line drawings (11% correct). Tests of visual imagery included drawing objects from memory, making judgments about the visual properties of objects (is this object taller than it is wide?), and letter transformation and reconstruction (see footnote 2). Drawings from memory were ranked better than drawings of real objects, which were ranked better than copies of line drawings. Performance was preserved on the tasks based on the long-term properties of objects, and possibly also on the letter transformation tasks, although very few trials were reported. Servos, Goodale, and Humphrey (1993) suggest that visual memories of objects, and visual imagery, are intact in DF.

3. Mme. D (Bartolomeo, Bachoud-Lévi, & Denes, 1997; Bartolomeo et al., 1998) suffered sequential bilateral occipital lobe lesions and was subsequently impaired at perceiving objects, letters, colors, and faces. The deficit appeared to have a perceptual origin, since object identification was worse with overlapping relative to nonoverlapping figures. Despite these impairments across broad classes of stimuli, performance was intact on a range of imagery tasks including the verification of high-imagery sentences; judgments of animal size; recognition of object and letter shape, colors, face properties (see case 6 below); and drawing of objects from memory.

4. MD (Jankowiak, Kinsbourne, Shalev, & Bachman, 1992) suffered a gunshot wound at 29 years of age, which resulted in bilateral occipital lesions involving lingual and fusiform gyri extending to posterior portions of the inferior and middle temporal gyri. He was impaired at object naming (e.g., scoring 42/60 on the Boston Naming test) and in recognizing famous faces. Only a mild deficit was present in color naming, and color sorting was relatively good. MD also showed generally spared visual memory and imagery abilities. Drawing from memory was good for inanimate objects, but less good for animate objects. He could also remember which items he had earlier identified, and he could name his own drawings when tested around 1 hour later, but he could not rename his own drawings when retested after several weeks. This may represent a distinction between recognition based on relatively short-term visual memories compared to recognition requiring matching to LTM, but it could also be that performance over the short-term improved because MD maintained a verbal memory for the objects he was presented with and could use this knowledge in a top-down fashion to aid his impaired visual object recognition (giving more accurate interpretation of partial visual cues; see Riddoch & Humphreys, 1987a).

5. HJA (Riddoch & Humphreys, 1987a) was profoundly agnosic following lesions to inferior prestriate cortex (fusiform, lingual, and inferior
temporal gyri). When initially tested, he named only 62% of common
real objects from vision, relative to a level of 86% naming from touch.
Similarly to other patients, he too was worse at identifying line drawings than real objects (averaging about 40% correct depending on the
particular stimuli). His deficits were exacerbated under conditions that
stressed processes of perceptual grouping and integration (e.g., with
overlapping figures, with line drawings relative to silhouettes, with
fragmented forms, with multiple similar forms in visual search tasks;
Boucart & Humphreys, 1992; Giersch, Humphreys, Boucart, & Koviaks,
2000; Humphreys et al., 1992a; Riddoch & Humphreys, 1987a).
Riddoch and Humphreys (1987a) proposed that the deficit lay in integrating form information in an efficient, spatially parallel manner.
Despite these perceptual problems, HJA demonstrated good long-term
knowledge about objects. When describing objects from memory, he
produced detailed definitions that typically specified the visual as well
as functional properties of objects, and he produced accurate drawings
of items from memory (Fig. 9–2). With objects that he could no longer
identify from vision, he was able to recall whether they had large or

Exemplars   HJA's copies

Figure 9–2. HJA's copies of line drawings from the Snodgrass and Vanderwart (1980) set of pictures.

small parts, and he could mentally manipulate and transform letters to form new emergent stimuli (Riddoch et al., 2003).

6. One other case in which imagery abilities have been reported to be superior to the perceptual abilities in a patient with an apparent high-level perceptual problem has been reported by Michelon and Biederman (2003). Their patient, MJH, suffered damage to the left visual cortex (area 18) and the fusiform gyrus in childhood. When tested some 19 years later, MJH was particularly poor at face processing, showing deficits in naming famous faces, in making familiarity decisions, and in matching unfamiliar faces. Michelon and Biederman assessed face imagery using tasks in which participants heard the names of famous people and had to judge how similar their faces were to each other. On this version of the task, MJH fell at the lower end of the control range. When required to perform the same task but with the faces present, the performance of the controls improved, whereas that of MJH remained the same, so that he was now clearly impaired. Thus, MJH's impairment on the imagery version of this task was relatively less than that on the perceptual version.

In each of these cases, a dissociation occurs, with imagery appearing to be better than visual perception. This dissociation goes against one of the basic tenets of the framework presented in Figure 9–1, namely that a close overlap should exist between disorders of perception and disorders of VSTM/imagery. Can the overlapping representation account be salvaged? A closer inspection of at least some of the listed cases suggests that the dissociations may be less pronounced than at first appears. For example, HJA had cerebral achromatopsia (Humphreys et al., 1992b). Coincident with this, he had a deficit in remembering the colors of objects, but this was apparent only when verbal knowledge of color was separated from more visual knowledge of object color. For example, HJA knew that indigenous squirrels in the United Kingdom are red, consistent with their common name, but he was impaired at recalling the real color of white wine (cf. Beauvois, 1982). This suggests that, when common processes are probed (visual color processing and specific, visual color knowledge), evidence for a consistent deficit can be derived. A similar example comes from a study of the relationships between HJA's face recognition impairment and his memory for faces. When asked to make judgments about individual features of people's faces (e.g., *did Harold MacMillan have a moustache?*), HJA performed well (Young et al., 1994). However, he was impaired when asked to make judgments about the configural properties of faces (e.g., *who looks more like Elizabeth Taylor: Joan Collins or Barbara Windsor?*). This deficit in imagery ran parallel to his problem in online face identification, where he showed a piecemeal approach to which individual features were used while there was poor perception of face configurations (Boutsen & Humphreys, 2002; Riddoch & Humphreys, 1987a). Thus, HJA was poor at making judgments from imaged representations of the same facial properties that he was impaired at using in online visual identification (Young et al., 1994). This suggests that, if studies use tests of imagery that target the particular processes affected in perception, then evidence for common representations will emerge.

Unfortunately, although we think that there is merit to this argument, we also doubt that it can be the full story. In particular, Mme. D (Bartolomeo et al., 1997; Bartolomeo et al., 1998) presents a case whose performance is difficult to attribute to a lack of common tests. Mme. D performed well on tests of imagery that appeared to require long-term visual memory for color (e.g., *which is darker, the inside of a potato or a pineapple?*), even though she was very impaired at perceptual matching visually presented colors. In addition, both Mme. D and MJH (Michelon & Biederman, 2003) succeeded on tasks in which images of faces needed to be retrieved from LTM, similar to the tests used with HJA to assess images for facial configurations derived from LTM. For these cases, at least, it cannot be argued that imagery appeared to be preserved because it demanded less precise visual representations. Other possibilities need to be examined. We now consider two: dynamic change in visual LTM over time, and differences between top-down and bottom-up support in task performance. We suggest that both factors are important in determining how well visual imagery tasks are performed; furthermore, the evidence on long-term dynamic change in memory points to an interaction between incoming perceptual representations of stimuli and LTM utilized in imagery retrieval.

8.2.2.2 Top-down versus bottom-up processes in imagery

In all of the examples in which patients with impaired object recognition have performed well on imagery tasks, the tasks have been cued via modalities other than vision. For example, patients may be asked to image whether a rabbit has a relatively short or long tail, or they may be asked to segment a letter and then to add additional features to create a new form (cf. Moscovitch, Behrman, & Winocur, 1994). In such cases, any short-term visual representations supporting imagery performance are induced in a top-down manner. Moreover, the top-down constraints provided through instructions may specifically overcome some of the problems in bottom-up visual processing that characterize the patients' poor object recognition. For example, instructions such as those used in the letter manipulation task tell the patients how to segment the forms (Moscovitch et al., 1994). In contrast, when visual object recognition is required, segmentation and grouping procedures operate without such constraints and are very often faulty (e.g., Giersch et al., 2000; see Behrmann et al., 1999, for this argument). It may be, then, that common representations are involved in visual perception and imagery, but that the processes leading to impaired perception are by-passed in the imagery tasks.

Some evidence for patients being more impaired in using VSTM in a bottom-up compared with a top-down manner comes from a paper by Riddoch et al. (2003), documenting the patient HJA. Riddoch et al. contrasted HJA's copying of visually presented stimuli with his immediate drawing of the same items from VSTM. In one task, HJA had to copy multicomponent drawings

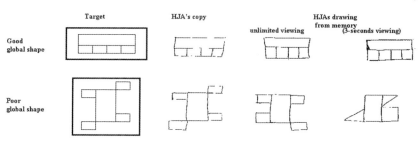

Figure 9–3. Multicomponent stimuli with either good or poor global qualities from Riddoch et al. (2003).

that either had a good or poor outline shape (Fig. 9–3).[4] Although his copying was relatively good, his immediate drawing from memory was poor, and this was particularly the case for the stimuli with a poor outline shape. His reproduction from memory of objects with poor outline shapes was better (although still impaired compared with controls) if he had unlimited viewing time, but it decreased dramatically when the time was reduced. This suggests that HJA had difficulty encoding patterns with poor global shapes into VSTM, despite having intact drawing abilities and perceptual information to support copying. The encoding problem was exacerbated when the exposure duration was limited. Riddoch et al. (2003) also had HJA copy and reproduce from visual memory *possible* and *impossible* line drawings (where impossible figures had incongruent structures across different parts; Fig. 9–4). Although HJA was relatively able to draw possible figures from memory, he was poor at drawing the impossible figures (e.g., frequently failing to represent the joints that made the figures structurally impossible), and this problem was again increased when he had to draw from memory rather than copy. To account for this, Riddoch et al., suggested that copying could be supported by low-level visual information that could be relatively unstructured. In contrast, to draw a complex form from memory requires that its structure is organized and encoded into a short-term store; it is just this bottom-up process of perceptual organization that is impaired in HJA's case. The interesting point about HJA's case is that he is able to structure and manipulate visual representations of objects when cued

---

4   It might be argued here that the memory representation involved in drawing such shapes from memory requires a form of visual memory representation with more capacity than that typically studied in VSTM studies in the laboratory (see Chapters 3 and 8). On the other hand, laboratory studies more typically examine memory for independent objects, rather than how connected elements are represented. As we go on to elaborate, we suggest that, normally, the individual elements of shapes are grouped, so that any VSTM is not based on a representation of individual elements but on organized "chunks," which impose a lower load on any capacity. It is precisely this "chunking" process (requiring perceptual organization) that we suggest is impaired in HJA.

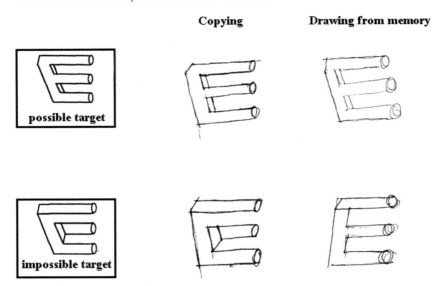

Figure 9–4. Possible and impossible figures from Riddoch et al. (2003).

in a top-down fashion (as in the letter manipulation task; Riddoch et al., 2003). This supports the argument that imagery may be preserved in many cases because of the dissociation in top-down and bottom-up grouping and segmentation.

We can make one other interesting suggestion from this[5]: The representation used to support drawing from memory is *more* sensitive to perceptual organization than the representation used to support copying. This follows because HJA, a patient with impaired perceptual organization (Giersch et al., 2000; Riddoch & Humphreys, 1987a), was significantly better at copying than at drawing from memory, and showed reduced effects of perceptual organization (effects of whether figures had incongruent parts) in copying. Interestingly, the same pattern—of stronger effects of perceptual organization on drawing from memory relative to copying—was also apparent in the control participants in this study (although to a much lesser extent than for HJA); when drawing accuracy was rated, the controls showed no difference between possible and impossible figures when copying, but an advantage occurred for possible figures when drawing from memory. If this proposal is correct, then it would run counter to the framework set out in Figure 9–1, in which copying and

---

5   This proposal must be cautious. It is possible that some of the advantage for possible over impossible figures in drawing from memory arose when participants forgot the stimulus, but used general knowledge of objects to correctly reproduce the possible but not the impossible figure. That is, the advantage is in reconstruction rather than memory. On the other hand, we would then expect the errors on impossible figures to be drawings of possible figures; this was not the case (see Fig. 9–4).

drawing from memory should both depend on a common representation in the input buffer. Instead of this, we suggest that drawing from memory is influenced by higher-level, structured representations in VSTM. This is supported by evidence from normal participants suggesting that VSTM involves representations in which different object features are integrated and grouped (Luck & Vogel, 1997; Woodman, Vecera, & Luck, 2003; see also Chapters 3 and 5 of this volume). In the section on Distributed Dynamics of Visual Short-term Memory, we return to elaborate on how structured representations may play a role in addition to more primitive representations in tasks requiring VSTM.

8.2.2.3 Dynamic changes over time

Time since lesion is one further factor that appears to influence the relationships between perception and imagery in patients with perceptual deficits. When he was initially tested after his brain lesion, HJA produced very accurate drawings from memory of objects that he could no longer visually identify (Fig. 9–2), and he had excellent knowledge of the visual attributes of objects when probed through verbal questions (with the exception of color; see earlier description). Riddoch et al. (1999) re-examined visual memory in HJA some 17 years after his lesion. They found a deterioration in HJA's memory for the visual properties of objects. In particular, there was a worsening in his ability to draw objects from memory, and he tended to give fewer visual details in his definitions of items. HJA's performance did not reflect a general deterioration, since the number of verbal/functional details increased in his verbal definitions.

The finding that HJA's visual knowledge had degraded over time is consistent with the idea that perceptual and memorial processes interact in vision. Thus, perceptual processing of objects may lead to a consistent updating of visual memories over time, so that these memories remain tuned to the visual properties of objects in the world. Such consistent tuning of memorial processes to vision fits with connectionist accounts of cognition, in which recognition systems change adaptively to the inputs they receive over time (Ellis & Humphreys, 1999). When perceptual inputs are impaired, as in an agnosic patient such as HJA, visual memorial processes may gradually show some decline, with there being less fine tuning of the system to the visual properties of objects. In this case, some coupling can be observed between the perceptual processes that are impaired and the effect on particular memorial processes (Young et al., 1994). Similar results have been reported by Thomas, Forde, Humphreys, and Graham (2002) in a long-term follow-up of another agnosic patient.

HJA's data suggest that long-term visual memory representations, and images of objects formed when memory retrieval takes place, can initially remain quite robust in the face of a severe perceptual impairment and that the effects of impoverished perceptual updating only become apparent over a longer time period. This initial robustness, however, should not be taken to indicate that perceptual and memorial processes are functionally dissociated, and particularly when the imagery tasks used to probe visual memory are supported by top-down constraints to a greater degree than online perceptual tasks (see the earlier section on top-down versus bottom-up processes in imagery). Interestingly, in other reports in which patients have had relatively preserved imagery over perceptual performance, imagery has been tested nearer the time of lesion than was the case in the follow-up of H.A. Hence, some of the discrepancy between findings of associated deficits linked to particular processes common to perception and imagery tasks, and findings of dissociations, may reflect dynamic changes in LTM for objects over time. These dynamic changes reflect problems in recalibrating long-term visual memories when perceptual processing is impaired.

Finally, we also note some of the strongest evidence for VSTM being influenced by long-term visual knowledge. This comes from patients who show poor VSTM specifically for objects with impaired representations in LTM. For example, Lambon-Ralph, Howard, Nightingale, and Ellis (1998) reported data from a patient with impaired LTM for the appearance of objects (e.g., on tasks requiring drawing from LTM). Although the patient was able to copy drawings of the same objects, his immediate reproductions of the drawings deteriorated back to the level found when drawing from LTM. Thus, even though the patient should have been capable of redrawing the objects from a VSTM coded from perception, there was very poor maintenance of information in VSTM without support from LTM. The patient LH (Etcoff, Freeman, & Cave, 1992) also showed poor LTM for the visual properties of objects (see also Lambon-Ralph et al., 1998). Visual short-term memory to new, bottom-up input was tested by presenting photographs of faces and then having the patient choose which of two alternative faces had just been seen. He scored 65% correct, not significantly different from chance. In contrast, accuracy levels were around 90% when the faces were presented simultaneously. This contrast suggests that LH was unable to maintain a short-term visual representation of objects he could not identify. The data suggest that long-term associative memories are not merely accessed in a bottom-up manner from the image (as in Figure 9–1), but feed back to support short-term visual memory representations. This is consistent with the proposal, described in Chapter 3 of this volume, that VSTM representations consist of activated LTM representations.

8.2.3 Summary

The neuropsychological evidence we have reviewed does indicate that there can be some dissociations between the visual representations involved in imagery and perception, throwing into doubt the proposal that imagery and perception depend on a common representation (the input buffer, Figure 9–1). On the other hand, no conclusive evidence suggests that there is spared imagery in patients with abolition of primary visual cortex, and dissociations between impaired perception and intact imagery in patients with higher-level lesions can at least partly be linked to top-down knowledge being used to support imagery tasks. Longitudinal studies also suggest that perception and long-term visual memory are interactive, so that images derived from LTM deteriorate over time when perceptual representations are impaired. Moreover, when long-term knowledge is impaired, even immediate memory representations formed to visual stimuli can be shown to be deficient. Hence there remains a case for arguing that at least some common processes are involved not just in imagery and perception, but also in the visual memory representations used in imagery and perceptual-memory tasks. The evidence also points to VSTM being dependent on representations that are structured (Riddoch et al., 2003) and permeated by LTM (Lambon-Ralph et al., 1998). A more complex account than that outlined in Figure 9–1 begins to emerge.

8.3 OBJECTS AND SPACE

8.3.1 Neurological Impairments in Spatial Imagery

The model presented in Figure 9–1 does make a clear prediction for some dissociations arising in imagery performance, according to whether spatial or object-based processes operate on the visual buffer. Neuropsychological data are consistent with this. Several current reports in the literature feature patients who have been documented with apparent problems in spatial imagery but not in imagery for object properties. The patient ELD (Hanley, Young, & Pearson, 1991) suffered a middle cerebral artery aneurism in the right hemisphere that resulted in a subarachnoid hematoma in the prefrontal sylvian fissure. Although her object recognition was relatively spared, she had difficulties with learning new visuospatial material (e.g., routes she did not know premorbidly). She also performed poorly on tasks requiring spatial VSTM for new visual input. For example, she had a reduced Corsi block span, and she was impaired at remembering sequences of pictorial material.[6] She was also poor at mental rotation. In contrast to her poor ability to maintain visuospatial sequences and to perform visuospatial manipulations, her visual memory for object attributes was relatively good (remembering object color, size, whether animals had long or short tails, city locations, and the faces of celebrities). Similar data have been reported by Carlesimo et al. (Carlesimo et al., 2001); Levine, Warach, and Farah (Case 2, 1985); and by Papagno (2002).

In contrast to these last cases are patients who have impaired imagery for object properties but retain apparently intact spatial imagery abilities. Farah, Hammond, Levine, and Calvanio (1988a) and Levine et al. (Case 1, 1985) present two patients who showed this pattern, with an intact ability to mentally rotate and manipulate letters, draw floor and street maps, and the like, accompanied by an inability to image the structural properties of objects (e.g., when asked to draw objects from memory or to recall whether animals had long or short tails). HJA, at the time of his reanalysis, also falls into this category, since his drawings from memory had deteriorated although he remained able to spatially manipulate the parts of letters (Riddoch et al., 2003; Riddoch et al., 1999).

---

6   ELD was presented with sequences of four unfamiliar faces. Following the initial presentation, the faces were presented again simultaneously, and ELD had to indicate the original order of presentation. Her performance was several SDs below that of the controls; that is, she was impaired at remembering sequences of visual and spatial stimuli.

The different patterns of impairment here, with selective impairment of the ability to spatially manipulate images and to image object properties, fits with the argument that procedures for processing the spatial and nonspatial (object) properties of stimuli can dissociate. Also, in patients with selective impairments on tasks such as Corsi blocks and remembering sequences of images, it can be argued that the impairment is specific to the ability to manipulate the spatial properties of the stimuli. Hence, there may be common representation of an image in the visual buffer (Fig. 9–1), but differential damage to the spatial and object processing procedures that act on the image. This would be consistent with arguing that the *inner cache* of VSTM is spared while there is impairment to the *inner scribe*, in the adaptation of Baddeley's working memory model proposed by Logie (1995, 2003; see earlier discussion).

There are difficulties with last argument, however. The patient MG (Morton & Morris, 1995) was unimpaired at visual imagery for object properties (e.g., object colors, animal tails, size comparisons, judging the similarity of faces of celebrities) following a left occipito-parietal-temporal lesion. On the other hand, she performed poorly on tests of mental rotation (Ratcliff, 1979; Shepherd & Metzler, 1971; Thurstone & Jeffrey, 1956) and at other tasks requiring the manipulation of the spatial positions of imagined stimuli (Brooks, 1968; Kosslyn, Ball, & Reiser, 1978). This looks like another case distinguishing intact imagery for object properties along with impaired spatial processing procedures. Interestingly, though, MG had no impairment in visual working memory when the tasks did not require that the material was manipulated or transformed, including the Corsi blocks span test (Canavan et al., 1989; see also Brooks, 1967, for a further task). Thus, patients with impairments on these last tasks, in addition to tasks such as mental rotation (where images must be transformed), seem to have a second problem (cf. Riddoch et al., 2003; Riddoch et al., 1999), presumably in maintaining the image representation itself. If this is the case, however, then it is not clear why object perception is preserved in such patients and why images can be created for object properties, if imagery and perception are mediated by a common representation (the visual buffer; Fig. 9–1). Possibly the short-term representations used for spatial manipulations of images differ from those used to maintain structural properties of objects in images.

This last argument gains support from cases such as that reported by Carlesimo et al. (2001). Their patient, MV, was impaired not only at tasks requiring the spatial manipulation of images, but also when the experiment demanded only visual memory for object locations (stimuli were presented in various locations followed by a grid, and the task was to report where the items fell within the grid). Interestingly, visual memory for shapes was spared. The data suggest that information about spatial position is maintained in images separately from representations of object shape, and it may well be that spatial transformations operate using the separately coded (hence contentless) spatial representations. If spatial transformations operate selectively on these spatial representations, then there may be selective loss of the transformation processes without affecting the basic representation of either object properties or space, as in the case of MG (Morton & Morris, 1995). Further evidence that spatial and object information are stored in separate VSTM subsystems is described in Chapter 3 of this volume.

8.3.2 Image Generation Deficits

One further refinement, suggested by the neuropsychological literature, is that the process of image generation can be distinguished from the maintenance of both the spatial and structural properties of objects in images. The patient RM (Farah, Levine, & Calvanio, 1988b) suffered a left occipital and medial temporal lobe infarct, and his object naming was intact on the small number of items tested. In contrast to this, he was unable to draw from memory or to describe the visual appearance of objects, and he was impaired at naming the colors of objects from memory. He was also impaired at verifying high-imagery sentences. Nevertheless, performance on drawing from memory did improve when he was given pictures of objects with missing parts to complete, and from this, Farah and colleagues argued that visual memories for objects were spared (in line with his object naming performance). To account for the pattern of good object recognition along with impaired imagery, Farah et al. (1988) suggested that a problem existed in image generation.

The patient DW (Riddoch, 1990) suffered a left temporoparietal lesion following a stroke. Like RM, visual object recognition was spared but his imagery abilities were impaired. For example, he was unable to draw objects from memory, to determine whether uppercase letters have curves or not, or to decide whether animals had long or short tails. In contrast to these deficits, DW did succeed on a task in which it can be argued that images were constructed in a bottom-up rather than top-down manner. On the *animal heads* task, a picture of a headless animal is positioned beneath four heads, and the task requires the patient to judge which head goes with the body (cf. Riddoch & Humphreys, 1987b). Here accurate performance may involve moving each head "in the mind's eye," so that it aligns with the body. DW was able to perform this matching task, suggesting that this mental transformation process was possible provided the stimuli were visually presented. Even more direct evidence for the ability to maintain a short-term visual representation came from tasks in which DW succeeded at copying visual patterns after varying delays. This last result indicates that any visual buffer was spared, whereas DW's spared object recognition indicates that he had intact long-term visual memories. To account for the results, Riddoch proposed that the problem was one of top-down image generation; for instance, a lack of top-down feedback from stored object memories may lead to a lack of activation within any visual buffer. This again suggests a need for top-down as well as bottom-up links from a visual input buffer to stored object memories (contra to Fig. 9–1).

Cases also exist that doubly dissociate from patients with good maintenance of visual images from perception, but poor generation from LTM. Problems in maintaining short-term visual memory representations, but with image generation being spared, were noted by Riddoch and Humphreys (1995).

Patient M was able to perform simple visual imagery tasks for object properties (e.g., the animal tails test), and he showed accurate immediate memory for visual material. However, he was abnormally poor at maintaining visual information from both LTM and perception as the interval between stimulus presentation and the response was delayed. These data point to there being a rapid dissipation of representations in VSTM, although images could be generated in both a top-down and bottom-up manner.

The argument for there being selective deficits in image generation and maintenance, which are distinct from one another and also from image transformation processes, fits with proposals made by Kosslyn, Behrmann, and Jeannerod (1995). They postulated separate functions of image generation, maintenance, and transformation. The neuropsychological evidence bears this out, while again pointing to common processes being required to maintain imaged representations derived from LTM and to maintain new VSTM representations from perceptual input.

8.3.3 Visual Memory Deficits in Other Syndromes: Visual Neglect

In developing arguments about the nature of VSTM and its relation to visual perception, an important part has been played by patients whose primary symptoms are not problems in VSTM itself (such as those patients with cortical blindness and patients with visual agnosia discussed earlier). *Visual neglect* provides another syndrome in which the deficits of patients are informative about VSTM. Visual neglect is a relatively common clinical syndrome associated primarily with patients with right hemispheric damage involving parietal and superior temporal cortex (Karnath, Himmelbach, & Kücher, 2003; Mort et al., 2003). Classically, such patients fail to notice stimuli presented on the side of space contralateral to their lesion.

One interesting clinical aspect of the performance of many neglect patients is that they may frequently come back to reanalyze objects already inspected on the ipsilesional side of space. Husain et al. (2001) describe the case of GK, who presented with left neglect after suffering an infarct of the right inferior parietal lobe. On tasks of spatial memory and visual scanning, GK made abnormally large numbers of revisits to previously inspected locations on the right-hand side. Moreover, when these revisits occurred, GK was unable to indicate whether or not he had previously inspected these left-side items. Husain et al. proposed that these reinspections could represent an impairment in VSTM for the positions of objects. They suggest that a reduced capacity in VSTM may be a significant component of the neglect syndrome. An interesting aspect of this argument is that the impairment in VSTM must affect the ipsi- as well as the contralesional side of space, given that patients reinspect ipsilesional items. That is, the deficit in VSTM may not be isolated to one side of space.

One problem with inferring a deficit in VSTM from evidence on reinspections is that the reinspections can be caused by a number of factors. For example, several demonstrations suggest that patients with parietal damage show impaired *inhibition of return* (IOR) in simple cueing tasks. Normally, after attention is cued to one location and then shifted away, a bias exists not to attend again to the initially attended location (Posner & Cohen, 1984). Bartolomeo, Sieroff, Chokron, and Decaix (2001) and Vivas, Humphreys, and Fuentes (2006) found that no IOR to locations occurred on the ipsilateral side of the lesion. Indeed, instead of there being a bias to attend away from a previously attended location on the ipsilesional side, patients could remain biased to reattend there. Given that, in these cueing tasks, only one location is often used on each side of space, it seems unlikely that an impairment in VSTM for the ipsilesional stimulus is causative here; and any bias to reattend to the ipsilesional location further indicates that some memory lingers after this location is cued. Vivas et al. attribute the lack of IOR to an imbalance in spatial attention to the contra- and ipsilesional sides of space, which is not outweighed even if an ipsilesional location is suppressed; hence, the ipsilesional position continues to attract attention.

Clearer evidence for a deficit in VSTM linked to the neglect syndrome comes from Malhotra et al. (2004, 2005). These investigators examined visual memory using a vertical variant of the Corsi blocks task, in which elements in a vertical array were highlighted sequentially.[7] They found an association between impaired visual memory for probed locations in the vertical arrays and a tendency for the neglect patients to reinspect ipsilesional locations in scan tasks. In addition, the magnitude of the VSTM deficit predicted the degree of neglect.

Converging evidence for VSTM deficits associated with the neglect syndrome comes from studies that have applied a particular mathematical model of visual report to patient data. Bundesen's *Theory of Visual Attention* (TVA) provides a mathematical account of our ability to report either whole arrays of visual elements or cued subsets of those elements (whole- and partial-report; cf. Sperling, 1960) (Bundesen, 1990). The model provides a number of parameters specifying bottom-up and top-down attentional biases, processing capacity, and VSTM capacity. Duncan et al. (1999) and Peers et al. (2005) applied TVA to groups of patients with parietal or frontal lesions. These authors report that parietal damage is associated with reduced processing capacity and VSTM estimates in patients, and this also correlates with measures of neglect. The reduced measures of capacity were found for stimuli on both the ipsi- and contralesional sides of space.

One noteworthy aspect of the data on VSTM deficits linked to the neglect syndrome is that memory is not deficient for all types of visual information. In a study of implicit memory in a search task, Kristjánsson et al. (2005) found that neglect patients can show speeded responses when the color of a target is repeated across trials. However, they found no carry-over for targets in repeated spatial positions. Pisella, Berberovic, and Mattingley (2004) examined neglect patients either with or without damage to posterior parietal cortex (four per group) on a task requiring explicit memory across sequentially presented visual arrays. The task was to match the arrays to decide whether one of four objects changed position, shape, or color. Pisella et al. found that patients with parietal

---

7   A vertical array was used here to avoid spatial biases due to neglect.

lesions performed poorly when required to match the spatial locations of stimuli, irrespective of where the stimuli fell in the visual field. However, they were
much less impaired at matching color and shape changes. This deficit in
memory for spatial location was not found in patients with neglect whose
lesion spared posterior parietal cortex. This last result indicates that the problem in VSTM may not be a necessary part of the neglect syndrome, since Pisella
et al.'s non–parietal lesion group of neglect patients did not present with the
memory deficit. In addition, the deficit appears to be associated with parietal
damage (although a definitive conclusion on this last point awaits testing with
a larger group of patients).

The selective deficit in memory for spatial location in parietal patients supports the argument we made earlier, that evidence exists for a VSTM for object
location that is distinct from a VSTM for object properties. Moreover, in the
case of neglect patients, the deficit is for visual short-term memories formed to
new perceptual information, rather than for memories used in imagery-based
retrieval from long-term storage (see also Chapter 3 of this volume). This is
inconsistent with the view that a single visual buffer exists to support both
object location and object structure in VSTM (Fig. 9–1). In the next section, we
consider the case for a contrasting view of VSTM to that offered in Figure 9–1,
in which VSTM relies on interactions between a set of distributed visual representations in different neural regions.

8.3.4 Summary

The evidence just presented fits with a broad distinction between operations
that process spatial properties in images and those dealing with object properties. However, rather than suggesting that these two different types of process
operate on a common visual representation (the visual buffer, Fig. 9–1), the
evidence points to there being separate representations of object location and
representations sensitive to the content of the stimuli (their shape, color, and so
forth). On top of this, distinct aspects of image processing concerned with
image generation, transformation, and maintenance can be identified. Finally,
deficits in representing visual information in the short-term are not solely associated with damage to primary occipital cortex, and impairments for spatial
representations are found after parietal damage, too. These results suggest
that we need to revise the proposals outlined in Figure 9–1 to accommodate
the data.

8.4 DISTRIBUTED DYNAMICS OF VISUAL SHORT-TERM MEMORY

The neuropsychological evidence that we have presented indicates that there
can be a loss of representations supporting short-term visual memory after
damage to either primary occipital cortex and/or to posterior parietal cortex. In
addition, damage to ventral visual cortex (associated with visual agnosia) leads
to a loss of bottom-up structuring of visual representations in memory. The
data suggest that multiple sites may be involved in supporting VSTM, perhaps
depending on the specific information being represented (location, shape,

color) and the task. For example, tasks such as drawing from memory, which are frequently used in neuropsychological studies, may well require support from more structured representations than tasks such as visual matching, which may be based on correspondences between relatively unstructured (early) visual representations. Note, however, that visual matching tasks have frequently been used to explore short-term visual memory in studies with normal participants, and here evidence has emerged for the involvement of integrated representations, in which different visual dimensions are bound together (Luck & Vogel, 1997; Woodman et al., 2003) (see also Chapter 3 of this volume). It appears that, with normal participants, it may be difficult to avoid integrating different features (at least once stimuli are attended, cf. Treisman, 1998), whereas with patients, the representations can be fractionated apart so that, for example, patients with parietal lesions maintain color and shape but not stimulus location (Pisella et al., 2004). In the latter case, matching performance may be based on unintegrated representations of particular features.

One way to conceptualize how VSTM may be supported by these different representations is to suggest that memory performance is contingent on dynamic interactions across different neural areas. For example, activation from long-term associative memories (e.g., in temporal cortex) may feed-back to provide top-down support for short-term representations of particular features in occipital cortex, which are otherwise fleeting and easily lost. In patients with impaired stored knowledge, this support decreases or even distorts the early representations, so that patients are impaired at immediate reproduction of stimuli they have lost memories for, even when they have just seen the objects involved (cf. Etcoff et al., 1992; Lambon-Ralph et al., 1998). Similarly, activation of visual areas concerned with structuring and organizing perceptual input (e.g., prestriate regions damaged in visual agnosia) may be critical for supporting representations of new visual stimuli, so that possible organizations are better maintained than impossible organizations (Riddoch et al., 2003). In contrast, activation in parietal cortex appears to be important for maintaining (as well as manipulating) location information. Dynamic changes between the different patterns of activity, varying across different tasks and over time (when patients enter a chronic state) alter the exact structures supporting VSTM. On this view, then, there exists no single visual buffer within primary occipital cortex (Fig. 9–1), but rather a network of interactive regions that lead to short-term recall from perception and imagery (drawing information from LTM). A framework illustrating this idea is presented in Figure 9–5.

These arguments for several brain regions contributing to VSTM are supported by data from functional brain imaging using normal observers. For example, although evidence exists for activation of primary occipital cortex during mental imagery (see Kosslyn & Thompson, 2003, for a review), this is particularly the case when relatively fine-grained visual discriminations must be made. Interestingly, primary visual cortex is not necessarily activated when fine-grained *spatial* discriminations are required (e.g., based on the positions of elements; see Mazard et al., 2004), whereas posterior parietal cortex is. A good deal of evidence also indicates activation of posterior parietal cortex in

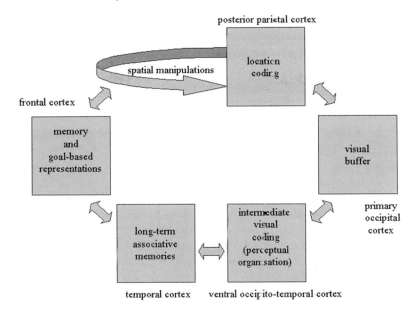

Figure 9–5. Interactive model of visual short-term memory.

maintaining short-term memory representations from visual input. For example, increased activation occurs in dorsal parieto-occipital regions when the locations of faces have to be remembered relative to the face identities (Ungerleider, Courtney, & Haxby, 1998). In contrast to this, more ventral regions concerned with pattern recognition are active when content-specific properties of stimuli have to be maintained (e.g., face identities; Druzgal & D'Esposito, 2003; Postle, Druzgal, & D'Esposito, 2003; Ranganath, Cohen, Dam, & D'Esposito, 2004a). Within inferior ventral cortex, differential activity also occurs when there is maintenance of different categories of stimuli (the fusiform gyrus for faces and the parahippocampal gyrus for buildings; Gazzaley et al., 2005; Ranganath, DeGutis, & D'Esposito., 2004b). Furthermore, the category- and location-specific regions of ventral and posterior dorsal cortex also increase their activity as, respectively, more items and locations have to be maintained (Druzgal & D'Esposito, 2003; Todd & Marois, 2004).

In addition to these posterior brain regions, however, imaging studies also point to a variety of areas within the frontal cortex that show sustained activity when visual stimuli have to be maintained (see Chapter 8 of this volume for an extensive discussion of the role of prefrontal cortex in VSTM). Within the frontal cortex, in some regions, the maintained activity seems to be content-specific, whereas in others, the activity is content-independent (see Haxby, Petit, Ungeleider, & Courtney, 2000, for a summary). These data for frontal lobe involvement in memory are consistent with results from single-cell recordings in monkeys (e.g., Goldman-Rakic, 1996; Goldman-Rakic & Leung, 2002) demonstrating activation, particularly in lateral areas when information must be temporarily held in memory as a task is being performed. Neuropsychological evidence certainly exists that patients with lateral prefrontal lesions can be impaired in working memory tasks when there is a delayed response (Freedman & Oscar-Berman, 1996), when information may no longer be maintained by rehearsal (Baddeley, 1986). However, this research has often failed to tackle the issue of visual memory in particular, although there is emerging evidence for both frontal and parietal regions being critical for short-term visual maintenance of location information, gained through TMS (e.g., Brandt et al., 1998; Koch et al., 2005; Muri et al., 1996; Pascal-Leone & Hallett, 1994). The extent to which the frontal areas play a critical role because they are better than more posterior regions at maintaining activity across more prolonged intervals, or because they carry other critical information for the task (such as the task rule; see Wallis, Anderson, & Miller, 2001), remains to be separated. Nevertheless some suggestive data come from Soto, Humphreys, and Heinke (2006), who examined how the contents of working memory affect an independent search task. Participants had to hold an item in working memory while they undertook the search task. Sometimes the working memory item appeared in the search display, located either by the target for the search task or by a distractor. Frontal lobe patients were as likely as controls to be guided to stimuli matching the contents of working memory, but the patients were then slowed in rejecting any matching item when it was not the search target. This suggests a problem in highlighting the *goal template* for the search task, rather than any reduced effect of the working memory item on attention. Clearly, it will be of interest for future work to examine the functional role played by frontal lobe structures in short-term visual memory, and their role in implementing task rules in maintenance of the basic representations or manipulation of the underlying information. For now, we propose that these data from imaging and TMS studies in normal participants fit with a picture of a distributed working memory system. The data from neuropsychology indicate that this system can be fractionated, according to the specific lesion affecting the patients.

ACKNOWLEDGMENTS

This work was supported by grants from the BBSRC, the MRC, and the Stroke Association UK.

REFERENCES

Baddeley A. (2000). The episodic buffer: A new component of working memory? *Trends in Cognitive Sciences* 11:417–423.

Baddeley, A. (1986). *Working Memory*. Oxford: Oxford University Press.

Bartolomeo P. (2002). The relationship between visual perception and visual mental imagery: Appraisal of the neuropsychological evidence. *Cortex* 38:357–378.

Bartolomeo, P., Bachoud-Lévi, A.-C., and Denes G. (1997). Preserved imagery for colors in a patient with cerebral achromatopsia. *Cortex* 33:369–378.

Bartolomeo, P., Bachoud-Lévi, A. C., de Gelder, B., Denes, G., Dalla Barba, G., Brugière, P. et al. (1998). Multiple-domain dissociation between impaired visual perception and preserved mental imagery in a patient with bilateral extrastriate lesions. *Neuropsychologia* 36:239–249.

Bartolomeo, P., Sieroff, E., Chokron, S., and Decaix C. (2001). Variability of response times as a marker of diverted attention. *Neuropsychologia* 39:358–363.

Beauvois M.-F. (1982). Optic aphasia: A process of interaction between vision and language. *Philosophical Transactions of the Royal Society* B289:35–47.

Behrmann, M., Moscovitch, M., and Winocur G. (1994). Intact visual imagery and impaired visual perception in a patient with visual agnosia. *Journal of Experimental Psychology: Human Perception and Performance* 20:1068–1087.

Behrmann, M., Moscovitch, M. and Winocur, G. (1999). Vision and visual mental imagery. In *Case Studies in the Neuropsychology of Vision*, eds. G. W. Humphreys. Hove: Psychology Press.

Boucart, M., and Humphreys, G. W. (1992). The computation of perceptual structure from collinearity and closure: Normality and pathology. *Neuropsychologia* 30(6):527–546.

Boutsen, L., and Humphreys G. W. (2002). Face context interferes with local part processing in a prosopagnostic patient. *Neuropsychologia* 40:2305–2313.

Brandt, S. A., Ploner, C. J., Meyer, B. U., Leistner, S., and Villringer A. (1998). Effects of repetitive transcranial magnetic stimulation over dorsolateral prefrontal and posterior parietal cortex on memory-guided saccades. *Experimental Brain Research* 118:197–204.

Brooks L. R. (1967). The suppression of visualisation by reading. *Quarterly Journal of Experimental Psychology* 19:289–299.

Brooks L. R. (1968). Spatial and verbal components of the act of recall. *Canadian Journal of Psychology* 22:349–368.

Bundesen, C. (1990). A theory of visual attention. *Psychological Review* 97:523-527.

Butter, C. M., Kosslyn, S. M., Mijovic-Prelec, D., and Riffle A. (1997). Field-specific deficits in visual imagery following hemianopia due to unilateral occipital infarcts. *Brain* 120:217–228.

Canavan, A. G. M., Passingham, R. E., Marsden, C. D., Quinn, N., Wyke, M., and Polkey C. E. (1989). Sequencing ability in parkinsonian patients with frontal lobe lesions and patients who have undergone unilateral temporal lobectomies. *Neuropsychologia* 27:787–798.

Carlesimo, G. A., Perri, R., Turriziani, P., Tomaiuolo, F., and Caltagirone C. (2001). Remembering what but not where: Independence of spatial and visual working memory in the brain. *Cortex* 36:519–534.

Chattergee, A., and Southwood M. H. (1995). Cortical blindness and visual imagery. *Neurology* 45:2189–2195.

Conrad, R. (1964). Acoustic confusion in immediate memory. *British Journal of Psychology*, 75–84.

Druzgal, T. J., and D'Esposito M. (2003). Dissecting contributions of prefrontal cortex and fusiform face area to face working memory. *Journal of Cognitive Neuroscience* 15:771–784.

Duncan, J., Bundesen, C., Olson, A., Humphreys, G. W., Chavda, S., and Shibuya H. (1999). Systematic analysis of deficits of visual attention. *Journal of Experimental Psychology: General* 128:450–478.

Ellis, R., and Humphreys. G. W. (1999). *Connectionist psychology*. London, UK: Erlbaum.

Etcoff, N. L., Freeman, R , and Cave, K. R. (1992). Can we lose memories of faces? Content specificity and awareness in a prosopagnosic. *Journal of Cognitive Neuroscience* 3(1), 25–41.

Farah, M. J., Hammond, K. M., Levine, D. N., and Calvanio R. (1988a). Visual and spatial mental imagery: Dissociable systems of representation. *Cognitive Psychology* 20:439–462.

Farah, M. J., Levine, D. N., and Calvanio R. (1988b). A case study of a mental imagery deficit. *Brain and Cognition* 8:147–164.

Farah, M. J., Soso, M. J., and Dasheiff R. M. (1992). Visual angle of the mind's eye before and after occipital lobectomy. *Journal of Experimental Psychology: Human Perception and Performance* 18:241–246.

Finke, R. A., and Pinker S. (1982). Spontaneous imagery scanning in mental extrapolation. *Journal of Experimental Psychology: Learning Memory and Cognition* 8:142–147.

Freedman, M., and Oscar-Berman M. (1996). Bilateral frontal lobe disease and selective delayed response deficits in humans. *Behavioural Neuroscience* 100:337–342.

Gazzaley, A., Cooney, J. W., McEvoy, K., Knight, R. T., and D'Esposito M. (2005). Top-down enhancement and suppression of the magnitude and speed of neural activity. *Journal of Cognitive Neuroscience* 17:507–517.

Giersch, A., Humphreys, G. W., Boucart, M., and Koviáks I. (2000). The computation of occluded contours in visual agnosia: Evidence of early computation prior to shape binding and figure-ground coding. *Cognitive Neuropsychology* 17:731–759.

Goldenberg, G., Mullbacher, W., and Nowak A. (1995). Imagery without perception: A case of anosagnosia for cortical blindness. *Neuropsychologia* 33:1373–1382.

Goldman-Rakic P. S. (1996). The prefrontal landscape: Implications of functional architecture for understanding human mentation and the central executive. *Philosophical Transactions of the Royal Society* B351:1445–1453.

Goldman-Rakic, P. S., and Leung, H.-C. (2002). Functional architecture of the dorsolateral prefrontal cortex in monkeys and humans. In *Principles of Frontal Lobe Function*, eds. D. T. Stuss and R. T. Knight, 85–95. Oxford: Oxford University Press.

Hanley, R. J., Young, A. W., and Pearson, N. (1991). Impairment of the visuo-spatial sketch pad. *Quarterly Journal of Experimental Psychology* 43A:101–125.

Haxby, J. V., Petit, L., Ungeleider, L. G., and Courtney S. M. (2000). Distinguishing the functional roles of multiple regions in distributed neural systems for visual working memory. *Neuroimage* 11:380–391.

Heilman, K. M. (1979). Neglect and related disorders. In *Clinical Neuropsychology*, eds. K. M. Heilman and E. Valenstein. New York: Oxford University Press.

Humphreys, G. W., Riddoch, M. J., Donnelly, N., Freeman, T., Boucart, M., and Müller, H. (1992a). Intermediate visual processing and visual agnosia. In *The Neurophysiology of High-Level Vision*, eds. M. J. Farah and G. Ratcliff. Hillsdale, N. J.: Lawrence Erlbaum.

Humphreys, G. W., Troscianko, T., Riddoch, M. J., Boucart, M., Donnelly, N., and Harding, G. F. A. (1992b). Covert processing in different visual recognition systems. In *The Neuropsychology of Consciousness*, eds. A. D. Milner and M. D. Rugg. London: Academic Press.

Husain, M., Mannan, S. K., Hodson, T., Wojciulik, E., Driver, J., and Kennard C. (2001). Impaired spatial memory across saccades contributes to abnormal search in parietal neglect. *Brain* 124:941–952.

Jankowiak, J., Kinsbourne, M., Shalev, R. S., and Bachman D. L. (1992). Preserved visual imagery and categorisation in a case of associative visual agnosia. *Journal of Cognitive Neuroscience* 4:119–131.

Karnath, H.-O., Himmelbach, M., and Kûker W. (2003). The cortical substrate of visual extinction. *NeuroReport* 14:437–442.

Koch, G., Oliveri, M., Torriero, S., Carlesimo, G. A., Turriziani, P., and Caltagirone C. (2005). RTMS evidence of different delay and decision processes in a fronto-parietal neuronal network activated during spatial working memory. *NeuroImage* 24:34–39.

Kosslyn S. M. (2005). Mental images and the brain. *Cognitive Neuropsychology* 22: 333–347.

Kosslyn, S. M., Ball, T. M., and Reiser B. J. (1978). Visual images preserve metric spatial information: Evidence from studies of image scanning. *Journal of Experimental Psychology: Human Perception and Performance* 4:47–60.

Kosslyn, S. M., Behrmann, M., and Jeannerod M. (1995). The cognitive neuroscience of mental imagery. *Neuropsychologia* 33:1335–1344.

Kosslyn, S. M., Pascual-Leone, A., Felician, O., Camposano, S., Keenan, J. P., Thompson, W. L. et al. (1999). The role of area 17 in visual imagery: Convergent evidence from PET and RTMS. *Science* 284:167–170.

Kosslyn, S. M., and Thompson W. L. (2003). When is early visual cortex activated during visual mental imagery? *Psychological Bulletin* 129:723–746.

Kristjánsson, Á., Vuilleumier, P., Malhotra, P., Husain, M., and Driver J. (2005). Priming of colour and position during visual search in unilateral spatial neglect. *Journal of Cognitive Neuroscience* 17:859–873.

Lambon-Ralph, M., Howard, D., Nightingale, G., and Ellis A. W. (1998). Are living and non-living category-specific deficits causally linked to impaired perceptual or associative knowledge? Evidence from a category-specific double dissociation. *Neurocase* 4:311–338.

Levine, D. N., Warach, J., and Farah M. J. (1985). Two visual systems in mental imagery: Dissociation of "what" and "where" in imagery disorders due to bilateral posterior cerebral lesions. *Neurology* 35:1010–1018.

Logie, R. H. (1995). *Visuo-spatial Working Memory*. Hove, UK: Lawrence Erlbaum.

Logie, R. H. (2003). Spatial and visual working memory. In *The Psychology of Learning and Motivation (Vol. 42)*, eds. D. Irwin and B. Ross. San Diego: Academic Press.

Luck, S. J., and Vogel E. K. (1997). The capacity of visual working memory for features and conjunction. *Nature* 390:279–281.

Malhotra, P., Jäger, H. R., Parton, A., Greenwood, R., Playford, E. D., Brown, M. M. et al. (2005). Spatial working memory capacity in unilateral neglect. *Brain* 128: 424–435.

Malhotra, P., Mannan, S. K. Driver, J., and Husain M. (2004). Impaired spatial working memory: One component of the visual neglect syndrome? *Cortex* 40:667–676.

Mazard, A., Tzourio-Mazoyer, N., Crivello, F., Mazoyer, B., and Mellet E. (2004). A pet meta-analysis of object and spatial mental imagery. *European Journal of Cognitive Psychology* 16:673–695.

Michelon, P., and Biederman I. (2003). Less impairment in face imagery than face perception in early prosopagnosia. *Neuropsychologia* 1516:1–21.

Mort, D. J., Malhotra, P., Mannan, S. K., Rorden, C., Pambakian, A., Kennard, C. et al. (2003). The anatomy of visual neglect. *Brain* 126:1986–1997.

Morton, N., and Morris R. G. (1995). Image transformation dissociated from visuospatial working memory. *Cognitive Neuropsychology* 12:767–791.

Moscovitch, M., Behrman, M., and Winocur G. (1994). Do pets have long or short ears? Mental imagery and neuroimaging. *Trends in Neuroscience* 17:292–294.

Muri, R. M., Vermersch, A. I., Rivaud, S., Gaymard, B., and Pierrot-Deseilligny C. (1996). Effects of single-pulse transcranial magnetic stimulation over the prefrontal and posterior parietal cortices during memory guided saccades in humans. *Journal of Neurophysiology* 76:2102–2106.

Papagno C. (2002). Progressive impairment of constructional abilities: A visuospatial scratchpad deficit? *Neuropsychologia* 40:1858–1867.

Pascal-Leone, A., and Hallett M. (1994). Induction of errors in a delayed response task by repetitive transcranial magnetic stimulation of the dorsolateral prefrontal cortex. *Neuroreport* 5:2517–2520.

Peers, P. V., Ludwig, C. J. H., Rordan, C., Cusack, R., Bonfiglio, C., and Bundesen C. (2005). Attentional functions of parietal and frontal cortex. *Cerebral Cortex* 15:1469–1484.

Pisella, L., Berberovic, N., and Mattingley J. B. (2004). Impaired spatial memory for location but not for colour or shape in visual neglect: A comparison of parietal and non-parietal lesions. *Cortex* 40:379–390.

Policardi, E., Perani, D., Zago, S., Grassi, F., Fazio, F., and Làdavas E. (1996). Failure to evoke visual images in a case of long-standing cortical blindness. *Neurocase* 2:381–394.

Posner, M. I., and Cohen, Y. (1984). Components of visual orienting. In *Attention and Performance: Control of Language Processes*, eds. H. Bouma and D. G. Bouwhuis. Hillsdale, N. J.: Lawrence Erlbaum.

Postle, B. R., Druzgal, T. J., and D'Esposito M. (2003). Seeking the neural substrates of working memory storage. *Cortex* 39:927–946.

Ranganath, C., Cohen, M. X., Dam, C., and D'Esposito, M. (2004a). Inferior temporal prefrontal and hippocampal contributions to working memory maintenance and associative memory retrieval. *Journal of Neuroscience* 24:3917–3925.

Ranganath, C., DeGutis, J., and D'Esposito M. (2004b). Category-specific modulation of inferior temporal activity during working memory encoding and maintenance. *Cognitive Brain Research* 20:37–45.

Ratcliff, G. (1979). Spatial thought mental rotation and the right cerebral hemisphere. *Neuropsychologia* 17:49–54.

Riddoch M. J. (1990). Loss of visual imagery: A generation deficit. *Cognitive Neuropsychology* 7:249–273.

Riddoch, M. J., Humphrey, G. W., Hardy, E., Blott, W., and Smith A. (2003). Visual and spatial short-term memory in visual agnosia. *Cognitive Neuropsychology* 20:641–671.

Riddoch, M. J., and Humphreys G. W. (1987a). A case of integrative agnosia. *Brain* 110:1431–1462.

Riddoch, M. J., and Humphreys G. W. (1987b). Visual object processing in optic aphasia: A case of semantic access agnosia. *Cognitive Neuropsychology* 4:131–185.

Riddoch, M. J., and Humphreys, G. W. (1995). 17 +14 = 41? Three cases of working memory impairment. In *Broken Memories: Case Studies in Memory Impairment*, eds. R. Campbell and M. A. Conway. Hove: Lawrence Erlbaum.

Riddoch, M. J., Humphreys, G. W., Gannon, T., Blott, W., and Jones V. (1999). Memories are made of this: The effects of time on stored visual knowledge in a case of visual agnosia. *Brain* 122:537–559.

Servos, P., and Goodale M. A. (1995). Preserved visual imagery in visual form agnosia. *Neuropsychologia* 33:1383–1394.

Servos, P., Goodale, M. A., and Humphrey G. K. (1993). The drawing of objects by a visual form agnosic: Contribution of surface properties and memorial representations. *Neuropsychologia* 31:251–259.

Shepherd, R. N., and Metzler J. (1971). Mental rotation of three-dimensional objects. *Science* 171:701–703.

Soto, D., Humphreys, G. W., and Heinke, D. G. (2006). Dividing the mind: The necessary role of the frontal lobes in separating memory from search. *Neuropsychologia* 44 1282–1289.

Sperling G. (1960). The information available in brief visual presentations. *Psychological Monographs: General and Applied* 74:1–29.

Thomas, R. M., Forde, E. M. E., Humphreys, G. W., and Graham K. S. (2002). The effects of the passage of time on a patient with category-specific agnosia. *Neurocase* 8:466–479.

Thurstone, L. L., and Jeffrey, T. E. (1956). *Flags: A Test of Spatial Thinking*. Illinois: Industrial Relations Centre.

Todd, J. J., and Marois R. (2004). Capacity limit of visual short-term memory in human posterior parietal cortex. *Nature* 428:748–751.

Treisman, A. (1998). Feature binding attention and object perception. *Philosophical Transactions of the Royal Society* 353:1295–1306.

Ungerleider, L. G., Courtney, S. M., and Haxby J. V. (1998). A neural system for human visual working memory. *Proceedings of the National Academy of Sciences USA* 95:883–890.

Vallar, G., and Shallice, T. (1990). *Neuropsychological Impairments of Short-term Memory*. Cambridge: Cambridge University Press.

Vivas, A. B., Humphreys, G. W., and Fuentes, L. J. (2006). Abnormal inhibition of return: A review and new data on patients with parietal damage. *Cognitive Neuropsychology* 23:1049–1064.

Wallis, J. D., Anderson, K. C., and Miller E. K. (2001). Single neurons in prefrontal cortex encode abstract rules. *Nature* 411:953–956.

Woodman, G. F., Vecera, S. P., and Luck, S. J. (2003). *Psychonomic Bulletin and Review* 10:80–87.

Young, A. W., Humphreys, G. W., Riddoch, M. J., Hellawell, D. J., and de Haan E. H. F. (1994). Recognition impairments and face imagery. *Neuropsychologia* 32:693–702.

Author Index

Subject Index